Red Dot Design Yearbook 2017/2018

Edited by Peter Zec

reddot award
product design

About this book

"Doing" presents more than 400 award-winning products for an active life. All of the products in this book are of outstanding design quality and have been successful in one of the world's largest and most renowned design competitions, the Red Dot Design Award. This book documents the results of the current competition in the field of "Doing", also presenting its most important players – the design team of the year, the designers of the best products and the jury members.

Über dieses Buch

„Doing" präsentiert mehr als 400 ausgezeichnete Produkte für ein aktives Leben. Alle Produkte in diesem Buch sind von herausragender gestalterischer Qualität, ausgezeichnet in einem der größten und renommiertesten Designwettbewerbe der Welt, dem Red Dot Design Award. Dieses Buch dokumentiert die Ergebnisse des aktuellen Wettbewerbs im Bereich „Doing" und stellt zudem seine wichtigsten Akteure vor – das Designteam des Jahres, die Designer der besten Produkte und die Jurymitglieder.

Contents
Inhalt

Professor Dr Peter Zec
Preface of the editor
Vorwort des Herausgebers

Dear Readers,

This "Doing" yearbook volume that you are currently holding in your hands showcases today's best products from the areas of hobbies and leisure, babies and children as well as fashion, accessories and jewellery. As different as these product groups may initially appear, they share common ground in one major respect, namely a conscious approach to materials. In this regard, design with natural and with new materials is in no way limited to aesthetic considerations. For example, in order to achieve the robustness and resilience frequently required for sports-related products, high-quality and innovative textiles and materials are often refined down to the finest detail, thus helping to achieve extremely high product quality. In addition, by integrating sensors and new technologies and connecting products to the Internet of Things, we ensure that they are constantly gaining in intelligence. All of these developments reflect the higher standards we are setting for leisure products and for ourselves.

By contrast, a fast-growing awareness of ecological aspects and sustainable, environmentally friendly and fair production can be observed for textiles used in fashion or for babies' and children's items. Jewellery and watches have long since provided a realm for experimentation with premium materials and processing technologies. Here, a sensitive approach to materials often goes hand in hand with a particularly scrupulous finish. On the one hand we are observing a return to traditional handicrafts, alongside the use of state-of-the-art manufacturing technologies on the other hand. Both of these approaches are justified.

On the following pages, we will introduce you to the "Doing" products that won over our expert jury this year with their design quality. They are all of excellent design quality and have won an award in one of the world's largest and most renowned design competitions. You will find winning products from other aspects of life in the remaining three yearbook volumes, "Living", "Working" and "Enjoying".

I wish you an inspiring read.

Sincerely, Peter Zec

Liebe Leserin, lieber Leser,

der Jahrbuchband „Doing", den Sie gerade in den Händen halten, zeigt die aktuell besten Produkte aus den Bereichen Hobby und Freizeit, Baby und Kind sowie Mode, Accessoires und Schmuck. So unterschiedlich diese Produktgruppen auch erscheinen mögen – ein großes Thema zieht sich durch all diese Bereiche: der bewusste Umgang mit Materialien. Dabei spielen bei der Gestaltung mit natürlichen ebenso wie mit neuen Materialien keineswegs nur ästhetische Gesichtspunkte eine Rolle. Um etwa die im Sportbereich oft notwendige Robustheit und Widerstandsfähigkeit zu erreichen, werden hochwertige und innovative Textilien und Materialien oft bis ins kleinste Detail verfeinert und tragen so zu einer extrem hohen Produktqualität bei. Die Integration von Sensoren und neuen Technologien und die Einbindung ins Internet der Dinge sorgen auf der anderen Seite dafür, dass die Produkte immer intelligenter werden. All das ist Ausdruck gestiegener Ansprüche an Freizeitprodukte und uns selbst.

Im Bereich von Textilien für Mode oder Baby- und Kinderartikel ist dagegen ein stark wachsendes Bewusstsein für ökologische Aspekte und eine nachhaltige, umweltschonende und faire Produktion zu konstatieren. Bei Schmuck und Uhren wird ohnehin schon seit sehr langer Zeit mit hochwertigen Materialien und Verarbeitungstechniken experimentiert. Der sensible Umgang mit Materialien geht dabei häufig mit einer besonders sorgfältigen Verarbeitung einher. Hier lässt sich einerseits eine Rückbesinnung auf traditionelle Handwerkstechniken und andererseits eine Nutzung neuester Produktionstechnologien feststellen – und beides hat seine Berechtigung.

Auf den folgenden Seiten zeigen wir Ihnen die Produkte aus dem Bereich „Doing", die unsere Expertenjury in diesem Jahr mit ihrer Designqualität überzeugen konnten. Sie alle sind von herausragender gestalterischer Güte, ausgezeichnet in einem der größten und renommiertesten Designwettbewerbe der Welt. Siegerprodukte aus anderen Lebensbereichen finden Sie in den drei weiteren Jahrbuchbänden „Living", „Working" und „Enjoying".

Ich wünsche Ihnen eine inspirierende Lektüre.

Ihr Peter Zec

The title "Red Dot: Design Team of the Year"
is bestowed on a design team that has
garnered attention through its outstanding
overall design achievements. This year,
the title goes to the Canyon Design Team
led by Lars Wagner and Peter Kettenring.
This award is the only one of its kind in the
world and is extremely highly regarded
even outside of the design scene.

Mit der Auszeichnung „Red Dot: Design Team
of the Year" wird ein Designteam geehrt,
das durch seine herausragende gestalterische
Gesamtleistung auf sich aufmerksam ge-
macht hat. In diesem Jahr geht sie an das
Canyon Design Team unter der Leitung von
Lars Wagner und Peter Kettenring. Diese
Würdigung ist einzigartig auf der Welt und
genießt über die Designszene hinaus höchstes
Ansehen.

In recognition of its feat, the Red Dot:
Design Team of the Year receives the "Radius"
trophy. This sculpture was designed and
crafted by Weinstadt-Schnaidt based
designer Simon Peter Eiber.

Als Anerkennung erhält das Red Dot: Design
Team of the Year den Wanderpokal „Radius".
Die Skulptur wurde entworfen und angefertigt
von dem Designer Simon Peter Eiber aus
Weinstadt-Schnaidt.

Red Dot: Design Team of the Year 2017
Canyon Design Team

For the first time in the history of the competition, the "Red Dot: Design Team of the Year" honorary award and the "Radius" challenge trophy are being bestowed on a design team in the bicycle industry. Led by Lars Wagner and Peter Kettenring, the Canyon Design Team is being honoured for its consistently high design achievements which are pioneering for the cycling sector and bicycle design. Honoured with numerous prizes within the Red Dot Design Award, Canyon Bicycles, like no other company in the bicycle industry, stands for the combination of technology, design and quality.

Erstmals in der Geschichte des Wettbewerbs gehen die Ehrenauszeichnung „Red Dot: Design Team of the Year" und der Wanderpokal „Radius" an ein Designteam aus der Fahrradindustrie. Unter der Leitung von Lars Wagner und Peter Kettenring wird das Canyon Design Team für seine kontinuierlich hohe Gestaltungsleistung ausgezeichnet, die wegweisend ist für die Radsportbranche und das Fahrraddesign. Mit zahlreichen Auszeichnungen im Red Dot Design Award steht Canyon Bicycles wie kein anderes Unternehmen in der Fahrradindustrie für die Verbindung von Technologie, Design und Qualität.

Building the best bike
Das beste Fahrrad bauen

"To me, influencing the design of a product means the realisation of a dream: to be able to express myself through my own products."
„Die Einflussnahme auf die Gestaltung eines Produkts bedeutet für mich die Verwirklichung eines Traumes: mich über die eigenen Produkte ausdrücken zu können."

Roman Arnold, Founder and Managing Director Canyon Bicycles

When Roman Arnold founds Canyon Bicycles GmbH in 2002, his claim is no less than to build the best bicycles in the world. With Canyon, he realises his dream to be able to express himself through his own products. In doing so, the technical and creative quality of the bicycles presents itself as calm and unobtrusive as Roman Arnold himself. Each Canyon bike appears simple and clear. At the same time, form and visual design of the bicycles convey a high degree of precision and dynamics, also reflected in Roman Arnold's uncompromising will to succeed.

Born at the racetrack, grew up in the garage

Canyon is a prime example of how the success of companies and brands can be inseparably linked to the life story of their founder. Roman Arnold, born in 1963, learns to ride a bicycle at the age of three. Still today, he clearly recalls the feeling of riding a used "Puky" bicycle all by himself and without support for the first time. It was a feeling of great freedom. For his 15th birthday, however, he indicates his wish for a moped. Two years of anticipation and looking forward to this birthday gift pass by. Then, in the summer vacation, shortly before his birthday and on the way to Italy, he observes a group of cyclists on their way through the Alps with sporty bicycles. From now on, his interest is awakened. Back in Germany, his father buys him a racing bike: a Peugeot PY10.

From now on, interest turns into passion. Roman Arnold trains on his racing bike and participates in cycle races. His father as well as his two brothers, Franc and Lothar, accompany him. The more passionate and successful Roman Arnold goes racing, the more difficult it becomes to obtain better accessories and fitting spare parts for his racing bike. And as Roman's father doesn't want to just stand around by the roadside during his son's cycle races, he decides to buy accessories and spare parts in Italy. Back home in the family garage, the bicycles are "made fit" for the races. And while Roman Arnold takes part in contests, his father starts a business of selling spare parts and accessories from a small trailer. The result is a small family business as a sideline enterprise.

Als Roman Arnold im Jahr 2002 die Canyon Bicycles GmbH gründet, hat er keinen geringeren Anspruch, als die besten Fahrräder der Welt zu bauen. Mit Canyon verwirklicht er seinen Traum, sich über die eigenen Produkte ausdrücken zu können. Die technische und gestalterische Qualität der Fahrräder präsentiert sich dabei so unaufgeregt und unaufdringlich wie Roman Arnold selbst. Jedes Canyon-Bike wirkt einfach und klar. Zugleich vermitteln die Form und die visuelle Gestaltung der Fahrräder eine hohe Präzision und Dynamik, die sich auch im unbedingten Erfolgs- und Siegeswillen von Firmengründer Roman Arnold widerspiegeln.

An der Rennstrecke geboren, in der Garage aufgewachsen

Canyon ist ein Musterbeispiel dafür, wie der Erfolg von Unternehmen und Marken untrennbar mit der Lebensgeschichte ihres Gründers verbunden sein kann. Roman Arnold, geboren 1963, lernt mit drei Jahren, Fahrrad zu fahren. An das Gefühl, als er zum ersten Mal ganz allein und ohne Halt auf einem gebrauchten Puky-Rad fährt, erinnert er sich bis heute. Es ist ein Gefühl großer Freiheit. Zu seinem fünfzehnten Geburtstag wünscht er sich zunächst ein Mofa. Zwei Jahre lang fiebert er darauf hin. Im Sommerurlaub, kurz vor seinem Geburtstag, sieht er dann auf dem Weg nach Italien eine Gruppe von Radfahrern, die in den Alpen mit sportlichen Zweirädern unterwegs sind. Von nun an ist sein Interesse geweckt. Zurück in Deutschland, kauft sein Vater ihm ein Rennrad: ein Peugeot PY10.

Aus Interesse wird Leidenschaft. Roman Arnold trainiert auf seinem Rennrad und nimmt an Radrennen teil. Sein Vater und seine beiden Brüder Franc und Lothar begleiten ihn. Je leidenschaftlicher und erfolgreicher Roman Arnold Rennen fährt, desto schwieriger wird es, besseres Zubehör und passende Ersatzteile für sein Rennrad zu bekommen. Und weil Romans Vater bei den Radrennen seines Sohnes nicht nur am Straßenrand stehen will, entschließt er sich, in Italien Zubehör und Fahrradteile einzukaufen. In der Garage der Familie werden die Fahrräder für die Rennen fit gemacht. Und während Roman Arnold Wettkämpfe bestreitet, startet sein Vater mit dem Verkauf von Ersatzteilen und Zubehör aus einem kleinen Anhänger. Es entwickelt sich ein kleiner Familienbetrieb im Nebenerwerb.

The design of the simplest things is often most complicated. The trend is towards system integration.
Die Gestaltung der einfachsten Dinge ist oft am kompliziertesten. Der Trend geht in Richtung Systemintegration.

Growing and growing up

With good quality and a service specifically oriented to the needs of customers, the Arnold family is soon making a name for itself in the scene. But shortly after Roman Arnold's high school graduation, the family is hit by a stroke of fate: the father dies. At this point, Roman Arnold has just turned 18 years old. Together with his brother Franc, he decides to continue the garage business. For this objective, Roman Arnold completes an apprenticeship as a wholesales and export/import merchant, immediately followed by an apprenticeship as a bicycle mechanic. In 1985, after the completion of the apprenticeship, Roman and Franc Arnold open up a shop with the name "Rad Sport Arnold" in Koblenz, Germany. Behind the shop counter and in the workshop, they directly experience the hour of birth and growth phase of the mountain bikes. With their sale of exclusive branded bicycles, spare parts and accessories as well as their bicycle repair service, the small business becomes known not only to amateur cyclists. The Koblenz-based company becomes an insider's tip among pros and top athletes as well. In 1990, the brothers decide to pursue different career paths. Franc Arnold founds the company RTI Sports. By the end of the 1990s, RTI Sports focuses exclusively on high-quality bicycle accessories for the specialist retail trade.

Roman Arnold takes a step-by-step approach to the manufacture of in-house bicycles. The first mountain bikes are produced in Asia according to Roman Arnold's ideas and concepts. They enter the market in 1996. Based on his experiences in cycling and in the immediate contact with customers, he develops a special sense for new models. Without any detour via the commercial trade channels, the bicycles are coming directly

Wachsen und erwachsen werden

Mit guter Qualität und einem Service, der unmittelbar auf die Bedürfnisse der Kunden abgestimmt ist, macht sich die Familie Arnold in der Szene bald einen Namen. Doch kurz nach dem Abitur von Roman Arnold trifft die Familie ein Schicksalsschlag. Der Vater stirbt. Roman Arnold ist gerade einmal 18 Jahre alt. Er entscheidet gemeinsam mit seinem Bruder Franc, den Garagenbetrieb weiterzuführen. Für dieses Ziel absolviert Roman Arnold zunächst eine Ausbildung zum Groß- und Außenhandelskaufmann und unmittelbar darauf zum Zweiradmechaniker. Nach Abschluss der Ausbildung eröffnen Roman und Franc Arnold im Jahr 1985 ein Ladenlokal mit dem Namen „Rad Sport Arnold" in Koblenz. Hinter der Ladentheke und in der Werkstatt erleben die beiden die Geburtsstunde und Wachstumsphase der Mountainbikes hautnah mit. Der Verkauf exklusiver Markenfahrräder, von Ersatz- und Zubehörteilen sowie die Reparatur von Fahrrädern macht das kleine Unternehmen nicht nur bei Hobbyradfahrern bekannt. Auch unter Profis und Spitzensportlern avanciert das Koblenzer Unternehmen zu einem Geheimtipp. 1990 trennen sich die beruflichen Wege der Brüder. Franc Arnold gründet die Firma RTI Sports, die sich Ende der 1990er Jahre ausschließlich auf hochwertige Fahrrad-Zubehörteile für den Fachhandel konzentriert.

Roman Arnold tastet sich Schritt für Schritt an die Herstellung eigener Fahrräder heran. Die ersten Mountainbikes werden nach Roman Arnolds Vorstellung in Asien produziert. Sie kommen 1996 auf den Markt. Aufbauend auf seinen Erfahrungen im Radsport und im unmittelbaren Kontakt mit den Kunden entwickelt er ein Gespür für neue Modelle. Ohne Umweg über den Handel kommen die Fahrräder direkt vom Hersteller zum Kunden.

Engineering and design in perfection: Ultimate CF Evo LTD. Precision and simplicity at the highest level.
Ingenieurskunst und Design in Perfektion: Ultimate CF Evo LTD. Präzision und Einfachheit auf höchstem Niveau.

from the manufacturer to the customer. Roman Arnold's breakthrough to success is paved with his move to the Internet. In 1998, he manages to secure the international domain name canyon.com for his company, thereby being well ahead of his time. In 2002, Radsport Arnold is renamed to Canyon Bicycles GmbH based in Koblenz. To improve the characteristics and quality of his bicycles, Roman Arnold is looking for a new material. He follows a recommendation to try it at the Institute for Composite Materials in Kaiserslautern, Germany. The young doctoral candidate Michael Kaiser is working at the Institute when, in 2003, Roman Arnold stands in front of the door of the research institute. He needs a racing bike made of carbon – namely and if possible, the world's best racing bike. Michael Kaiser works for weeks and months, even late nights and weekends. The final result is the Canyon F10 racing bike which obtains score values that have never been achieved before.

At the international bicycle trade fair Eurobike 2004, the bike is presented for the first time. It weighs merely 3.7 kg – unimaginable at that time. The carbon frame weighs merely 818 grams. The new development is a technical crossing of borders with which Canyon underlines its aspiration as a technology leader in the industry. In an interview, former Canyon design engineer Hans-Christian Smolik explains: "The bike is a carrier of technology. We want to show how light and stable a racing bike can be." In 2005, the "Canyon F10 Carbon Ultimate" serial product, derived from this pioneer product, is honoured in the Red Dot Design Award. In retrospect, Michael Kaiser explains the influence of the material on bicycle design: "In the final analysis, carbon is carbon fibre reinforced plastic. It is a composite material because two materials are combined with each other: carbon fibres, on the one hand, which are embedded into a matrix, on the

Der Durchbruch gelingt Roman Arnold mit dem Schritt ins Internet. 1998 sichert er sich die internationale Domain canyon.com und ist seiner Zeit damit weit voraus. 2002 wird aus Radsport Arnold die Canyon Bicycles GmbH mit Sitz in Koblenz. Um die Eigenschaften und die Qualität seiner Fahrräder zu verbessern, ist Roman Arnold auf der Suche nach einem neuen Werkstoff. Er folgt einer Empfehlung, es am Institut für Verbundwerkstoffe in Kaiserslautern zu versuchen. Dort arbeitet der junge Doktorand Michael Kaiser, als im Jahr 2003 Roman Arnold vor der Tür des Forschungsinstituts steht und ein Rennrad aus Carbon braucht – und zwar das beste Rennrad der Welt, wenn möglich. Michael Kaiser arbeitet über Wochen und Monate, bis im Jahr 2004 mit dem Canyon F10 ein Rennrad entsteht, das nie erreichte Werte erzielt.

Erstmals vorgestellt wird das Rad auf der Eurobike 2004. Es bringt gerade einmal 3,7 kg auf die Waage. Unvorstellbar für die damalige Zeit. Der Carbonrahmen wiegt lediglich 818 g. Die Neuentwicklung ist ein technischer Grenzgang, mit dem Canyon seinen Anspruch auf Technologieführerschaft in der Branche unterstreicht. In einem Interview erläutert der damalige Canyon-Konstrukteur Hans-Christian Smolik: „Das Rad ist ein Technologieträger, mit dem wir zeigen wollen, wie leicht und stabil ein Rennrad sein kann." 2005 wird das aus diesem Pionierprodukt abgeleitete Serienprodukt „Canyon F10 Carbon Ultimate" im Red Dot Design Award ausgezeichnet. Michael Kaiser erläutert rückwirkend den Einfluss des Materials auf das Fahrraddesign: „Letztlich ist Carbon ein kohlenstofffaserverstärkter Kunststoff. Es ist ein Verbundwerkstoff, weil man zwei Materialien miteinander kombiniert: Das sind Kohlenstofffasern, die man in eine Matrix einbettet", so Michael Kaiser. „Das Schöne an diesem Werkstoff ist, dass man eine unendliche Anzahl an Gestaltungsmöglichkeiten hat.

other," Michael Kaiser explains. "The beauty of this material is that it gives you a sheer unlimited number of design options. I can combine thousands of different fibres with thousands of different plastics systems. One can render the material either very stiff or very soft, one can make it flexible, elastic or plastic, even thermally or electrically conductive. Actually one can do anything with it." After the success of the Canyon F10, Michael Kaiser considers a job switch from the Institute for Composite Materials to Canyon. By now, he feels a close bond between himself and the company, as he has long since been inspired by the passion expressed by staff and company. In 2007, the moment has arrived. Michael Kaiser becomes the first permanent employee to work in the development department of Canyon Bicycles. What follows is the successive build-up of the development department, the testing laboratory and the quality assurance management. Today, there are nearly 100 staff employed in these areas.

Staying in motion to keep the balance

The Canyon F10 does not yet wear the striking logo of the Canyon bikes, yet it marks a milestone in the bicycle industry and company history of Canyon with regard to technology and design. The teamwork performed by Michael Kaiser as engineer, Hans-Christian Smolik as constructor and Lutz Scheffer as designer clearly states the working principle pursued by Canyon: engineers and designers engage in mutual collaboration to arrive at the best solution. Lutz Scheffer at that time takes care of the development of the product portfolio und the bicycle design. After researching and applying the composite material carbon, Roman Arnold adds more designers to the team. Starting in 2005, the Munich-based KMS Team oversees the complete Canyon brand development which also includes a new corporate design with a new logo and new corporate typeface. In 2007, the corporate design is honoured in the Red Dot Award: Communication Design. In 2009, the award for the new Canyon Home follows. The new building not only reflects the dynamic growth of the company; in the "showroom", the customer learns to understand the areas of technology, design and quality and can directly experience the products and the brand. And the customers' interest in high-quality bicycles with regard to technology and design is growing unstoppably.

In retrospect, Michael Kaiser recalls: "To us, the subject of design in product development has always been an important factor. In 2009, we decided to redefine industrial design as a strategic subject with the objective to play a leading role in the entire industry. Subsequently, we have expanded our product and graphic design team successively, celebrating many successes since then." The design results are impressive. In the last six years, Canyon has won the Red Dot: Best of the Best award six times for, among others, the Speedmax CF SLX triathlon bike and the Aeroad CF SLX racing bike whose design was masterminded by Darmstadt-based Artefakt design studio. The team around Tomas Fiegl and Achim Pohl develops a reduced design language for the racing bikes and time trial machines made of carbon, underlying the attributes of the brand.

Ich kann Tausende von verschiedenen Fasern mit Tausenden von verschiedenen Kunststoffsystemen zusammenbringen. Man kann das Material sehr steif oder sehr weich machen, man kann es flexibel, elastisch oder plastisch, ja sogar wärme- oder elektrisch leitfähig machen. Man kann eigentlich alles machen." Nach dem Erfolg der Canyon F10 denkt Michael Kaiser lange über den Wechsel vom Institut für Verbundwerkstoffe in Kaiserslautern zu Canyon nach. Er fühlt sich inzwischen eng mit dem Unternehmen verbunden, weil ihn die Leidenschaft der Mitarbeiter und die des Unternehmens schon längst angesteckt haben. Im Jahr 2007 ist es so weit. Michael Kaiser wird der erste fest angestellte Mitarbeiter in der Entwicklung von Canyon Bicycles. Was folgt, ist der sukzessive Aufbau der Entwicklungsabteilung, des Prüflabors und des Qualitätswesens. Heute sind knapp 100 Mitarbeiter in diesen Bereichen beschäftigt.

In Bewegung bleiben, um die Balance zu halten

Das Canyon F10 trägt noch nicht den markanten Schriftzug der Canyon-Bikes, markiert aus technologischer und gestalterischer Sicht aber einen wichtigen Meilenstein in der Fahrradbranche und in der Unternehmensgeschichte von Canyon. Die Teamarbeit von Michael Kaiser als Ingenieur, Hans-Christian Smolik als Konstrukteur und Lutz Scheffer als Designer macht das Arbeitsprinzip von Canyon deutlich: Ingenieure und Designer arbeiten gemeinsam an der besten Lösung. Lutz Scheffer kümmert sich damals um die Entwicklung des Produktportfolios und des Fahrraddesigns. Nach der Erforschung und Anwendung des Verbundwerkstoffs Carbon zieht Roman Arnold weitere Designer hinzu. Ab 2005 gestaltet KMS Team aus München die komplette Markenentwicklung von Canyon, die auch ein neues Corporate Design mit neuem Logo und eigener Hausschrift beinhaltet. Das Corporate Design wird 2007 im Red Dot Award: Communication Design ausgezeichnet. 2009 folgt die Auszeichnung für das neue „Canyon Home". Der Neubau spiegelt nicht nur das dynamische Wachstum des Unternehmens wider, im Showroom lernt der Kunde auch die Bereiche Technologie, Design und Qualität verstehen. Hier kann er die Produkte und die Marke hautnah erleben. Und das Interesse der Kunden an technologisch wie gestalterisch hochwertigen Fahrrädern wächst unaufhaltsam.

Rückblickend erinnert sich Michael Kaiser: „Uns war das Thema ‚Design' in der Produktentwicklung schon immer sehr wichtig. Im Jahre 2009 haben wir uns entschlossen, Industriedesign als strategisches Thema neu zu definieren, mit dem Ziel, hier führend in der gesamten Branche werden zu wollen. Wir haben danach sukzessive unser Produkt- und Grafikdesignteam ausgebaut und seitdem viele Erfolge feiern dürfen." Die Designbilanz ist beeindruckend. In den letzten sechs Jahren wird Canyon sechs Mal mit dem Red Dot: Best of the Best ausgezeichnet, unter anderem für das Triathlonrad „Speedmax CF SLX" und das Rennrad „Aeroad CF SLX", die aus der Feder des Darmstädter Designbüros Artefakt stammen. Das Team um Tomas Fiegl und Achim Pohl entwickelt eine reduzierte Formensprache für die Rennräder und Zeitfahrmaschinen aus Carbon, die die Attribute der Marke unterstreichen.

Design captures the city. With integrated LED lighting as well as theft-proof wheels and saddle, the Commuter is ideal for the urban space.
Design erobert die Stadt. Mit integrierter LED-Beleuchtung sowie diebstahlsicheren Laufrädern und Sattel ist der Commuter ideal für den urbanen Raum.

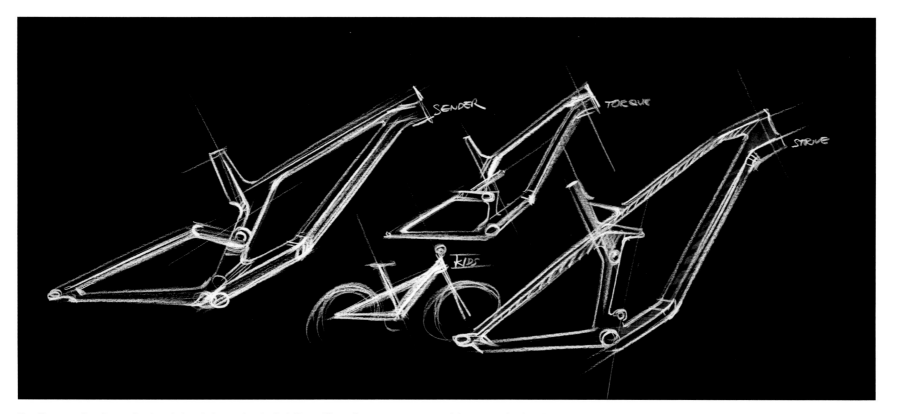

The first step involves a freehand sketch. Later the draft follows. Then, line management and frame aesthetics play a highly crucial role.
Im ersten Schritt wird frei von Hand entworfen. Später folgt der Entwurf. Die Linienführung und Ästhetik des Rahmens spielen dann eine entscheidende Rolle.

In 2017, the Canyon in-house design team receives not one but two "Red Dot: Best of the Best" awards: for the Roadlite CF fitness bike by Fedja Delic and for the Inflite CF SLX, designed by Alexander Forst and Lars Wagner. Numerous awards for the mountain bikes Strive CF, Sender CF and Nerve AL by Canyon designer Peter Kettenring and constructor Vincenz Thoma, as well as for the Commuter urban bike, round off the picture and demonstrate that Canyon, like hardly any other manufacturer in the industry, is outstandingly successful in combining the different bicycle types under a singular design and brand language. The form of each bicycle, whether for the road or for off-road, conveys simplicity, precision and dynamics. As Senior Industrial Designer, Lars Wagner is in charge of the Road Bikes section. He has been active for Canyon since 2010. Senior Industrial Designer Peter Kettenring is responsible for the Mountain Bikes section; he joined Canyon in 2012. Both Lars Wagner and Peter Kettenring studied industrial design in Darmstadt and speak the same language with regard to the design of Canyon bikes. Bringing the bicycles into an aesthetic form that renders the brand attractive yet making the design unobtrusive is the exciting task of the Canyon Design Team. The self-image and aspiration to always develop, design and build the best bicycle is a challenge and motivation, as the single models always have to combine a mixture of different development objectives. Racing cyclists, for instance, always strive for a bike as lightweight as possible which is supposed to be stiff and thus efficient in propulsion at the same time, yet it must not be uncomfortable. Triathletes want the aerodynamically optimised model, while mountain bikers want perfect kinematics.

Im Jahr 2017 wird das Canyon In-house Design Team dann gleich zweimal mit dem Red Dot: Best of the Best ausgezeichnet: für das Fitness-Bike „Roadlite CF" von Fedja Delic und für das „Inflite CF SLX" aus der Feder von Alexander Forst und Lars Wagner. Zahlreiche Auszeichnungen für die Mountainbikes „Strive CF", „Sender CF" und „Nerve AL" von Canyon-Designer Peter Kettenring und Konstrukteur Vincenz Thoma sowie für das Urban Bike „Commuter" runden das Bild ab und veranschaulichen, dass es Canyon wie kaum einem anderen Hersteller der Branche gelingt, die unterschiedlichen Fahrradtypen unter einer Design- und Markensprache zu verbinden. Die Form jedes Fahrrads, ob für die Straße oder für das Gelände, vermittelt Einfachheit, Präzision und Dynamik. Als Senior Industrial Designer verantwortet Lars Wagner den Bereich „Roadbikes". Er ist seit 2010 für Canyon tätig. Verantwortlich für den Bereich „Mountainbikes" ist Senior Industrial Designer Peter Kettenring, der 2012 zu Canyon kommt. Lars Wagner und Peter Kettenring haben beide Industriedesign in Darmstadt studiert und sprechen dieselbe Sprache, wenn es um die Gestaltung der Canyon-Bikes geht. Die Fahrräder in eine ästhetische Form zu bringen, die die Marke attraktiv, das Design aber unaufdringlich macht, ist die spannende Aufgabe des Canyon Design Teams. Das Selbstverständnis und der Anspruch, immer das beste Fahrrad entwickeln, gestalten und bauen zu wollen, ist Herausforderung und Motivation, müssen die einzelnen Modelle doch immer einen Mix aus verschiedenen Entwicklungszielen in sich vereinen. Rennradfahrer etwa streben stets nach einem möglichst leichten Bike, das zugleich steif und somit vortriebseffizient sein soll, andererseits aber nicht unkomfortabel sein darf. Triathleten suchen das aerodynamisch optimierte Modell, Mountainbiker die perfekte Kinematik.

3D rendering and result. By means of computer modelling, a virtual model results that constitutes the materiality and functionality.
The result is a high-quality carbon frame which captivates through aesthetic form and innovative features.
3D-Darstellung und Ergebnis. Mittels der Modellierung am Computer entsteht ein virtuelles Modell, das die Materialität und Funktionalität
darstellt. Das Resultat ist ein hochwertiger Carbonrahmen, der durch ästhetische Form und innovative Funktionen besticht.

All these parameters are gauged by Canyon in static and dynamic quality controls; moreover, the designers are in the wind tunnel for regular testing. With the endoscope and the first computer tomography images in the bicycle industry, all safety-relevant components are literally x-rayed. This applies to the development of new component parts, but the serially produced carbon forks and cockpits are also tested to 100 per cent. Canyon mounts its own bikes in a state-of-the-art facility in Koblenz and sells them via the Internet. The customers are able to experience the wide range of products online or in the Canyon Home, and eventually, for instance, to ride the same bicycle as the numerous professionals under contract with Canyon. The Canyon websites are available in 16 different languages. The bikes are shipped worldwide.

Something that, in retrospect, reads like a self-evident and natural course of things is by no means a straightforward path. Any cyclist knows that, in the face of obstacles and uncertainties, technical defects or material weaknesses, the shortest route from start to finish is not a straight line. This is in no way different for Roman Arnold and Canyon. And this is precisely what makes the success for Canyon so remarkable, because in the areas of technology, quality and design, the company repeatedly arrives at solutions no one had foreseen – not even industry insiders.

All diese Parameter werden von Canyon in statischen und dynamischen Qualitätsprüfungen gemessen, zudem sind die Entwickler regelmäßig für Tests im Windkanal. Mit einem Endoskop und dem ersten Computertomographen in der Fahrradbranche werden alle sicherheitsrelevanten Bauteile zudem buchstäblich durchleuchtet. Das trifft auf die Entwicklung neuer Teile zu, aber auch die in Serie gefertigten Carbongabeln und Cockpits werden zu 100 Prozent geprüft. Canyon montiert seine Bikes in einer hochmodernen Fabrik in Koblenz und vertreibt sie über das Internet. Die Kunden können online oder im Canyon Home die verschiedenen Produktwelten erleben und am Ende zum Beispiel sogar das gleiche Fahrrad wie die zahlreichen Profis fahren, die bei Canyon unter Vertrag stehen. Die Internetseiten von Canyon sind heute in 16 verschiedenen Sprachen verfügbar. Die Fahrräder werden weltweit verschickt.

Was sich rückwirkend wie selbstverständlich liest, ist kein geradliniger Weg. Jeder Radsportler weiß, dass angesichts von Hindernissen und Unwägbarkeiten, technischen Defekten oder Materialschwächen die kürzeste Verbindung zwischen Start und Ziel keine gerade Linie ist. Das ist für Roman Arnold und Canyon nicht anders. Gerade das macht den Erfolg für Canyon so bemerkenswert, weil das Unternehmen im Bereich Technologie, Qualität und Design immer wieder auf Lösungen kommt, mit denen keiner gerechnet hat, nicht einmal Brancheninsider.

Vincenz Thoma, Sandro Groll, Christian Hellmann, Wanjo Koch, Michael Kaiser, Lars Wagner, Peter Kettenring, Roman Arnold,
Fedja Delic, Sebastian Hahn, Dennis Fiedler, Christopher Herd

Interview
Peter Kettenring, Senior Industrial Designer Mountain Bikes
Lars Wagner, Senior Industrial Designer Road Bikes

Mr Kettenring, Mr Wagner, what does cycling actually mean?

P. Kettenring: Roman Arnold, the founder and CEO of Canyon once said: "When I learned to cycle, I felt great freedom for the first time." Basically, cycling is about moving oneself forward independently.

That sounds like a philosophy for life. Cycling to find out something about oneself!

L. Wagner: Absolutely. Almost everyone remembers the first time they rode a bike on their own. It's an emotional moment: the first time cycling alone, without your parents, just on your own steam. Bicycles are an important part of our life experience.

This year was the first time that a children's bike, the Offspring by Canyon, won in the Red Dot Design Award, and two years ago an urban bike called the Commuter won the award. How do these types of bikes fit with the Canyon brand with its origins in race bikes?

L. Wagner: Of course we did consider whether a kid's bike or a lifestyle product like the Commuter fits with our history and our brand. But this step can make absolute sense and be successful if we pay very close attention to transferring the design and quality features that characterise our brand and identity to new areas.

How can you know what kind of bicycle might be in demand in the future?

L. Wagner: That's mainly the job of the product manager, who forms a team together with the designer and the engineer and continuously looks at new types of bikes. The development may well start from scratch, or new trends emerge on the market. Customers are also a source of ideas for entirely new types of bikes. We then use these ideas to create a new overall concept.

Herr Kettenring, Herr Wagner: Fahrrad fahren – was bedeutet das eigentlich?

P. Kettenring: Roman Arnold, der Gründer und CEO von Canyon, hat einmal gesagt: „Als ich Rad fahren lernte, hatte ich erstmals das Gefühl großer Freiheit." Im Prinzip dreht es sich darum, sich selbst zu bewegen, selbst voranzukommen.

Das klingt nach Lebensphilosophie. Rad fahren, um etwas über sich selbst zu erfahren!

L. Wagner: Durchaus. Fast jeder weiß noch, wann er das erste Mal alleine mit dem Fahrrad gefahren ist. Das ist ein emotionaler Moment: das erste Mal allein unterwegs sein, ohne die Eltern, ganz einfach aus eigener Kraft. Das Fahrrad ist ein wichtiger Teil unserer Lebenserfahrung.

In diesem Jahr wurde mit dem Offspring erstmals ein Kinderfahrrad von Canyon im Red Dot Design Award ausgezeichnet, vor zwei Jahren ein Urban Bike, das Commuter. Wie passen diese Fahrradtypen zur Marke Canyon, die aus dem Radsport kommt?

L. Wagner: Natürlich haben wir überlegt, ob ein Kinderrad oder ein Lifestyle-Produkt wie das Commuter zu unserer Geschichte und Marke passen. Wenn man aber sehr genau darauf achtet, die Design- und Qualitätsmerkmale, die unsere Marke und Identität prägen, auf neue Bereiche zu übertragen, dann kann dieser Schritt durchaus sinnvoll und erfolgreich sein.

Woher weiß man, welches Fahrrad in der Zukunft gefragt sein könnte?

L. Wagner: Das ist im Wesentlichen die Arbeit des Produktmanagers, der zusammen mit dem Designer und dem Ingenieur ein Team bildet und sich immer wieder mit neuen Fahrradtypen auseinandersetzt. Die Entwicklung kann durchaus bei null beginnen, oder es entwickeln sich neue Trends im Markt. Auch die Kunden kommen mit Ideen für ganz neue Fahrradtypen. Und wir entwickeln aus diesen Ideen dann ein neues Gesamtkonzept.

So it is possible to reinvent the wheel?

P. Kettenring: Maybe not the wheel, but certainly the bicycle. Bike design has undergone a lot of change, and this will continue to be the case.

L. Wagner: Interestingly, the bicycle is much older than the car, but the classic ideas of industrial design came comparatively late to the bicycle industry. Bicycle design is still a relatively new discipline. This means that we have not yet reached a stage where no more innovation is possible. Development is a continuous process.

P. Kettenring: For example, we developed a Shapeshifter function for the Strive mountain bike. The bike looks like a traditional mountain bike but allows the rider to choose between two different geometries at the touch of a button and to tune the bike to different trail conditions on the fly: uphill and downhill. It's like having two bikes in one.

How would you describe the difference between the past and the present?

P. Kettenring: In the past, when bike frames were still welded together using individual tubes, the work of the designer was limited to the artwork. Nowadays we receive a geometric sketch made up of lines. The geometric sketch provides a framework for us to move within, but as designers we can also make our own suggestions for turning points, kinematics or tube cross-sections. We have become very confident about what we do.

Das Rad lässt sich also doch neu erfinden?

P. Kettenring: Das Rad vielleicht nicht, das Fahrrad schon. Im Fahrraddesign hat sich viel geändert, und es wird sich noch vieles ändern.

L. Wagner: Interessanterweise ist das Fahrrad viel älter als das Automobil. Der klassische Gedanke des Industriedesigns ist aber relativ spät in der Fahrradindustrie angekommen. Das Fahrraddesign ist eine noch relativ junge Disziplin. Wir sind also noch nicht an einem Punkt angekommen, der keine Innovationen mehr zulässt. Die Entwicklung geht immer weiter.

P. Kettenring: Für das Mountainbike „Strive" haben wir beispielsweise eine Shapeshifter-Funktion entwickelt. Das Rad sieht aus wie ein traditionelles Mountainbike, erlaubt dem Fahrer aber, ganz einfach per Knopfdruck zwischen zwei unterschiedlichen Geometrien zu wählen und das Rad während der Fahrt auf unterschiedliche Geländesituationen abzustimmen: bergauf und bergab. Man hat im Prinzip zwei Räder in einem.

Wie lässt sich der Unterschied zwischen gestern und heute beschreiben?

P. Kettenring: Früher, als die Fahrradrahmen noch aus einzelnen Rohren zusammengeschweißt wurden, reduzierte sich die Arbeit des Designers auf das Artwork. Heute erhalten wir eine Geometrieskizze, die aus Linien besteht. Die Geometrieskizze ist einerseits ein Rahmen, in dem wir uns bewegen, andererseits können wir als Designer eigene Vorschläge machen für Drehpunkte, Kinematik oder Rohrquerschnitte. Inzwischen wissen wir sehr gut, was wir tun.

"Simplicity, precision and dynamics are basic elements of our design language."

„Einfachheit, Präzision und Dynamik sind elementare Bestandteile unserer Designsprache."

Lars Wagner, Senior Industrial Designer Road Bikes

L. Wagner: If you look at frame development alone, you will understand that technology also creates whole new design possibilities for the designer and whole new shapes for the bike.

What is the role of the bicycle frame? It combines aesthetics with function.

L. Wagner: Yes, exactly. The bicycle frame is form and structure, volume and sculpture. If you imagine that everything we design always also affects the function, then there is a lot hanging on the frame, quite literally. Basically we draw the frame and structure it with areas of differing brightness so that the light edges and surfaces become visible. In general we try to use edges sparingly but very consciously, as the edges always also symbolise technical precision. The freeform surfaces stand for the distribution of power and the rigidity as well as for bionic shapes.

P. Kettenring: On the one hand we want to reduce the frame to the essentials, but that doesn't mean we simply weld round tubes together. If we apply the ideas of simplicity, precision and dynamics to the frame in a formal aesthetic way, then we emphasise a light edge that connects the rear end of the frame with the main frame. This is an essential point. We can reduce other downstream or subordinate edges a little using lower contrast. Basically, contrast is created where light and shade converge.

L. Wagner: Wenn man sich allein die Rahmenentwicklung anschaut, dann versteht man, dass sich durch die Technologie auch ganz neue Gestaltungsmöglichkeiten für den Designer und ganz neue Formen für das Fahrrad ergeben.

Welche Rolle spielt der Fahrradrahmen? Er vereint ja Ästhetik und Funktion.

L. Wagner: Ja, genau. Der Fahrradrahmen ist Form und Struktur, Volumen und Skulptur. Wenn man sich vorstellt, dass alles, was wir gestalten, immer auch Auswirkungen auf die Funktion hat, dann hängt buchstäblich sehr viel am Rahmen. Im Prinzip ist es so, dass wir den Rahmen zeichnen und mit unterschiedlich hellen Flächen strukturieren, sodass die Lichtkanten und Flächen sichtbar werden. Wir versuchen grundsätzlich, mit den Kanten sparsam, aber sehr deutlich umzugehen, da die Kanten immer auch die technische Präzision symbolisieren. Die Freiformflächen stehen für die Kraftverteilung und die Steifigkeit sowie für bionische Formen.

P. Kettenring: Einerseits wollen wir den Rahmen auf das Wesentliche reduzieren, andererseits bedeutet das nicht, dass wir einfach Rundrohre miteinander verschmelzen. Wenn wir die Gedanken der Einfachheit, Präzision und Dynamik formalästhetisch auf den Rahmen übertragen, dann betonen wir eine Lichtkante, die den Hinterbau und den Hauptrahmen verbindet. Das ist etwas Wesentliches. Andere Kanten, die nach- oder untergeordnet sind, können wir durch einen geringeren Kontrast etwas zurücknehmen. Der Kontrast bildet sich im Prinzip dort, wo sich Licht und Schatten treffen.

"Canyon succeeds better than almost any other manufacturer in combining the different bikes under one design and brand language."
„Canyon gelingt es wie kaum einem anderen Hersteller, die unterschiedlichen Fahrräder unter einer Design- und Markensprache zu verbinden."

Peter Kettenring, Senior Industrial Designer Mountain Bikes

How would you describe the design process at Canyon?

P. Kettenring: We start with a rough 3D sketch. Then we make a 3D print. Next we can use picture editing to change gradients. After that, the draft design goes back into the CAD system.

L. Wagner: The 3D print allows us to check the design. We don't use traditional modelling. Instead we print smaller true-to-scale models and components in house. The parts are then assembled in the technical workshop. After all, we work with very different components, and each one has to fit. As designers we also create the final shapes, and the engineer is responsible for the interfaces to the other mounting parts. As a result, we know exactly what the bike ultimately has to look like and will look like.

P. Kettenring: Artwork is still a very important topic, because the lettering, logos and colours are linked very closely to the design. The lines and the edges of the frame are reflected in and enhanced through the artwork, preventing them from disappearing during the painting stage. But we never create effects that do not exist in the form. By the time the finished bike is wheeled into our office, it's already like an old friend.

L. Wagner: Yes, it's already familiar, we have seen each other before.

Wie lässt sich der Designprozess bei Canyon beschreiben?

P. Kettenring: Wir beginnen mit einer groben Skizze. Dann wird ein 3D aufgebaut. Anschließend besteht die Möglichkeit, im Bildbearbeitungsprogramm Verläufe zu ändern. Von da aus geht der Entwurf dann wieder ins CAD-System.

L. Wagner: Der 3D-Druck dient uns dann zur Überprüfung des Designs. Wir haben keinen klassischen Modellbau, sondern drucken kleinere Maßstabsmodelle und Bauteile bei uns im Haus. In der Technikwerkstatt werden dann die Teile zu einem Ganzen zusammengefügt. Wir arbeiten ja mit ganz unterschiedlichen Komponenten. Und die müssen alle passen. Da wir als Designer auch die finalen Formen gestalten und der Ingenieur die Schnittstellen zu den anderen Anbauteilen übernimmt, wissen wir sehr genau, wie das Fahrrad am Ende aussehen muss und wird.

P. Kettenring: Auch das Thema „Artwork" ist nach wie vor sehr wichtig, da Schrift, Grafik und Farbgebung sehr eng mit der Formgebung verbunden sind. Die Linienführung und die Kanten der Rahmen werden aufgegriffen und durch das Artwork verstärkt, sodass sie nicht durch den Lackiervorgang verschwinden. Es werden aber niemals Effekte erzeugt, die formal nicht da sind. Wenn dann irgendwann das fertige Fahrrad in unser Büro rollt, ist es schon ein alter Bekannter.

L. Wagner: Ja, man kennt sich. Man hat sich schon mal gesehen.

The corporate design stems from the brand agency KMS Team in Munich. The Canyon lettering emphasises the simplicity, precision and dynamics of the bikes.

L. Wagner: The lettering is a real stroke of luck. It doesn't wear over time and never gets boring.

But Canyon design involves even more than that.

L. Wagner: Depending on the type of bike, there are different requirements in terms of aerodynamics, weight, rigidity and comfort. Bringing these opposing factors into harmony with each other is what we do, and that's what makes it exciting.

P. Kettenring: At the same time, Canyon succeeds better than almost any other manufacturer in combining the different bikes under one design and brand language. Every line, every detail and every shape should convey simplicity and precision.

Yet designing simplicity can be very complex.

L. Wagner: Of course we do always try to simplify the bikes. The frame is the structure that keeps the different elements and parts in place. That automatically leads to a certain complexity, because certain connections have to be made. We try to reduce this complexity.

P. Kettenring: The best simplification is one that not only reduces the design but also improves the function. That is a challenge and a difficulty at the same time. Not only do you take something away, you also create an improvement.

How does the idea for a functional yet aesthetic solution come about?

P. Kettenring: At Canyon, there is a very close working relationship between designers and engineers. This team work is hugely instructive. Designers learn from engineers, and engineers learn from designers. And we also always explain why we want to find different solutions for certain details from a design perspective.

L. Wagner: We generally create a team of three persons who are responsible for a project: the product manager, the engineer and the designer. The product manager has the last word if the engineer and the designer can't agree on something.

Is this team structure specific to Canyon?

P. Kettenring: Other companies are generally organised into departments. But often the project teams organised in departments don't sit together at one table from the beginning. So that is a very specific way of working at Canyon.

Das Corporate Design stammt von der Markenagentur KMS Team aus München. Der Schriftzug „Canyon" unterstreicht die Einfachheit, die Präzision und die Dynamik der Fahrräder.

L. Wagner: Der Schriftzug ist ein absoluter Glücksfall. Er verschleißt sich nicht und wird nie langweilig.

Das Canyon-Design umfasst aber noch mehr.

L. Wagner: Je nach Fahrradtyp geht es um unterschiedliche Anforderungen mit Blick auf Aerodynamik, Gewicht, Steifigkeit und Komfort. Diese Gegensätze zu einem harmonischen Ganzen zu verbinden, macht unsere Arbeit aus und bringt die Spannung.

P. Kettenring: Gleichzeitig gelingt es Canyon wie kaum einem anderen Hersteller, die unterschiedlichen Fahrräder unter einer Design- und Markensprache zu verbinden. Jede Linie, jedes Detail, jede Form soll Einfachheit und Präzision vermitteln.

Die Gestaltung der Einfachheit kann aber durchaus komplex sein.

L. Wagner: Natürlich versuchen wir auch immer, die Fahrräder zu vereinfachen. Der Rahmen ist die Struktur, die verschiedene Elemente und Teile an Ort und Stelle hält. Das führt automatisch zu einer gewissen Komplexität, weil bestimmte Verbindungen hergestellt werden müssen. Wir versuchen, diese Komplexität zu reduzieren.

P. Kettenring: Die beste Vereinfachung ist die, die nicht nur eine gestalterische Reduktion, sondern auch eine verbesserte Funktion erzielt. Das ist Herausforderung und Schwierigkeit zugleich. Man nimmt nicht nur etwas weg, sondern schafft auch noch eine Verbesserung.

Wie entsteht die Idee zu einer ebenso funktionalen wie ästhetischen Lösung?

P. Kettenring: Bei Canyon gibt es eine sehr enge Zusammenarbeit zwischen Designern und Ingenieuren. Diese Teamarbeit schult ungemein. Designer lernen von Ingenieuren, und Ingenieure lernen von Designern. Und wir erklären auch immer, warum wir bestimmte Details aus gestalterischer Sicht gerne anders gelöst hätten.

L. Wagner: Wir bilden in der Regel ein Team aus drei Personen, die für ein Projekt verantwortlich sind: Produktmanager, Ingenieur und Designer, wobei der Produktmanager das letzte Wort hat, wenn sich Ingenieur und Designer einmal nicht einigen sollten.

Ist diese Teamstruktur eine Besonderheit bei Canyon?

P. Kettenring: Aus anderen Unternehmen kennt man vorrangig die Organisation in Form von Abteilungen. Die in Abteilungen organisierten Projektteams sitzen aber häufig nicht von Anfang an an einem Tisch. Das ist schon sehr spezifisch für die Arbeit bei Canyon.

So the common understanding of the project team shortens communication channels?

L. Wagner: I think so. We know immediately what the other person is talking about. There are lots of things we don't even need to talk about, because they are obvious for us, particularly amongst designers.

P. Kettenring: I agree. Of course there are always situations where we need to discuss details and have different opinions, but the basic understanding of the brand and the design is a given.

To what extent does the management influence design?

L. Wagner: We are lucky in that our CEO Roman Arnold has a strong affinity for design. His overarching motto of "Building the best bike" emphasises how he sees himself and what he expects. He is the one who motivates all of us over and over again to develop the best bike.

P. Kettenring: Roman Arnold also expressly requested that the bikes should be of high quality and consistent in their appearance. In the same way that the frame should not only be the aesthetic form but also the functional structure, we aim to design even the smallest of details in a functional and aesthetic way. As an owner-managed business, we have the advantage that Roman Arnold truly embraces the overarching motto of "Building the best bike" in practise. This claim is not based simply on economic considerations alone. Instead, it stems from his passion for cycling.

So what role does the design play for customers?

L. Wagner: To help our customers better understand how a bike is created, we have presented examples on the topics of technology, design and quality in our showroom. For us, there is also a moment of acknowledgement when we see the joy and satisfaction on the faces of our customers as they leave the showroom with their new Canyon bike. Cycling simply has an emotional dimension.

P. Kettenring: Our customers are delighted with their new bikes. And happy customers are always also a confirmation of the work we do. Of course we also design bikes that we would like to ride ourselves. And when a new bike comes on the market, it's nice to observe the intense discussions in social media and Internet forums about the design, and not just about the test reports of trade journals. Canyon has recognised this, and maybe even contributed to this perception. It simply demonstrates the general importance of design today.

Is customers' interest in design also reflected in the specialist magazines? Is the topic of design also a topic discussed in the specialist media?

P. Kettenring: Unfortunately, design is not one of the assessment criteria used in the tests by the trade journals. It is a topic that has not yet made it to the print media, but it is very present in social media.

Das gemeinsame Verständnis des Projektteams verkürzt die Kommunikation?

L. Wagner: Ich habe schon das Gefühl. Wir wissen ja sofort, worüber der andere spricht. Über viele Dinge müssen wir gar nicht reden, weil sie für uns selbstverständlich sind, insbesondere zwischen uns Designern.

P. Kettenring: Das sehe ich auch so. Natürlich gibt es immer auch Situationen, in denen es um Details geht und man anderer Meinung ist, aber das grundsätzliche Verständnis für die Marke und das Design ist einfach gegeben.

Inwieweit nimmt die Geschäftsführung auf die Gestaltung Einfluss?

L. Wagner: Wir haben das Glück, dass unser Geschäftsführer Roman Arnold sehr designaffin ist. Sein Leitgedanke „Building the best bike" unterstreicht sein Selbstverständnis und seinen Anspruch. Er ist es, der uns alle immer wieder motiviert, das beste Fahrrad zu entwickeln.

P. Kettenring: Roman Arnold hat auch den konkreten Wunsch geäußert, dass die Fahrräder hochwertig und wie aus einem Guss aussehen. So, wie der Rahmen nicht nur ästhetische Form, sondern auch funktionale Struktur sein soll, haben wir auch den Anspruch, die kleinsten Details funktional und ästhetisch zu gestalten. Als inhabergeführtes Unternehmen haben wir den Vorteil, dass Roman Arnold den Leitgedanken „Building the best bike" lebt. Dieser Anspruch geht nicht einfach nur auf wirtschaftliche Überlegungen zurück, sondern resultiert aus seiner Leidenschaft für das Radfahren.

Welche Rolle spielt denn das Design für die Kunden?

L. Wagner: Damit auch unsere Kunden die Entwicklung eines Fahrrads besser verstehen, haben wir die Themen „Technologie", „Design" und „Qualität" beispielhaft in unserem Showroom dargestellt. Für uns ist es zudem ein Moment der Bestätigung, wenn man die Freude und Zufriedenheit in den Gesichtern der Kunden sehen kann, die mit ihrem neuen Canyon-Fahrrad den Showroom verlassen. Rad fahren ist einfach etwas Emotionales.

P. Kettenring: Unsere Kunden freuen sich riesig über ihr neues Fahrrad. Und die Freude der Kunden ist immer auch eine Wertschätzung unserer Arbeit. Natürlich gestalten wir auch Fahrräder, die wir selbst gerne fahren möchten. Wenn dann aber ein neues Fahrrad auf den Markt kommt, lässt sich sehr schön beobachten, wie in den Sozialen Medien und in den Internetforen intensiv über das Design diskutiert wird und nicht nur über die Testberichte der Fachzeitschriften. Canyon hat das erkannt. Vielleicht hat Canyon diese Wahrnehmung auch gefördert. Es zeigt einfach, welche generelle Bedeutung das Thema „Design" heute hat.

Spiegelt sich das Designinteresse der Kunden auch in den Fachmagazinen wieder? Ist Design auch ein Thema in den Fachmedien?

P. Kettenring: In den Tests der Fachmagazine ist Design leider kein Bewertungskriterium. Das Thema ist in den Printmedien noch nicht angekommen, in den Sozialen Medien dagegen schon.

Dr Michael Kaiser, Technical Managing Director Canyon Bicycles GmbH

Roman Arnold, Founder and Managing Director Canyon Bicycles GmbH

L. Wagner: The traditional media are of course important for Canyon's success. For race bikes, Tour magazine publishes a well-known Tour Test. And when we start a new project, everyone knows that we want to win that test. But we don't design new bikes just to have a new sales argument. The technical or design changes we make are based on the desire to build the best bike.

What role does the material play in bicycle design?

L. Wagner: The low-end models include bikes with an aluminium frame, while the higher-end models have carbon frames.

P. Kettenring: Normally we design the carbon model first, and apply the carbon model to the different segments. The impetus comes from the high-end models.

Traditionally it has been relatively easy to tell a bike with an aluminium frame from one with a carbon frame on account of the welded seams, isn't that so?

P. Kettenring: But the new models are making this optical distinction increasingly difficult, because the aluminium frames now also look like they are made from a single cast part.

L. Wagner: It goes without saying that we design new models without transitions and welded seams, using technology to try to get aluminium frames closer to the ideal, which is a carbon frame.

L. Wagner: Natürlich sind auch die klassischen Medien für den Erfolg von Canyon wichtig. Im Rennradbereich veröffentlicht das Tour-Magazin einen bekannten Tour-Test. Und wenn wir ein neues Projekt beginnen, ist jedem klar, dass wir diesen Test gewinnen wollen. Wir gestalten aber keine neuen Fahrräder, nur um ein neues Verkaufsargument zu haben. Die technischen oder gestalterischen Veränderungen, die wir vornehmen, basieren auf dem Anspruch, das beste Fahrrad zu bauen.

Welche Rolle spielt das Material für das Fahrraddesign?

L. Wagner: Bei den Einsteigermodellen findet man Fahrräder mit Aluminiumrahmen. Im gehobenen Segment kommen Carbonrahmen zum Einsatz.

P. Kettenring: Im Normalfall gestalten wir zuerst das Carbonmodell und übertragen das dann auf die unterschiedlichen Segmente. Der Impuls geht vom High-End-Bereich aus.

Traditionell lassen sich die Fahrräder mit Aluminiumrahmen aufgrund der Schweißnähte relativ leicht von den Fahrrädern mit Carbonrahmen unterscheiden, oder?

P. Kettenring: Die neuen Modelle machen diese optische Unterscheidung aber zusehends schwieriger, da die Aluminiumrahmen auch schon wie aus einem Guss aussehen.

L. Wagner: Wir gestalten neue Modelle natürlich übergangslos und ohne Schweißnähte und versuchen mithilfe der Technologie auch im Aluminiumbereich, uns dem Idealzustand der Carbonrahmen anzunähern.

What conditions does Canyon use to test its own bikes? The question of material quality is always also relevant for safety.

L. Wagner: Generally there are between 10 and 20 bikes assembled that are ridden and tested on road or off road by professionals, but also of course by the development team.

P. Kettenring: In addition, the quality of the pre-series production models is tested on static and dynamic test stations in the lab in order to meet norms and standards and to have similar testing stands to the bike magazines that test our bikes.

L. Wagner: What we want to achieve is a frame that is flexible vertically and rigid horizontally. The direction of the fibre in the carbon is designed accordingly. In the tests on the test station, we can see very clearly how the individual components work under pressure or tensile forces.

P. Kettenring: For example, there is a dedicated test station for the Strive with its Shapeshifter function. This station tests the durability of the bearings and seals in continuous rain and in off-road conditions with mud running down the tubes.

L. Wagner: We literally look right through the frames, and we were the first company in the bike industry to use computer tomography for quality testing.

What trends are you currently watching in bicycle design?

P. Kettenring: One trend is definitely system integration. Nowadays the customer gets a bike specially tailored to his or her needs, and no longer has to replace the components.

L. Wagner: E-bikes will also have a role to play in the future of Canyon. But of course that does mean abandoning the fundamental idea of cycling, which is to move oneself forward on one's own steam. It is almost a philosophical question.

All the more astounding how strongly Canyon has grown so far without e-bikes.

L. Wagner: If your motivation is to build the better product, you don't necessarily have to be the first on the market with a whole new type of bike.

P. Kettenring: The key moment is when you ride an e-bike for the first time. It is a completely new and different feeling. And that requires a new solution.

Mr Wagner, Mr Kettenring, thank you for speaking with us and congratulations on the title of honour, "Red Dot: Design Team of the Year".

Unter welchen Bedingungen testet Canyon die eigenen Fahrräder? Die Frage der Materialqualität ist ja immer auch sicherheitsrelevant.

L. Wagner: In der Regel sind 10 bis 20 Fahrräder aufgebaut, die von Profis, aber natürlich auch von der Entwicklungsabteilung auf der Straße oder im Gelände gefahren und getestet werden.

P. Kettenring: Zudem werden im Prüflabor die Modelle der Vorserienproduktion auf statischen und dynamischen Prüfständen mit Blick auf ihre Qualität überprüft, um Normen und Standards zu erfüllen und um ähnliche Prüfbedingungen zu haben wie die Fahrradmagazine, die unsere Fahrräder testen.

L. Wagner: Wir wollen ja erreichen, dass der Rahmen vertikal flexibel und horizontal steif ist. Entsprechend wird die Faserrichtung des Carbons darauf ausgelegt. Und in den Tests auf dem Prüfstand sieht man sehr genau, wie die einzelnen Bauteile unter Druck oder Zug arbeiten.

P. Kettenring: Für das Strive mit Shapeshifter-Funktion gibt es beispielsweise einen eigenen Prüfstand. Hier geht es um die Haltbarkeit der Lager und Dichtungen, wenn es dauerhaft regnet und im Gelände der Schlamm an den Rohren herunterläuft.

L. Wagner: Wir durchleuchten die Rahmen regelrecht und waren das erste Unternehmen in der Fahrradindustrie, das einen Computertomographen zur Qualitätsprüfung eingesetzt hat.

Welche Trends verfolgen Sie aktuell im Fahrraddesign?

P. Kettenring: Ein Trend ist sicherlich in der Systemintegration zu sehen. Heute erhält der Kunde ein speziell auf ihn abgestimmtes Fahrrad und muss gar nicht mehr die Komponenten austauschen.

L. Wagner: E-Bikes werden auch bei Canyon in Zukunft eine Rolle spielen. Allerdings verabschiedet man sich dann natürlich von dem grundsätzlichen Gedanken des Fahrrads, sich selbst aus eigener Kraft fortzubewegen. Das ist schon fast eine philosophische Frage.

Umso erstaunlicher ist, wie stark Canyon bisher ohne das Thema „E-Bike" gewachsen ist.

L. Wagner: Wenn man den Anspruch hat, das bessere Produkt zu bauen, muss man nicht unbedingt als erster mit einem ganz neuen Fahrradtyp auf dem Markt vertreten sein.

P. Kettenring: Der Schlüsselmoment ist halt der, wenn man das erste Mal E-Bike fährt. Es ist ein ganz anderes, neues Gefühl. Und das verlangt nach einer neuen Lösung.

Herr Wagner, Herr Kettenring, vielen Dank für das Gespräch und herzlichen Glückwunsch zur Ehrenauszeichnung „Red Dot: Design Team of the Year".

"The cyclist must be convinced by the product.
Only when the cyclist is convinced that it is a
fast bike will he really go fast."
„Der Fahrer muss vom Produkt überzeugt sein.
Nur wenn der Fahrer überzeugt ist, dass es ein
schnelles Rad ist, wird er auch schnell fahren."

Dr Michael Kaiser, Technical Managing Director Canyon Bicycles GmbH

Canyon Speedmax CF SLX
Design: Artefakt industriekultur, Darmstadt & Canyon Bicycles GmbH, Koblenz

Red Dot: Best of the Best
The best designers of their category
Die besten Designer ihrer Kategorie

The designers of the Red Dot: Best of the Best
Only a few products in the Red Dot Design Award
receive the "Red Dot: Best of the Best" accolade.
In each category, the jury can assign this award to
products of outstanding design quality and innovative
achievement. Exploring new paths, these products are
all exemplary in their design and oriented towards the
future.

The following chapter introduces the people who have
received one of these prestigious awards. It features
the best designers and design teams of the year 2017
together with their products, revealing in interviews
and statements what drives these designers and what
design means to them.

Die Designer der Red Dot: Best of the Best
Nur sehr wenige Produkte im Red Dot Design Award
erhalten die Auszeichnung „Red Dot: Best of the
Best". Die Jury kann mit dieser Auszeichnung in jeder
Kategorie Design von außerordentlicher Qualität
und Innovationsleistung besonders hervorheben. In
jeder Hinsicht vorbildlich gestaltet, beschreiten diese
Produkte neue Wege und sind zukunftsweisend.

Das folgende Kapitel stellt die Menschen vor, die diese
besondere Auszeichnung erhalten haben. Es zeigt
die besten Designer und Designteams des Jahres 2017
zusammen mit ihren Produkten. In Interviews und
Statements wird deutlich, was diese Designer bewegt
und was ihnen Design bedeutet.

Kris Van Puyvelde
Royal Botania

"If perfection does not exist, then at least try to get as close to it as possible."

„Wenn es Perfektion nicht gibt, sollte man wenigstens versuchen, ihr so nah
wie möglich zu kommen."

What inspires you?
Beauty and functionality, and the combination of both.

How do you define quality?
Details make quality, but quality is not a detail. It is initially defined by the design of a product, but then it can be found in every step of its production, from the choice of the best possible materials, the fittings, the assembly details to the final finish and the packaging.

What do you see as being the biggest challenges in your industry at present?
Firstly, staying ahead of copycats. Protecting new ideas and designs is a big job and consumes a lot of money. Secondly, there are new challenges due to the rise of e-commerce which is jeopardising existing sales channels.

Was inspiriert Sie?
Schönheit und Funktionalität, und die Kombination von beiden.

Wie definieren Sie Qualität?
Kleinigkeiten machen die Qualität aus, aber Qualität ist keine Kleinigkeit. Qualität wird zunächst vom Design eines Produktes bestimmt, findet sich dann aber in jedem Schritt seines Herstellungsprozesses wieder, von der Wahl der bestmöglichen Materialien, der Ausstattung, der Montagedetails bis hin zum letzten Schliff und der Verpackung.

Worin sehen Sie aktuell die größten Herausforderungen in Ihrer Branche?
Erstens den Nachahmern immer einen Schritt voraus zu sein. Neue Ideen und Designs zu schützen, ist eine große und kostspielige Aufgabe. Zweitens stellt uns der zunehmende E-Commerce vor neue Herausforderungen, da er bestehende Vertriebskanäle gefährdet.

reddot award 2017
best of the best

Manufacturer
Royal Botania, Nijlen, Belgium

PALMA
Garden Umbrella
Sonnenschirm

See page 78
Siehe Seite 78

Heston Blumenthal

"Question everything!"
„Hinterfrage alles!"

What was your goal when you designed your award-winning product?
I wanted to capture the joy I get from cooking round a BBQ – the whole theatrical multi-sensory experience of it – and make the process very simple: the latest technology combined with modern design aesthetics.

What inspires you?
Confucius said that: "The man who asks a question is a fool for a minute, the man who does not ask is a fool for life." I'm inspired by all questions, great and small.

What does winning the Red Dot: Best of the Best mean to you?
I'm very happy to have won this award. A lot of thought went into every aspect of this range and it's wonderful to have that celebrated by such a prestigious jury.

Welches Ziel verfolgten Sie bei der Gestaltung Ihres ausgezeichneten Produktes?
Ich wollte den Spaß, den mir das Kochen mit einem Grill bereitet, festhalten – das gesamte dramatische, multisensorische Erlebnis dabei – und den Vorgang des Grillens ganz einfach machen: neueste Technik kombiniert mit moderner Designästhetik.

Was inspiriert Sie?
Konfuzius sagte: „Wer fragt, ist ein Narr für eine Minute. Wer nicht fragt, ist ein Narr sein Leben lang." Mich inspirieren alle Fragen, große und kleine.

Was bedeutet die Auszeichnung mit dem Red Dot: Best of the Best für Sie?
Ich habe mich sehr über die Auszeichnung gefreut. An jedem Aspekt dieser Produktreihe wurde hart gearbeitet. Es ist großartig, dass das die Anerkennung einer so renommierten Jury gefunden hat.

reddot award 2017
best of the best

Manufacturer
Shriro Australia, Kingsgrove,
New South Wales, Australia

Everdure by Heston Blumenthal – HUB
Charcoal BBQ
Holzkohlengrill

See page 88
Siehe Seite 88

34

Fiskars Design Team

What inspires you?
Nordic nature.

**What does winning the Red Dot:
Best of the Best mean to you?**
It is an indication of good design quality.

Was inspiriert Sie?
Die nordische Natur.

**Was bedeutet die Auszeichnung mit
dem Red Dot: Best of the Best für Sie?**
Sie ist ein Zeichen guter Designqualität.

"Watch, learn, collaborate and iterate."
„Beobachten, lernen, zusammenarbeiten und wiederholen."

reddot award 2017
best of the best

Manufacturer
Fiskars Finland Oy Ab, Helsinki, Finland

Fiskars PowerGear™ X
Pruners
Gartenscheren

See page 92
Siehe Seite 92

Mitsuo Nakajima, Hiroyuki Asano, Chikara Fujita
Nikon Corporation

"We strive for designs that resonate with people, and their desires and emotions."

„Wir streben Gestaltungen an, die bei Menschen, ihren Wünschen und Emotionen Widerhall finden."

What was your goal when you designed your award-winning product?
We wanted to offer users a new imaging experience.

Was your award-winning product based on a particular design approach?
We inspected prototypes based on use case analysis.

How do you maintain a work-life balance?
Incorporating our hobby into our work, we are able to work and have fun at the same time.

What does winning the Red Dot: Best of the Best mean to you?
Winning this award will increase the morale of the entire design department, and also reflect positively on Nikon's brand image.

Welches Ziel verfolgten Sie bei der Gestaltung Ihres ausgezeichneten Produktes?
Wir wollten Nutzern eine neue Erfahrung der Bildgebung bieten.

Liegt Ihrem ausgezeichneten Produkt ein bestimmter Gestaltungsansatz zugrunde?
Wir haben Prototypen mithilfe einer Use-Case-Analyse untersucht.

Wie erhalten Sie sich Ihre Work-Life-Balance?
Die Einbindung unserer Hobbys in die Arbeit erlaubt es uns, zu arbeiten und gleichzeitig Spaß zu haben.

Was bedeutet die Auszeichnung mit dem Red Dot: Best of the Best für Sie?
Die Auszeichnung mit diesem Award wird die Moral der gesamten Designabteilung heben und sich auch positiv auf das Markenimage von Nikon auswirken.

reddot award 2017
best of the best

Manufacturer
Nikon Corporation, Tokyo, Japan

KeyMission 360
Action Camera
Actionkamera

See page 104
Siehe Seite 104

Huy Nguyen, Seung Lee, Rich Gioscia, John Muhlenkamp, Senka Bergman, Ben Parfitt, Michael Paterson
GoPro Industrial Design Team

"Design the future GoPro flagship camera, honour the heritage of GoPro's past."

„Die Gestaltung der GoPro Vorzeige-Kamera der Zukunft und die Bewahrung des kulturellen Erbes von GoPro."

Was your award-winning product based on a particular design approach?
Our approach to designing the HERO5 Black looked forward to the future while paying due respect to the past. The form and shape of the new camera was inspired by work done on previous-generation cameras, but it also pushes towards a friendlier, more modern, and more approachable design.

How do you define design quality?
Design is a method of communication. Any physical object should show evidence of the time, effort and care behind the design's original intent. With the HERO5 Black, we wanted durability and robustness to be conveyed from the moment the user first handles the product.

Liegt Ihrem ausgezeichneten Produkt ein bestimmter Gestaltungsansatz zugrunde?
Unser Gestaltungsansatz für die HERO5 Black blickte in die Zukunft, zollte aber gleichzeitig auch der Vergangenheit den gebührenden Respekt. Die Form der neuen Kamera wurde in Anlehnung an Kameras früherer Generationen gestaltet, wobei das Design jetzt freundlicher, moderner und zugänglicher ist.

Wie definieren Sie Designqualität?
Design ist eine Methode der Kommunikation. Jedes physische Objekt sollte Spuren der Zeit, des Aufwands und der Sorgfalt, die in die ursprüngliche Intention der Gestaltung investiert wurden, aufzeigen. Wir wollten, dass die HERO5 Black vom ersten Augenblick an, in dem der Nutzer mit dem Produkt umgeht, Haltbarkeit und Robustheit vermittelt.

reddot award 2017
best of the best

Manufacturer
GoPro, Inc., San Mateo, California, USA

GoPro HERO5 Black
Action Camera
Actionkamera

See page 106
Siehe Seite 106

Guanqun Zhang, Mengqiu Wang, Tong Zhang, Zhaozhe Wang, Lixin Liu
Zero Zero Robotics Inc.

"Do what you love most and enjoy the pleasure and honour it brings you."

„Tu das, was du am meisten liebst, und genieße die Freude und Anerkennung, die es dir bringt."

What was your goal when you designed your award-winning product?
What we wanted to provide was a new photo and video capturing experience. The product should be safe, portable and easy to use. And it should be able to take photos and videos from various angles to capture the most natural and precious moments of your life, just like your personal photographer.

What do you see as being the biggest challenges in your industry at present?
Particularly in the flying camera and drone industry, the biggest challenge is to harmonise aesthetic perception and product functionality. There are always trade-offs and decisions to make e.g. weight requirements for a flying device are critical.

Welches Ziel verfolgten Sie bei der Gestaltung Ihres ausgezeichneten Produktes?
Wir wollten ein neues Erlebnis der Foto- und Videoaufnahme bieten. Das Produkt sollte sicher, tragbar und einfach anzuwenden sein. Und es sollte Fotos und Videos aus verschiedenen Winkeln aufnehmen können, um so die wichtigsten Momente im Leben auf natürlichste Weise einzufangen, genau wie ein persönlicher Fotograf es tun würde.

Worin sehen Sie aktuell die größten Herausforderungen in Ihrer Branche?
Für die Drohnen-Branche besteht die größte Herausforderung insbesondere darin, die ästhetische Wahrnehmung mit der Funktionalität des Produktes in Einklang zu bringen. Man muss immer wieder Kompromisse machen und Entscheidungen treffen, beispielsweise sind bei einem fliegenden Objekt die Gewichtsvorgaben äußerst wichtig.

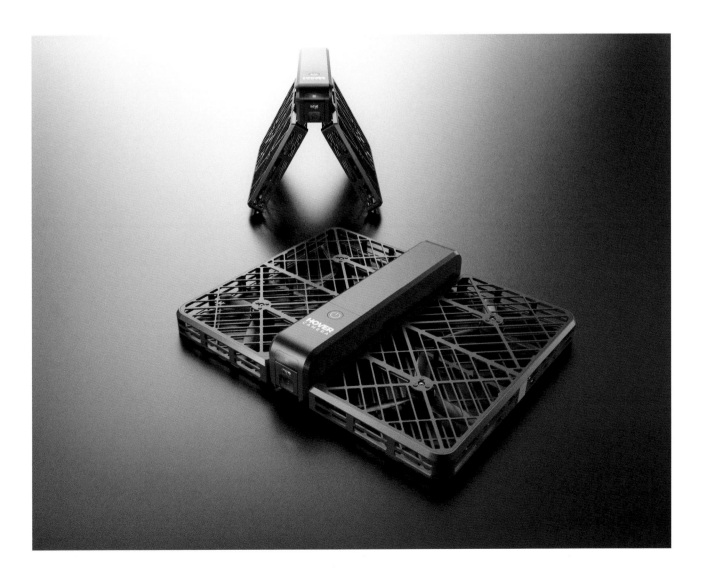

reddot award 2017
best of the best

Manufacturer
Zero Zero Robotics Inc., Beijing, China

Hover Camera
Drone
Drohne

See page 112
Siehe Seite 112

GoPro Industrial Design Team

"Design more than a drone and enable stabilised GoPro footage
from land or air."

„Es ist mehr als nur der Entwurf einer Drohne, es ist die Ermöglichung
stabilisierter GoPro-Aufnahmen sowohl an Land als auch in der Luft."

Was your award-winning product based on a particular design approach?
With Karma, we wanted to design a system of products that work together to get the best possible shot – on land or in the air. The ability to switch the image stabilisation gimbal from the drone to the handheld mount makes the Karma system a unique design.

What do you see as being the biggest challenges in your industry at present?
The speed at which technology and products are developed. Trying to keep up with such an incredibly fast pace, you run the risk of bending to compromise. But as designers need time to be deliberate and thoughtful we try to do fewer things, but do them better and better.

Liegt Ihrem ausgezeichneten Produkt ein bestimmter Gestaltungsansatz zugrunde?
Mit Karma wollten wir ein System von Produkten gestalten, die zusammenarbeiten, um die bestmögliche Aufnahme – ob an Land oder in der Luft – zu realisieren. Die Möglichkeit, den Tragrahmen zur Bildstabilisierung von der Drohne auf Hand-Halterung umzuschalten, macht die Gestaltung des Karma-Systems einzigartig.

Worin sehen Sie aktuell die größten Herausforderungen in Ihrer Branche?
Das Tempo, in dem Technologie und Produkte entwickelt werden. Bei dem Versuch, mit diesem rasanten Tempo Schritt zu halten, geht man das Risiko ein, sich auf Kompromisse einzulassen. Da Designer aber Zeit brauchen, um bewusst und umsichtig vorzugehen, versuchen wir, weniger Aspekte anzugehen, diese aber dafür immer besser zu machen.

reddot award 2017
best of the best

Manufacturer
GoPro, Inc., San Mateo, California, USA

GoPro Karma System
Drone
Drohne

See page 116
Siehe Seite 116

Philip Tavell, Anne Lise Kanestrøm, Katrine Jopperud, Ralf Kirner
Helly Hansen AS

"We make professional grade gear to help people stay and feel alive."

„Wir produzieren professionelle Ausrüstung, die hilft, am Leben zu bleiben und sich lebendig zu fühlen."

Was your award-winning product based on a particular design approach?
The design concept for this jacket is inspired by the masculine style of men's tailoring mixed with strong futuristic aesthetics. The goal is for the wearer to feel powerful, masculine and stylish, while being protected from the elements.

How do you define design quality?
Something consumers are willing to pay full price for, that makes them feel satisfied that they have got something they love for a long time.

What do you see as being the biggest challenges in your industry at present?
We do believe that the skier demographic will be the same in ten years, but we are increasingly challenged by the ever-changing climate and the unpredictable weather patterns.

Liegt Ihrem ausgezeichneten Produkt ein bestimmter Gestaltungsansatz zugrunde?
Das Gestaltungskonzept für diese Jacke ist inspiriert von einer Kombination aus dem maskulinen Stil der Herrenkonfektion einer überzeugend futuristischen Ästhetik. Das Ziel ist, dass sich die Nutzer stark, männlich und schick fühlen und gleichzeitig bei Unwetter geschützt sind.

Wie definieren Sie Designqualität?
Als etwas, wofür Konsumenten bereit sind, den vollen Preis zu zahlen, das ihnen ein Gefühl von Zufriedenheit gibt, dass sie etwas haben, was sie lange lieben werden.

Worin sehen Sie aktuell die größten Herausforderungen in Ihrer Branche?
Wir sind davon überzeugt, dass die Zielgruppe der Skifahrer in zehn Jahren gleich groß sein wird, die ständig wechselnden Klimaverhältnisse und unberechenbaren Wetterlagen hingegen zunehmend eine Herausforderung darstellen werden.

reddot award 2017
best of the best

Manufacturer
Helly Hansen AS, Oslo, Norway

Icon
Ski Jacket
Skijacke

See page 122
Siehe Seite 122

Lars Wagner
Canyon Bicycles GmbH

"Take Flite."

Was your award-winning product based on a particular design approach?
Racing and cyclocross bikes are pieces of very efficient sports equipment. Simplicity and clarity are particularly important and fundamental design goals, because we want our design idiom to express the high value of our bikes.

How do you maintain a work-life balance?
Before I started in the bicycle business, I used to ride a bike to relax. When I ride a bike now, I think about "work" all the time and every ride is a test ride. That's why we rather like to call it a work-bike balance.

How do you define design quality?
When a product exudes self-evidence, in a way that it conveys the feeling to have hit the nail on the head.

Liegt Ihrem ausgezeichneten Produkt ein bestimmter Gestaltungsansatz zugrunde?
Renn- und Cyclocrossräder sind sehr effiziente Sportgeräte. Da wir möchten, dass unsere Designsprache die hohe Wertigkeit unserer Räder zum Ausdruck bringt, sind Einfachheit und Klarheit besonders wichtige und grundlegende Designziele.

Wie erhalten Sie sich Ihre Work-Life-Balance?
Bevor ich in der Fahrradbranche anfing, bin ich zum Ausgleich Rad gefahren. Wenn ich jetzt bike, sehe ich ständig „Arbeit" und jede Fahrt ist eine Testfahrt. Wir sprechen daher eher von der Work-Bike-Balance.

Wie definieren Sie Designqualität?
Wenn ein Produkt eine Selbstverständlichkeit ausstrahlt, sozusagen das Gefühl vermittelt, etwas auf den Punkt getroffen zu haben.

reddot award 2017
best of the best

Manufacturer
Canyon Bicycles GmbH, Koblenz, Germany

Inflite CF SLX
Cyclocross Bike

See page 136
Siehe Seite 136

Fedja Delic
Canyon Bicycles GmbH

"Ride Your Workout."

What was your goal when you designed your award-winning product?
Our goal was to build the best fitness bike in the world – and that's what we did. We paid attention to every detail; the bicycle is a convincing symbiosis of engineering and design.

How do you define design quality?
Timelessness, functionality and clarity are the major attributes. In our daily life, we must not forget what a responsibility we as designers have for our environment.

Where will your industry be in ten years?
In the future, a product without a connectivity function will be almost unthinkable. The bike will communicate with us, will navigate for us and give us advice for our next cycling tour.

Welches Ziel verfolgten Sie bei der Gestaltung Ihres ausgezeichneten Produktes?
Unser Anspruch war es, das beste Fitness-bike der Welt zu bauen – und das haben wir gemacht. Wir haben jedem Detail viel Aufmerksamkeit gewidmet: Engineering und Design bilden eine überzeugende Symbiose.

Wie definieren Sie Designqualität?
Zeitlosigkeit, Funktionalität und Klarheit sind die höchsten Attribute. Im Arbeitsalltag darf man nicht vergessen, welche Verantwortung wir als Designer für unsere Umwelt haben.

Wo wird Ihre Branche in zehn Jahren stehen?
In Zukunft wird ein Produkt ohne Konnektivitätsfunktion kaum denkbar sein. Das Rad wird mit uns kommunizieren, uns navigieren und uns Empfehlungen für die nächste Radtour geben.

reddot award 2017
best of the best

Manufacturer
Canyon Bicycles GmbH, Koblenz, Germany

Roadlite CF
Fitness Bike

See page 140
Siehe Seite 140

Nick Broadbent
Tailfin

"I shall either find a way or make one."

„Entweder ich finde einen Weg oder ich baue einen."

Hannibal

What was your goal when you designed your award-winning product?
Traditional metal bike racks and panniers have barely changed in 50 years. Our goal was to completely re-engineer them for the 21st century whilst simultaneously launching a new brand that develops incredible, disruptive cycling and sports products.

How do you maintain a work-life balance?
I am by no means an expert, but having clear boundaries of work-time and play-time are crucial in helping me achieve a happy and fun home life whilst staying focused and passionate at work.

Welches Ziel verfolgten Sie bei der Gestaltung Ihres ausgezeichneten Produktes?
Traditionelle Metall-Fahrradgepäckträger und -taschen haben sich in den letzten 50 Jahren kaum verändert. Unser Ziel war es, sie für das 21. Jahrhundert vollkommen umzurüsten und gleichzeitig eine neue Marke einzuführen, die unglaubliche, aufregende Rad- und Sportprodukte entwickelt.

Wie erhalten Sie sich Ihre Work-Life-Balance?
Ich bin keineswegs Experte auf diesem Gebiet, doch sind klare Grenzen zwischen der Arbeitszeit und der Freizeit äußerst wichtig. Sie erlauben mir, daheim ein glückliches und angenehmes Leben zu haben und erhalten gleichzeitig die Leidenschaft und den Fokus bei der Arbeit.

reddot award 2017
best of the best

Manufacturer
Tailfin, Bristol, Great Britain

Tailfin Carbon Rack and
Waterproof Panniers
Pannier Rack and Panniers
Gepäckträger und Fahrradtaschen

See page 146
Siehe Seite 146

Shanghai Orangeade Health Technology Co., Ltd.

"To inspire people to be optimistic about a life with fitness."
„Wir wollen die Menschen inspirieren, eine positive Einstellung
zu einem Leben mit Fitness zu haben."

What was your goal when you designed your award-winning product?
We wanted dramatically to improve the indoor cycling experience that our clients and their families have. That's why we designed a product which can offer customers an immersive experience.

How do you maintain a work-life balance?
By learning from observations and experiences in our daily life and applying that to work.

What does winning the Red Dot: Best of the Best mean to you?
Our company is a start-up team. The award has offered us great encouragement. This is a memorable event for us which marks a very important new stage along our path to business success.

Welches Ziel verfolgten Sie bei der Gestaltung Ihres ausgezeichneten Produktes?
Wir wollten das Indoor-Radfahrerlebnis unserer Kunden und ihrer Familien drastisch verbessern. Deshalb haben wir ein Produkt konzipiert, das ihnen ein intensives Erlebnis bietet.

Wie erhalten Sie sich Ihre Work-Life-Balance?
Dadurch, dass wir von Beobachtungen und Erfahrungen in unserem Alltag lernen und diese in unsere Arbeit mit einfließen.

Was bedeutet die Auszeichnung mit dem Red Dot: Best of the Best für Sie?
Wir sind ein Start-up-Unternehmen. Die Auszeichnung ist für uns eine großartige Ermutigung und ein denkwürdiges Ereignis, das für uns den Beginn einer sehr wichtigen neuen Etappe auf unserem Weg zu geschäftlichem Erfolg bedeutet.

reddot award 2017
best of the best

Manufacturer
Shanghai Orangeade Health Technology
Co., Ltd., Shanghai, China

Yesoul Smart Cycling
Indoor Bike

See page 154
Siehe Seite 154

Xiaomi Design Team

"Simplicity is the ultimate sophistication."

„Einfachheit ist die höchste Stufe der Vollendung."

What was your goal when you designed your award-winning product?
Our goal was to create an alternative green, urban mobile solution for medium-range transport – an electric scooter with carefully designed mechanical parts, well thought through user interaction and an appealing exterior with style.

Is there a product that you have always dreamed about realising someday?
Our passion is to turn everyday objects into smart devices powered by cutting-edge technologies, and redesign them with a rational, minimalist style.

How do you maintain a work-life balance?
To us designers, work and life are not opposites. We learn from and are inspired by everyday things and life.

Welches Ziel verfolgten Sie bei der Gestaltung Ihres ausgezeichneten Produktes?
Unser Ziel war es, eine alternative, grüne Lösung für mittlere Transportstrecken im Stadtverkehr zu entwickeln – einen elektrischen Roller mit durchdacht gestalteten mechanischen Teilen, einer wohlüberlegten Nutzerinteraktion und einem ansprechenden, stilvollen Äußeren.

Welches Produkt würden Sie gerne einmal realisieren?
Wir verwandeln Alltagsprodukte leidenschaftlich gern in intelligente Geräte, die mit hochmodernen Technologien angetrieben werden, und geben ihnen einen rationalen, minimalistischen Stil.

Wie erhalten Sie sich Ihre Work-Life-Balance?
Für uns Designer sind Arbeit und Leben keine Gegensätze. Wir lernen von und finden Inspiration in alltäglichen Dingen und dem Leben.

reddot award 2017
best of the best

Manufacturer
Xiaomi Inc., Beijing, China

Mi Electric Scooter
Mi Elektroroller

See page 178
Siehe Seite 178

Joohee Lee, Volker Pflueger, Piotr Stolarski, Michael Tropper, Mark Jones, Toshihide Suzuki
forpeople / Yamaha Design Laboratory

"Integrity: design that respects the essence of the object."

„Integrität: Design, das die Essenz des Objekts respektiert."

What was your goal when you designed your award-winning product?
We wanted to reignite the love for Yamaha guitars by celebrating the unique Japanese culture and rich company heritage.

Was your award-winning product based on a particular design approach?
Endless conversations with musicians and experts provided us with the insights on which we based our design for an instrument that could become an inspirational tool for guitarists.

How do you define quality?
Quality comes in combination with honesty. We have to respect the function, express it with a genuine form and be sincere about the materials and finishes used.

Welches Ziel verfolgten Sie bei der Gestaltung Ihres ausgezeichneten Produktes?
Wir wollten die Liebe zu Yamaha-Gitarren neu entfachen, indem wir das Augenmerk auf die einzigartige Kultur Japans und die lange Tradition des Unternehmens richteten.

Liegt Ihrem ausgezeichneten Produkt ein bestimmter Gestaltungsansatz zugrunde?
Unzählige Gespräche mit Musikern und Fachleuten und die daraus hervorgegangenen Erkenntnisse bildeten die Grundlage für das Design eines Instruments, das zu einem inspirierenden Hilfsmittel für Gitarristen werden soll.

Wie definieren Sie Qualität?
Qualität ist immer mit Ehrlichkeit verbunden. Wir müssen die Funktion respektieren, sie in Verbindung mit einer authentischen Form zum Ausdruck bringen und offen sein bezüglich der verwendeten Materialien und Veredelungen.

reddot award 2017
best of the best

Manufacturer
Yamaha Corporation,
Hamamatsu, Shizuoka, Japan

Revstar
Electric Guitar
Elektrogitarre

See page 186
Siehe Seite 186

David Sprengers, Eric Dumortier, Jana Onzo, Tibo Grandry, Dominik Klampfl, Steven Plomteux
GBO Innovation Makers

"Meaningful design creates success!"

„Aussagekräftiges Design führt zum Erfolg!"

What was your goal when you designed your award-winning product?
Our goal was to create a timeless design vocabulary that defines a clear brand image for the FP product family and that also underlines the new powerful sound quality of the instrument. We wanted to improve ease of use with a more logic button sequence and clear lettering. The buttons, with integrated lights, different finishes or surface shapes, were all designed with reflection in mind, creating the best possible instrument for the artist.

How do you define design quality?
Honest products that deliver what they promise as opposed to shiny boxes that trick you into buying them.

Welches Ziel verfolgten Sie bei der Gestaltung Ihres ausgezeichneten Produktes?
Unser Ziel war es, eine zeitlose Formensprache zu entwickeln, die ein klares Markenimage für die FP-Produktfamilie festlegt und zugleich die neue, kraftvolle Klangqualität des Instruments betont. Wir wollten durch ein logischeres Arrangement der Schaltknöpfe und eine klare Beschriftung die Benutzerfreundlichkeit verbessern. Die Schaltknöpfe, mit eingebauter Beleuchtung, Oberflächenveredelungen oder verschiedenen Oberflächenformen, wurden alle mit der Intention gestaltet, für Künstler das bestmögliche Instrument zu entwerfen.

Wie definieren Sie Designqualität?
Ehrliche Produkte, die leisten, was sie versprechen, im Gegensatz zu glänzend verpackten, die einen nur durch ihr Äußeres zum Kauf verleiten.

reddot award 2017
best of the best

Manufacturer
Roland Corporation, Hamamatsu, Shizuoka, Japan

Roland FP-90
Digital Piano

See page 192
Siehe Seite 192

Ralf Holleis, Petra Napier
CYBEX GmbH

"The details are not just the details. The details make the design."
„Die Details sind nicht einfach nur Details. Die Details machen das Design aus."

What was your goal when you designed your award-winning product?
Urban mobility newly defined: We want to enable trend-oriented and modern parents to continue to pursue their previous lives in an urban environment with the help of our stylish and functional products.

What do you see as being the biggest challenges in your industry at present?
For us, it is important to design essential, complex and functional products in a simple and appealing way according to the CYBEX-D.S.F. innovation principle, "The combination of a unique design, unsurpassed security as well as quality and intelligent functionality".

What does winning the Red Dot: Best of the Best mean to you?
It is a confirmation of the work and passion we as a team have put into the product.

Welches Ziel verfolgten Sie bei der Gestaltung Ihres ausgezeichneten Produktes?
Urbane Mobilität neu definiert: Wir möchten mit unseren stylischen und funktionalen Produkten trendbewussten und modernen Eltern ermöglichen, ihr bisheriges Leben in einem urbanen Umfeld fortzuführen.

Worin sehen Sie aktuell die größten Herausforderungen in Ihrer Branche?
Für uns ist es wichtig, bedeutende, komplexe und funktionale Produkte simpel und ansprechend nach dem CYBEX-D.S.F.-Innovationsprinzip „Die Kombination von einzigartigem Design, unübertroffener Sicherheit wie auch Qualität und intelligenter Funktionalität" zu gestalten.

Was bedeutet die Auszeichnung mit dem Red Dot: Best of the Best für Sie?
Es ist für uns eine Bestätigung für die Arbeit und Liebe, die wir als Team in das Produkt gesteckt haben.

reddot award 2017
best of the best

Manufacturer
CYBEX GmbH, Bayreuth, Germany

MIOS
Stroller
Kinderwagen

See page 212
Siehe Seite 212

Jort Nijhuis, Imre Jacobs, Gert-Jan van Breugel
Vanderveer Designers

"Creating products with character."

„Kreiere Produkte mit Charakter."

What was your goal when you designed your award-winning product?
Our main goal when designing a product is to create a strong character that has a clear "right to exist". People should automatically understand the added value of the product when seeing it for the first time and appreciate the quality of all aspects during use.

Was your award-winning product based on a particular design approach?
We strongly believe that products are like people: character makes believers and creates followers. A product with character speaks for itself and does more than just "contribute to sales". It is the foundation stone of a business.

Welche Zielsetzung verfolgten Sie bei der Gestaltung Ihres ausgezeichneten Produktes?
Wenn wir ein Produkt gestalten, ist unser Hauptziel immer, ihm einen starken Charakter zu geben, der eine ganz eindeutige „Existenzberechtigung" hat. Menschen, die das Produkt zum ersten Mal sehen, sollen automatisch seinen Mehrwert erfassen können und im Umgang mit ihm die Qualität aller Aspekte unmittelbar spüren.

Liegt Ihrem ausgezeichneten Produkt ein bestimmter Gestaltungsansatz zugrunde?
Wir sind der festen Überzeugung, dass Produkte Menschen ähneln: Charakter schafft die Grundlage dafür, an etwas zu glauben und darauf zu vertrauen. Ein Produkt mit Charakter spricht für sich selbst und erreicht mehr als nur „zum Umsatz beizutragen". Es bildet den Grundstein eines Unternehmens.

reddot award 2017
best of the best

Manufacturer
Thule Group, Malmö, Sweden

Thule Yepp Nexxt Maxi
Child Bike Seat
Fahrrad-Kindersitz

See page 220
Siehe Seite 220

Emma Sandberg, Nina Warburton
Philips Design

"The Philips AVENT design team has a responsibility and passion to deliver meaningful, trusted solutions."

„Das Philips AVENT Design Team ist sich seiner Verantwortung bewusst und hat ein leidenschaftliches Bedürfnis, sinnvolle und zuverlässige Lösungen zu liefern."

What inspires you?
Meaningful design solutions that solve parenting challenges with smart, simple and responsive designs.

Where will your industry be in ten years?
Philips is moving into the HealthTech space, focusing on the delivery of complete solutions across the health continuum. In Philips Avent we will see more integration between product, digital and service propositions that work across the entire parenting journey, with stronger connections between consumers and health care professionals.

Was inspiriert Sie?
Sinnvolle Designlösungen, die die Herausforderungen, vor die sich Eltern gestellt sehen, durch cleveres, einfaches und reaktionsstarkes Design lösen.

Wo wird Ihre Branche in zehn Jahren stehen?
Philips rückt zunehmend in den HealthTech-Markt vor und konzentriert sich auf die Bereitstellung von Komplettlösungen für das gesamte Gesundheitswesen. Bei Philips Avent werden wir eine größere Integration von Produkt-, Digital- und Service-Angeboten sehen, die Eltern in der gesamten Erziehungsphase begleiten, sowie eine stärkere Verbindung zwischen Verbrauchern und Fachkräften des Gesundheitswesens.

reddot award 2017
best of the best

Manufacturer
Philips, Eindhoven, Netherlands

Philips Avent
Natural Electric Breast Pump Range
Breast Pump
Milchpumpe

See page 240
Siehe Seite 240

Ralf Kropf, Gabriel Kirschner, Simon Klein, Mike Milkowski
GABE Eyewear

"Surprise people and have the courage to think unconventionally."

„Überraschen und Mut zum unkonventionellen Denken haben."

What was your goal when you designed your award-winning product?
It was clear that we wanted to create something special and not just produce the 100th rehash of some RayBan or nerd-like model. We wanted to develop hand-made glasses from a natural material whose aesthetics allow them to stand out from the crowd and meet the highest quality demands.

How do you maintain a work-life balance?
A healthy work-life balance tends to be wishful thinking, particularly in the start-up phase of a company. You need passion, motivation, but also the willingness to make some personal sacrifices in order to develop a product that is unique and do everything that is required. Our big advantage is that we were good friends long before the project started.

Welches Ziel verfolgten Sie bei der Gestaltung Ihres ausgezeichneten Produktes?
Für uns stand fest, dass wir etwas Einzigartiges machen wollten und eben nicht den 100sten Aufguss irgendwelcher RayBan- oder Nerd-Modelle aus Holz heraussägen. Wir wollten eine handgefertigte Brille aus Naturmaterialien entwickeln, die sich ästhetisch von den anderen abhebt und den höchsten Qualitätsansprüchen gerecht wird.

Wie erhalten Sie sich Ihre Work-Life-Balance?
Gerade zu Beginn eines Unternehmens ist eine gesunde Work-Life-Balance meist eine Wunschvorstellung. Ein einzigartiges Produkt zu entwickeln und alles, was damit zusammenhängt, erfordert Leidenschaft, Motivation, aber auch die Bereitschaft, persönlich Opfer zu bringen. Unser großer Vorteil ist, dass wir schon vor dem Start des Projektes langjährige beste Freunde waren.

reddot award 2017
best of the best

Manufacturer
GABE Eyewear, Strom Eyewear GmbH,
Linz, Austria

REI – A symphony of wood and horn
Handcrafted Eyewear
Handgefertigte Brillen

See page 250
Siehe Seite 250

David McKenzie
PUMA SE

"The greatest source of happiness is the ability to be grateful at all times."
„Die größte Quelle des Glücks ist die Fähigkeit, zu jeder Zeit dankbar zu sein."

What was your goal when you designed your award-winning product?
The goal was to create a waterproof backpack that contoured the runner's body, fusing athlete and product whilst providing zoned ventilation. It was important that we achieved a balance between a clean aesthetic and the perfect volume whilst protecting gear from the elements.

Is there a product that you have always dreamed about realising someday?
I'd love to hand-build my own custom bike frame one day.

How do you maintain a work-life balance?
PUMA recognises that flexible working hours, the environment and embracing people's sporting interests positively influence design.

Welches Ziel verfolgten Sie bei der Gestaltung Ihres ausgezeichneten Produktes?
Das Ziel war es, einen wasserfesten Rucksack zu entwerfen, der sich den Körperkonturen des Läufers anpasst, Athlet und Produkt miteinander verschmelzen lässt und gleichzeitig Belüftung in bestimmten Zonen bietet. Uns war wichtig, ein Gleichgewicht zwischen einer klaren Ästhetik und dem perfekten Volumen zu erreichen und dabei die Ausrüstung vor Witterungseinflüssen zu schützen.

Welches Produkt würden Sie gerne einmal realisieren?
Ich würde eines Tages gerne mal meinen eigenen maßgefertigten Fahrradrahmen von Hand bauen.

Wie erhalten Sie sich Ihre Work-Life-Balance?
PUMA ist sich bewusst, dass flexible Arbeitszeiten, die Umwelt und die Förderung der sportlichen Interessen von Mitarbeitern einen positiven Einfluss auf das Design haben.

reddot award 2017
best of the best

Manufacturer
PUMA SE, Herzogenaurach, Germany

PUMA Winterized Backpack
Backpack
Rucksack

See page 260
Siehe Seite 260

Victor Santiago, Silvia Giovanardi, Matteo Ward
WRAD Srl

"Our raw state is our rad state – and WE, together,
take action for #LivableChange."

„Unser Rohzustand ist unser großartiger Zustand –
und WIR engagieren uns gemeinsam für #LivableChange."

What was your goal when you designed your award-winning product?
The first goal of our movement and brand was to inspire people to express intangible values in tangible ways. To raise awareness about the true cost of the fashion system, one of the most polluting industries worldwide second only to the oil industry.

How do you define design quality?
Our era is characterised by a structural redefinition of what we have always taken for granted regarding the creation of products. We live in a time marked by three macro-revolutions in action: a spiritual one, a social one and an ecological one. In this scenario of crisis we believe design quality must also be inclusive. Because by allowing the market to participate in the making of a product, consumers become active players invested in the realisation of the brand's higher purpose.

Welches Ziel verfolgten Sie bei der Gestaltung Ihres ausgezeichneten Produktes?
Das erste Ziel unserer Bewegung und Marke war, Menschen zu inspirieren, nicht greifbare Werte greifbar zum Ausdruck zu bringen. Menschen auf die wahren Kosten der Modebranche aufmerksam zu machen, einer der Industrien, die der Umwelt weltweit am meisten schadet. Nur die Ölindustrie verursacht mehr Umweltbelastung.

Wie definieren Sie Designqualität?
Unsere Epoche ist von einer strukturellen Neudefinition dessen gekennzeichnet, was wir bezüglich Produktgestaltung für selbstverständlich gehalten haben. Wir leben in einer Zeit, die von drei aktuellen Makro-Revolutionen, einer spirituellen, sozialen und ökologischen, geprägt ist. In dieser Krisensituation glauben wir, dass Designqualität alle mit einbeziehen muss. Indem wir es dem Markt erlauben, an der Herstellung eines Produktes teilzuhaben, werden Konsumenten zu Akteuren, die sich an der Verwirklichung des höheren Zwecks der Marke beteiligen.

reddot award 2017
best of the best

Manufacturer
WRAD Srl, Monticello Conte Otto
(Vicenza), Italy

WRAD Graphi-Tee
T-Shirt

See page 282
Siehe Seite 282

Ricardo Guadalupe
Hublot SA

"Hublot – being first, unique and different."

Was your award-winning product based on a particular design approach?
We wanted to focus on a new movement, manufactured in-house, the Meca-10. It is a mechanical movement with a power reserve of ten days. This movement required more than two years of development. In order to showcase it perfectly, we present it in our unique and patented scratchproof Magic Gold version.

Is there a product that you have always dreamed about realising someday?
A Ferrari car.

What does winning the Red Dot: Best of the Best mean to you?
It is truly a great honour because the award is the most important in the design community. Seeing Hublot with the Meca-10 as one of the laureates makes me really proud of the work we all do in the manufacture.

Liegt Ihrem ausgezeichneten Produkt ein bestimmter Gestaltungsansatz zugrunde?
Wir wollten das intern hergestellte neue Uhrwerk, das Meca-10, in den Vordergrund stellen. Es ist ein mechanisches Uhrwerk mit einer Gangreserve von zehn Tagen. Seine Entwicklung hat mehr als zwei Jahre in Anspruch genommen. Um es perfekt zur Schau zu stellen, präsentieren wir es in unserer patentierten kratzfesten Magic Gold-Version.

Welches Produkt würden Sie gerne einmal realisieren?
Einen Ferrari.

Was bedeutet die Auszeichnung mit dem Red Dot: Best of the Best für Sie?
Es ist wirklich eine große Ehre, da die Auszeichnung die wichtigste in der Designwelt ist. Hublot mit der Meca-10 als Preisträger zu sehen, macht mich sehr stolz auf die Arbeit, die wir alle während des Herstellungsprozesses geleistet haben.

reddot award 2017
best of the best

Manufacturer
Hublot SA, Nyon, Switzerland

Big Bang Meca-10 Magic Gold
Wristwatch
Armbanduhr

See page 296
Siehe Seite 296

Nina Georgia Friesleben
Niessing Manufaktur GmbH & Co. KG

"The fairest fortune that can fall to a thinking man is to have searched out the searchable, and restfully to adore the unsearchable."

„Das schönste Glück des denkenden Menschen ist, das Erforschliche erforscht zu haben und das Unerforschliche ruhig zu verehren."

What was your goal when you designed your award-winning product?
We wondered if precious metal could be used in a way that would give it a shimmering and translucent appearance, creating the illusion of a mirage. We wanted to see if it could appear to be almost weightless and not as solid as it normally is. Our vision was to reinvent gold.

Was your award-winning product based on a particular design approach?
I adore a clear design vocabulary which conveys a poetic meaning. It is very important for me to be sensitive to the properties of the prototype, of the material being used and of the form being created. Only then will my design be comprehensible and will be consciously or subconsciously understood by its observers.

Welches Ziel verfolgten Sie bei der Gestaltung Ihres ausgezeichneten Produktes?
Wir haben uns gefragt, ob sich Edelmetall so verarbeiten lässt, dass es schillernd und durchscheinend wirkt, die Illusion einer Luftspiegelung erzeugt. Ob es fast schwerelos sein kann, nicht massiv wie üblich. Unsere Vision war es, Gold ganz neu zu erfinden.

Liegt Ihrem ausgezeichneten Produkt ein bestimmter Gestaltungsansatz zugrunde?
Ich liebe eine klare Formensprache mit poetischer Sinnhaftigkeit. Für mich ist sehr wichtig, sensibel zu sein für die Eigenschaften des Entwurfs, des jeweiligen Materials und der jeweiligen Form. Nur dann wird meine Gestaltung nachvollziehbar, teilt sich dem Betrachter unbewusst oder bewusst mit.

reddot award 2017
best of the best

Manufacturer
Niessing Manufaktur GmbH & Co. KG,
Vreden, Germany

Niessing Mirage
Pendant
Anhänger

See page 304
Siehe Seite 304

Garden
Garten

PALMA
Garden Umbrella
Sonnenschirm

Manufacturer
Royal Botania, Nijlen, Belgium

In-house design
Kris Van Puyvelde

Web
www.royalbotania.com

reddot award 2017
best of the best

Luxury shade

Garden umbrellas evoke images of a special ambiance and are generally associated with sitting in the shade on a sunny day, maybe on a beach near the sea. PALMA seamlessly ties in with such associations. This garden umbrella was designed with the objective of reflecting the various ways of relaxing in the shade in its form and functionality. At first glance, it impresses with a minimalist language of form, yet maintains an overly solid impression. Equally luxurious and purist in appearance, the umbrella is marked by the fact that there are no visible mechanical details interfering with its overall clear lines. Based on a patented concept, the opening and closing mechanism contained within remains completely hidden. At the same time, this delivers very high user convenience. A single lifting action suffices to activate the mechanism in the base for driving a pneumatic strut innovatively integrated into the shaft. This makes the canopy either open or close automatically in an elegant movement. This also eliminates the need, as with conventional models, to stand right under the umbrella and wrestle to open or close it, as the mechanism sets in motion almost by itself. The design of PALMA has thus emerged as an impressive unity of aesthetic inspiration and mechanical innovation – the garden umbrella is reinterpreted through lending it a highly elegant appeal.

Luxuriös beschattet

Der Sonnenschirm repräsentiert ein besonderes Ambiente, das man im Allgemeinen mit Sonne, Strand und Meer assoziiert. PALMA knüpft nahtlos an solche Szenarien an. Gestaltet wurde dieser Sonnenschirm mit der Zielsetzung, die vielfältigen Möglichkeiten des Relaxens in der Sonne in seiner Form und Funktionalität widerzuspiegeln. Er beeindruckt auf den ersten Blick mit einer minimalistischen Formensprache und wirkt zugleich sehr solide auf den Betrachter. Prägend für die ebenso luxuriöse wie puristische Anmutung des Schirms ist, dass keine sichtbaren mechanischen Details seine klare Linienführung stören. Basierend auf einem patentierten Konzept, konnte der Verstellmechanismus vollständig verborgen werden. Dieser Sonnenschirm ist deshalb auch überaus komfortabel im Gebrauch. Mit einer einzigen Hebebewegung kann der Nutzer die auf innovative Weise integrierte, pneumatisch betriebene Verstrebung aktivieren, die das selbsttätige, sich elegant vollziehende Öffnen und Schließen des Schirms bewirkt. Es ist daher auch nicht notwendig wie bei üblichen Modellen, irgendwie direkt unter dem Schirm zu stehen und mühsam zu hantieren, alles geschieht wie von selbst. Der Gestaltung von PALMA gelingt damit eine beeindruckende Einheit aus ästhetischer Inspiration und mechanischer Innovation – der Sonnenschirm erfährt hier eine sehr stilvolle Neuinterpretation.

Statement by the jury

This garden umbrella fascinates with an overly eye-catching, minimalist language of form, as well as a cleverly integrated, innovative functionality that is truly special and astounding. The formally integrated, pneumatic mechanism allows easy, automatic opening and closing of the canopy. Complemented by a beautifully coordinated colour concept, the PALMA garden umbrella is highly convincing and enriches the ambiance at any time.

Begründung der Jury

Dieser Sonnenschirm begeistert mit einer ins Auge fallenden, minimalistischen Formensprache. Bemerkenswert ist zudem seine clevere, innovative Funktionalität, die ihn zu etwas Besonderem macht. Ein formal integrierter, pneumatischer Mechanismus erlaubt ein müheloses, automatisches Öffnen und Schließen des Schirms. Auch mit seinem schön abgestimmten Farbkonzept überzeugt der Sonnenschirm PALMA und bereichert jederzeit das Ambiente.

Designer portrait
See page 30
Siehe Seite 30

Duck
Arm Awning
Gelenkarmmarkise

Manufacturer
Gibus S.p.A., Saccolongo (Padua), Italy
Design
Meneghello Paolelli Associati, Milan, Italy
Web
www.gibus.com
www.meneghellopaolelli.com

Duck is an innovatively designed arm awning with a compact, cylindrical cassette made of powder-coated extruded aluminium. It protects the fabric and ensures a long service life, since it is less exposed to the effects of weather. The awning can be mounted on the wall or ceiling. It has been designed as a synthesis of functionality and form that harmoniously fits into its architectural environment.

Duck ist eine innovativ gestaltete Gelenkarmmarkise mit einer kompakten zylinderförmigen Kassette aus extrudiertem, pulverbeschichtetem Aluminium. Diese schützt den Stoff und sichert ihm eine lange Lebensdauer, da er den Witterungseinflüssen dadurch weniger stark ausgeliefert ist. Die Markise kann an der Wand oder der Decke angebracht werden und wurde gezielt als eine Synthese aus Funktionalität und Design gestaltet, die sich harmonisch in ihr architektonisches Umfeld einfügt.

Statement by the jury
The arm awning Duck strikes the eye by the inventive design of a cylindrical aluminium cassette; it also offers a high standard regarding functionality.

Begründung der Jury
Die Gelenkarmmarkise Duck fällt durch eine originelle Gestaltung mit einer zylinderförmigen Aluminiumkassette ins Auge und bietet auch funktional einen hohen Standard.

T-Hide
Sun Awning
Markise

Manufacturer
Pratic F.lli Orioli S.p.A., Fagagna (Udine), Italy
In-house design
Dino Orioli, Edi Orioli, Loris Mindotti
Web
www.pratic.it

The sun awning T-Hide is characterised by aesthetic rigidity and a reduced form. The cassette is mounted on the wall and conceals the awning, the functional elements and the electric system. It can reach a length of up to seven metres and extend to up to four metres. The sunscreen can be inclined between 6 and 40 degrees. The motorised valance and the dimmable light source at the bottom along the entire length create a distinguished ambience.

Der Sonnenschutz T-Hide zeichnet sich durch ästhetische Strenge und reduzierte Formgebung aus. Die an der Wand zu montierende Kassette verbirgt die Markise, die funktionalen Bestandteile und die elektrische Anlage. Sie kann eine Länge von bis zu sieben Metern erreichen und bis zu vier Meter weit ausfahren. Die Neigung des Sonnenschutzes lässt sich von 6 bis 40 Grad variieren. Ausgestattet mit motorisiertem Volant und einer dimmbaren Lichtquelle unter der gesamten Länge, lässt sich eine gehobene und entspannte Atmosphäre herstellen.

Statement by the jury
The electric awning T-Hide is characterised by a timeless aesthetic appearance thanks to its strict design and atmospheric lighting.

Begründung der Jury
Eine zeitlos ästhetische Anmutung dank strenger Formgebung und eine atmosphärische Beleuchtung zeichnen die elektrische Markise T-Hide besonders aus.

CAMABOX BX4000
Box Awning with Cubic Box
Kassettenmarkise

Manufacturer
STOBAG AG, Muri, Switzerland
In-house design
Web
www.stobag.com

The Camabox BX4000 is a box awning with a reduced and shapely design that fits elegantly into existing architecture. An LED lightning can be optionally integrated into the box so that the shady space can be used even in the evening hours. The non-corroding aluminium box protects the cloth and the articulated arms against weathering and dirt and thus ensures a long service life. The variable console position allows flexible, simple and time-saving mounting on the wall, under the ceiling or on rafters. The Camabox BX4000 can alternatively be driven with a hand crank or with an electric motor.

Die Camabox BX4000 ist eine reduziert gestaltete, formschöne Kassettenmarkise, die sich elegant in die vorhandene Architektur einfügt. Optional kann eine LED-Beleuchtung in den Kasten integriert werden, sodass sich der Schattenplatz auch in den Abendstunden nutzen lässt. Die korrosionsbeständige Aluminiumkassette schützt das Tuch und die Gelenkarme effektiv vor Witterungseinflüssen und Schmutz und sorgt so für eine lange Lebensdauer. Die variable Konsolenposition ermöglicht eine flexible, einfache und zeitsparende Montage an der Wand, unter der Decke oder an Dachsparren. Die Camabox BX4000 kann wahlweise mit einer Handkurbel oder mit einem Elektromotor angetrieben werden.

Statement by the jury
The box awning Camabox BX4000 appeals by a stylish elegance and impresses with the use of durable and skilfully processed materials.

Begründung der Jury
Die Kassettenmarkise Camabox BX4000 strahlt eine stilvolle Eleganz aus und besticht zudem durch den Einsatz langlebiger und hochwertig verarbeiteter Materialien.

w17 easy
Sliding Glass Panel
Glas-Schiebewand

Manufacturer
weinor GmbH & Co. KG, Cologne, Germany
In-house design
Web
www.weinor.de

The w17 easy is a sliding glass wall that can be used as a substructure system for virtually all types of roofing. It provides reliable weather protection and allows full transparency thanks to its frameless construction. The all-glass elements can be opened and closed very quietly and easily by means of a soft-closing system. Due to the "standing construction", static adjustments of the roof of the terrace or the pergola awning are in the most cases not necessary. The sliding glass wall can also be used as a divider in interior rooms – without any obstructing thresholds. The design of the handles, rails and the lock is characterised by clear and transparent lines.

Bei w17 easy handelt es sich um eine Glas-Schiebewand, die sich als Unterbausystem für praktisch alle Arten von Überdachungen eignet. Sie bietet zuverlässigen Wetterschutz und ermöglicht dank rahmenloser Bauweise volle Transparenz. Die Ganzglaselemente lassen sich mittels Soft-Closing-System leise und sehr leicht öffnen wie schließen. Aufgrund der „stehenden Konstruktion" entfallen beim Nachrüsten meist statische Anpassungen des Terrassendachs oder der Pergolamarkise. Die Glas-Schiebewand kann aber auch als Raumteiler in Innenräumen – hier ganz ohne Stolperschwelle – zum Einsatz kommen. Das Design der Griffe, Profile und des Schlosses ist durch eine klare Linienführung gekennzeichnet.

Statement by the jury
The sliding glass wall w17 easy pleases aesthetically with its clear elegance. Functionally, it scores with a construction thanks to which it fits into almost any architecture both inside and outside.

Begründung der Jury
Die Glas-Schiebewand w17 easy punktet ästhetisch durch klare Eleganz und funktional durch eine Konstruktion, dank derer sie sich in nahezu jede Architektur sowohl innen wie außen einfügen lässt.

No Rock Esplanade
Table Base
Tischgestell

Manufacturer
No Rock Technology, Dunsborough, Australia
In-house design
Toby Heyring
Web
www.no-rock.com

The No Rock Esplanade table base provides a distinctive solution to table instability. Using a simple mechanical system with four pivoting legs, it meets the everyday needs of cafes and restaurants. Its bases self-stabilise on uneven indoor and alfresco surfaces, while exhibiting an innovative and contemporary design aesthetic. The Esplanade table base is classic and architectural. It is suited to the sophisticated dining experience and available in range of powder coated finishes.

Der Tischfuß No Rock Esplanade ist eine markante Antwort auf das Problem instabiler Tische. Seine Lösung beruht auf dem einfachen mechanischen System von vier beweglichen Füßen und liefert Stabilität und Sicherheit für Cafés und Restaurants. Das Gestell passt sich jedem unebenen Untergrund im Inneren wie im Freien an und ist durch eine innovative und zeitgemäße Ästhetik gekennzeichnet. Der Esplanade hat eine klassisch architektonische Form und eignet sich für anspruchsvolle kulinarische Erlebnisse. Erhältlich ist er in unterschiedlichen Farbbeschichtungen.

Statement by the jury
The table base No Rock Esplanade solves the problem of uneven ground in the open air not only in a functionally but also in an aesthetically impressive way.

Begründung der Jury
Das Problem unebener Böden im Freien löst das Tischgestell No Rock Esplanade auf nicht nur funktional überzeugende Weise, sondern auch auf ästhetische.

HAVSTEN
Outdoor Sofa

Manufacturer
IKEA, Älmhult, Sweden
In-house design
Andreas Fredriksson
Web
www.ikea.com

Havsten is a modular seating furniture to be used in the garden and the outdoor area in general and is available in many colours. It can be extended at discretion and arranged as a two-, three- or four-seater with or without armrest. It is not only modern, functional and practical but also sustainable and can be completely recycled. The sofa can be built up quickly by assembling the steel frame, covering it with the fabric and finally fixing it with a strap. Thick upholstery and cushions make Havsten a very comfortable piece of furniture.

Havsten ist ein modulares und in zahlreichen Farben erhältliches Sitzmöbel für den Garten und den Outdoor-Bereich allgemein. Es lässt sich nach Belieben verbreitern und zu einem 2er-, 3er- oder auch 4er-Sofa mit oder ohne Seitenlehne aufbauen. Dabei ist es nicht nur modern, funktional und praktisch, sondern auch nachhaltig und später komplett recycelbar. Das Sofa kann rasch aufgebaut werden, indem der Stahlrahmen zusammengefügt, mit dem Gewebe überspannt und anschließend mit dem Gurt fixiert wird. Dicke Polster und Kissen machen Havsten außerdem sehr bequem.

Statement by the jury
The design of the garden sofa Havsten impresses with its modularity. It offers a wide scope of individual configurations for this comfortable furniture.

Begründung der Jury
Die Gestaltung des Gartensofas Havsten überzeugt durch ihre Modularität. Sie lässt für die individuelle Konfiguration des bequemen Möbels großen Spielraum.

Riverside
Lounge Chair
Loungesessel

Manufacturer
Tonon & C. SpA, Manzano, Italy
Design
Massive Design (Mac Stopa),
Warsaw, Poland
Web
www.tononitalia.com
www.massivedesign.pl

Riverside is a lounge chair whose organic design is inspired by nature. Its sculptural shape and curved lines resemble the pattern that wind and water leave on the banks of a river. It is weatherproof and lightweight so it can easily be moved. Thanks to a water drain, it is very suitable for outdoor use. The material Soft Touch Plus consists of a two-component polyurethane, which is especially hard-wearing, hygienic and non-toxic. Riverside is available in a variety of current trend colours.

Riverside ist ein Loungesessel, dessen organische Gestaltung von der Natur inspiriert ist. Seine skulpturale Form und die geschwungenen Linien ähneln dem Muster, das Wind und Wasser am Uferstrand eines Flusses hinterlassen. Er ist wetterfest und leicht, sodass er sich einfach bewegen lässt. Auch dank eines Wasserablaufs ist er sehr gut für den Einsatz im Freien geeignet. Das Material Soft Touch Plus ist ein aus zwei Komponenten bestehendes Polyurethan, das besonders widerstandsfähig, hygienisch und ungiftig ist. Riverside ist in einer Vielzahl aktueller Trendfarben erhältlich.

Statement by the jury
The lounge chair Riverside fascinates with its conspicuously organic appearance. Both lightweight and robust, it is a fancy furniture for relaxed sitting in the open air.

Begründung der Jury
Der Loungesessel Riverside begeistert durch sein auffallend organisches Erscheinungsbild. Zugleich leicht und robust, ist er ein originelles Möbel für entspanntes Sitzen im Freien.

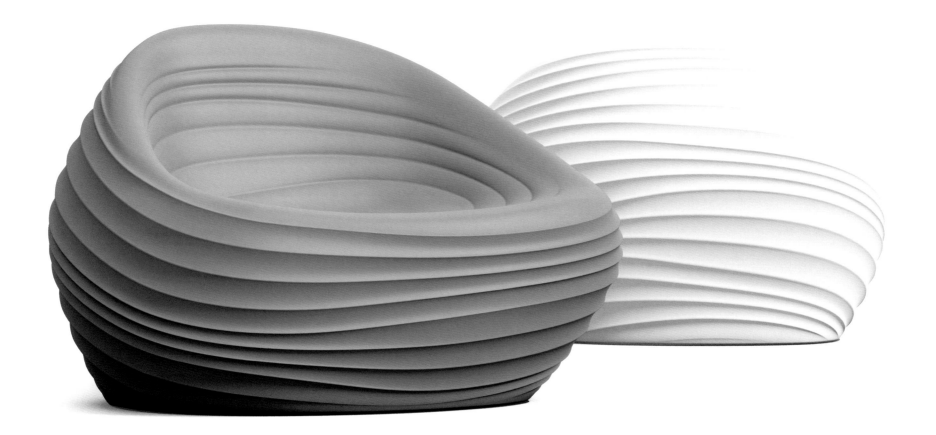

Twins Collection
Lounge Armchair
Loungesessel

Manufacturer
Expormim, Moixent, Spain
Design
MUT Design (Alberto Sánchez),
Valencia, Spain
Web
www.expormim.com
www.mutdesign.com

The Twins Collection includes a low arm-chair with soft round shapes and a larger more rectilinear one with a high back-rest. The designer's intention was to trans-fer a feeling of warmth to the outdoor area and to offer versatility through the use of new technical fabrics. The arm-chairs are covered with 3D Mesh Omega Outdoor, a material specifically devel-oped for the company. The fabric is so robust that it withstands the most various climatic conditions as well as the demanding requirements of the cater-ing sector. In addition, it is particularly soft and very comfortable due to its three-dimensional structure. This allows to use the outdoor collection, which is available in attractive colours, also in interior spaces such as waiting rooms or lobbies.

Die Twins Collektion besteht aus einem nie-drigen Sessel mit runder, weicher Formge-bung und einem größeren geradlinigen mit hoher Rückenlehne. Die Intention der Ge-staltung war es, ein Gefühl von Wärme in den Außenbereich zu übertragen und durch die Verwendung neuer technischer Stoffe Vielseitigkeit zu bieten. Die Sessel sind mit „3D Mesh Omega Outdoor", einem eigens für das Unternehmen entwickelten Material, bezogen. Dieses Gewebe ist so wi-derstandsfähig, dass es den verschiedens-ten klimatischen wie den anspruchsvollen Bedingungen des Gastronomiesektors standhält. Es ist zudem besonders weich und aufgrund seiner dreidimensionalen Struktur sehr bequem. Dadurch lässt sich die in attraktiven Farben erhältliche Out-door-Kollektion auch in Innenräumen wie Wartezimmern oder Lobbys einsetzen.

Statement by the jury
The Twins Collection is distinguished by its classic appearance of a comfortable armchair, which has been designed with high-quality materials for the outdoor area but equally shows to advantage in indoor environments.

Begründung der Jury
Die Twins Collektion sticht durch ihre klassische Anmutung eines komfortablen Sessels hervor, der mit hochwertigen Materialien für den Outdoor-Bereich konzi-piert wurde, aber in Innenräumen ebenso gut zur Geltung kommt.

Everdure by Heston Blumenthal – HUB
Charcoal BBQ
Holzkohlengrill

Manufacturer
Shriro Australia, Kingsgrove,
New South Wales, Australia

Design
Design + Industry, Balmain,
New South Wales, Australia

Web
www.everdurebyheston.com
www.design-industry.com

reddot award 2017
best of the best

Enjoyment in style

Grilling requires not only thorough skills in delicious food preparation but, above all, also the right equipment. The HUB charcoal BBQ combines a clear design idiom with a very well thought-out functionality, enabling users to create a variety of BBQ dishes. The grill exudes an elegant high-quality appeal. It showcases formal details such as sleek, tapered legs and smooth-looking chrome handles, complemented by advanced technical innovations such as a Fast Flame Ignition System that solves the problem of fuelled-charcoal burning. Thanks to these integrated electronics, the charcoal starts burning at the right cooking temperature in just ten minutes. The cleverly integrated patented Rotiscope Technology promotes high user convenience. It provides an authentic experience of rotisserie grilling by means of a discreet motor tucked inside as well as jaw-like forks, which ensure that everything from chickens to suckling pigs are firmly kept in place over the coals at three different adjustable heights. Following the maxim of a high-quality and durable design, all elements are easy and comfortable to clean. The inspired design of the HUB charcoal BBQ delivers the experience of stylish enjoyment outdoors thanks to its perfectly user-oriented implementation – a consistent design for visualising such a lifestyle.

Stilvoller Genuss

Grillen erfordert ein fundiertes Wissen über die geschmackvolle Zubereitung und vor allem das richtige Grillgerät. Der Holzkohlengrill HUB vereint dafür eine klare Formensprache mit einer sehr gut durchdachten Funktionalität und ermöglicht so eine Vielzahl von Grillkreationen. Mit Details wie schmalen, sich nach unten verjüngenden Beinen und weich anmutenden Griffen aus Chrom wirkt er elegant und hochwertig. Er verfügt zudem über eine hochentwickelte technische Ausstattung. So wird die Problematik des Anfachens der Holzkohle durch das Fast Flame Ignition System gelöst. Dank eines elektrischen Elements kann der Nutzer innerhalb von zehn Minuten die gewünschte Temperatur erreichen. Ein Erlebnis ist zudem die geschickt integrierte, patentierte Rotiscope Technology. Diese erlaubt ein authentisches Rotisseriegrillen mittels eines eingebauten Motors, wobei krallenähnlich geformte Gabeln auch größeres Grillgut fest an Ort und Stelle halten und auf drei verschiedene Höhen über der Kohle eingestellt werden können. Der Maxime einer hochwertigen und langlebigen Gestaltung entsprechend, lassen sich alle Komponenten leicht und komfortabel reinigen. Die inspirierte Gestaltung des Holzkohlengrills HUB ermöglicht durch ihre perfekt am Nutzer orientierte Umsetzung ein stilvolles Genießen im Freien – durch gutes Design wird hier ein Lebensgefühl inszeniert.

Statement by the jury

The HUB charcoal BBQ projects a perfect unity of form and functionality. It is highly elegant and offers many possibilities for uncomplicated grilling. The entire system is thoroughly thought through to the last detail and fully geared toward user convenience. It offers rotisserie grilling over the coals at three different heights for different foods or grilling times, while the storage space underneath can also be used as a holding rack for keeping the food warm until serving.

Begründung der Jury

Der Holzkohlengrill HUB zeigt sich als perfekte Einheit von Form und Funktionalität. Er ist überaus elegant und bietet viele Möglichkeiten für das unkomplizierte Grillen. Das gesamte System ist bis ins Detail durchdacht und lässt sich sehr bedarfsgerecht nutzen. So ist ein Rotisseriegrillen auf drei verschiedenen Höhen über der Kohle für eine unterschiedliche Gardauer möglich, und der Stauraum unter dem Grill kann auch als Warmhaltefach zum zeitgerechten Servieren genutzt werden.

Designer portrait
See page 32
Siehe Seite 32

FUSION
Charcoal BBQ
Holzkohlegrill

Manufacturer
Shriro Australia, Kingsgrove,
New South Wales, Australia
Design
Design + Industry, Balmain,
New South Wales, Australia
Web
www.everdurebyheston.com
www.design-industry.com

Thanks to the Fast Flame Ignition System, it is very easy to get the charcoal on the Fusion barbecue started. Equipped with an integrated electric element, the charcoal burns at the right cooking temperature in just ten minutes. Thanks to the patented Rotiscope technology, a reliable rotisserie can be set up quickly at three different heights. The Cliplock Forks ensure that chickens or suckling pigs are kept firmly in place above the cooking surface.

Statement of the jury
The charcoal barbecue Fusion is ready for operation in a very short time, which is just as appealing as its design, which has been thought through in every detail.

Der Holzkohlegrill Fusion macht das Anzünden der Holzkohle mithilfe des Fast-Flame-Ignition-Systems ausgesprochen einfach. Ausgestattet mit einem integrierten elektrischen Element, brennt die Holzkohle in nur zehn Minuten in der gewünschten Temperatur. Dank der patentierten Rotiscope-Technologie lässt sich schnell ein zuverlässiger Drehgrill in drei verschiedenen Höhen einrichten. Die Cliplock Forks halten Huhn oder Ferkel sicher über der Kochfläche fest.

Begründung der Jury
Die Tatsache, dass der Holzkohlegrill Fusion in kürzester Zeit betriebsbereit ist, überzeugt ebenso wie seine bis in die Details durchdachte Konstruktion.

FURNACE
Gas BBQ
Gasgrill

Manufacturer
Shriro Australia, Kingsgrove,
New South Wales, Australia
Design
Design + Industry, Balmain,
New South Wales, Australia
Web
www.everdurebyheston.com
www.design-industry.com

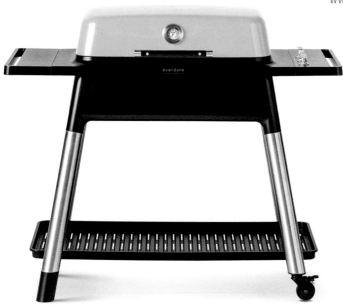

The stylish, compact Furnace barbecue was designed to bring the performance of modern kitchen appliances to the outdoors. It is ready for use in just five minutes and allows instant searing of the food. Variable flame control is managed by the slender, ergonomically designed taps. The body of the barbecue is made of easy-to-clean, die-cast aluminium and is available in a range of contemporary colours. The extra high hood is ideal for convection cooking creating wonderful flavours with the 360-degree circulation.

Statement by the jury
The barbecue Furnace has a stylish design and is easy to handle thanks to its flowing transitions; it also appeals by its differentiated functionality.

Der stilvolle, kompakte Barbecue-Grill Furnace wurde entworfen, um sich auch im Freien der Leistung moderner Küchengeräte bedienen zu können. In nur fünf Minuten ist das Gerät einsatzbereit und ermöglicht ein sofortiges Anbraten des Grillguts. Die Flamme lässt sich mit schlanken, ergonomisch gestalteten Gashähnen einstellen. Das aus leicht zu reinigendem Spritzgussaluminium gefertigte Gehäuse ist in verschiedenen modernen Farben erhältlich. Die besonders hohe Haube lenkt die aufsteigende Hitze optimal zurück und garantiert durch die 360-Grad-Zirkulation überzeugende Aromen.

Begründung der Jury
In der Formgebung stilvoll und mit seinen fließenden Übergängen praktisch zu handhaben, besticht der Gasgrill Furnace auch durch eine ausdifferenzierte Funktionalität.

AURORA
Table Top BBQ
Tischgrill

Manufacturer
Enders Colsman AG, Werdohl, Germany
In-house design
Nils Cala
Web
www.enders-germany.com

Aurora is a smart charcoal-fuelled table grill, which allows to grill quickly, simply and – thanks to an innovative e-fan technology – with less smoke. It is easy to place everywhere and in the centre of attention. The metallic surface in black chrome/copper or pastel shades makes the grill a striking eye-catcher. The development of the grill is based on the idea of "one table, one conversation, one barbecue" making the Aurora suitable for any social gathering.

Aurora ist ein smarter, mit Holzkohle betriebener Tischgrill, mit dem man einfach, schnell und raucharm grillen kann, und zwar dank einer innovativen E-Fan-Lüfter-technologie. Er lässt sich überall unkompliziert auf- und in den Mittelpunkt stellen. Die metallische Oberfläche – in Black Chrome/Copper oder Pastelltönen – macht den Grill zum auffälligen Blickfang. Seiner Entwicklung liegt die Idee „ein Tisch, ein Talk, ein Grill" zugrunde, sodass sich der Aurora für jegliche gesellige Runde eignet.

Statement by the jury
The table grill Aurora impresses with its compact ergonomic design that integrates an easy-to-handle technology and makes grilling a relaxed pleasure.

Begründung der Jury
Der Tischgrill Aurora beeindruckt durch seine kompakte ergonomische Gestaltung, die eine einfach zu handhabende Technologie integriert und Grillen so zum entspannten Vergnügen macht.

Fiskars PowerGear™ X
Pruners
Gartenscheren

Manufacturer
Fiskars Finland Oy Ab,
Helsinki, Finland

In-house design
Fiskars Finland Oy Ab

Web
www.fiskarsgroup.com

reddot award 2017
best of the best

The perfect cut

Trimming bushes into shape and cutting branches in the garden can turn out to be a highly time-consuming task. The new Fiskars PowerGear X pruners have been designed especially to deliver more cutting power to take the effort out of garden work tasks. The design combines highly developed ergonomics with aesthetically balanced proportions. The pruners offer tools for cutting both fresh and dry wood. They provide a high degree of user comfort and make it easier for any user to cut for longer, such as in autumn, without experiencing fatigue. This is made possible by the patented PowerGear mechanism, which delivers a three-fold increase in cutting power. The innovative rotating handle ensures that the power of all fingers is engaged on every cut, exerting an equal but reduced pressure to deliver maximised power output with minimal user effort. The pruners are equipped with sharp, corrosion-resistant steel blades. The lightweight durable handles are made of glass fibre reinforced plastic and rest perfectly in the hand. The slip-resistant SoftGrip material and the 3D contouring of the handles prevent slipping. The ergonomic handle sizes are optimised for small to large hands. With their ingenious innovative ergonomics and a design idiom of dynamic look, these pruners aestheticise work in the garden – their functionality makes them a pleasure to use.

Der perfekte Schnitt

Im Garten die Äste der Bäume zu schneiden oder die Büsche in Form zu trimmen, ist eine mitunter zeitaufwendige Arbeit. Die Fiskars PowerGear X Gartenscheren wurden in besonderem Maße für eine höhere Schneidleistung bei geringerem Krafteinsatz entwickelt. Ihre Gestaltung vereint eine hochentwickelte Ergonomie mit ästhetisch ausgewogenen Proportionen. Konzipiert wurden die Scheren zum Schneiden von frischem sowie trockenem Holz. Dabei bieten sie ein hohes Maß an Komfort, durch den sie auch bei längerem Schneiden, etwa im Herbst, ermüdungsfrei eingesetzt werden können. Ermöglicht wird dies durch den patentierten PowerGear-Mechanismus, der die Schneidleistung verdreifacht. Der innovative Rollgriff nutzt bei jedem Schnitt die Kraft aller Finger. Der dadurch entstehende gleichmäßige, reduzierte Druck sorgt für eine optimierte Schneidleistung bei nur minimaler Anstrengung. Die Gartenscheren sind ausgestattet mit scharfen, korrosionsbeständigen Stahlklingen. Mit ihren leichten, langlebigen Griffen aus glasfaserverstärktem Kunststoff liegen sie perfekt in der Hand des Nutzers. Das rutschfeste SoftGrip-Material und die 3D-Konturierung der Griffe verhindern dabei ein Abrutschen. Die ergonomischen Griffgrößen sind für kleine bis große Hände optimiert. Mit ihrer ausgeklügelten, innovativen Ergonomie und dynamisch anmutenden Formensprache ästhetisieren diese Gartenscheren die Arbeit im Garten – ihre Funktionalität bereitet dabei viel Spaß.

Statement by the jury

These pruners by Fiskars are convincing in every respect, featuring a patented mechanism that simplifies cutting task considerably and thus makes garden work easier. The mechanism represents a cleverly designed solution and fits perfectly into the form. Significantly increasing user comfort, the innovative handle grips engage the power of all fingers on every cut. Everything merges into an outstandingly clear, concise and ergonomic design.

Begründung der Jury

Diese Gartenscheren von Fiskars überzeugen in jeder Hinsicht mit ihrem patentierten Mechanismus, der das Schneiden erheblich vereinfacht und dem Nutzer so die Arbeit erleichtert. Dieser Mechanismus ist gestalterisch clever gelöst und perfekt in die Form integriert. Bei jedem Schnitt wird durch den innovativen Rollgriff die Kraft aller Finger genutzt, was den Komfort merklich erhöht. Alles fügt sich hier zusammen zu einem sehr klaren, integrativen und ergonomischen Design.

Designer portrait
See page 34
Siehe Seite 34

Fiskars PowerGear™ X
Tree Pruners
Baumschere

Manufacturer
Fiskars Finland Oy Ab, Helsinki, Finland
In-house design
Web
www.fiskarsgroup.com

The Fiskars PowerGear X tree pruners offer a particularly high cutting performance for branches at high altitudes. The version with adjustable telescopic handle reaches up to a height of six metres. The efficient bypass cutting mechanism takes up to 12 times less effort than standard pruning shears without support. With a practical lock, the cutting angle can be adjusted up to 230 degrees. An orange-coloured blade support improves visibility. Hard-wearing, anti-slip handles provide excellent hold and comfort. The anti-slip material prevents slipping during upright storage.

Die Fiskars PowerGear X Schneidgiraffen bieten eine besonders hohe Schneidleistung für Zweige in großer Höhe. Die Version mit einstellbarem Teleskopstiel reicht bis zu sechs Meter hoch. Dabei erfordert der effiziente Bypass-Schneidmechanismus bis zu zwölfmal weniger Kraftaufwand im Vergleich zu Standard-Baumscheren ohne Unterstützung. Der Schneidewinkel lässt sich mit einer praktischen Verriegelung bis 230 Grad einstellen. Eine orangefarbene Klingenstütze verbessert die Sichtbarkeit und strapazierfähige, rutschfeste Griffe sorgen für hervorragenden Halt und Komfort. Die Antirutschbeschichtung verhindert ein Wegrutschen während der Aufbewahrung.

Statement by the jury
The pruning shears Fiskars PowerGear X combine a well-devised mechanism with an ergonomic design to create a functional, effective unit.

Begründung der Jury
Die Baumschere Fiskars PowerGear X verbindet einen durchdachten Mechanismus mit einer auf Ergonomie ausgerichteten Gestaltung zu einer funktionalen, effektiven Einheit.

WORX Hydroshot
Pressure Washer
Hochdruckreiniger

Manufacturer
Positec Technology, Suzhou, China
In-house design
Web
www.positecgroup.com
www.worx.com

Worx Hydroshot is a battery-operated pressure washer that is flexibly to move and can use water from various sources. It is suitable for numerous tasks at home and on the way, for instance to clean bicycles, sports equipment, terraces, windows or garden furniture. The pump is integrated into the appliance and delivers water pressure up to 320 psi (22 bar) – ten times stronger than from the water line. Just like the spray head, this pressure can be adjusted according to the respective task.

Statement by the jury
The pressure washer Worx Hydroshot impresses with its compact size and an operation mode that is independent of a power source, thanks to which it can be used in manifold ways.

Worx Hydroshot ist ein flexibel bewegbarer, akkubetriebener Hochdruckreiniger, der Wasser aus verschiedensten Quellen nutzen kann und für eine Vielzahl von Anwendungen zuhause wie unterwegs geeignet ist; etwa um Fahrräder, Sport-Equipment, Terrassen, Fenster oder Gartenmöbel zu reinigen. Die Pumpe ist im Gerät integriert und liefert Wasserdruck bis zu 320 psi (22 Bar) – zehnmal stärker als aus der Leitung. Dieser Druck kann der jeweiligen Aufgabe entsprechend, ebenso wie der Sprühkopf, eingestellt werden.

Begründung der Jury
Der Hochdruckreiniger Worx Hydroshot überzeugt durch seine kompakte Größe und den stromunabhängigen Betrieb, dank derer er sich sehr vielseitig einsetzen lässt.

WORX 20V
Turbine Blower
Laubbläser

Manufacturer
Positec Technology, Suzhou, China
In-house design
Web
www.positecgroup.com
www.worx.com

Worx 20V is a powerful battery leaf blower with electric motor and a high-performance machine that is driven by a turbine impeller system. It is operated at 10,000 revolutions per minute as opposed to petrol-driven models that reach approx. 3,000 rotations. The result is a blowing speed of 245 km/h and an airflow of 10.5 cbm. The brushless engine ensures high efficiency and an extended running time. The lightweight construction and the ergonomic design allow operation with only one hand.

Statement by the jury
The outstanding innovation of the leaf blower Worx 20V is its technical performance, which generates enormous speeds by means of a turbine impeller system.

Worx 20V ist ein kraftvoller Akku-Laubbläser mit Elektromotor und einem Hochleistungsgebläse, das mit Turbinentechnik betrieben wird. Es operiert mit 10.000 Umdrehungen pro Minute im Unterschied zu benzinbetriebenen Modellen, die auf ca. 3.000 Rotationen kommen. Das Ergebnis ist eine Blasgeschwindigkeit von 245 km/h und ein Luftstrom von 10,5 cbm. Der bürstenlose Motor sorgt für hohe Effizienz und eine verlängerte Laufzeit. Die leichte Bauweise und die ergonomische Gestaltung ermöglichen die Bedienung mit nur einer Hand.

Begründung der Jury
Die herausragende Innovation des Laubbläsers Worx 20V ist seine technische Leistungsfähigkeit, die mittels Turbinengebläse enorme Geschwindigkeiten erzeugt.

Gardena Hedge Trimmer
Heckenschere

Manufacturer
GARDENA GmbH, Ulm, Germany
In-house design
Jens Näslund, Taras Czornyj
Web
www.husqvarnagroup.com
www.gardena.com

The hedge trimmer by Gardena not only allows for easy handling but is impressively powerful. Its design is characterised by a compact motor with rounded edges and two ergonomic handles, the distance between which has been carefully balanced. Thus, the closed front handle offers optimum support when hedges are trimmed with vertical movements. Dark colours give the impression of solidity, while turquoise-coloured elements, such as the clearly visible knife protection tip, bring lightness into the design.

Statement by the jury
A harmonious ergonomic design with a focus on user-friendliness and safety is the striking feature of this hedge trimmer.

Diese Heckenschere von Gardena ermöglicht eine bewegliche Handhabung und ist zudem leistungsstark. Ihre Gestaltung ist durch einen kompakten Motor mit abgerundeten Kanten und zwei ergonomische Griffe geprägt, deren Abstände zueinander sorgfältig ausbalanciert wurden. Dadurch bietet der geschlossene Vordergriff beim Heckenschnitt in vertikaler Bewegung optimale Unterstützung. Dunkle Farben vermitteln Solidität, während die türkis eingefärbten Elemente, wie die dadurch gut sichtbare Messerschutz-Spitze, Leichtigkeit in die Gestaltung bringen.

Begründung der Jury
Eine ausgewogene ergonomische Gestaltung mit Fokus auf Benutzerfreundlichkeit und Sicherheit ist das hervorstechende Kennzeichen dieser Heckenschere.

Frutte
Winnowing Basket
Sammel- und Sortierkorb

Manufacturer
Cainz Corporation, Honjō, Japan
In-house design
Web
www.cainz.com

Frutte redefines the traditional Japanese Temi and is used in gardening for collecting, transport and disposal. In the typical rounded form with sieve, harvested vegetables can be washed right away. When used as dustpan, water and soil can be shaken off the leaves. The curved handle is easy to manage so that Frutte can be held and carried with just one hand. Elements such as hanger holes or the basic shape were taken from the classic Temi and transferred into a modern design.

Statement by the jury
Frutte is a new interpretation of the traditional Temi from Japan and gives it a very form-fit and modern appearance.

Frutte definiert das traditionelle japanische Temi neu und wird beim Gärtnern zum Sammeln, Transportieren und Entsorgen verwendet. Dank der typischen Rundung mit Sieb kann geerntetes Gemüse gleich darin gewaschen werden. Als Kehrschaufel genutzt, lassen sich damit auch Wasser und Erde von Laub abschütteln. Der gebogene Griff macht es handlich, sodass man Frutte mit nur einer Hand halten und ganz einfach transportieren kann. Elemente wie Aufhängelöcher oder die Grundform wurden vom klassischen Temi übernommen und in eine moderne Gestaltung übertragen.

Begründung der Jury
Frutte stellt eine Neuinterpretation des traditionellen Temi aus Japan dar und verleiht ihm ein überaus formschlüssiges und modernes Erscheinungsbild.

Landroid S
Mowing Robot
Mähroboter

Manufacturer
Positec Technology, Suzhou, China
In-house design
Web
www.positecgroup.com
www.worx.com

The mowing robot Landroid S is suitable for lawns up to 500 sqm and can be individually programmed using an app. Due to its laterally relocated cutting mechanism, the edges of lawns, which mowing robots usually do not reach, need not be manually trimmed. Thanks to AIA technology, it saves approx. 30 per cent mowing time compared to competing products. It can be easily navigated through narrow places and crooked lawn areas. Its charging station is barely visible.

Statement by the jury
The elaborate design with its laterally displaced cutting mechanism and innovative technology distinguish the mowing robot Landroid S as a highly functional appliance.

Der Mähroboter Landroid S eignet sich für Rasenflächen bis zu 500 qm und ist via App individuell programmierbar. Aufgrund seines seitlich versetzten Schnittmechanismus müssen die Kanten von Rasenflächen, an die Mähroboter üblicherweise nicht herankommen, nicht manuell nachgetrimmt werden. Dank AIA-Technologie spart er ca. 30 Prozent Mähzeit im Vergleich zu Konkurrenzprodukten und navigiert mühelos auch durch Engstellen und verwinkelte Rasenbereiche. Seine Ladestation ist kaum sichtbar.

Begründung der Jury
Die Gestaltung mit seitlich versetztem Schnittmechanismus ist durchdacht und hebt den Mähroboter Landroid S samt seiner innovativen Technologie als hochfunktional hervor.

Tornado Pro 9118 XWS 4WD
Lawn Tractor
Rasentraktor

Manufacturer
Global Garden Products Italy S.p.A.,
Castelfranco Veneto, Italy
Design
Delineo Design (Giampaolo Allocco),
Montebelluna, Italy
Web
www.stiga.com
www.delineodesign.it

The lawn tractor Tornado Pro 9118 XWS 4WD is versatile, robust and powerful. Due to its four-wheel drive, it is suitable for demanding gardens and for difficult terrain. Thanks to a lateral eject function, it mows high grass quickly and easily. The cutting deck is equipped with three blades and six wheels. The 15-litre tank and a 2-cylinder 725 cc Kawasaki motor ensure high performance. The large wheels offer secure grip. A display shows all important data. Charger, mulch kit and tow coupling are included.

Statement by the jury
Powerful, compact and very suitable for intractable subsoils – these are the outstanding features of the striking lawn tractor Tornado Pro 9118 XWS 4WD.

Der Rasentraktor Tornado Pro 9118 XWS 4WD ist vielseitig, stabil und kraftvoll. Er eignet sich für anspruchsvolle Gärten und aufgrund des Allradantriebs auch für schwieriges Gelände. Dank Seitenauswurffunktion mäht er hohes Gras schnell und leicht. Das Mähdeck ist mit drei Messern und sechs Rädern ausgestattet und der 15-Liter-Tank und ein 2-Zylinder-726-cbcm-Kawasaki-Motor sorgen für hohe Leistung. Die großen Räder bieten sicheren Grip und ein Display zeigt alle wichtigen Daten an. Ladegerät, Mulchkit und Anhängevorrichtung sind inklusive.

Begründung der Jury
Leistungsstark, kompakt und sehr gut für heikle Untergründe geeignet – das sind die herausragenden Merkmale des markanten Rasentraktors Tornado Pro 9118 XWS 4WD.

Grundfos Scala2
Water Booster Pump
Hauswasserwerk

Manufacturer
Grundfos GmbH, Erkrath, Germany
In-house design
Morten Sofussen
Web
www.grundfos.de

The domestic water pump Grundfos Scala2 is a compact, versatile solution for indoor and outdoor water supply. Thanks to constant pressure control, it does not need a membrane pressure vessel and requires only a quarter of the usual space. The water-cooled permanent magnet motor provides the same hydraulic performance as a traditional domestic water pump. It is very quiet and extremely energy-efficient with a maximum of 550 watts of power input. Scala2 can be installed without tools in no time and features ten safety and comfort functions for protection against dry-running or overvoltage/undervoltage.

Das Hauswasserwerk Grundfos Scala2 stellt eine kompakte, vielseitige Lösung für die Wasserversorgung im Innen- und Außenbereich dar. Dank Konstantdruckregelung kommt es ohne Membrandruckbehälter aus und benötigt nur ein Viertel des üblichen Platzes. Der wassergekühlte Permanentmagnetmotor liefert die gleiche hydraulische Leistung wie ein traditionelles Hauswasserwerk, ist dabei aber sehr leise und mit maximal 550 Watt Leistungsaufnahme äußerst energieeffizient. Scala2 lässt sich in kürzester Zeit werkzeuglos installieren und verfügt über zehn Sicherheits- und Komfortfunktionen zum Schutz gegen Trockenlauf oder Über-/ Unterspannung.

Statement by the jury
Scala2 wins over with remarkably compact dimensions and such high performance that it stands out clearly from comparable domestic water pumps.

Begründung der Jury
Scala2 beeindruckt durch bemerkenswert kompakte Maße bei zugleich derart hoher Leistungsfähigkeit, dass es sich von vergleichbaren Hauswasserwerken deutlich abhebt.

Pendularis®
Floating Indoor Garden
Schwebende Innenraum-
begrünung

Manufacturer
Pendularis®, ZHAW/IUNR,
Wädenswil, Switzerland
In-house design
Erich Stutz
Design
Designpunkt GmbH (Bernd Danhamer),
Niederweningen, Switzerland
Web
www.pendularis.ch
Honourable Mention

Pendularis is a modular system that can be planted and hung up individually in interior spaces. It can be used as a room divider or fixed along walls, above work places, furniture and railings. In the specially developed planters, which feature a sophisticated clip system, the plants can be rearranged quickly and easily. Larger installations, which are variable in form, length and shape, are attended to by an automatic irrigation system.

Pendularis ist ein modulares Baukasten-system, das sich bepflanzen und individuell in Innenräumen aufhängen lässt. Es kann als Raumteiler fungieren oder entlang von Wänden, über Arbeitsplätzen, Möbeln und Geländern befestigt werden. In den speziell entwickelten Pflanzgefäßen, die über ein raffiniertes Clip-System verfügen, lassen sich die Pflanzen schnell und einfach neu arrangieren. Größere Installationen, die in Form, Länge und Farbe variabel sind, können durch eine automatisierte Bewässerung unterhalten werden.

Statement by the jury
The idea of Pendularis to stylishly upgrade spaces as green oases is fascinating and offers much creative freedom thanks to its variability.

Begründung der Jury
Die Idee von Pendularis, Räume als grüne Oasen stilvoll aufzuwerten, ist faszinierend und bietet dank ihrer Variabilität einen hohen Gestaltungsspielraum.

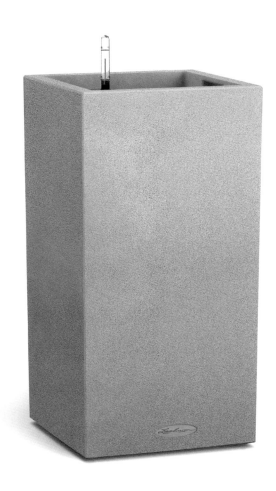

CANTO Color Column
Self-Watering Planter
Pflanzgefäß mit
Erdbewässerung

Manufacturer
LECHUZA, geobra Brandstätter Stiftung &
Co. KG, Zirndorf, Germany
In-house design
Web
www.lechuza.com

The Canto Color Column planter is made of robust and weatherproof plastic and features a planter liner and the proven Lechuza sub-irrigation system. Its three-litre reservoir optimally supplies the plants with water. The removable planter liner with colour-coordinated frame and integrated handles offers sufficient leeway for creative ideas. Featuring a natural stone look, the planter presents itself as a modern, flexible design element for interior as well as outdoor spaces, since excess rainwater can simply drain with the help of a removable drain plug.

Statement by the jury
The Canto Color Column not only impresses with its clear, plain elegance but also with its integrated sub-irrigation system as well its suitability for indoor and outdoor use.

Das Pflanzgefäß Canto Color Säule ist aus robustem und witterungsbeständigem Kunststoff gefertigt und mit einem Pflanzeinsatz und dem bewährten Lechuza-Erdbewässerungssystem ausgestattet. Über das Wasserreservoir mit drei Litern Fassungsvermögen werden die Pflanzen optimal versorgt. Der herausnehmbare Pflanzeinsatz mit Rahmen in Gefäßfarbe und Griffmulde ermöglicht kreativen Spielraum. Das Gefäß in Natursteinoptik präsentiert sich so als modernes und flexibles Gestaltungselement für Innenräume wie auch im Freien, da überschüssiges Regenwasser über eine herausnehmbare Bodenschraube problemlos ablaufen kann.

Begründung der Jury
Die Canto Color Säule beeindruckt nicht nur durch ihre klare, schlichte Eleganz, sondern auch durch ihr integriertes Bewässerungssystem sowie ihre Eignung für innen und außen.

CANTO Color Cube
Self-Watering Planter
Pflanzgefäß mit
Erdbewässerung

Manufacturer
LECHUZA, geobra Brandstätter Stiftung &
Co. KG, Zirndorf, Germany
In-house design
Web
www.lechuza.com

Like the Canto Color Column, the Canto Color Cube planter features a removable planter liner and an integrated Lechuza sub-irrigation system. The rough natural stone look makes the very lightweight cube a timeless eyecatcher. Made of robust and weatherproof plastic, it is suited for both indoors and outdoors as well as a wide range of planting options. In the open, the drain plug can be removed, which allows rainwater to drain off. The planter liner with colour-coordinated frame and integrated handles can be easily changed and offers countless creative possibilities.

Statement by the jury
The design of the Canto Color Cube is based on clear lines and a stylish aesthetics, which sets no limits to individual planting.

Ebenso wie die Säule ist das Pflanzgefäß Canto Color Würfel mit einem herausnehmbaren Pflanzeinsatz und einem integrierten Lechuza-Erdbewässerungssystem ausgestattet. Die raue Natursteinoptik macht den zugleich sehr leichten Würfel zu einem zeitlosen Blickfang. Aus robustem und wetterfestem Kunststoff gefertigt, ist er für den Innen- und Außenbereich und für unterschiedlichste Bepflanzungen geeignet. Im Freien kann dank einer herausdrehbaren Bodenschraube überschüssiges Regenwasser ablaufen. Der Pflanzeinsatz mit Rahmen in Gefäßfarbe und einer Griffmulde ist leicht wechselbar und ermöglicht zahlreiche Gestaltungsmöglichkeiten.

Begründung der Jury
Das Design des Canto Color Würfels setzt auf klare Linien und eine stilvolle Ästhetik, die der individuellen Bepflanzung keine Grenzen setzt.

Natura 2in1
Water Butt
Regentonne

Manufacturer
Otto Graf GmbH Kunststofferzeugnisse,
Teningen, Germany
In-house design
Web
www.graf-online.de

The water butt Natura 2in1 is characterised by an unusual surface, which has a three-dimensional effect thanks to convex and concave areas. When light falls on the waved outer face, the aesthetics of the container comes particularly into its own. It is made of high-quality weather-resistant plastic, is UV-stable and available in different colours. With a height of 1.5 metres, the reservoir has a volume of 350 litres with small space requirements. In addition, it can be arranged individually as a planting bowl.

Statement by the jury
Natura 2in1 reinterprets the conventional water butt and becomes an eye-catcher not only because of its elegant appearance but also through the innovative possibility of planting it.

Die Regentonne Natura 2in1 ist durch eine ungewöhnliche Oberfläche gekennzeichnet, die durch konvexe und konkave Flächen dreidimensional wirkt. Wenn Licht auf die wellenförmig gestaltete Außenseite fällt, kommt die Ästhetik des Behälters besonders gut zur Geltung. Dieser ist aus hochwertigem, witterungsbeständigem Kunststoff hergestellt, UV-stabil und in verschiedenen Farben erhältlich. 1,5 Meter hoch, besitzt der Speicher ein Volumen von 350 Litern bei zugleich geringem Platzbedarf. Darüber hinaus lässt er sich als Pflanzschale individuell gestalten.

Begründung der Jury
Natura 2in1 interpretiert die klassische Regentonne neu und wird nicht nur durch ihr elegantes Erscheinungsbild zum Blickfang, sondern auch durch die innovative Möglichkeit ihrer Bepflanzung.

Clever Pots Holder
Pot Holder
Blumentopfhalter

Manufacturer
W'innovate Ltd, Worksop, Great Britain
In-house design
Web
www.winnovate.co.uk
Honourable Mention

This small garden pot holder has been designed to attach to drainpipes with ease. The product responds to the trend for vertical planting providing a solution for those with limited space for gardening. Several holders can be added to a drainpipe one above the other to create a decorative group of flowers and herbs. The inclusive design offers height flexibility, to all users regardless of mobility or age.

Statement by the jury
This garden pot holder scores with the creative idea to be hung effortlessly on drainpipes making plantation possible in the simplest way.

Der kleine Blumentopfhalter wurde entworfen, um ihn ganz mühelos an Regenrohren anbringen zu können. Er stellt eine Antwort auf den Trend der vertikalen Bepflanzung dar und bietet gerade für diejenigen eine gute Lösung an, die nur über begrenzten Platz zur Begrünung verfügen. Es können auch mehrere Halter übereinander gefügt werden, um dekorative Ensembles aus Blumen und Kräutern zu gestalten. Das inklusive Design ermöglicht ein Anbringen in jeder gewünschten Höhe für alle Benutzer, unabhängig ihrer Mobilität und ihres Alters.

Begründung der Jury
Dieser Blumentopfhalter punktet durch die gestalterische Idee, ihn ohne Anstrengung an Regenrohre hängen zu können und so höchst einfach eine Begrünung zu ermöglichen.

Wilko Tool Handle
Tool Handle
Werkzeuggriff

Manufacturer
Winnovate Ltd., Worksop, Great Britain
In-house design
Web
www.winnovate.co.uk

This product is a universal handle that can be attached easily to any long-handled garden tool. The fixing-less design enables for simple transfer from one tool to the next. The Tool Handle provides an additional axis, enabling the user to create a firm grip to assist with the more labour-intensive gardening tasks, where greater leverage is often required for activities such as raking, hoeing or turning over heavy soil. It enables both pushing and pulling actions in either direction.

Statement by the jury
The idea behind the Wilko Tool Handle was implemented in a very simple and innovative solution, which makes tiresome gardening much easier.

Dieser Universalgriff lässt sich umstandslos an allen langstieligen Gartengeräten anbringen. Da die Gestaltung des Produkts ohne Fixierung auskommt, kann man den Griff einfach von einem Werkzeug auf ein anderes umstecken. Die Verlängerung der Stielachse garantiert einen festen Griff bei arbeitsintensiveren Aufgaben im Garten wie Rechen, Hacken und Umstechen, die oft mehr Hebelwirkung brauchen. Der Griff hilft sowohl bei schiebenden wie auch ziehenden Tätigkeiten in beide Richtungen.

Begründung der Jury
Die Idee, die dem Werkzeuggriff Wilko Tool Handle zugrunde liegt, wurde in einer überaus einfachen wie innovativen Lösung umgesetzt, die ermüdende Gartenarbeit deutlich erleichtert.

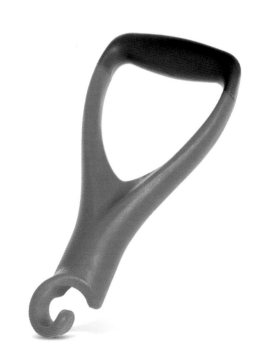

Action cameras	Actionkameras
Air mattresses	Cityräder
Baskets and containers	E-Bikes
Bike equipment	Fahrradzubehör
Binoculars	Ferngläser
City bikes	Fitnessgeräte
Clasp knives and hunting knives	Fitnesszubehör
Diving	Fun-Drohnen
E-bikes	Funktionsbekleidung
Fitness devices	Golf und Golfzubehör
Fitness equipment	Haustierbedarf
Fun drones	Helme
Functional clothing	Hobby
Golf and golf accessories	Körbe und Behälter
Helmets	Luftmatratzen
Hobbies	Mountainbikes
Locks	Musik-Equipment
Mountain bikes	Musikinstrumente
Musical equipment	Öffentliches Spielzeug
Musical instruments	Outdoorausrüstung
Outdoor equipment	Profi-Drohnen
Pet supplies	Rennräder
Professional drones	Roller
Public playing equipment	Schlösser
Racing bikes	Sextoys
Scooters	Skateboards
Sex toys	Sportartikel
Skateboards	Sportbekleidung
Sports articles	Sportschuhe
Sports bottles	Taschen- und Jagdmesser
Sports clothing	Tauchsport
Sports shoes	Trendsport und -zubehör
Tents	Trinkflaschen
Trend sports and equipment	Wassersport und -zubehör
Water sports and equipment	Wintersport und -zubehör
Winter sports and equipment	Zelte

Leisure, sport and games
Freizeit, Sport und Spiel

KeyMission 360
Action Camera
Actionkamera

Manufacturer
Nikon Corporation, Tokyo, Japan

In-house design
Hiroyuki Asano, Chikara Fujita,
Mitsuo Nakajima

Web
www.nikon.com

reddot award 2017
best of the best

Inspiring design

Modern action cameras offer many possibilities, since the maxim of flexibility is already inherent in their design. The KeyMission 360 expands on the use spectrum of such cameras by lending it a highly user-friendly design. The camera is equipped with an image sensor and a Nikkor lens on both the front and back. It thus facilitates 4K UHD video recording in a 360-degree format. This innovative recording possibility is complemented by path-breaking functional features. The camera is not only waterproof to a depth of up to 30 metres, but also resistant to shock, freeze and dust. In addition, it is compatible with a number of accessories, inviting users to experience new approaches to outdoor recording. The camera boasts a highly solid construction for extreme demands, based on materials that guarantee its durability. In terms of form it impresses with a symmetric shape that identifies it as an omnidirectional camera. The sophisticated design concept also encompasses the possibility to share images quickly. The support of the SnapBridge 360/170 app means that users can easily transfer the images they record with the camera to a smart device. Showcasing a solid as well as aesthetic look that is enhanced by new user possibilities, the KeyMission 360 provides an active recording experience – it inspires users to test and go beyond their own limits.

Inspirierendes Design

Moderne Actionkameras bieten viele Möglichkeiten, da die Maxime der Flexibilität bereits in ihrem Konzept verinnerlicht ist. Die KeyMission 360 erweitert deren Einsatzspektrum und verbindet dies mit einer sehr nutzerfreundlichen Gestaltung. Sie ist auf der Vorderseite und Rückseite mit einem Bildsensor sowie einem Nikkor-Objektiv ausgestattet. Damit ermöglicht sie es dem Fotografen, 4K-UHD-Aufnahmen im 360-Grad-Format zu machen. Diese innovative Aufnahmeoption verbindet sich mit wegweisenden funktionalen Eigenschaften. Die Kamera ist wasserdicht bis zu einer Tiefe von 30 Metern, sie ist stoßfest, frostsicher und vor eindringendem Staub geschützt. Da sie zudem über zahlreiche Ausrüstungsoptionen verfügt, kann sich der Fotograf mit ihr neue Bereiche im Outdoor-Einsatz erschließen. Die Kamera ist für extreme Anforderungen sehr solide konstruiert, die verwendeten Materialien verleihen ihr Langlebigkeit. Formal beeindruckt sie mit ihrem symmetrischen Aufbau, der ihre omnidirektionalen Eigenschaften erkennen lässt. Ihr ausgereiftes Gestaltungskonzept schließt außerdem die Möglichkeit ein, die Aufnahmen unkompliziert zu versenden. Sie unterstützt die SnapBridge 360/170-App, weshalb User auf einfache Weise die aufgenommenen Bilder auf ein Smart Device übertragen können. Mit ihrer soliden wie ästhetischen Gestaltung und im Einklang mit neuen Anwendungseigenschaften bietet die KeyMission 360 ein aktives Aufnahmeerlebnis – der Fotograf kann mit ihr seine Grenzen austesten und darüber hinausgehen.

Statement by the jury

The compact design of the KeyMission 360 embodies the classic Nikon quality. Its design idiom visualises functionality in a simple and easy-to-understand approach. Perfectly executed to the very last detail, the camera is highly suitable for outdoor use. It offers fantastic 360-degree picture quality and is equipped with an image sensor and a Nikkor lens on both the front and back. This action camera fascinates with sophisticated features for demanding recording scenarios.

Begründung der Jury

Die kompakt gestaltete KeyMission 360 verkörpert die klassische Qualität von Nikon. Ihre Formensprache visualisiert ihre Funktionalität auf einfache und verständliche Weise. Für den Einsatz im Outdoor-Bereich ist sie bis in die Details perfekt ausgeführt. Ausgestattet mit einem Bildsensor und einem Nikkor-Objektiv auf beiden Kameraseiten, bietet sie eine phantastische Bildqualität im 360-Grad-Format. In anspruchsvollen Aufnahmesituationen begeistert diese Actionkamera mit ihren ausgereiften Features.

Designer portrait
See page 36
Siehe Seite 36

GoPro HERO5 Black
Action Camera
Actionkamera

Manufacturer
GoPro, Inc., San Mateo,
California, USA

In-house design
GoPro Industrial Design Team

Design
HUGE Design LLC,
San Francisco, USA

Web
www.gopro.com
www.huge-design.com

reddot award 2017
best of the best

Form for lifestyle
The uncomplicated creation of high-quality photos and video recordings is part of the technically highly advanced lifestyle of our time. The GoPro HERO5 Black action camera has been designed for convenient recording and sharing of our experiences. It offers a stabilised HD video recording function, stereo sound as well as a resolution of 12 MP for professional photos. Its innovative language of form results from the goal of creating a camera that remains waterproof up to ten metres of depth without the need of a separate housing. Due to its compact housing made of high-quality materials, it is robust with all controls arranged to be easily accessible for the photographer. The GoPro HERO5 Black also impresses with sophisticated operating comfort. One push of the shutter button suffices to switch the camera on and have it start recording automatically. A 2" LCD touchscreen on the rear as well as voice-activated operating controls make it easy to pick up the camera, quickly adjust the settings and start capturing images immediately. To help users get satisfying shots from virtually any activity or perspective, this camera is fully backwards compatible with all existing 30-plus GoPro mounts. Embodying a holistic design approach, the GoPro HERO5 Black is an impressive reinterpretation of the action camera – its special aesthetic is an enrichment to our contemporary lifestyle.

Form für den Lifestyle
Das unkomplizierte Erstellen qualitativ hochwertiger Fotos und Videoaufnahmen ist Teil des technisch hochentwickelten Lebensstils unserer Zeit. Die Actionkamera GoPro HERO5 Black wurde für das bequeme Aufnehmen und Teilen unserer Erlebnisse konzipiert. Sie bietet eine stabilisierte HD-Video-Aufnahmefunktion, Stereoton sowie eine Auflösung von 12 MP für professionelle Fotos. Ihre innovative Formensprache ist das Resultat der Zielsetzung, eine bis zehn Meter wasserdichte Kamera ohne ein zusätzliches Gehäuse zu gestalten. Durch ihr kompaktes Gehäuse aus hochwertigen Materialien ist sie robust, und alle Bedienelemente sind für den Fotografen leicht zugänglich angeordnet. Die GoPro HERO5 Black begeistert dabei durch ihren ausgereiften Bedienkomfort. So schaltet man sie durch einmaliges Drücken der Auslösetaste ein und startet damit automatisch die Aufnahme. Ein 2"-LCD-Touchscreen auf der Rückseite sowie eine sprachgesteuerte Bedienung erleichtern es, die Kamera in die Hand zu nehmen, die Einstellungen anzupassen und die Aufnahme zu starten. Um es den Nutzern zu ermöglichen, gute Aufnahmen von ihren Aktivitäten aus nahezu jeder Perspektive zu erhalten, ist diese Kamera mit den vorhandenen 30-plus GoPro-Halterungen vollständig kompatibel. Auf der Basis eines rundum durchdachten Designs entstand mit der GoPro HERO5 Black eine beeindruckende Neuinterpretation der Actionkamera – ihre besondere Ästhetik bereichert den aktuellen Lebensstil.

Statement by the jury
The GoPro HERO5 Black action camera is marked by an impressive design with which it achieves a new, iconic quality. Its elegant design idiom is the result of a perfectly thought-through, user-friendly concept. Equipped with features such as a stabilised high-definition video recording function, 12-MP photo resolution and stereo audio, it delivers capturing experiences of exquisitely high standard.

Begründung der Jury
Die Actionkamera GoPro HERO5 Black zeichnet sich durch eine beeindruckende Gestaltung aus, mit der sie eine neue, ikonische Qualität erlangt. Ihre elegante Formensprache ist das Ergebnis eines perfekt durchdachten, nutzerfreundlichen Konzepts. Ausgestattet mit Features wie einer stabilisierten HD-Video-Aufnahmefunktion, Stereoton und einer Fotoauflösung von 12 MP, bietet sie dem Nutzer ein Erlebnis auf exklusivem Niveau.

Designer portrait
See page 38
Siehe Seite 38

GoPro HERO5 Session
Action Camera

Manufacturer
GoPro, Inc., San Mateo, California, USA
In-house design
GoPro Industrial Design Team
Web
www.gopro.com

GoPro Hero5 Session is a very robust and compact camera with 38 x 38 x 36.4 mm enclosure size and is suitable for shots from impressive perspectives. With its mounts it can be attached to almost anything and thanks to a single-button, or simple voice-activated control, it can be operated hands-free. The picture quality for videos is 4K and for photos 10 MP in three modes: single, burst and time-lapse. This camera, designed for longevity, is waterproof to ten metres.

Statement by the jury
The design of the action camera GoPro Hero5 Session fascinates with its reduced size, which accommodates an impressive performance spectrum.

GoPro Hero5 Session ist eine sehr robuste und kompakte Kamera von 38 x 38 x 36,4 mm Größe und für Aufnahmen aus beeindruckenden Perspektiven geeignet. Mit ihren Halterungen lässt sie sich nahezu überall befestigen und dank Ein-Tasten-Bedienung oder einfacher Sprachsteuerung freihändig steuern. Die Bildqualität beträgt bei Videos 4K und bei Fotos 10 MP in den drei Modi Einzelfotos, Serienaufnahme und Zeitraffer. Die auf Langlebigkeit ausgelegte Kamera ist bis zehn Meter Tiefe wasserdicht.

Begründung der Jury
Die Gestaltung der Action-Kamera GoPro Hero5 Session fasziniert durch ihre reduzierte Größe, in der ein beeindruckendes Leistungsspektrum untergebracht ist.

Paralenz Dive Camera
Unterwasserkamera

Manufacturer
Paralenz ApS, Copenhagen, Denmark
Design
MOEF A/S (Martin Holmberg),
Copenhagen, Denmark
Web
www.paralenz.com
www.moef.dk

The Paralenz underwater camera is particularly lightweight, robust and easy to handle. Designed for adventure, it delivers very good footage, even at extreme depths, and it can automatically adjust the colours according to depth. The camera features a pressure and temperature sensor; it logs the dives and links data with photos and videos. The corresponding app generates a depth profile in which it links the footage with depth and time. The dive diary can be shared on social networks.

Statement by the jury
The Paralenz underwater camera accommodates high-grade technology in a stable housing and facilitates the easy documentation of diving adventures.

Die Unterwasserkamera Paralenz ist besonders leicht, robust und einfach zu bedienen. Auf Abenteuer ausgelegt, liefert sie auch in extremen Tiefen sehr gute Aufnahmen, wobei ein eingebauter Tiefenmesser die Farben automatisch anpasst. Ausgestattet mit einem Druck- und Temperatursensor, loggt die Kamera den Tauchgang und versieht Fotos und Videos mit Daten. Die dazugehörige App erstellt ein Tiefenprofil, in dem sie die Aufnahmen mit Tiefe und Zeit verlinkt. Das Tauchlogbuch lässt sich in den sozialen Netzwerken teilen.

Begründung der Jury
Die Unterwasserkamera Paralenz bringt hochwertige Technik in einem stabilen Gehäuse unter und macht das Abenteuer Tauchgang ganz leicht dokumentierbar.

VIVID
Gimbal Stabilised Camera
Kamera mit Gimbal-
Stabilisierung

Manufacturer
Autel Robotics Co., Ltd., Shenzhen, China
In-house design
Prof. Juntian Jiang, Prof. Yongshuai Wang
Web
www.autelrobotics.com

Vivid is a powerful ultra HD 4K compact camera, with quick release mount and three-axis gimbal. High quality video recordings and photos can be easily achieved. During recording or shooting, a mobile device can be used for live video feeds, playback or immediate sharing with others. The different gimbal modes: lock, follow, semi-follow and selfie, offer additional options for a personal creative expression.

Statement by the jury
The compact camera Vivid scores not only in terms of its high performance and quality but also with additional benefits that can be used synchronously.

Vivid ist eine leistungsstarke Ultra-HD-4K-Kompaktkamera, die mit einem Schnellspanner und einem 3-Achsen-Gimbal ausgestattet ist. Mit ihr gelingen Video- und Fotoaufnahmen leicht und in hoher Qualität. Während der Aufnahme lässt sich ein Mobilgerät zur Live-Videoübertragung, zum Abspielen oder zum sofortigen Teilen mit anderen einsetzen. Die verschiedenen Gimbal-Modi Lock, Follow, Semi-Follow und Selfie bieten zusätzlich die Möglichkeit des individuellen kreativen Ausdrucks.

Begründung der Jury
Die Kompaktkamera Vivid punktet nicht nur durch hohe Leistungsfähigkeit und Qualität, sondern auch durch synchron mögliche Zusatznutzen.

KeyMission 80
Action Camera

Manufacturer
Nikon Corporation, Tokyo, Japan
In-house design
Shu Suzuki, Mitsuo Nakajima
Web
www.nikon.com

The KeyMission 80 is a lightweight, flexible and user-friendly action camera which captures exciting situations in real time. It is ready to record in less than a second and features a housing that is waterproof to one metre for 30 minutes, making it a versatile companion. Developed for demanding conditions, dust and dirt don't stand a chance. The housing withstands falls from a height of up to 1.5 metres and it is cold-resistant up to minus ten degrees Celsius. The camera is available in black or silver and features an 80-degree Nikkor fixed focal length lens that can record details and textures in high resolution.

Statement by the jury
With its outstanding stability and compact as well as user-friendly size, the KeyMission 80 meets its users' high demands for a versatile application.

Die KeyMission 80 ist eine leichte, bewegliche und bedienfreundliche Action-Kamera, die spannende Situationen live aufnimmt. Sie ist in weniger als einer Sekunde aufnahmebereit und mit ihrem in bis zu einem Meter Tiefe 30 Minuten lang wasserdichten Gehäuse ein vielseitiger Begleiter. Für anspruchsvolle Bedingungen entwickelt, bleiben Staub und Schmutz außen vor. Das Gehäuse hält Stürzen aus einer Höhe von bis zu 1,5 Meter stand und ist bis minus zehn Grad Celsius kältebeständig. Die Kamera ist in Schwarz und Silber erhältlich und mit einem 80-Grad-Nikkor-Festbrennweitenobjektiv ausgestattet, das Details und Texturen hochauflösend aufzeichnen kann.

Begründung der Jury
Mit ihrer herausragenden Stabilität und zugleich kompakten, nutzerfreundlichen Größe wird die KeyMission 80 den hohen Ansprüchen ihrer Benutzer an einen vielseitigen Einsatz gerecht.

TP-Link Quarter Camera
Wearable Camera
Tragbare Kamera

Manufacturer
TP-Link Technologies Co., Ltd.,
Shenzhen, China
Design
Whipsaw Inc, San Jose, USA
Web
www.tp-link.com
www.whipsaw.com

The TP-Link Quarter Camera is a wearable digital video camera the size of a quarter (an American 25 cent coin). It is operated through a mobile charging base that features an interactive display and a memory card slot. The cylindrical camera can be removed from its base and used as is, or with one of three sophisticated attachment solutions: a suction cup to mount on stationary objects, a magnetic system for thicker materials, or a spring steel clip to attach to clothing.

Statement by the jury
The powerful wide-angle HD camera impresses with its compact dimensions and its various accessories, allowing it to be attached almost anywhere.

Die TP-Link Quarter Camera ist eine tragbare digitale Videokamera in der Größe eines Quarters (amerikanische 25-Cent-Münze). Sie wird mittels mobiler Ladebasis betrieben, die über ein interaktives Display und einen Speicherkarteneinschub verfügt. Die zylindrisch geformte Kamera kann von der Basis abgenommen und allein verwendet werden oder mit einer von drei ausgeklügelten Befestigungslösungen: einem Saugnapf zur Befestigung an ortsfesten Objekten, einem Magnetsystem für dickere Materialien oder einem Federstahlclip zur Anbringung etwa an Kleidung.

Begründung der Jury
Die leistungsstarke HD-Weitwinkelkamera überzeugt durch ihre kompakten Maße sowie verschiedene Zusätze, mit denen sie sich nahezu überall befestigen lässt.

OCLU
Action Camera

Manufacturer
OCLU Limited, London, Great Britain
In-house design
Hugo Martin
Web
www.oclu.com

Oclu is an action camera designed to overcome a number of use-related challenges. It has a low profile, aerodynamic form factor making it less intrusive and less likely to be accidentally knocked out of position. Highly durable and water resistant to a depth of five metres outside of its dive chamber, it ensures high quality audio recording. It has image stabilisation and records 4K video at 30 frames per second and full HD at 120 frames per second to achieve smooth 4x slow motion. Intuitive software on both camera and app has many patent pending features including "LiveCut", making it easy to cut unwanted footage on the fly.

Oclu ist eine Action-Kamera, die darauf ausgelegt ist, eine Reihe funktionaler Herausforderungen zu meistern. Dank ihres flachen Profils und ihrer aerodynamischen Form ist sie unaufdringlich und kann nicht so leicht versehentlich aus ihrer Position gebracht werden. Widerstandsfähig und außerhalb ihrer Tauchkammer bis in eine Tiefe von fünf Metern wasserdicht, gewährleistet sie qualitativ hochwertige Tonaufnahmen. Sie verfügt über einen Bildstabilisator und zeichnet 4K-Videos mit 30 Bildern pro Sekunde sowie Full-HD-Videos mit 120 Bildern pro Sekunde auf, um Aufnahmen mit ruhiger Vierfachzeitlupe zu ermöglichen. Die intuitiv bedienbare Software von Kamera und App weist mehrere zum Patent angemeldete Features wie das Programm LiveCut auf, mit dem sich verwackelte Aufnahmen spontan herausschneiden lassen.

Statement by the jury
The design of the action camera Oclu impresses with its easily manageable size and latest technical features for sound and image recordings.

Begründung der Jury
Die Gestaltung der Action-Kamera Oclu überzeugt durch eine komfortabel zu handhabende Größe und modernste technische Ausstattung für Ton- und Bildaufnahmen.

iSHOXS Power Force Cup
Actioncam Suction Cup
Actioncam-Saughalter

Manufacturer
Tormaxx GmbH, Mönchengladbach, Germany
In-house design
Hubert Koch
Web
www.tormaxx.de

The patent pending iSHOXS Power Force Cup has a square area in the centre of its oval form, which is larger than the rounded lateral areas ensuring high stability. Two cam levers were integrated in the suction plate so that action cameras and other devices can be mounted centrally. This reduces vibrations and improves the quality of the recordings. The suction cup mount is made of glass-fibre reinforced ABS and features a slider for mounting GoPro systems.

Statement by the jury
This suction cup impresses with its design concept of a square surface on an oval base, which, with its compact size, ensures high stability and therefore high quality recordings.

Die zum Patent angemeldete iSHOXS Power Force Cup hat in der Mitte ihrer ovalen Form eine quadratische Fläche, die größer ist als die abgerundeten Flächen an der Seite und so eine hohe Standfestigkeit erreicht. In die Saugplatte wurden zwei Exzenterhebel integriert, sodass Actioncams und andere Geräte mittig montiert werden können. Dadurch werden Vibrationen vermindert und die Qualität der Aufnahmen verbessert. Der Saughalter ist aus glasfaserverstärktem ABS-Material gefertigt und verfügt über eine mit dem GoPro-System kompatible Slider-Aufnahme.

Begründung der Jury
Der Saughalter besticht durch die formale Idee einer quadratischen Fläche auf ovalem Grund, was bei kompakter Größe für eine hohe Standfestigkeit und damit eine hohe Qualität der Aufnahmen sorgt.

iSHOXS Active Pole Sealed
Selfie Stick

Manufacturer
Tormaxx GmbH, Mönchengladbach, Germany
In-house design
Hubert Koch
Web
www.tormaxx.de

Since the telescopic elements of selfie sticks are often not protected against the penetration of sand, dust or mud, a patent pending sealing technology was developed for the iSHOXS Active Pole Sealed, which prevents impurities as well as snow or ice from penetrating the telescopic tubes. The clip-on modular technology, with two modules, is integrated in the handle: the ProFork and GoPro Smart Remote clip-on modules can be firmly and safely locked into place at the handle, which also accommodates the Activity Lock.

Statement by the jury
A technical innovation of the design of this selfie stick is the seal that protects it against external influences.

Da die Teleskopelemente von Selfie Sticks häufig nicht vor dem Eindringen von Sand, Staub oder Matsch geschützt sind, wurde für den iSHOXS Active Pole Sealed eine zum Patent angemeldete Dichtungstechnologie entwickelt, die verhindert, dass Verschmutzungen sowie Schnee oder Eis in die Rohre eindringen. Im Griffmodul des Active Pole ist die Clip-on-Modultechnik mit zwei Modulen enthalten: einem ProFork- und einem GoPro-Smart-Remote-Clip-on-Modul, die sicher und fest am Griff eingerastet werden können. Darin ist auch das Activity Lock integriert.

Begründung der Jury
Mit der Gestaltung dieses Selfie Sticks gelingt die technische Innovation, ihn so mit einer Dichtung auszustatten, dass er gegen Einflüsse von außen geschützt ist.

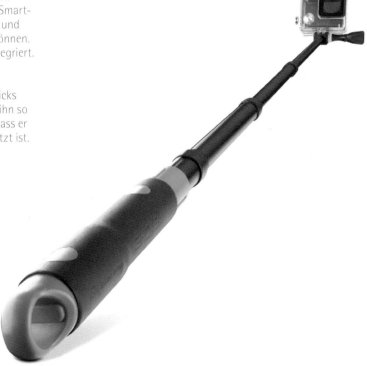

Hover Camera
Drone
Drohne

Manufacturer
Zero Zero Robotics Inc.,
Beijing, China

In-house design
Mengqiu Wang, Guanqun Zhang

Web
www.gethover.com

reddot award 2017
best of the best

Interactive companion

Pictures and in particular selfies have become a ubiquitous part of our world. They play a central role and even serve to interactively share private trip experiences with others. Against the backdrop that many pictures are only possible thanks to accessories such as selfie sticks, the Hover Camera offers fascinating new options. Integrated into a self-flying drone, this camera delivers a picture quality with a resolution of 4K and 13 MP. It is fully enclosed by a foldable, cage-like housing made of carbon fibre, which is very light and compact. Thanks to its patented construction, it protects against open propellers and folds up to a size no larger than a Moleskine notebook. The solid housing thus guarantees safe and uncomplicated transportation, yet is easy to handle as well as mechanically strong and robust. Interacting with the Hover Camera is a highly entertaining and exciting experience. It floats softly in the air, reacts to commands and shoots pictures. This is made possible through proprietary embedded AI technology that allows for the drone to operate autonomously using facial and body recognition. The Hover Camera follows and accompanies its user almost anywhere like a friendly and interactive companion – an object that is just as futuristic as it is emotionalising.

Interaktiver Begleiter

Bildaufnahmen und besonders Selfies sind in der aktuellen Lebenswelt allgegenwärtig und spielen eine zentrale Rolle, auch Reisen werden so zum interaktiv geteilten Erlebnis. Vor dem Hintergrund, dass viele Aufnahmen erst durch Accessoires wie Selfie-Sticks ermöglicht werden, bietet die Hover Camera faszinierend neue Optionen. Integriert in eine autonom fliegende Drohne, erlaubt diese Kamera Aufnahmen mit einer Auflösung von 4K und 13 MP. Umschlossen ist sie dabei von einem zusammenklappbaren, käfigartigen Gehäuse aus Carbonfaser, das sehr leicht und kompakt ist. Dank seiner patentierten Konstruktion schützt es vor offenliegenden Propellern und ist kaum größer als ein Moleskine-Notizbuch. Das stabile Gehäuse gewährleistet daher ein sicheres und unkompliziertes Transportieren, es ist angenehm zu handhaben und zugleich sehr belastbar. Ein unterhaltsamer, spannender Vorgang ist die Art der Interaktion mit der Hover Camera. Sachte schwebend, reagiert sie auf Befehle und macht ihre Aufnahmen. Ermöglicht wird dies durch eine proprietäre, integrierte KI-Technologie, die, eine Gesichts- und Körpererkennung nutzend, für den autonomen Betrieb der Drohne sorgt. Die Hover Camera folgt und begleitet ihren Nutzer überall hin wie ein freundliches und dienstbereites Objekt – das auf seine Umgebung ebenso futuristisch wie emotionalisierend wirkt.

Statement by the jury

Showcasing a fascinating design, the Hover Camera represents a new type of drone. The closed and compact construction of the housing ensures safe and easy operation. One can approach the device and even hold it in the hand while it is on, without fear of injury. The unit works perfectly and can easily be turned off with a simple gesture. This drone is uncomplicated, versatile and promotes a high fun factor.

Begründung der Jury

Mit ihrer faszinierenden Konstruktion stellt die Hover Camera eine neue Art von Drohne dar. Ihr geschlossen und kompakt gestaltetes Gehäuse bietet dem Nutzer eine einfache und sichere Art des Gebrauchs. Man kann sich ihr nähern und sie auch in Betrieb in der Hand halten, ohne Angst haben zu müssen, sich zu verletzen. Sie funktioniert perfekt, und mit einer einfachen Handgeste lässt sie sich wieder stoppen. Diese Drohne ist unkompliziert, vielseitig und hat einen hohen Funfaktor.

Designer portrait
See page 40
Siehe Seite 40

Inspire 2
Drone
Drohne

Manufacturer
DJI, Shenzhen, China

In-house design
DJI

Web
www.dji.com

reddot award 2017
best of the best

Autonomous flying

Photo and film recordings have always drawn inspiration from the possibilities inherent in the cameras used. The Inspire 2 drone has been designed for professional aerial photography, offering photographers a wide range of new freedoms. Featuring a grey magnalium shell, it impresses with an elegant and futuristic look, as well as with a higher strength and a lighter weight than the predecessor model. Its innovative image processing system records at up to 5.2K in formats such as CinemaDNG RAW, Apple ProRes and others. The drone accelerates from 0 to 80 km/h in five seconds, reaches a maximum speed of 94 km/h and has a maximum descent speed of 9 m/s, making it very fast for an aircraft of this size. A powerful dual-battery system prolongs the flight time to a maximum of 27 minutes, while an innovative self-heating technology allows it to fly even in low temperatures. The drone is highly agile thanks to the integrated FlightAutonomy system, providing obstacle avoidance and sensor redundancy in two directions. Equipped with multiple intelligent flight modes, including Spotlight Pro, the device gives even single pilots the ability to create complex, dramatic shots. With its high performance and innovative agility, this drone inspires anyone working with it to new projects and impressive cinematic achievements.

Freier Flug

Foto- und Filmaufnahmen beziehen ihre Inspiration immer auch aus den vorhandenen Möglichkeiten der Kamera. Die Drohne Inspire 2 wurde für die professionelle Luftfotografie konzipiert und bietet Fotografen eine Vielzahl neuer Freiheiten. Gestaltet mit einem Magnaliumgehäuse, beeindruckt sie durch eine elegante und futuristische Anmutung, wobei sie eine höhere Festigkeit sowie ein leichteres Gewicht als das Vorgängermodell hat. Mit einem innovativen Bildverarbeitungssystem zeichnet sie mit einer Auflösung von bis zu 5,2K in Formaten wie CinemaDNG RAW oder Apple ProRes auf. Sie beschleunigt dabei von 0 auf 80 km/h in fünf Sekunden, erreicht eine Höchstgeschwindigkeit von 94 km/h und verfügt mit einer maximalen Abstiegsgeschwindigkeit von 9 m/s über eine sehr hohe Geschwindigkeit für ein Fluggerät dieser Größe. Ein leistungsfähiges Doppel-Batteriesystem erlaubt ihr eine Flugzeit von maximal 27 Minuten, wobei eine innovative Technologie zur Eigenerwärmung auch den Einsatz bei niedrigen Temperaturen ermöglicht. Überaus manövrierfähig ist sie durch das integrierte FlightAutonomy-System, da dieses in zwei Richtungen Hindernisvermeidung und eine Sensor-Redundanz bietet. Ausgestattet mit mehreren intelligenten Flugmodi, einschließlich Spotlight Pro, versetzt sie auch Einzelpiloten in die Lage, überaus komplexe und dramatische Aufnahmen zu machen. Mit ihrer innovativen Wendigkeit und Leistungsfähigkeit inspiriert diese Drohne die mit ihr arbeitenden Menschen zu neuen Projekten und filmischen Höchstleistungen.

Statement by the jury

The Inspire 2 drone inspires with its powerful performance and possesses strong visual expressivity. It showcases a novel design language as the higher performance requirements for more professional use called for a more robust structure. It is obvious that design had high priority here. The construction impressively conveys both the notion of reliability and the detailed professionalism of this drone.

Begründung der Jury

Die Drohne Inspire 2 begeistert mit ihrer leistungsfähigen Performance und besitzt dabei eine starke visuelle Ausdruckskraft. Sie zeigt eine neuartige Formensprache, da ihre höheren Leistungsanforderungen für professionellere Ansprüche eine stabilere Struktur bedingen. Es zeigt sich deutlich, dass das Design hier einen hohen Stellenwert hatte. Es bringt auf beeindruckende Weise die Zuverlässigkeit und die bis ins Detail reichende Professionalität dieser Drohne zum Ausdruck.

GoPro Karma System
Drone
Drohne

Manufacturer
GoPro, Inc., San Mateo,
California, USA

In-house design
GoPro Industrial Design Team

Web
www.gopro.com

reddot award 2017
best of the best

Aesthetic continuity

Drones are used extensively in the field of photography, where they have also created a new image aesthetic. GoPro Karma is a very light, self-contained system compatible with GoPro cameras. It was conceived for use with action cameras to capture smooth, stabilised video. Showcasing a stringently executed design idiom, the main components of the system include the controller, an aerial drone, a stabiliser with harness, a charger, a battery, six propellers, a handheld grip, a mounting ring as well as a matching case. The lightness of how the system is operated is highly impressive. The controller comes as an easy-to-use, gamestyle flight and camera control, while the ergonomic mounting ring allows users to connect the Karma Grip to the full line of existing 30-plus GoPro mounts. Another characteristic defining the versatility of the system is that it is not only a solution for taking aerial pictures but also embraces a handheld and mountable gimbal solution. Combining all these options into a self-contained life capture solution, the system allows for a versatile range of approaches towards getting good shots and building compelling stories from all vantage points. GoPro Karma delivers a new kind of lightness and versatility in the field of action cameras – a perfectly designed system that can even be comfortably folded together and worn as a backpack.

Ästhetische Kontinuität

Drohnen werden vielseitig im Bereich der Fotografie eingesetzt, wo sie zugleich eine neue Bildästhetik begründen. GoPro Karma ist ein sehr leichtes, mit den Kameras von GoPro kompatibles und in sich schlüssiges System. Konzipiert für Actionkameras, eignet es sich insbesondere für die Erfassung wackelfreier, stabilisierter Videoaufnahmen. In einer stringent umgesetzten Formensprache umfasst es einen Controller, eine Flugdrohne, einen Stabilisator mit Gurthalterung, ein Ladegerät, einen Akku, sechs Propeller, einen Griff, einen Befestigungsring und eine Verstaumöglichkeit. Beeindruckend ist dabei die Leichtigkeit der Steuerung dieses Systems. Der Controller ist eine einfach zu bedienende Flug- und Kamerasteuerung im Game-Stil, während der ergonomische Befestigungsring es ermöglicht, den Karma Grip mit allen vorhandenen 30-plus GoPro-Halterungen zu verbinden. Eine die Vielseitigkeit des Systems prägende Eigenschaft ist, dass es nicht nur eine Lösung für Aufnahmen aus der Luft, sondern auch von Hand oder von einer Körperhalterung aus ist. In seinem Selbstverständnis als eine Life-Capture-Lösung eröffnet es in der Kombination aller Möglichkeiten so ein vielseitiges Spektrum an Anwendungen für gute Aufnahmen und das Filmen perspektivisch überzeugender Stories. GoPro Karma bietet eine neue Leichtigkeit und Vielseitigkeit beim Einsatz einer Actionkamera – mit einem perfekt gestalteten System, das man bequem zusammengepackt auch als Rucksack tragen kann.

Statement by the jury
The design of GoPro Karma is astounding for the fact that all elements of the system are perfectly matched in terms of form and function. This has lent it an aesthetically pleasing and highly continuous appearance. Moreover, it has also emerged as a unified system with a functionality that allows sounding out the possibilities of drones. Easy-to-handle and user-oriented, it not only facilitates recording aerial images but also integrates a handheld and easily mountable gimbal solution.

Begründung der Jury
Die Gestaltung von GoPro Karma besticht vor allem darin, dass alle Elemente des Systems in Form und Funktion perfekt aufeinander abgestimmt sind. Dies gibt ihm eine ästhetisch ansprechende, sehr kontinuierlich wirkende Anmutung. Es entstand zudem ein auch in seiner Funktionalität sehr einheitliches System, das die Möglichkeiten einer Drohne auslotet. Leicht handhabbar und nutzerfreundlich, erlaubt es nicht nur, Aufnahmen aus der Luft zu machen, sondern auch von Hand oder vom Körper aus mit einer einfach montierbaren Kardanlösung.

Designer portrait
See page 42
Siehe Seite 42

MAVIC PRO
Drone
Drohne

Manufacturer
DJI, Shenzhen, China
In-house design
Web
www.dji.com

Mavic Pro is a drone which is designed to be small and powerful, and capable of easily transforming the sky into a creative canvas. Its compact size conceals technically sophisticated features: 24 high performance central processing units, a dual satellite link telling the user what is in front of or below the camera, a revised transmission system with a range of 4.3 miles (7 km), five vision sensors and a 4K camera, which is stabilised by a three-axis gimbal. They can all be controlled by simply pressing a button on the remote control, of gamepad size.

Mavic Pro ist eine klein und kraftvoll gestaltete Drohne, die den Himmel ganz leicht in eine kreative Leinwand verwandelt. Ihre kompakte Größe verbirgt eine hohe technische Komplexität: 24 Hochleistungsrecheneinheiten, eine duale Satellitenverbindung, die dem Benutzer mitteilt, was vor oder unter ihr liegt, ein überarbeitetes Übertragungssystem mit einer Reichweite von 4,3 Meilen (7 km), fünf Vision-Sensoren und eine 4K-Kamera, die durch einen dreiachsigen mechanischen Gimbal stabilisiert wird, lassen sich schlicht per Knopfdruck auf die Fernbedienung in Gamepad-Größe steuern und kontrollieren.

Statement by the jury
The drone Mavic Pro fascinates with a very wide spectrum of technical features, which are skillfully concealed in its compact design.

Begründung der Jury
Die Drohne Mavic Pro begeistert mit einem sehr hohen technischen Leistungsumfang, den ihre kompakte Gestaltung gekonnt kaschiert.

PHANTOM 4 PRO
Drone
Drohne

Manufacturer
DJI, Shenzhen, China
In-house design
Web
www.dji.com

The Phantom 4 Pro drone is characterised by exceptional design and technology. Its powerful camera features a 2.5 cm 20 MP sensor, which can record 4K videos at 60 frames per second and stills in burst mode at 14 frames per second. Highly developed sensors provide detailed images with all the necessary data. The construction is made of a titanium magnesium alloy to increase the rigidity of the aircraft and, at the same time, reduce weight. The FlightAutonomy system of the drone features two rear vision sensors and an infrared sensor technology allowing obstacles to be captured in five directions and circled in four directions.

Die Drohne Phantom 4 Pro ist durch eine ausgefallene Gestaltung und Technologie gekennzeichnet. Ihre leistungsstarke Kamera verfügt über einen 2,5 cm großen 20-MP-Sensor, mit dem 4K-Videos mit 60 Bildern pro Sekunde und im Burst-Modus 14 Standbilder pro Sekunde aufgenommen werden können. Hochentwickelte Sensoren sorgen für detailgetreue Aufnahmen mit allen erforderlichen Daten. Die Konstruktion aus einer Titan-Magnesium-Legierung verstärkt die Festigkeit des Flugkörpers und reduziert gleichzeitig das Gewicht. Das FlightAutonomy-System stattet die Drohne mit zwei Sensoren für die Sicht nach hinten und einer Infrarotsensorik aus, sodass Hindernisse in fünf Richtungen erfasst und in vier Richtungen umflogen werden können.

Statement by the jury
The differentiated design of the drone Phantom 4 Pro reflects the high performance of the aircraft, which is equipped with the latest technology.

Begründung der Jury
Die differenzierte Gestaltung der Drohne Phantom 4 Pro spiegelt die hohe Leistungsfähigkeit des mit aktuellster Technik ausgestatteten Flugobjekts wider.

PowerEgg
Quadrocopter
Quadrokopter

Manufacturer
PowerVision Robot Inc., Beijing, China
In-house design
Feng Fan
Web
www.powervision.me
www.powervision.cn

The PowerEgg is an egg-shaped quadcopter with 4K camera – and its shape is a real eye-catcher. In addition to a large propeller for stable flight and more power, the case accommodates the landing gear, arms and motors, which automatically pull out after being switched-on. The development phase of the PowerEgg not only focused on aesthetics but also on a high degree of functionality. Pictures with the 360-degree camera are therefore stabilised with a gimbal and thanks to special sensors, the PowerEgg can also fly indoors.

Statement by the jury
This quadcopter combines an impressive design with well-conceived integrated functions to create an original and powerful flying device.

Das PowerEgg ist ein eiförmiger Quadrokopter mit 4K-Kamera – und seine Formgebung ein echter Eyecatcher. Das Gehäuse enthält neben einem großen Propeller für stabilen Flug und mehr Kraft das Landegestell, die Arme bzw. Ausleger sowie die Motoren, die nach dem Einschalten automatisch aus dem Gehäuse fahren. Außer auf Ästhetik zielte die Entwicklung des PowerEgg auf hohe Funktionalität. So werden die Aufnahmen mit der 360-Grad-Kamera durch einen Gimbal stabilisiert, und dank spezieller Sensoren kann das PowerEgg auch indoor fliegen.

Begründung der Jury
Dieser Quadrokopter verknüpft eine beeindruckende Formgebung mit durchdacht integrierten Funktionen zu einem originellen und leistungsfähigen Fluggerät.

PowerEye
Quadrocopter
Quadrokopter

Manufacturer
PowerVision Technology Co., Ltd.,
Beijing, China
In-house design
Brian Yuan
Web
www.powervision.me
www.powervision.cn

The PowerEye is a quadcopter characterised by high performance, with a 4K camera, and minimalist design. The range of functions includes an anti-collision system and two cameras. One is installed at the front and provides the FPV image, which is transmitted in real time to the smartphone of the pilot, so that the device can be flown and controlled from a cockpit perspective. The other camera is mounted on a three-axis gimbal below the quadcopter and is responsible for shake-free aerial photographs.

Statement by the jury
With two high-quality cameras, embedded in a housing which is simple and straightforward in design, the PowerEye has an extraordinary range of features to offer.

Das PowerEye ist ein Quadrokopter, der durch hohe Leistung mit 4K-Kamera und eine minimalistische Gestaltung gekennzeichnet ist. Zum Funktionsumfang zählen etwa ein Antikollisionssystem und gleich zwei Kameras. Die eine ist in der Front verbaut und liefert das FPV-Bild, das in Echtzeit auf das Smartphone des Piloten gesendet wird, sodass er das Gerät aus einer Cockpitperspektive fliegen und steuern kann. Die andere Kamera ist an einem Drei-Achsen-Gimbal unterhalb des Quadrokopters montiert und für wackelfreie Luftaufnahmen zuständig.

Begründung der Jury
Mit zwei hochwertigen Kameras, eingebettet in ein schlicht gestaltetes Gehäuse, hat das PowerEye einen außergewöhnlichen Leistungsumfang zu bieten.

WhiteShark MAX
Remotely Operated
Underwater Vehicle
Ferngesteuertes
Unterwasserfahrzeug

Manufacturer
Tianjin Deepfar Ocean Technology,
Tianjin, China
In-house design
Design
Tianjin 712 Communication & Broadcasting
Co., Ltd., Tianjin, China
Web
www.sublue.com
www.idesign712.com

WhiteShark Max is a remote-controlled submarine vehicle which can dive up to 100 metres in depth. It has a solid driving unit and a nine-axis motion compensation system that allows full manoeuvrability, and it can automatically track sonar beacons through image recognition algorithms. The special material used for its construction is called "Schulmann PC+GF30", which reduces the risk of disturbing sensitive marine animals, such as sharks. The vehicle is suitable for underwater inspection, cleaning contaminated areas or supporting salvage and rescue initiatives.

Statement by the jury
The technology and the construction are carefully adapted to the requirements under water, making WhiteShark Max a powerful and versatile underwater vehicle.

WhiteShark Max ist ein ferngesteuertes Unterwasserfahrzeug für bis zu 100 Meter Tiefe. Es besitzt ein solides Antriebssystem und ein neunachsiges Bewegungsausgleichssystem, das volle Manövrierbarkeit gestattet, und kann Sonarbaken automatisch durch Bilderkennungsalgorithmen verfolgen. Das für seinen Bau verwendete Spezialmaterial heißt „Schulman PC+GF30" und mindert das Risiko, empfindliche Meereslebewesen wie Haie zu stören. Das Fahrzeug eignet sich zur Unterwasserinspektion, zur Reinigung schadstoffbelasteter Bereiche oder zur Begleitung von Bergungs- und Rettungsmaßnahmen.

Begründung der Jury
Die sensibel auf die Erfordernisse unter Wasser abgestimmte Technik und Konstruktion des WhiteShark Max machen es zum leistungsstarken und vielseitig einsetzbaren Unterwasserfahrzeug.

Airblock
Drone for Education
Drohne für Lehrzwecke

Manufacturer
Makeblock Co., Ltd., Shenzhen, China
In-house design
Mingzhe Guo, Jimmy Qin, Wenhua Wang
Web
www.makeblock.com

Airblock is a drone made of seven hexagonal modules of identical size, including a main control module and six power modules with electric motors and propellers. Without needing any tools, and thanks to magnetic fasteners, the modules are easily assembled, to form various shapes, and dismantled. With the two operation modes: hexacopter drone and hovercraft, the drone can be employed freely in the air or directly over the ground or a water surface. The housing is made of a lightweight, machine-made foam padding that is soft, sturdy and resistant. The propeller blades are protected by the hexagonal structure and ensure safe operation, even for children.

Airblock ist eine Drohne aus sieben sechseckigen Modulen identischer Größe, darunter einem Hauptkontrollmodul und sechs Leistungsmodulen mit Elektromotoren und Propellern. Die Module sind dank Magnetbefestigungen leicht und ohne Werkzeuge in verschiedensten Formen zusammensetzbar und zerlegbar. Mit den beiden Betriebsmodi Hexakopterdrohne und Hovercraft kann die Drohne frei in der Luft oder direkt über dem Boden oder einer Wasseroberfläche eingesetzt werden. Das Gehäuse ist aus leichtem maschinellem Schaumpolster gefertigt, das weich, stabil und widerstandsfähig ist. Die von der Sechseckstruktur geschützten Propellerblätter gewährleisten auch für Kinder einen sicheren Betrieb.

Statement by the jury
The Airblock drone is a stable, functional educational tool and is particularly eye-catching due to its modularity, thanks to which it can be assembled in a variety of different ways.

Begründung der Jury
Die Drohne Airblock stellt ein stabiles, funktionales Lehrinstrument dar und fällt besonders durch ihre Modularität ins Auge, dank derer sie sich individuell zusammensetzen lässt.

Icon
Ski Jacket
Skijacke

Manufacturer
Helly Hansen AS, Oslo, Norway

In-house design
Katrine Jopperud

Web
www.hellyhansen.com

reddot **award** 2017
best of the best

Good climate

Ski slopes are often challenging due to extreme conditions for skiers and materials. The Icon ski jacket offers new possibilities of temperature regulation in the form of the H2Flow™ temperature regulation system. This innovative technology, which channels and directs cold air via air ports along the inside to cool the body of the wearer, enhances the cooling efficiency of this jacket by 20 per cent. The design concept for this jacket is inspired by the masculine style of men's tailoring mixed with futuristic aesthetics to skilfully visualise the high-tech aspect of the jacket. For additional comfort, it features slick face fabric panels on the inside to create a frictionless lining between jacket and base layer. Another innovative feature is the Life Pocket which was designed to protect mobile phones safely from the cold. Due to its specific construction, this pocket is three times warmer than a regular chest outer pocket and thus preserves the mobile battery life span for longer. The contemporary design of this jacket is further underlined by a foldaway hi-vis brim on the hood to help minimise and avoid collisions on crowded slopes through improved visibility. With all these innovative functional features, the Icon jacket fascinates ski aficionados under all conditions.

Gutes Klima

Auf den Skipisten herrschen oftmals extreme Bedingungen für Mensch und Material. Die Skijacke Icon bietet hier neue Möglichkeiten der Temperaturregulierung in Form des H2Flow™-Systems. Diese innovative Technologie lenkt und leitet kalte Luft über Luftöffnungen entlang der Innenseite, um den Körper des Trägers zu kühlen, und erhöht so die Kühleffizienz dieser Jacke um 20 Prozent. Das Gestaltungskonzept für diese Jacke ist inspiriert von einer Kombination aus dem maskulinen Stil der Herrenkonfektion und futuristischer Ästhetik, um den Hightech-Aspekt der Jacke geschickt zu visualisieren. Ihren Komfort erhöhen zudem glatte Stoffoberflächen, die für ein reibungsfreies Innenfutter sorgen. Eine weitere Innovation der Jacke ist ihre Life Pocket-Ausstattung, um das Mobiltelefon sicher vor Kälte zu schützen. Diese besonders isolierte Brustaußentasche ist dreimal wärmer als bei anderen Jacken und verhindert so einen Abfall der Batterieleistung bei Kälte. Die zeitgemäße Gestaltung dieser Jacke wird außerdem durch eine faltbare Hi-Viz-Krempe an der Kapuze unterstrichen, die durch verbesserte Sichtbarkeit Kollisionen auf überfüllten Pisten vermeiden hilft. Mit all diesen innovativen, funktionalen Features begeistert Icon Skisportler in jeder Situation.

Statement by the jury

An innovative, technical principle from the world of performance sports car technology has lent this ski jacket its outstanding insulation properties. Equipped with the H2Flow™ temperature regulation system as well as an outer chest Life Pocket, it delivers a new approach toward comfort. The body temperature is ideally regulated on the slope and the mobile phone battery stays ready for use for longer. The Icon ski jacket fascinates with a distinctive expressivity based on a highly consistent design.

Begründung der Jury

Ein innovatives technisches Prinzip aus der Welt der Hochleistungssportwagen verleiht dieser Skijacke ihre besonderen Isoliereigenschaften. Ausgestattet mit dem H2Flow™-System zur Temperaturregulierung sowie einer Life Pocket-Brustaußentasche bietet sie eine neue Art von Komfort. Die Körpertemperatur wird während des Skifahrens optimal reguliert, und das Mobiltelefon bleibt lange leistungsfähig. Die Skijacke Icon fasziniert mit ihrem prägnanten Ausdruck, der auf einer sehr stringenten Gestaltung basiert.

Designer portrait
See page 44
Siehe Seite 44

NINJA PILLOW JACKET
Outdoor Jacket
Outdoor-Jacke

Manufacturer
TMAX strategy & marketing,
Taipei, Taiwan
In-house design
Hong Grong Peng
Web
www.slooc.com.tw

The Ninja Pillow Jacket is a highly functional outdoor jacket with eye and face mask, ear muffs, scarf and hat. In addition, an insulated mid-layer jacket can serve as a travel pillow. The material is water-repellent, and the zippers are water-resistant. The additional face mask offers special protection against coldness and rain. The large side pockets provide space for water bottles, goggles and gloves. The two-way zipper on the side can be pulled up to regulate the body temperature.

Statement by the jury
The Ninja Pillow Jacket inspires by its numerous features and functional finesse, which makes it ideal for outdoor activities.

Ninja Pillow Jacket ist eine hochfunktionale Outdoor-Jacke mit Augen- und Gesichtsmaske, Ohrenschützern, Schal und Hut. Eine isolierte Zwischenjacke kann zudem als Reisekissen dienen. Das Material ist wasserabweisend, die Reißverschlüsse sind wasserbeständig. Die zusätzliche Gesichtsmaske bietet besonderen Schutz gegen Kälte und Regen und die großen Seitentaschen Platz für Wasserflaschen, Schutzbrillen oder Handschuhe. Zur Regulierung der Körpertemperatur lässt sich der seitliche 2-Wege-Reißverschluss aufziehen.

Begründung der Jury
Die Ninja Pillow Jacket begeistert durch ihre zahlreichen Beigaben und funktionalen Finessen, dank derer sie sich bestens für Outdoor-Aktivitäten eignet.

Cloud Jacket
Ski Jacket
Skijacke

Manufacturer
Mountain Force, Rotkreuz, Switzerland
In-house design
Web
www.mountainforce.com

Cloud Jacket is an ultra-light ski jacket and part of the new A.Sign clothes collection, which adapts quickly to weather and skiing conditions. Its urban look makes the jacket an all-rounder suitable for both the ski slopes and the city. The high-quality down comes from a sustainable manufacture. The Prima Loft Gold insulation provides additional warmth and high breathability, keeping the wearer warmer and drier. The elastic waistband ensures a comfortable fit and the blouson cut enhances the casual look.

Statement by the jury
The ski jacket Cloud Jacket is a real all-rounder: it is light and warm and thanks to its breathability is suitable for all kinds of ski conditions and, moreover, it is aesthetically appealing.

Cloud Jacket ist eine ultraleichte Skijacke und Teil des neuen Kleidungskonzepts A.Sign, das sich rasch an aktuelle Wetter- und Skifahrbedingungen anpassen lässt. Ihre urbane Anmutung macht die Jacke zum Allrounder für Piste und Stadt. Die hochwertigen Daunen stammen aus einer nachhaltigen Produktion. Die „PrimaLoft Gold"-Isolierung bietet zusätzliche Wärme, hohe Atmungsaktivität und hält den Träger noch wärmer und trockener. Der elastische Bund sorgt für überzeugenden Tragekomfort und der Blouson-Schnitt unterstreicht die Casual-Optik.

Begründung der Jury
Die Skijacke Cloud Jacket ist ein echtes Multitalent: Sie ist leicht und warm, dank Atmungsaktivität eignet sie sich für verschiedenste Skibedingungen und ist dabei ästhetisch ansprechend.

Evoknit Move Infinite (Evoknit M.I.)
Jacket
Jacke

Manufacturer
PUMA SE, Herzogenaurach, Germany
In-house design
Adele Pei Ying Goh
Web
www.puma.com

The Evoknit Move Infinite is a stylish, multifunctional jacket manufactured with cutting-edge technology. It causes little waste, is produced quickly and offers great benefits. The versatile jacket is easy to wear and adapts to different situations and temperatures. The lightweight polyester yarn has been designed to provide a seamless and comfortable knit fabric. Specifically inserted panels, made of breathable fabric, ensure very good moisture regulation.

Statement by the jury
The designers of the Evoknit Move Infinite jacket have focused not only on producing a really handy garment, suitable for everyday use, but also on observing the principles of sustainability.

Die Evoknit Move Infinite ist eine mit modernster Technologie gefertigte schicke, multifunktionale Jacke, die nur wenig Abfall verursacht, schnell zu produzieren ist und hohen Nutzen bietet. Die vielseitige Jacke lässt sich unkompliziert tragen und passt sich unterschiedlichen Situationen und Temperaturen an. Das leichte Polyestergarn wurde so bearbeitet, dass es in nahtloses und bequemes Strickmaterial ergibt. Gezielt angebrachte Einsätze aus atmungsaktivem Gewebe sorgen für eine sehr gute Feuchtigkeitsregulation.

Begründung der Jury
Bei der Gestaltung der Jacke Evoknit Move Infinite wurde Wert auf die Fertigung eines wirklich praktischen Alltagsbegleiters gelegt und darüber hinaus auf nachhaltige Prinzipien.

Women's Annecy 3in1 Coat II
Winter Jacket
Wintermantel

Manufacturer
VAUDE Sport GmbH & Co. KG, Tettnang, Germany
In-house design
Web
www.vaude.com

The winter jacket Annecy 3in1 Coat II is entirely made from environmentally friendly materials. The removable inner down coat with stitching can be worn alone. In combination with the weatherproof outer layer material it provides effective protection against the cold. The adjustable cuffs on the hood and sleeves serve to hold off wind and rain in bad weather. In addition, the reflective prints on the sleeves can be folded up to make sure that the wearer is highly visible in the dark. The outer coat is laminated with a waterproof, breathable membrane and is very comfortable to wear.

Statement by the jury
Eco-friendly materials that are perfectly suitable for cold conditions as well as two layers, which can also be worn separately, make the winter jacket Annecy 3in1 Coat II a true all-rounder.

Der Wintermantel Annecy 3in1 Coat II wurde aus durchweg umweltfreundlichen Materialien gefertigt. Der herausnehmbare Daunen-Innenmantel mit Steppung lässt sich auch solo tragen und bietet in Verbindung mit dem wetterfesten Material einen wirksamen Schutz gegen Kälte. Die verstellbaren Abschlüsse an Kapuze und Ärmel halten bei schlechtem Wetter Wind und Regen ab und im Ärmel befindliche Reflektordrucke zum Hochklappen sorgen außerdem dafür, dass die Trägerin auch in der Dämmerung gut gesehen wird. Der mit einer wasserdichten, atmungsaktiven Membran laminierte Außenmantel schafft einen hohen Tragekomfort.

Begründung der Jury
Materialien, die umweltfreundlich und uneingeschränkt kältetauglich sind, und zwei Lagen, die sich beide auch einzeln tragen lassen, machen den Wintermantel Annecy 3in1 Coat II zum echten Allrounder.

Cirrus
Women's Ultralight Down Jacket
Ultraleichte Damendaunenjacke

Manufacturer
Yeti GmbH, Görlitz, Germany
In-house design
Oliver Reetz
Web
www.yetiworld.com

Cirrus consists of outstanding components such as the ultralight "Next to Nothing" fabric, a 7x7 denier ripstop fabric, weighing only 19g/sqm and a high-quality insulating Crystal Down filling with a mix ratio of 95/5 and a fill power of 900+ cuin. The down jacket weighs only 134 grams and can be easily stowed away in its own front left pocket. Two zipper pockets, two inside pockets, an integrated pack sack as well as elastic inserts at the waist and sleeve ends complete this robust jacket.

Statement by the jury
The especially lightweight Cirrus down jacket for women impresses with its high quality materials as well as with its innovative manufacturing to create highly functional garment.

Cirrus besteht aus herausragenden Komponenten wie dem ultraleichten „Next to Nothing"-Stoff, einem nur 19g/qm wiegenden 7x7-Denier-Ripstop-Gewebe, und hochwertig isolierender Crystal-Daune mit einem Mischungsverhältnis von 95/5 und einer Bauschkraft von 900+ cuin. Die 134 Gramm leichte Daunenjacke lässt sich in ihre eigene linke Fronttasche packen und damit einfach verstauen. Zwei Reißverschlusstaschen, zwei Innentaschen, ein integrierter Packsack und elastische Einsätze an Bund und Ärmelabschlüssen komplettieren diese widerstandsfähige Jacke.

Begründung der Jury
Die besonders leichte Damendaunenjacke Cirrus überzeugt durch ihre hohe Materialqualität sowie die innovative Verarbeitung zu einem hochfunktionalen Kleidungsstück.

Camelbak Quick Stow Flask
Soft Water Bottle
Softwasserflasche

Manufacturer
Camelbak, Petaluma, USA
In-house design
Kaydee Boone
Web
www.camelbak.com

The Quick Stow Flask is a very light-weight, foldable and thermally insulated water bottle which is very suitable for joggers and marathon runners. Thanks to its positive and leak-proof lock, the functional drinking vessel with its special insulating system creates a pleasant hydration experience. The elastic bottle fits comfortably in the hand; it is easy to clean and even fits in tight pockets. Thus, it fulfils the requirements for a high-performance drinking vessel.

Statement by the jury
The design of the water bottle Camelbak Quick Stow Flask combines important functional details such as light weight and elasticity with excellent manage-ability for athletes.

Die Quick Stow Flask ist eine sehr leichte, faltbare und thermisch isolierte Trink-flasche, die sich sehr gut für Jogger und Marathonläufer eignet. Ihr formschlüssi-ger und auslaufsicherer Verschluss macht die Flüssigkeitszufuhr aus dem funktio-nalen Trinkgefäß in Kombination mit einem besonderen Isoliersystem zum komfor-tablen Vergnügen. Die elastische Flasche liegt außerdem gut in der Hand, lässt sich einfach reinigen und passt selbst in enge Taschen. So erfüllt sie die Anforde-rungen an ein leistungsfähiges Trinkgefäß.

Begründung der Jury
Die Gestaltung der Trinkflasche Camelbak Quick Stow Flask verknüpft wichtige funktionale Details wie Leichtigkeit und Elastizität mit herausragender Handhab-barkeit für Sportler.

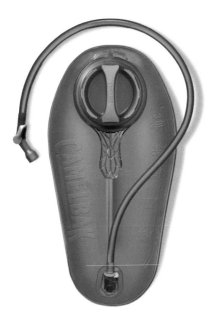

Camelbak Crux Reservoir
Hydration System
for Backpacks
Trinkbehälter für Rucksäcke

Manufacturer
Camelbak, Petaluma, USA
In-house design
Kaydee Boone
Web
www.camelbak.com

Crux Reservoir is a water tank that holds up to three litres of liquid and fits into almost every backpack. It allows 20 per cent more water flow per sip than previous systems. It features a Big-Bite mouthpiece, which closes safely after drinking. In addition, the valve can be manually closed. The hose is easily de-tachable thanks to a coupling and can be quickly filled en route. The light-weight drinking system is made from antibacterial, resistant polyurethane.

Statement by the jury
Exactly tailored to the needs of athletes, the easy-to-use Crux Reservoir is a user-friendly liquid dispenser for mobile use.

Crux Reservoir ist ein bis zu drei Liter Flüs-sigkeit fassender Wasserbehälter, der in fast jeden Rucksack passt. Er ermöglicht 20 Prozent mehr Wasserdurchfluss pro Schluck als vorige Systeme und ist mit dem Big-Bite-Mundstück ausgestattet, das nach dem Trinken sicher schließt. Zusätzlich lässt sich das Ventil einhändig auch manuell schließen. Der mittels Kupplung leicht ab-nehmbare Schlauch kann unterwegs rasch befüllt werden. Das leichtgewichtige Trink-system besteht aus antibakteriellem, wider-standsfähigem Polyurethan.

Begründung der Jury
Genau auf die Bedürfnisse von Sportlern zugeschnitten, ist der einfach zu hand-habende Crux Reservoir ein sehr anwen-derfreundlicher Flüssigkeitsspender für unterwegs.

YUUKI
Outdoor Water Filter
Outdoor-Wasserfilter

Manufacturer
Runner Group, Xiamen, China
In-house design
Zhiguo Jiang
Web
www.runner-corp.com.cn

Yuuki is a water filter for outdoor use. It is easy to operate, to clean and to col-lapse. It is particularly lightweight. With-out great effort, water can be collected and carried. By pressing once on the sili-cone body, which has a pleasantly soft feel, the water is purified. Yuuki is NSF-certified and removes bacteria, microbial cysts and other contaminations. It is easy to exchange and replace the filter.

Statement by the jury
The water filter Yuuki offers a convinc-ing solution for obtaining clean water in nature: It is easy to handle and carry.

Yuuki ist ein Wasserfilter für den Außen-bereich. Er lässt sich einfach bedienen, säubern und zusammenschieben und hat ein besonders leichtes Gewicht. Man kann das Wasser darin gut sammeln und tragen. Drückt man einmal auf den Silikonkörper, der eine angenehm weiche Haptik aufweist, wird das Wasser gereinigt. Yuuki ist NSF-zertifiziert und entfernt Bakterien, mikrobi-elle Zysten und andere Verunreinigungen. Sein Filter ist leicht auszutauschen und zu ersetzen.

Begründung der Jury
Der Wasserfilter Yuuki bietet eine über-zeugende Lösung für die Gewinnung von sauberem Wasser im Freien: Er ist einfach in der Handhabung und leicht zu tragen.

Aladdin Fresco Twist & Go
Vacuum Insulated Water Bottle
Vakuumisolierte Wasserflasche

Manufacturer
Aladdin, a brand of PMI,
Amsterdam, Netherlands
In-house design
Web
www.pmi-worldwide.com

The reusable vacuum insulated water bottle combines performance with durability and is characterised by an appealing colouring. Made of long-lasting stainless steel and Eastman Tritan, beverages stay cold in the bottle for several hours thanks to the vacuum insulation. The lid is specially formed so the spout allows for a great drinking experience. The Aladdin Fresco Twist & Go is dishwasher-safe, BPA-free and made of recyclable and reusable materials.

Statement by the jury
The water bottle Aladdin Fresco Twist & Go impresses by an attractive colour concept and high functionality coupled with sustainable manufacture.

Die wiederverwendbare vakuumisolierte Wasserflasche verbindet Leistung mit Haltbarkeit und zeichnet sich durch eine ansprechende Farbgebung aus. Hergestellt aus langlebigem Edeltstahl und Eastman Tritan, bleiben Getränke darin durch die Vakuumisolierung mehrere Stunden lang kalt. Der Deckel ist speziell geformt, sodass der Ausgießer ein besonderes Trinkerlebnis bietet. Aladdin Fresco Twist & Go ist spülmaschinenfest, BPA-frei und aus recyceltem und wiederverwendbarem Material gefertigt.

Begründung der Jury
Die Wasserflasche Aladdin Fresco Twist & Go überzeugt durch ein ansprechendes Farbkonzept und eine hohe Funktionalität, gepaart mit nachhaltiger Fertigung.

Stanley Master Series
Insulated Beverage Container Series
Isolierflaschenserie

Manufacturer
Stanley, a brand of PMI,
Amsterdam, Netherlands
In-house design
Web
www.pmi-worldwide.com

Thanks to The Stanley QuadVac construction that minimises heat loss via convection, conduction and heat radiation due to its four layers and a wall thickness of 1 mm plus the use of 18/8 stainless steel, the Master Series vacuum insulated bottles stand out by being extraordinarily robust and for being able to retain heat for up to 40 hours. These features, in combination with a vacuum-insulated closing lid with stainless steel coating and a pour-through stopper, which goes far into the bottle, result in a high quality insulated bottle. The Master Series products are also leak proof, BPA free and dishwasher safe.

Statement by the jury
The outstanding quality features of the Master Series are their high durability thanks to high-class material usage and their particularly good insulation performance.

Dank der Stanley QuadVac-Isolierung, die den Wärmeverlust mittels vier Schichten durch Konvektion, Konduktion und Wärmestrahlung sowie eine Wandstärke von 1 mm und einen 18/8-Edelstahl minimiert, zeichnen sich die Isolierflaschen der Master Series durch außerordentliche Robustheit und einen Wärmerückhalt von bis zu 40 Stunden aus. Zusammen mit einem vakuumisolierten Verschlussdeckel mit Edelstahlauskleidung und dem weit nach innen ragenden Verschlussstopfen ergibt sich eine Isolierflasche von ausgesprochen hoher Qualität. Die Produkte der Master Series sind zudem auslaufsicher, BPA-frei und spülmaschinenfest.

Begründung der Jury
Die hervorstechenden Qualitätsmerkmale der Master Series sind die hohe Stabilität dank hochwertigem Materialeinsatz und besonders gute Isolierwerte.

Tri-Lamp
Camping Lamp
Campingleuchte

Manufacturer
Ningbo Asia Leader Import & Export Co.,
Ltd., Ningbo, China
Design
Altplus Design Limited
(Jianpeng Zhang), Hong Kong
Web
www.nbexporter.com.cn
www.altplusdesign.com
Honourable Mention

Tri-Lamp is a multifunctional lighting set for outdoor activities such as hiking, camping or fishing. It consists of three individual flashlights with different lighting modes for diverse settings. Each unit can be detached for individual use and can serve as a torch, working light, ambient light or emergency signal. With built-in magnets, the units can be interconnected to a powerful torch, camping light and lantern all in one.

Statement by the jury
Tri-Lamp scores with the innovative idea of modularity. Thus, the set of three different lamps is suitable for a variety of purposes.

Tri-Lamp ist ein multifunktionales Beleuchtungsset für Outdoor-Aktivitäten wie Wandern, Zelten oder Angeln. Es besteht aus drei einzelnen Taschenlampen mit verschiedenen Beleuchtungsarten für unterschiedliche Szenerien. Jede Einheit lässt sich für den individuellen Gebrauch abtrennen und als Taschenlampe, Arbeitslicht, Umgebungslicht oder Notfallsignal verwenden. Mithilfe eingebauter Magnete lassen sie sich miteinander verknüpfen und dienen zusammen als zugleich leistungsstarke Taschenlampe, Campinglicht und Laterne.

Begründung der Jury
Tri-Lamp punktet durch die innovative Idee seiner Modularität. Dadurch eignet sich das Set aus drei verschiedenen Lampen für unterschiedliche Zwecke.

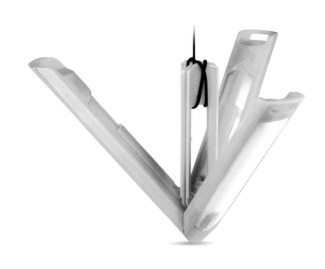

Enki Stove Wild
Portable Biomass
Outdoor Stove
Tragbarer Biomassekocher

Manufacturer
Enki Stove Srl, Lucca, Italy
In-house design
Ivan Mura
Web
www.enkistove.com
Honourable Mention

Enki Stove Wild is a portable pyrolytic stove that can be heated with any kind of dry biomass and is safe and easy to use. The patent-pending technology allows to transform the biomass into gas, creating a powerful, smoke-free flame. Feet and pot holder are integrated and give the stove a solid stand. The surface is made of anodized aluminium and AISI-316-inox steel, which makes it smooth as well as scratch- and heat-resistant.

Statement by the jury
The portable biomass stove appeals by its practical use; in a simple and safe manner, it allows cooking anywhere in the open air.

Enki Stove Wild ist ein tragbarer pyrolytischer Kocher, der sich mit jeder trockenen Biomasse beheizen und sich sicher und einfach bedienen lässt. Mithilfe der zum Patent angemeldeten Technologie wird die Biomasse in Gas umgewandelt, sodass eine kraftvolle, rauchfreie Flamme entsteht. Die Füße und der Gefäßhalter sind integriert und geben dem Kocher einen soliden Stand. Die Oberfläche besteht aus eloxiertem Aluminium und AISI-316-Inox-Stahl, was sie glatt sowie kratz- und hitzebeständig macht.

Begründung der Jury
Der tragbare Biomassekocher überzeugt durch seinen praktischen Nutzen, auf einfache und sichere Art und Weise überall im Freien eine Kochmöglichkeit zu gewährleisten.

Coleman® FyreStorm® Stove
Coleman® FyreStorm®-Kocher
Gas Stove
Gaskocher

Manufacturer
Coleman EMEA, Hattersheim, Germany
In-house design
David Nicholson
Web
www.coleman.eu

The sunken burner, the high quality Xtreme gas, and a specially designed patented wind protection system called the Wind Block, ensure that the Coleman FyreStorm stove delivers exceptional cooking performance. In fact, the boiling time can be reduced by half, even in windy conditions. The high-performance, stainless steel burner is particularly durable and comes with a textile bag. The compact pan support, with umbrella folding mechanism, provides for easy storing.

Statement by the jury
The appeal of the Coleman FyreStorm stove is the well thought through wind protection features combined with high quality materials, therefore ensuring a long service life.

Der versenkte Brenner, das hochwertige Xtreme-Gas und ein speziell konstruierter patentierter Windschutz, der Wind Block, sorgen dafür, dass der Kocher Coleman FyreStorm außergewöhnliche Kochleistung erbringt und sich die Siedezeit unter windigen Bedingungen sogar auf die Hälfte verkürzen lässt. Der mit Textiltasche gelieferte Hochleistungsbrenner aus Edelstahl ist besonders langlebig und sein Topfträger mit Regenschirm-Faltmechanismus so kompakt, dass er einfach zu lagern ist.

Begründung der Jury
Überzeugend an dem Kocher Coleman FyreStorm ist sein ausgereift gestalteter Windschutz, kombiniert mit hoher Materialqualität und damit einer langen Nutzungsdauer.

MONARCH HG 8x42/10x42
Binoculars
Fernglas

Manufacturer
Nikon Vision Co., Ltd., Tokyo, Japan
In-house design
Tatsuya Kobayashi
Web
www.nikon.com

Thanks to a field flattener lens system and ED glass, the Monarch HG 8x42/10x42 stands out with its clear and wide field of view and high optical performance, providing edge-to-edge sharpness. The highly reflective dielectric multilayer prism coating and the high-quality multilayer coating ensure impressive brightness, natural colour fidelity and sharpness of detail. Made from magnesium alloy, the housing enables the design to be compact, light and robust, so that the binoculars, which are also waterproof and fog-free, are ideally suited as a companion for a wide range of outdoor activities.

Statement by the jury
Outstanding optics with brilliant sharpness, a wide field of view and a simple and comfortable handling make the Monarch HG 8x42/10x42 binoculars a number one choice.

Das Monarch HG 8x42/10x42 zeichnet sich dank Bildfeldebnungslinsensystem und ED-Glas durch ein klares, großes Sehfeld und hohe optische Leistung mit Schärfe bis zum Bildrand aus. Die dielektrische Mehrschichtenverspiegelung des Prismas und die hochwertige Mehrschichtvergütung sorgen für eindrucksvolle Helligkeit, Farbtreue und Detailschärfe. Das aus einer Magnesiumlegierung hergestellte Gehäuse ermöglicht eine kompakte, leichte und robuste Formgebung, sodass sich das zudem wasserdichte und beschlagfreie Fernglas ideal als Begleiter für Aktivitäten im Freien eignet.

Begründung der Jury
Hervorragende Optik mit brillanter Schärfe, ein großes Sehfeld und eine einfache wie komfortable Handhabung machen das Monarch HG 8x42/10x42 zu einem Fernglas erster Wahl.

PROSTAFF 3S 8x42/10x42
Binoculars
Fernglas

Manufacturer
Nikon Vision Co., Ltd., Tokyo, Japan
In-house design
Ayumi Nagata
Web
www.nikon.com

The Prostaff 3S 8x42/10x42 binoculars are particularly compact and lightweight and very suitable for all kinds of leisure activities. The multilayer lenses and the highly reflective prism coating generate a sharp, bright image. The rubber armouring of the slim housing ensures increased shock resistance, a secure and comfortable grip and easy handling. The binoculars are waterproof, fog-free and suitable for all weather conditions. Their wide field of view makes it considerably easier to find objects, without compromising the distance of the exit pupil.

Statement by the jury
The Prostaff 3S 8x42/10x42 binoculars score highly with their outstanding lens technology for excellent clear-sightedness as well as for their simple and unwavering user-friendliness.

Das Fernglas Prostaff 3S 8x42/10x42 ist besonders kompakt und leicht und für Freizeitaktivitäten aller Art sehr gut geeignet. Die mehrschichtenvergüteten Linsen und die hochreflektive Verspiegelung des Prismas bewirken ein scharfes, helles Bild. Die Gummiarmierung des schlanken Gehäuses sorgt für erhöhte Stoßfestigkeit, einen sicheren, bequemen Griff sowie für eine einfache Handhabung. Das Fernglas ist wasserdicht und beschlagfrei und tauglich für jegliche Wetterbedingungen. Sein großes Sehfeld ohne Abstriche beim Abstand der Austrittspupille erleichtert das Finden von Objekten deutlich.

Begründung der Jury
Das Fernglas Prostaff 3S 8x42/10x42 punktet insbesondere mit einer herausragenden Linsentechnik für eine ausgezeichnete Scharfsicht sowie mit einer einfachen, konsequenten Nutzerfreundlichkeit.

OK4
Outdoor Knife
Outdoormesser

Manufacturer
Hultafors Group AB, Bollebygd, Sweden
In-house design
Nikita Golovlev
Design
Veryday (Pelle Reinius, Stefan Strandberg, Marcus Heenen), Bromma, Sweden
Web
www.hultaforsgroup.com
www.veryday.com

OK4 is a powerful, solid outdoor knife with nonslip handle for demanding work. It can be attached to belts up to 80 mm wide with a textile belt loop, while a further loop holds a fire steel. The Scandi grind blade is easy to sharpen; it is made of 3 mm thick carbon steel, hardened to 58–60 HRC and protected from corrosion by an electrophoretic dip coating. The grinded blade spine is suitable for starting a fire with a fire steel.

OK4 ist ein kraftvolles, stabiles Outdoormesser mit rutschsicherem Griff für anspruchsvolle Arbeiten. Mit einer textilen Gürtelschlaufe kann es an bis zu 80 mm breiten Gürteln befestigt werden; eine weitere Schlaufe nimmt einen Zündstab auf. Die Klinge mit Scandischliff lässt sich leicht nachschleifen. Sie wurde aus 3 mm starkem Carbonstahl gefertigt, auf 58–60 HRC gehärtet und mit einer elektrophoretischen Tauchlackierung gegen Korrosion geschützt. Der geschliffene Messerrücken eignet sich dafür, mit einem Zündstab Feuer zu machen.

Statement by the jury
With its high functionality and a variety of practical application possibilities, the extremely robust outdoor knife OK4 is an innovative tool for leisure and nature.

Begründung der Jury
Hohe Funktionalität und eine Vielzahl praktischer Anwendungsmöglichkeiten machen das überaus robuste Outdoormesser OK4 zum innovativen Werkzeug für Freizeit und Natur.

Walther Multi Tac 2
Knife
Messer

Manufacturer
Umarex GmbH & Co. KG, Arnsberg, Germany
In-house design
Seunghan Kang
Web
www.umarex.com

Walther Multi Tac 2 stands for a new generation of multifunctional knives combining a tactical knife and various tools. The matt black, partially serrated one-hand blade features a safe liner lock. The handle of the tactical knife accommodates the multifunctional tool. It consists of a bottle opener, can opener and screwdriver as well as a swing-out bit holder.

Walther Multi Tac 2 steht für eine neue Generation von Multifunktionsmessern, die ein Tactical Messer und verschiedene Tools miteinander kombinieren. Die mattschwarze Einhandklinge mit partiellem Wellenschliff weist eine sichere Liner-Lock-Verriegelung auf. Im Griff des Tactical Messers ist das Multifunktionswerkzeug untergebracht. Es setzt sich aus Flaschenöffner, Dosenöffner, Schraubendreher sowie einem ausschwenkbaren Bithalter zusammen.

Statement by the jury
Different functions in one tool – according to this design principle, the compact Walther Multi Tac 2 was created, which is more than just a knife.

Begründung der Jury
Unterschiedliche Funktionen in einem Werkzeug – nach diesem Gestaltungsprinzip wurde das kompakte Walther Multi Tac 2 entworfen, das mehr als nur ein Messer ist.

Lamzac® the Original 2.0
Lounge Bed
Lounge-Sofa

Manufacturer
Fatboy the original B.V.,
's-Hertogenbosch, Netherlands
In-house design
Marijn Oomen
Web
www.fatboy.com/lamzac

Lamzac the Original 2.0 is a seat or a sofa for two people that can be filled with air in a few seconds. The open sack is simply swung through the air to capture enough air, and then closed in no time at all. Just as easy to deflate after use, the large, comfortable air couch can be stowed away in the supplied carrying bag. Ideal for all outdoor activities, travel, festivals or the park, the air couch is made of lightweight nylon and is extremely hard-wearing.

Lamzac the Original 2.0 ist ein Sitz oder Sofa für zwei Personen, das sich in wenigen Sekunden mit Luft füllen lässt. Der geöffnete Sack wird einfach durch die Luft geschwungen, um genügend Luft einzufangen, und anschließend im Handumdrehen verschlossen. Nach der Nutzung ebenso einfach zu entleeren, kann die große bequeme Luftcouch platzsparend im mitgelieferten Tragebeutel verstaut werden. Ideal für sämtliche Outdoor-Aktivitäten, für Reisen, Festivals oder den Park, ist die aus leichtem Nylon gefertigte Air-Couch überaus strapazierfähig.

Statement by the jury
Lamzac the Original 2.0 inspires with its simple design and the high comfort that this lounge sofa offers. A smart companion for outdoor activities.

Begründung der Jury
Lamzac the Original 2.0 begeistert durch die einfache Konstruktion und den hohen Komfort, den dieses Lounge-Sofa bietet. Ein smarter Begleiter für Unternehmungen im Freien.

Coleman Rocky Mountain 5 Plus
Tent
Zelt

Manufacturer
Coleman EMEA, Hattersheim, Germany
In-house design
Stéphane Besse
Web
www.coleman.eu

The Coleman Rocky Mountain 5 Plus is a spacious and comfortable tunnel tent with ample room for the whole family, along with some tables and chairs. It features the patented BlackOut Bedroom, a new sleep system for campers that blocks out 99 per cent of daylight penetrating through the bedroom – ideal for parents or anyone who is sensitive to daylight. The lightweight, yet sturdy construction with fibreglass poles allows easy assembly in a few minutes. PVC windows with covers create a good balance of light and privacy. The water column of 4,500 mm can withstand heavy rain, and an integrated welded PE ground sheet ensures clean and dry conditions inside the tent.

Das Coleman Rocky Mountain 5 Plus ist ein geräumiges und komfortables Tunnelzelt mit Platz für die ganze Familie samt Tisch und Stühlen. Seine patentierte Black-Out-Bedroom-Technologie ist ein neues Schlafsystem für Camper, das 99 Prozent des in den Schlafraum dringenden Tageslichts abblockt und so ideal für Eltern wie lichtsensible Personen ist. Die leichte, dennoch stabile Konstruktion mit Fiberglasgestänge ermöglicht einen einfachen Aufbau in wenigen Minuten. PVC-Fenster mit Abdeckung schaffen eine gute Balance von Belichtung und Privatsphäre. Die Wassersäule von 4.500 mm hält Starkregen stand und ein verschweißter integrierter PE-Boden sorgt für saubere und trockene Verhältnisse im Inneren.

Statement by the jury
The design of the easy to handle Coleman Rocky Mountain 5 Plus family tent fully meets the requirements of campers in terms of spaciousness, comfort and protection.

Begründung der Jury
Die Gestaltung des einfach zu handhabenden Familienzelts Rocky Mountain 5 Plus wird den Ansprüchen des Campers an Geräumigkeit, Komfort und Schutz voll gerecht.

Invenio SUL 3P
Lightweight Tent
Leichtgewichtszelt

Manufacturer
VAUDE Sport GmbH & Co. KG,
Tettnang, Germany
In-house design
Philipp Ziegler
Web
www.vaude.com

Invenio SUL 3P is a very lightweight and wind-stable three season tent for trekkers, which can be erected quickly and easily thanks to its Mark wrap-around construction. The special arrangement of the pole creates a cubic interior with a comfortable seat height in a large part of this three-person tent. The possibility to open up the two lateral panorama entrances offers an unobstructed view of natural surroundings. Both vestibules feature sufficient space for the equipment and are a suitable space for cooking. Two coverable vents ensure a pleasant microclimate even with the entrances closed.

Statement by the jury
The Invenio SUL 3P lightweight tent scores with a sophisticated design approach which takes into consideration the spatial construction, materials and handling in equal measure.

Invenio SUL 3P ist ein sehr leichtes und windstabiles 3-Seasons-Zelt für Trekker, das sich dank seiner Mark-Wickelkonstruktion schnell und einfach aufbauen lässt. Die spezielle Anordnung des Gestänges erzeugt einen kubischen Innenraum mit komfortabler Sitzhöhe in einem Großteil des 3-Personen-Zelts. Durch die Möglichkeit, die zwei seitlichen Panorama-Eingänge weit zu öffnen, ergibt sich eine ungehinderte Aussicht in die Natur. Die beiden Vorräume bieten ausreichend Platz für die Ausrüstung und eignen sich zum Kochen. Zwei abdeckbare Belüftungsöffnungen sorgen für ein angenehmes Raumklima auch bei geschlossenen Zelteingängen.

Begründung der Jury
Das Leichtgewichtszelt Invenio SUL 3P besticht mit einem durchdachten Gestaltungsansatz, der die räumliche Konstruktion, die Materialien und die Handhabung gleichermaßen berücksichtigt.

Lofoten 1 ULW
Ultra Light Weight Tent
Ultraleichtes Zelt

Manufacturer
Nordisk Company A/S, Silkeborg, Denmark
In-house design
John Poulsen
Web
www.nordisk.eu

With only 11 x 22 cm the Lofoten 1 ULW exhibits an exceptionally small pack size, and with 490 grams an extremely low weight for a double-walled one person tent. Stable aluminium poles with particularly short segments enable the reduced pack size, and the seven denier nylon of 26g/sqm with a thread count of 580 the extreme low weight. On both sides the fabric is siliconised in three layers thus guaranteeing high elasticity, and the water column of 1,600 mm creates a pleasant microclimate.

Statement by the jury
In the Lofoten 1 ULW one person tent, low weight and small pack size combine to create an innovative functional unit, which is ground-breaking in the industry.

Mit nur 11 x 22 cm zeigt das Lofoten 1 ULW ein bestechend geringes Packmaß und mit 490 Gramm zudem ein äußerst niedriges Gewicht für ein doppelwandiges Einmannzelt. Für das reduzierte Packmaß sorgt das stabile Aluminiumgestänge mit besonders kurzen Segmenten und für das enorme Leichtgewicht ein 7-Denier-Nylon von 26 g/qm bei einer Fadendichte von 580. Das beidseitig in drei Lagen siliconisierte Gewebe gewährleistet eine hohe Elastizität, wobei die Wassersäule von 1.600 mm ein angenehmes Raumklima erzeugt.

Begründung der Jury
In dem Einmannzelt Lofoten 1 ULW verbinden sich geringes Gewicht und kleines Packmaß zu einer innovativen funktionalen Einheit, die in der Branche wegweisend ist.

KarTent
Tent
Zelt

Manufacturer
Smurfit Kappa Benelux, Netherlands
In-house design
Chico Aertsen
Design
KarTent, Amsterdam, Netherlands
Web
www.smurfitkappa.com
www.kartent.com

KarTent is an eco-friendly tent made entirely out of cardboard, a natural material. It is 100 per cent recyclable and a sustainable alternative to traditional tents that are often abandoned at the end of festivals. Delivery emissions are saved as KarTents can be produced locally, and people can rely on public transport as the KarTents are already on site. In addition, they can be manufactured for less CO_2 than conventional tents. Easy to assemble, this tent has been successfully used at over 150 events, even in heavy rain.

Statement by the jury
Using the KarTent at festivals to avoid a multiple of garbage is an excellent solution from a creative as well as an ecological point of view.

KarTent ist ein umweltfreundliches, gänzlich aus Pappe, einem natürlichen Material, hergestelltes Zelt. Es lässt sich hundertprozentig recyceln und stellt eine nachhaltige Alternative zu herkömmlichen Zelten dar, wie sie am Ende von Festivals oft zurückgelassen werden. Da es lokal produziert werden kann, entfallen die mit der Zustellung gegebenen Emissionen und die Besucher können öffentliche Verkehrsmittel nutzen, weil die KarTents bereits vor Ort sind. Zudem wird für ihre Herstellung weniger CO_2 verbraucht wie für gewöhnliche Zelte. Das leicht aufzubauende Zelt kam bereits bei über 150 Festen, auch in schwerem Regen, erfolgreich zum Einsatz.

Begründung der Jury
Mit dem KarTent auf Festivals ein Vielfaches an Müll zu vermeiden, stellt eine hervorragende Lösung, unter gestalterischen wie ökologischen Aspekten, dar.

Inflite CF SLX
Cyclocross Bike

Manufacturer
Canyon Bicycles GmbH,
Koblenz, Germany

In-house design
Alexander Forst, Lars Wagner

Web
www.canyon.com

reddot award 2017
best of the best

Precision of form

Cyclocross bikes have to satisfy the highest demands, as users want to ride them as fast as possible both on the road and off-road. The design of the Inflite CF SLX therefore has placed the adaptability to individual riding styles and the requirements regarding form and material centre stage. The bike impresses with a patent-pending carrying system, which as an important functional element simultaneously defines its overall appearance. In line with the coherent overall concept, the frame has been optimised with regard to the field of application, with all interfaces following a design approach of complete system integration. This bike showcases a flowing silhouette with light gleaming off its clean surfaces and distinctively honed edges. The sculpturally crafted joint connections are aimed at emphasising the unique character of the bike. The shape of the cockpit, in conjunction with other innovative solutions such as the integrated seat clamp, conveys a sense of simplicity and functional precision. Graphic elements are a fundamental element of the overall appearance of the bike. The visual "bracket" not only serves as an optical connection between the cockpit and seat post, but also highlights the bike's signature parallelogram. Black surfaces on the fork en-sure a flowing transition to the frame. The Inflite CF SLX has thus emerged as a cyclocross bike with a design language that coherently embodies and visualises a high level of precision.

Präzision der Form

Cyclocross-Bikes sind enormen Anforderungen ausgesetzt, da die Sportler mit ihnen ebenso schnell auf der Straße wie auch im Gelände fahren wollen. Beim Inflite CF SLX standen die damit verbundenen Herausforderungen an Form und Material sowie die Anpassungsfähigkeit an das Fahrerverhalten im Mittelpunkt. Es beeindruckt mit einem zum Patent angemeldeten Tragefeature, das als wichtiges funktionales Element zugleich seine Formensprache definiert. In einem schlüssigen Gesamtkonzept wurde der Rahmen in Bezug auf den Einsatzbereich hin optimiert, wobei alle Schnittstellen dem gestalterischen Ansatz der Systemintegration folgen. Dieses Rad hat eine fließende Silhouette, deutlich herausgearbeitete Flächenwinkel heben dabei die Lichtkanten hervor. Seine skulptural gestalteten Knotenpunkte sollen zugleich den unverwechselbaren Charakter des Rades betonen. Die Form des Cockpits sowie innovative Detaillösungen wie eine integrierte Sattelklemme transportieren wiederum visuell die Attribute der Einfachheit und funktionalen Präzision. Ein integrativer Teil der Gestaltung ist die auffallende Grafik des Rades. Die visuelle „Klammer" verbindet nicht nur den Lenker mit der Sattelstütze, sondern hebt auch das die Form kennzeichnende Parallelogramm hervor. Die Gabel findet mit ihren schwarzen Flächen einen fließenden Übergang zum Rahmen. Mit dem Inflite CF SLX entstand so ein Cyclocross-Bike, dessen Formensprache die Präzision seiner Gestaltung auf sehr stimmige Weise nach außen trägt.

Statement by the jury

The Inflite CF SLX cyclocross bike impresses with its stringently implemented design. Every detail seems to be geared towards a philosophy of the best possible functionality in combination with the highest aesthetic quality. Its elegant appearance incorporates an outstanding design solution. Its expressiveness is underlined by a striking graphic that ideally suits this kind of bike.

Begründung der Jury

Das Cyclocross-Bike Inflite CF SLX begeistert durch sein stringent umgesetztes Design. Alles an ihm scheint sich konsistent an der Philosophie einer möglichst optimalen Funktionalität bei gleichzeitig höchster ästhetischer Qualität auszurichten. Seine elegante Formensprache stellt dabei eine sehr gute Gestaltungslösung dar. Seine Ausdruckskraft wird unterstrichen von einer markanten Grafik, die gut zu dieser Art von Rad passt.

Designer portrait
See page 46
Siehe Seite 46

SpeedX Leopard Pro
Racing Bike
Rennrad

Manufacturer
SpeedX Inc., Beijing, China
In-house design
Zhen Sun
Web
www.speedx.com

Leopard Pro is a carbon fibre aero racing bike with completely hidden wiring – even the brakes – and with a performance which reflects competition level cycling. Using the latest technology, the training can be monitored in real-time thus helping athletes to improve immediately. Data such as speed, cadence, climb, heart rate and more, are simultaneously indicated. In addition, a bicycle light and a camera can be connected externally. Aerodynamic design elements integrated into the frame largely reduce the air resistance.

Leopard Pro ist ein Aero-Rennrad aus Carbon mit komplett versteckter Verkabelung – selbst der Bremsen – und mit einer Performance auf Wettkampfniveau. Mittels neuester Technik lässt sich das Training in Echtzeit überwachen und dem Sportler dadurch unmittelbar zu Fortschritten verhelfen. Daten wie Geschwindigkeit, Kadenz, Steigung, Herzfrequenz und mehr werden simultan angezeigt, zudem lassen sich extern Fahrradlicht und -kamera anschließen. In den Rahmen integrierte aerodynamische Formgebungselemente reduzieren den Luftwiderstand weitestgehend.

Statement by the jury
The design of the racing bike Leopard Pro inspires with its powerful elegance and design features which specifically target aerodynamics, such as brake cables which have been incorporated into the bike.

Begründung der Jury
Die Gestaltung des Rennrads Leopard Pro begeistert durch kraftvolle Eleganz und gezielt auf Aerodynamik ausgerichtete Elemente wie die nach innen verlegten Bremszüge.

UNICORN
Road Bike
Rennrad

Manufacturer
SpeedX Inc., Beijing, China
In-house design
Zhen Sun
Web
www.speedx.com

Unicorn is a smart endurance racing bicycle with integrated power meter. With concealed wiring, it is aerodynamic and features a frame that combines stiffness with a light weight – making the bike ideally suited for a training day on the road or on hilly terrain. The removable SpeedForce smart device monitors all necessary cycling data and, with seven built-in sensors, delivers real-time readable reports on its scratch-resistant 2.2" screen. Based on this data, this device can develop a professional training programme.

Unicorn ist ein intelligentes Ausdauer-rennrad mit integriertem Leistungsmesser. Es ist, die Verdrahtung verbergend, aero-dynamisch und mit einem Rahmen gestal-tet, der Steifigkeit und Leichtigkeit in sich vereint – bestens geeignet für einen Trainingstag auf der Straße oder in hü-geligem Gelände. Das abnehmbare, smarte Gerät SpeedForce verfolgt mit sieben eingebauten Sensoren alle nötigen Rad-daten und liefert auf seinem kratzfesten 2,2"-Bildschirm in Echtzeit ablesbare Be-richte. Darauf basierend kann es ein pro-fessionelles Trainingsprogramm erstellen.

Statement by the jury
In Unicorn, technically advanced engi-neering and modern digital technology combine to form a racy and exclusive professional bicycle.

Begründung der Jury
In Unicorn verbinden sich ausgereifte Ingenieursleistung und moderne Digital-technik zu einem schnittigen und ex-klusiven Profirennrad.

Roadlite CF
Fitness Bike

Manufacturer
Canyon Bicycles GmbH,
Koblenz, Germany

In-house design
Fedja Delic

Web
www.canyon.com

reddot award 2017
best of the best

Design for the workout

Anyone who rides a bike a lot or uses it to commute to work automatically increases the fitness. The design of the Roadlite CF is modelled on the values of "simple, precise & dynamic" and places the improvement of individual fitness centre stage through a focus on function. This carbon bike is outstandingly light and delivers a fast and highly agile riding experience. Its innovative qualities are based on a stiffness and flexibility that has been optimised in specific areas of the frame. This approach also manifests itself in the surface design and shows in its junction points and the distinctive head tube. Blending coherently into the overall design, the carbon cockpit features optimised aerodynamics and comfort. The expressivity of the bike stems from a design of visual contrasts. Hard angles are honed to meet soft surfaces, while alternating between narrow and wide tube profiles creates the impression of dynamic interaction. Precise parallel lines further support the clear design language. The design idea of visual contrast also reappears in the frame artwork. The diagonally oriented graphic visualises a precise and dynamic look, while it highlights the shape of the individual profiles and plays with the change form matte to glossy surfaces. The Roadlite CF has emerged as a carbon fitness bike for enhanced workout experiences and showcases a combination of thoughtful design and high-tech performance.

Design für den Workout

Wer viel mit dem Fahrrad fährt oder dieses für den Weg zur Arbeit nutzt, erhöht damit automatisch seine Fitness. Mit der Orientierung an den Werten „Simple, Precise & Dynamic" rückt die Gestaltung des Roadlite CF die Funktion und so die Steigerung des individuellen Workouts in den Vordergrund. Dieses Rad aus Carbon ist ausgesprochen leicht und ermöglicht ein sehr agiles und schnelles Fahren. Seine innovativen Eigenschaften basieren darauf, dass es an entscheidenden Stellen hinsichtlich der Steifigkeit und Flexibilität optimiert wurde. Dieser Ansatz wird durch die Flächengestaltung unterstützt und zeigt sich in skulptural anmutenden Knotenpunkten sowie einem markanten Steuerrohr. Das in Bezug auf Aerodynamik und Komfort optimierte Carbon-Cockpit fügt sich stimmig in das Gesamtkonzept ein. Die Ausdruckskraft dieses Rades beruht auch auf einem visuellen Kontrast. Harte Kanten treffen auf weiche Flächen, wobei der Wechsel schmaler und breiter Profile ein dynamisches Wechselspiel erzeugt. Präzise, parallel geführte Linien unterstützen die klare Formensprache. Das gestalterische Element des Kontrasts wiederholt sich auch in der Grafik. Der diagonal verlaufende grafische Schnitt visualisiert eine prägnante Dynamik und Präzision. Gleichzeitig unterstreicht er die Form der einzelnen Profile und spielt mit dem Wechsel zwischen matter und glänzender Oberflächenbeschaffenheit. Das Roadlite CF ist ein Carbon-Fitnessbike für erlebnisreiche Workouts, das mit seiner Kombination von durchdachtem Design und Fast-Forward-Performance beeindruckt.

Statement by the jury

The Roadlite CF fitness bike combines simplicity and clarity with exciting innovative features. Showcasing a stringent design, it does without redundant details. Its silhouette immediately attracts attention. Optimised in its stiffness and flexibility, the bike conveys dynamic elegance – all its elements are precisely crafted and well thought-out. It thus achieves a highly emotional appeal.

Begründung der Jury

Das Fitnessbike Roadlite CF verbindet Einfachheit und Klarheit mit spannenden innovativen Features. Dieses Rad ist auf den Punkt und ohne redundante Details gestaltet. Man gerät sofort in seinen Bann, wenn man seine Silhouette betrachtet. In seiner Steifigkeit und Flexibilität optimiert, kommuniziert es eine dynamische Eleganz – alle seine Elemente sind präzise geformt und wohldurchdacht. Es spricht damit direkt die Emotionen an.

Designer portrait
See page 48
Siehe Seite 48

KOGA F3 6.0
Bicycle
Fahrrad

Manufacturer
KOGA, Heerenveen, Netherlands
In-house design
Daniel Loot, Reina Osinga-van der Veen
Web
www.koga.com

The Koga F3 6.0 was specifically developed for commuters who attach importance to a sporty appeal and sustainable quality. The technically advanced frame, and the fork, with Koga Crown Connect technology, allow for concealed cable routing. This particularly emphasises the elegant appearance of the smooth welded frame, of silver smoke colour, with round and sharp-edged lines. Its high-quality features also include a belt drive, Shimano-Alfine internal gear hub and hydraulic disc brakes.

Statement by the jury
Simple elegance, sporty dimensions and high-quality technical components define the Koga F3 6.0 as a modern bicycle for an urban life.

Das Koga F3 6.0 wurde gezielt für Pendler entwickelt, die Wert auf Sportlichkeit und nachhaltige Qualität legen. Der technisch ausgeklügelte Rahmen und die Gabel mit Koga-Crown-Connect-Technologie ermöglichen es, alle Kabel unsichtbar zu verlegen. Dadurch wird das edle Erscheinungsbild des glatt verschweißten Rahmens im Silver-Smoke-Ton mit runden scharfkantigen Linien besonders betont. Zur hochwertigen Ausstattung zählen zudem der Riemenantrieb, die Shimano-Alfine-Nabenschaltung und hydraulische Scheibenbremsen.

Begründung der Jury
Schlichte Eleganz, eine sportliche Geometrie und hochwertige technische Komponenten definieren das Koga F3 6.0 als zeitgemäßes Rad für das urbane Leben.

Offspring
Children's Bike
Kinderrad

Manufacturer
Canyon Bicycles GmbH, Koblenz, Germany
In-house design
Peter Kettenring
Design
ARTEFAKT design, Darmstadt, Germany
Web
www.canyon.com
www.artefakt.de

With a dynamic shape and precise details the children's bike, Offspring, displays an independent design. When power is applied to the pedal, the rear wheel starts to rotate and movement is then converted into a forward thrust. This movement is reflected in the colour scheme, which enhances the feeling of acceleration. As the child grows older, the design of the bicycle and the access heights can be adjusted to the size of the cyclist. Thanks to its low weight an enjoyable ride and great control of the bike are ensured.

Statement by the jury
The design and construction of the children's bike Offspring are tailored to the requirements of the target group and display dynamism and pleasurable cycling.

Das Kinderrad Offspring zeigt mit einer dynamischen Formgebung und präzisen Details eine eigenständige Gestaltung. Kommt Kraft auf die Pedale, wird das Hinterrad in Rotation versetzt und diese in Vortrieb umgesetzt. Diese Bewegung spiegelt sich in der Farbgebung wider, die das Gefühl der Beschleunigung unterstreicht. Mit zunehmendem Alter des Kindes passt sich die Gestaltung des Rades an und die Einstiegshöhe verändert sich mit der Größe des Fahrers. Dank des geringen Gewichts sind Fahrspaß und zugleich die Kontrolle über das Rad sehr ausgeprägt.

Begründung der Jury
Konstruktion und Formgebung des Kinderrads Offspring sind ganz auf die Anforderungen der Zielgruppe zugeschnitten und vermitteln Dynamik und Fahrspaß.

KOGA E-Xite N8
E-Bike

Manufacturer
KOGA, Heerenveen, Netherlands
In-house design
Mark Dorlandt, Reina Osinga-van der Veen
Web
www.koga.com

The e-bike Koga E-Xite N8 combines a high performance with sportiness and an elegant look. The particularly smooth welded aluminium frame integrates brake cables and derailleur gears, such as the low maintenance Shimano Nexus 8 speed premium internal gear hub, as well as lighting cables and electric components, thus keeping them protected from the weather. The high-quality Koga Feathershock fork suspension and powerful Bosch motor, positioned in the centre of the bicycle, ensure optimal weight distribution and a good ride.

Statement by the jury
The combination of a high technical performance and top-quality manufacturing make the Koga E-Xite N8 a sporty and safe to ride e-bike.

Das E-Bike Koga E-Xite N8 verbindet hohe Leistungskraft mit Sportlichkeit und elegantem Look. Der besonders glatt verschweißte Alurahmen integriert Schalt- und Bremszüge wie die wartungsarme Shimano-Nexus-8-Gang-Premium-Nabenschaltung, außerdem Beleuchtungskabel und elektrische Komponenten hervorragend, geschützt vor Witterungseinflüssen. Die hochwertige Koga-Feathershock-Gabeldämpfung und ein leistungsstarker, in der Fahrradmitte platzierter Bosch-Motor gewährleisten eine bestmögliche Gewichtsverteilung und gute Fahreigenschaften.

Begründung der Jury
Die Kombination aus hoher technischer Leistung und qualitätvoller Verarbeitung weisen das Koga E-Xite N8 als sportlich und sicher zu fahrendes E-Bike aus.

Chenoa HS
E-Bike

Manufacturer
Simplon Fahrrad GmbH, Hard, Austria
In-house design
Web
www.simplon.com

The design goals of the Chenoa HS e-bike were to develop a bicycle with a particularly rigid, durable and light frame that offers high seating and riding comfort, as well as safety. The rechargeable battery not only fits harmoniously and aesthetically in the carbon frame, but it is also intended to have a stabilising effect through its central balance point. Specially designed cross sections for the chainstays, a carbon or suspension fork and 50 mm tyres, which safely master road curves, complete the high-class features of this e-bike.

Statement by the jury
The lightweight frame, which is a focus of the Chenoa HS, is combined with the stability to create an appealing, high-quality e-bike.

Die Entwicklung des E-Bikes Chenoa HS zielte auf ein Rad mit besonders steifem, haltbarem und leichtem Rahmen ab, der hohen Sitz- und Fahrkomfort sowie Fahrsicherheit bietet. In den aus Carbon hergestellten Rahmen fügt sich der Akku nicht nur harmonisch und formschön ein, er hat auch die Funktion, durch seinen zentralen Schwerpunkt stabilisierend zu wirken. Speziell konstruierte Kettenstreben-Querschnitte, eine Carbon- oder Federgabel und kurvensichere 50-mm-Bereifung runden die qualitätsorientierte Ausstattung dieses E-Bikes ab.

Begründung der Jury
Die beim Chenoa HS im Vordergrund stehende Leichtigkeit des Rahmens fügt sich mit der gleichzeitigen Stabilität gekonnt zu einem hochwertig gestalteten attraktiven E-Bike.

Klever X
E-Bike

Manufacturer
Klever Mobility, New Taipei City, Taiwan
Design
ARTEFAKT design, Darmstadt, Germany
Web
www.klever-mobility.com
www.artefakt.de

The Klever X e-bike stands out with its new approach: a rear wheel drive, and it creates a focal point of its rechargeable battery, which distinguishes it from traditional e-bikes. The loop frame successfully integrates the rechargeable battery, and its bent down top tube forms a unisex frame design with reduced standover height. The resulting dynamic appearance underscores the power of the Biactron drive. The frame architecture serves as a modular platform for several types of bicycle from the same brand.

Statement by the jury
The rechargeable battery of the e-bike Klever X is integrated into the circumferential frame in a harmonious as well as conspicuous manner, demonstrating a successful and unique design.

Das E-Bike Klever X sticht durch einen neuen Ansatz mit Hinterradmotor hervor und macht den Akku zum zentralen Thema, mit dem es sich von herkömmlichen E-Bikes unterscheidet. Der „loop frame" integriert den Akku formschlüssig, wobei sein nach unten abknickendes Oberrohr ein Unisex-Rahmendesign mit reduzierter Überstandshöhe ergibt. Das so entstehende dynamische Erscheinungsbild unterstreicht die Leistungskraft des Biactron-Antriebs. Die Rahmenarchitektur dient als modulare Plattform für unterschiedliche Fahrradtypen der Marke.

Begründung der Jury
Mit seinem gleichermaßen harmonisch wie augenfällig in den umlaufenden Rahmen integrierten Akku beweist das E-Bike Klever X eine gelungene eigenständige Gestaltung.

RBIKE R4
E-Folding Bike
E-Faltrad

Manufacturer
RBIKE Technology Development Co., Ltd.,
Shenzhen, China
In-house design
Jiannong Zhou
Design
LKK Design Shenzhen Co., Ltd. (Hao Tian,
Haizhou Zhang, Rui Wen, Shiyang Zhou),
Shenzhen, China
Web
www.rbike.com.cn
www.lkkdesign.com
Honourable Mention

The Rbike R4 folding bike, developed
for a young target group, is intended to
help reduce the high traffic volume,
especially in cities, and to promote eco-
friendly means of transport. Its range
is up to 50 km. Thanks to a dual sensor
for speed and torque the engine adapts
very well to the power output, making
it easy to master diverse terrain. When it
is folded, the stylish and comfortable
Rbike R4 has a pack size of only 0.15 sqm
and can therefore be easily transported.

Statement by the jury
The design of the foldable e-bike
Rbike R4 is modern and unconvention-
al, thus meeting the requirements
of its target group to a high degree.

Das für eine junge Zielgruppe entwickelte
Faltrad Rbike R4 soll dazu beitragen, das
hohe Verkehrsaufkommen vor allem innerhalb von Städten zu reduzieren und umweltschonende Fortbewegungsarten zu
fördern. Seine Laufleistung beträgt 50 km.
Dank eines Dual-Sensors für Geschwindigkeit und Drehmoment passt sich der Motor sehr gut an die abgegebene Leistung an
und erlaubt es, mühelos unterschiedliche
Geländearten zu meistern. Zusammenge-
klappt weist das schick und komfortabel
gestaltete Rbike R4 ein Packmaß von nur
0,15 qm auf und lässt sich dadurch einfach
transportieren.

Begründung der Jury
Die Gestaltung des E-Faltrads Rbike R4 ist
modern und unkonventionell und wird
den Ansprüchen seiner Zielgruppe damit in
hohem Maße gerecht.

Taga 2.0
Family Bike
Familienrad

Manufacturer
Taga Bikes BV, Bussum, Netherlands
In-house design
Web
www.tagabikes.com

Taga 2.0 is a cool, safe and highly versatile family bike, available in a standard
or an electric version. Designed for urban families, it has a cargo box, suitable
for one or two kids facing forwards,
backwards or towards each other. The
seats have adjustable headrests and
can be reclined for sleeping or folded to
seal the cargo box. Taga 2.0 offers a
wide range of accessories including car
seat adapter, sun hood and more and
can be folded easily to be stored in a car
trunk.

Statement by the jury
Taga 2.0 fascinates with multifunctional
fields of application, which are not only
well-devised and practical but also provide a fun ride with the e-bike.

Taga 2.0 ist ein cooles, sicheres und sehr
vielseitiges Familienrad, das in einer Stan-
dardversion und als E-Bike erhältlich ist.
Für Familien in der Stadt konzipiert, ist es
mit einer Lastenbox für ein oder zwei
Kinder ausgestattet, die vorwärts oder rückwärts sitzend oder einander zugewandt
transportiert werden können. Die Sitze haben verstellbare Kopfstützen, die zum
Schlafen nach hinten geklappt oder so um-
gelegt werden können, dass sie die Lastenbox verschließen. Taga 2.0 bietet zahlreiche
Zusätzen wie einen Autositzadapter und
ein Sonnendach, es lässt sich leicht zusammenklappen und im Kofferraum verstauen.

Begründung der Jury
Taga 2.0 begeistert mit seinen multifunktionalen Einsatzmöglichkeiten, die nicht
nur durchdacht und praktisch sind, sondern
auch für Fahrspaß mit dem E-Bike sorgen.

BMW Paralympic Racing Wheelchair
Paralympic Racing Wheelchair
Rennrollstuhl

Manufacturer
BMW North America, LLC,
Woodcliff Lake, New Jersey, USA
Design
BMW Group Designworks,
Newbury Park, California, USA
Web
www.bmwgroupna.com
www.bmwgroupdesignworks.com

For the world class athletes of the Rio 2016 Paralympic games BMW developed a racing wheelchair that is particularly aerodynamic lightweight and fast. In addition to a completely revised design, the model, made of carbon fibre, features a new seat which can be optimally tailored to the body of an individual athlete by means of 3D scanning and printing techniques. The ambitious ergonomic approach was also applied to the other points of contact, such as the steering mechanism and the brakes.

Statement by the jury
The design of this racing wheelchair inspires with its streamlined and lightweight appearance that elegantly conceals its technical top performance.

Für die Weltklasseathleten der Rio 2016 Paralympic Games entwickelte BMW einen Rennrollstuhl, der besonders aerodynamisch, leicht und schnell ist. Neben einem komplett überarbeiteten Design verfügt das aus Carbon gefertigte Modell über einen neu entwickelten Sitz, der sich mithilfe von 3D-Scan- und Drucktechniken optimal auf den Körper der einzelnen Sportler zuschneiden lässt. Der anspruchsvolle ergonomische Ansatz wurde auch bei den Berührungspunkten, etwa dem Lenkmechanismus und den Bremsen, angewandt.

Begründung der Jury
Die Gestaltung dieses Rennrollstuhls begeistert durch die stromlinienförmige und leichte Anmutung, die seine technische Spitzenleistung elegant kaschiert.

New HANDY
Handcycle (Tricycle)
Handbike (Dreirad)

Manufacturer
Pacific Cycles, Inc., Taoyuan, Taiwan
In-house design
Michael Lin, Oscar Chung
Web
www.pacific-cycles.com

The design of the handcycle New Handy is specifically compact and easy to carry. It can be folded up to half its size so that it is easy to store and transport. The height of the handlebar and the seating position can be adjusted to the individual body size. The e-motor system, for long-distance or up-hill support, has been especially developed for the handcycle, since the performance of the hands corresponds to only one-sixth of the leg performance. An elastomer suspension ensures high comfort and stability, even on bumpy roads.

Statement by the jury
The handcycle combines a modern functional appearance with a well-considered construction, thanks to which it can be collapsed to a manageable size and many components can be adjusted.

Das Handbike New Handy wurde gezielt kompakt und leicht tragbar gestaltet. Es lässt sich auf die Hälfte seiner Größe zusammenklappen, sodass es problemlos zu verstauen und zu transportieren ist. Die Höhe der Lenkstange oder die Sitzposition kann je nach Körpermaßen individuell eingestellt werden. Das E-Motor-System zur Unterstützung bei weiten Entfernungen oder Bergen wurde speziell für das Handbike entwickelt, da die Leistung der Hände nur einem Sechstel der Beinleistung entspricht. Eine Elastomerfederung sorgt für hohen Komfort und Stabilität auch auf holprigen Strecken.

Begründung der Jury
Beim Handbike New Handy verbindet sich die überlegte Konstruktion, dank derer es sich handlich zusammenklappen lässt und sich viele Komponenten einstellen lassen, mit einer modernen funktionalen Anmutung.

Tailfin Carbon Rack and Waterproof Panniers
Pannier Rack and Panniers
Gepäckträger und Fahrradtaschen

Manufacturer
Tailfin, Bristol, Great Britain

In-house design
Tailfin

Web
www.tailfin.cc

reddot award 2017
best of the best

Aesthetic transportation

Panniers and pannier racks lend themselves to easily turning a bicycle into a true means of transportation. However, they usually do not fit all types of bicycles and backpacks are only suitable for short distances and light loads. With the aim of creating pannier accessories that make riding easier, faster and more enjoyable, the design of this pannier rack and panniers by Tailfin followed a novel approach. This consistently engineered system comprises a pannier rack and two matching waterproof panniers. Made of light carbon material, the pannier rack fascinates users with its dynamic shape and appearance. It is inspired by the aesthetic of contemporary racing bicycles and fits them perfectly. The patent-pending system is both highly functional and ergonomically well thought-out. With a weight of only 650 grams per pannier and 350 grams for the rack, it is easy to use and engineered to fit almost any type of bicycle. As mounting the system is self-explanatory, users can mount it within seconds without the need for any tools. The pannier rack is certified to carry a weight of up to 18 kg (ISO 11243). It thus allows easy and uncomplicated carry-ing of all belongings, including all equipment needed for a weekend trip for example. Convincing in terms of logic and aesthetic design, this system embodies a new concept for a traditional bicycle accessory and exudes a strong impression of lightness and elegance.

Ästhetisch transportiert

Ein Gepäckträger und Fahrradtaschen machen das Fahrrad erst zu einem Transportmittel. Diese passen jedoch nicht zu jedem Fahrradtyp, und Rucksäcke sind für längere Strecken ungeeignet. Mit der Zielsetzung, das Radfahren mit solchen Accessoires einfacher, schneller und angenehmer zu machen, ging man bei der Gestaltung des Gepäckträgers und der Fahrradtaschen von Tailfin neue Wege. Dieses schlüssig gestaltete System besteht aus einem Gepäckträger sowie zwei wasserdichten Radtaschen. Geformt aus dem leichten Material Carbon, begeistert der Gepäckträger den Nutzer mit seiner dynamischen Formensprache. Er greift die Ästhetik zeitgemäßer Rennräder auf und passt sich diesen perfekt an. Dieses zum Patent angemeldete System ist zudem funktional wie auch ergonomisch gut durchdacht. Mit einem Gewicht von nur 650 Gramm pro Radtasche und 350 Gramm für den Gepäckträger ist es einfach zu handhaben und passend für fast jedes Fahrrad konstruiert. Da die Montage sich gut selbst erklärt, kann der Fahrer alles ohne Werkzeug in Sekunden am Rad montieren. Der Gepäckträger ist dabei für ein Gewicht von bis zu 18 kg (ISO 11243) zertifiziert. Auf diese Weise kann etwa auch die Ausrüstung für den Wochenendausflug leicht und unkompliziert mit dem Fahrrad transportiert werden. Mit einem in seiner Logik und Ästhetik bestechend neuen Konzept für ein traditionelles Fahrradzubehör entstand hier ein System von beeindruckender Leichtigkeit und Eleganz.

Statement by the jury

The waterproof panniers and pannier mounting rack system by Tailfin incorporates an outstanding solution for the bicycle. It has been crafted towards a consistently high design aesthetic, with all details supporting the concept of lightness and uncompromising user-friendliness. This system fits onto almost all bicycle models – even modern racing bikes. It is fun, has a fresh look and represents a welcome addition to the range of classic bicycle accessories.

Begründung der Jury

Das System aus Gepäckträger und wasserdichten Radtaschen von Tailfin verkörpert eine herausragende Lösung für das Fahrrad. Es besitzt eine durchgehend hohe Designästhetik, bei der alle Details gekonnt das Konzept der Leichtgewichtigkeit und kompromisslosen Nutzerfreundlichkeit unterstützen. Dieses System eignet sich für beinahe alle Fahrradmodelle – auch für ein modernes Rennrad. Es macht Spaß, hat einen frischen Look und bereichert in vielerlei Hinsicht das klassische Fahrradzubehör.

Designer portrait
See page 50
Siehe Seite 50

Active Line / Active Line Plus
Product Line
Produktlinie

Manufacturer
Robert Bosch GmbH, Bosch eBike Systems,
Reutlingen, Germany
Design
KISKA GmbH, Anif-Salzburg, Austria
Web
www.bosch-ebike.de

The Active Line and Active Line product lines combine technology and design. The drive unit and system components are coordinated for optimum efficiency. The Active Line is ideal for everyday rides and casual trips. The Active Line Plus is geared towards higher performance and well-suited for short trekking tours. The drive units work quietly and provide a harmonious and natural driving experience. Elegantly designed cover plates serve as a protective element and compliment the flowing shape of the components. Both versions are characterised by a robust and particularly compact construction. They are about 20 to 25 per cent smaller than previous models. This allows manufacturers to better integrate them into the bike frame.

Die beiden Produktlinien Active Line und Active Line Plus verbinden Technologie mit Design. Antriebseinheit und Systemkomponenten sind optimal aufeinander abgestimmt. Die Active Line ist ideal für alltägliche Fahrten und Ausflüge. Die kraftvollere Active Line Plus eignet sich darüber hinaus auch für kleinere Trekkingtouren. Die Antriebseinheiten sind leise und sorgen für ein harmonisches und natürliches Fahrgefühl. Elegant gestaltete Blenden dienen als schützende Abdeckung und nehmen die fließende Formgebung der Systemkomponenten auf. Beide Ausführungen zeichnen sich durch eine robuste und besonders kompakte Bauweise aus und sind ca. 20 bis 25 Prozent kleiner als bisherige Modelle. Herstellern wird damit eine bessere Integration in den Rahmen ermöglicht.

Statement by the jury
Both drive units are technically advanced and score with a compact design and softly rounded edges. They are therefore very easy to integrate into a wide variety of frame models.

Begründung der Jury
Die beiden Antriebseinheiten sind technisch ausgereift und punkten mit einer kompakten Formgebung und weich abgerundeten Kanten, womit sie sich sehr gut in verschiedenste Rahmenmodelle integrieren lassen.

149

HD-T910
Bicycle Component
Fahrradkomponente

Manufacturer
Tektro Technology Corporation,
Puyan Township, Changhua County, Taiwan
In-house design
Web
www.tektro.com
Honourable Mention

HD-T910 is a fully hydraulic disc brake specifically designed for time trial and triathlon bikes. It integrates the previously external master cylinder into the handlebar grip, thus fulfilling a further function as a driver contact point. The co-moulded rubber grip slides easily over the end of a standard 24.2 mm TT base bar, therefore no handlebar tape is needed. The modular grip system is designed to neatly connect to modern electronic gear shifting systems and does not require adjustment after assembly.

Statement by the jury
It is an excellent idea to integrate the formerly separate master cylinder of this fully hydraulic disc brake, combined with the shifting system, into the handle.

HD-T910 ist eine speziell für Zeitfahr-Triathlonräder entwickelte vollhydraulische Scheibenbremse. Den bisher externen Hauptzylinder integriert sie in den Lenkergriff und erfüllt so als Fahrer-Kontaktpunkt eine Doppelfunktion. Der zusammengegossene Gummigriff lässt sich direkt auf das Ende einer Standard-24,2-mm-TT-Basisstange anbringen, ohne dass Griffband nötig ist. Das modulare Griffsystem ist so konzipiert, dass es sauber mit modernen elektronischen Schaltsystemen verbunden werden kann und nach dem Zusammenbau nicht extra neu eingestellt werden muss.

Begründung der Jury
Die Idee dieser vollhydraulischen Scheibenbremse, den früher separaten Hauptzylinder in den Griff, verknüpft mit dem Schaltsystem, einzubauen, ist hervorragend.

Comyou Back Single
Rear Pannier
Satteltasche

Manufacturer
VAUDE Sport GmbH & Co. KG,
Tettnang, Germany
In-house design
Web
www.vaude.com

Comyou Back Single is an urban rear pannier with roll closure and bamboo handles, climate neutrally manufactured in Germany. The robust material is PVC-free and waterproof welded, making any additional rain cover unnecessary. The bag features a large main compartment with expansion bellows and zip pocket. It is mounted to the rear luggage rack with the QMR 2.0 system and a stable back plate. It is adjustable by small easy to use hand wheels and can be quickly removed and carried comfortably over the shoulder with a carrying strap.

Statement by the jury
The design of the Comyou Back Single stands out with its clever construction together with its climate neutral production; in addition, it is an aesthetic eye-catcher.

Comyou Back Single ist eine urbane, klimaneutral in Deutschland hergestellte Radtasche mit Wickelverschluss und Bambusgriffen. Das robuste Material ist PVC-frei und wasserdicht verschweißt und macht eine zusätzliche Regenhülle überflüssig. Die Tasche ist mit einem großen Hauptfach inkl. Staubalg mit Reißverschlusstasche ausgestattet und wird mit dem QMR-2.0-System und stabiler Rückenplatte am hinteren Gepäckträger befestigt. Sie ist über einfach bedienbare Handrädchen justierbar, lässt sich rasch abnehmen und mittels Tragegurt bequem über der Schulter tragen.

Begründung der Jury
Die Gestaltung der Comyou Back Single sticht durch ihre clevere Konstruktion samt klimaneutraler Herstellung hervor und ist auch ästhetisch ein Blickfang.

Lumos
Bicycle Helmet
Fahrradhelm

Manufacturer
Lumen Labs, Hong Kong
In-house design
Web
www.lumoshelmet.co

The Lumos bicycle helmet features lights, brake lights and indicators combined in an intelligent, stable and weatherproof model. The elegant solution, in order to provide a high degree of safety and visibility, is equipped with bright white LEDs at the front and red spotlights at the rear to ensure sufficient lighting on the road. The flashlight signals of the helmet can be controlled wirelessly via a remote control on the handlebar, while the brake lights are automatically activated via a motion sensor.

Statement by the jury
Lumos comes up with a special innovation: thanks to built-in LEDs the bicycle helmet can emit light signals, thus significantly increasing the safety of the cyclist.

Der Fahrradhelm Lumos weist Leuchtstrahler auf, die Bremslichter und Blinker in einem intelligenten, stabilen und wetterfesten Modell zusammenführen. Die elegante Lösung für hohe Sicherheit und Sichtbarkeit ist vorne mit hellen weißen LEDs und hinten mit roten Strahlern ausgestattet, sodass ausreichende Beleuchtung auf der Straße gewährleistet ist. Die Blinksignale des Helms lassen sich drahtlos über eine Fernbedienung an der Lenkstange steuern, während die Bremslichter automatisch über einen Bewegungssensor aktiviert werden.

Begründung der Jury
Lumos wartet mit einer besonderen Innovation auf: Dank eingebauter LEDs kann der Fahrradhelm Leuchtsignale aussenden und so die Sicherheit des Radfahrers erheblich steigern.

Arofly
Power Meter
Leistungsmesser

Manufacturer
TBS Group Corporation,
New Taipei City, Taiwan
In-house design
Web
www.arofly.com

Arofly is an all-in-one bike meter (including power meter) featuring a modern design in housing and advanced technology. It is easy to install and suitable for almost all bicycles. Moreover, it is user-friendly and equipped with an innovative algorithm. It provides cyclists with comprehensive data on speed, cadence, power, distance or climbs, and is even compatible with heart rate devices. Due to its compact size, it is easy to carry the device with you.

Statement by the jury
Handy in size, easy to operate – and, above all, technically sophisticated; the power meter Arofly collects a lot of important data during cycling.

Arofly ist ein All-in-one-Fahrradmessgerät (inklusive Leistungsmesser), das eine moderne Gestaltung von Gehäuse und Hochtechnologie aufweist. Es lässt sich leicht und an nahezu allen Fahrräder installieren, ist benutzerfreundlich sowie mit einem innovativen Algorithmus bestückt. Dieser liefert Radfahrern umfangreiche Daten über Geschwindigkeit, Pedalkraft, Kadenz, Fahrzeit, Entfernung oder Anstiege und ist selbst mit Herzfrequenzmessern kompatibel. Durch seine kompakte Größe kann man das Gerät mühelos mit sich führen.

Begründung der Jury
Handlich in der Größe, einfach zu bedienen – und vor allem technisch durchdacht erhebt der Leistungsmesser Arofly eine Vielzahl wichtiger Daten während des Radfahrens.

KT606
Mounting System for
Smartphone and Power Bank
Halterung für Smartphone
und Ladegerät

Manufacturer
Index Measuring Tape Co., Ltd.,
New Taipei City, Taiwan
In-house design
Jason Hwang, Marco Yang, Jack Lin
Web
www.index-gifts.com.tw

KT606 is a multifunctional tool for bicycles as it provides a mounting system for both a smartphone and a power bank. Due to its elastic material, it can integrate two differently sized devices and hold them both securely. This smartphone holder can also be mounted elsewhere and therefore used separately. Available in various modern colours, the products can be fixed to the handlebar of any type of bicycle; it is easily and securely fastened with an integrated loop.

Statement by the jury
Sophisticated and, at the same time, simple in terms of design, this elastic holder for a smartphone and a power bank proves to be an extremely practical everyday companion.

KT606 ist ein Multifunktionstool fürs Fahrrad: Halterung für das Smartphone sowie Ladegerät in einem. Aufgrund seines elastischen Materials kann es zwei verschieden große Geräte integrieren und beide sicher einfassen. Die Smartphone-Halterung lässt sich auch separat benutzen und anbringen. In verschiedenen aktuellen Farben erhältlich, lassen sich die Produkte innerhalb weniger Sekunden an der Lenkstange jedes Fahrradtyps fixieren und mit einer integrierten Schlaufe einfach und sicher befestigen.

Begründung der Jury
Ausgeklügelt und zugleich einfach konstruiert, erweist sich die elastische Halterung für Smartphone und Ladegerät KT606 als überaus praktischer Alltagsbegleiter.

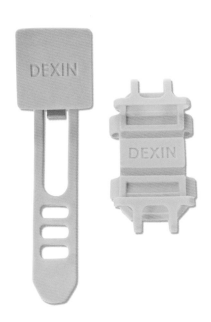

Varia Vision
In-Sight Display
Blickfeldanzeige

Manufacturer
Garmin, New Taipei City, Taiwan
In-house design
David Lammer-Meis, Sung-Chi Chen
Web
www.garmin.com.tw
Honourable Mention

Varia Vision is an in-sight display which enhances road awareness when cycling. It provides the cyclist with valuable information, such as performance data and navigation instructions, directly in the line of sight. This lightweight device can be attached flexibly to the temple of sunglasses, and it transfers data directly from a compatible Garmin device. Cyclists can therefore keep their focus on the road whilst looking for the next turn or when they want to keep an eye on cars approaching from behind. The display shows up to four important data fields and colour-coded graphic data. Vibration alarms alert the cyclist when a segment is being approached, a training zone is being left or a call is coming in. The convenient touch panel makes it easy to change between data pages, even with gloves on.

Varia Vision ist ein In-Sight-Display, mit dem sich das Situationsbewusstsein beim Radfahren erhöhen lässt und der Radfahrer wichtige Informationen wie Leistungsdaten oder Navigationsanweisungen direkt in Sichtlinie empfängt. Das leichte Gerät kann flexibel am Bügel der Sonnenbrille befestigt werden und überträgt die Daten unmittelbar vom kompatiblen Garmin-Gerät. Somit kann der Blick beim Fahren konzentriert auf der Straße bleiben, während man etwa die nächste Abbiegung sucht oder Autos, die von hinten kommen, im Auge behalten möchte. Das Display zeigt bis zu vier wichtige Datenfelder und farbcodierte Grafikdaten an. Vibrationsalarme signalisieren dem Fahrer, wenn er sich Segmenten nähert, einen Trainingsbereich verlässt oder einen Anruf erhält. Am praktischen Touch-Bedienfeld kann man bequem zwischen den Datenseiten wechseln, selbst mit Handschuhen.

Statement by the jury
It is a remarkable innovation to be able to see data, concerning the course or current heart rate, in the line of sight using Varia Vision; which is attached to a pair of glasses.

Begründung der Jury
Mit dem an einer Brille befestigten Varia Vision während der Fahrt Daten über die Strecke oder die aktuelle Herzfrequenz im Sichtfeld sehen zu können, stellt eine bemerkenswerte Innovation dar.

NutFix™
Component Lock
Komponentensicherung

Manufacturer
ABUS August Bremicker Söhne KG,
Wetter, Germany
In-house design
Web
www.abus.com
Honourable Mention

NutFix is an innovative solution for securing bicycle components. The system protects wheels as well as seat posts from theft. It features a mechanism that only releases the subjacent screw when the bicycle is lying on its side, otherwise no access is possible. In addition to a lock, which ideally fastens and locks the frame and wheels, NutFix offers an exceptional additional protection for the wheels and the saddle. If the bicycle is vertically fastened to an object, the NutFix caps cannot be removed, thus denying access to the nut, therefore ensuring that all components of the bicycle remain safely in place.

NutFix stellt eine innovative Lösung zur Sicherung von Fahrradkomponenten dar. Das System schützt sowohl Laufräder wie Sattelstützen vor Diebstahl und ist mit einem Mechanismus versehen, der die darunterliegende Mutter nur freigibt, wenn das Rad auf der Seite liegt. Ansonsten ist kein Zugriff möglich. Neben einem Schloss, das Rahmen und Laufräder idealerweise mit an- und abschließt, bietet NutFix eine außergewöhnliche Zusatzsicherung für Laufräder und Sattelstütze. Bei einem aufrecht angeschlossenen Fahrrad lassen sich die NutFix-Kappen eben nicht anheben und verweigern den Zugang zur Mutter, sodass alle Radkomponenten sicher an ihrem Platz bleiben.

Statement by the jury
The specialised functionality of NutFix is based on a well thought through design, which secures the wheels and the seat post particularly well.

Begründung der Jury
Der Gestaltungsansatz, der hinter der speziellen Funktionsweise von NutFix steckt, ist durchdacht und sichert Laufräder wie Sattelstütze besonders gut.

Yesoul Smart Cycling
Indoor Bike

Manufacturer
Shanghai Orangeade Health
Technology Co., Ltd.,
Shanghai, China

Design
Shanghai Titane Design
Consultant Co., Ltd.,
Shanghai, China

Web
www.yesoulchina.com
www.titanedesign.com

reddot award 2017
best of the best

Design in motion

Working out at home to keep healthy and fit has many benefits because it allows sticking to one's own schedule. The Yesoul Smart Cycling indoor bike has been designed and matched perfectly for use at home. It offers users a myriad of comfortable possibilities to enhance health and fitness, as the unit can innovatively connect to the Internet and allows users to take part in fitness courses via live streaming. The interaction is facilitated via a 19.5" smart touchscreen with a user-friendly design integrated into the bike's head. With the Yesoul App users can access the live streaming of a coach or opt for courses on demand, and even manage their exercise data. Fascinatingly, all data and guidance are displayed in real time. In addition, this home fitness device delivers sophisticated technology and ergonomics with its belt transmission and magnetic brake. The pull-type resistance-regulating stem embedded in the bike head helps avoid the movement track of the legs. The Yesoul Smart Cycling indoor bike fascinates with a highly self-sufficient design language, which is unusual for this type of device and primarily based on a design approach that hides all mechanical parts. Featuring a V-shaped structure frame, it provides high stability and compactness. With its comfort and path-breaking elegance, this home fitness device sets new standards and, at the same time, enhances any interior.

Design in Bewegung

Sich zu Hause fit zu halten, hat viele Vorteile, da man sich dort immer seine Zeit selbst einteilen kann. Das Indoor-Bike Yesoul Smart Cycling wurde perfekt auf den Einsatz in den eigenen vier Wänden abgestimmt. Es bietet dem Nutzer eine Vielzahl komfortabler Möglichkeiten, um die eigene Fitness zu steigern. Innovativ kann er über das Internet und Live-Streaming beispielsweise direkt an Fitnesskursen teilnehmen. Die Interaktion wird über einen an der Kopfseite integrierten, nutzerfreundlich gestalteten 19,5" großen Touchscreen ermöglicht. Mittels der Yesoul App können per Livestream die Anleitungen des Fitnesstrainers, On-Demand-Kurse sowie die Verwaltung von Trainingsdaten erfolgen. Verblüffend ist dabei, dass alle Daten in Echtzeit dargestellt werden. Das Fitnessgerät bietet dem Trainierenden zudem eine ausgereifte Technik und Ergonomie mit einer Riemenübertragung sowie einer Magnetbremse. Der Regulierungshebel für den Widerstand an der Kopfseite des Bikes sichert den Beinen Bewegungsfreiheit. Das Yesoul Smart Cycling fasziniert mit einer für solche Geräte sehr geschlossen anmutenden Formensprache, die auch darauf basiert, dass bei der Gestaltung die Mechanik komplett verborgen wurde. Ausgestattet mit einem V-förmigen Strukturrahmen ist es zudem sehr stabil und kompakt. Mit seinem Komfort und seiner bahnbrechenden Eleganz setzt dieses Fitnessgerät neue Standards und bereichert zugleich das Interieur.

Statement by the jury

The Yesoul Smart Cycling optimises the possibilities of indoor bikes. Innovative Internet connectivity and live streaming deliver direct interaction with a coach. This fitness device convinces with sophisticated technology and ergonomics, its user-friendly functionality as well as a highly elegant design language unusual for this product segment. Exacting and reduced to essential features, its design improves the performance of this type of devices to lasting effect.

Begründung der Jury

Das Yesoul Smart Cycling optimiert die Möglichkeiten eines Indoor-Bikes. So erlaubt innovatives Internet-Live-Streaming die direkte Interaktion mit dem Fitnesstrainer. Dieses Fitnessgerät gefällt mit seiner ausgefeilten Technik und Ergonomie, seiner nutzerfreundlichen Funktionalität sowie einer für den Fitnessbereich ungewöhnlich eleganten Formensprache. Seine exakt auf die notwendigen Features reduzierte Gestaltung verbessert die Performance eines solchen Gerätes nachhaltig.

Designer portrait
See page 52
Siehe Seite 52

SPIN BIKE
Spinning Bike

Manufacturer
Kaesun Sports, Paju, South Korea
Design
designwow & partners, Seoul, South Korea
Web
www.kaesun.com

This professional spinning bike, with magnetic resistance, was designed with a particular focus on user-friendliness. It differs from conventional devices due to its compact design. With its solid frame, it imparts a high degree of stability. The design vocabulary of the handlebars supports the various postures required by individual users; additionally the handlebar and saddle can be adjusted to suit their size and preferred seat position. Therefore, a comfortable and efficient posture is possible for every athlete.

Das magnetoresistive professionelle Spinning Bike wurde mit besonderem Fokus auf die Benutzerfreundlichkeit entworfen und unterscheidet sich von herkömmlichen Geräten durch seine kompakte Gestaltung. Mit seinem kräftigen Rahmen vermittelt es ein hohes Maß an Stabilität. Die Formensprache der Lenkstange berücksichtigt unterschiedliche Haltungen der einzelnen Nutzer und erlaubt die jeweilige Anpassung von Lenkstange und Sattel an deren Größe und Sitzposition. Für jeden Sportler ist damit eine bequeme und effiziente Haltung möglich.

Statement by the jury
The compact design of the Spin Bike scores with a functional performance: height and position can be individually adjusted to the user.

Begründung der Jury
Die kompakte Gestaltung des Spin Bike punktet mit der funktionalen Leistung, dass es sich in der Höhe und Position individuell an den Nutzer anpassen lässt.

SKILLMILL
Fitness Equipment
Fitnessgerät

Manufacturer
Technogym SpA, Cesena (Forli-Cesena), Italy
In-house design
Web
www.technogym.com

Skillmill assists sportspeople in effectively improving their strength, speed, stamina and agility. With a variety of training routines all energy systems of the body can be trained and top performances achieved. Since it is non-motorised, the device is directly driven and controlled by the user. From a cold start, it accelerates quickly and adapts itself to the individual's speed. By moving forward on the treadmill, speed is increased and decreased by moving backwards.

Skillmill bietet Breitensportlern die Möglichkeit, ihre Kraft, Schnelligkeit, Ausdauer und Beweglichkeit effektiv zu verbessern. Mit einer Vielzahl von Trainingsprogrammen lassen sich sämtliche Energiesysteme des Körpers trainieren und Spitzenleistungen erzielen. Da es keinen eigenen Motor besitzt, wird das Gerät direkt vom Benutzer angetrieben und gesteuert. Vom Kaltstart aus beschleunigt es schnell und passt sich dann der individuellen Geschwindigkeit an. Durch Bewegung nach vorn auf der Lauffläche wird die Geschwindigkeit gesteigert und umgekehrt verringert.

Statement by the jury
With its numerous training options for both proficient athletes and beginners, the innovative and easy to handle treadmill Skillmill is extremely effective.

Begründung der Jury
Mit seinen zahlreichen Trainingsmöglichkeiten für Geübte wie Anfänger zeigt sich das innovative und einfach zu handhabende Fitnessgerät Skillmill als außerordentlich wirksam.

motusBASEBALL
Biomechanics Wearable
Biomechanisches Wearable

Manufacturer
Motus Global, Massapequa, USA
Design
Product Creation Studio, Seattle, USA
Web
www.motusglobal.com
www.productcreationstudio.com

motusBaseball specialises in 3D motion capture assessments and biomechanical calculations using the latest monitoring technology to protect athletes from serious injuries within the sport of baseball. The smart, versatile and robust wearable was inspired by natural stone. It feels good both in the hand and on the body. A USB connection enables travelling athletes to synchronise their data and charge the device. In addition, all interactions are automated, from turning on to powering down, allowing athletes to stay focused on play.

Statement by the jury
The intelligent, handy motusBaseball has it all: it allows users to monitor and analyse the movement data of athletes comprehensively and precisely.

Auf die Erfassung und Bewertung von 3-D-Bewegungen und biomechanische Berechnungen spezialisiert, bedient sich motusBaseball hochmoderner Aufzeichnungstechnologie, um Sportler im Bereich Baseball vor schweren Verletzungen zu schützen. Das smarte, vielseitige und robuste Wearable ist Naturstein nachempfunden und fühlt sich in der Hand und am Körper gut an. Mittels USB-Verbindung können die Sportler unterwegs ihre Daten synchronisieren und das Gerät aufladen. Zudem sind alle Interaktionen vom Ein- bis zum Ausschalten automatisiert, damit die Spieler auf das Spiel konzentriert bleiben können.

Begründung der Jury
Der intelligente, handliche motusBaseball hat es in sich: Mit ihm lassen sich die Bewegungsdaten des Sportlers umfassend und präzise überwachen wie analysieren.

TRATAC Active Ball
Vibration Exercise Ball
Vibrationsübungsball

Manufacturer
Naum Care Corp, Seongnam, South Korea
In-house design
Gabriel Lim
Web
www.naum.biz

The Tratac Active Ball is a vibration device whose high intensity serves to relax muscles and fascias. With its compact size, it is easy to carry; it offers three vibration levels that can be changed by pressing the power button. In the form of a peanut, the Active Ball has the optimal shape to address the difficult to reach stabilizing muscles on the vertebrae and spine. The 4-mm thick silicone layer ensures outstanding elasticity, thermal stability and padding when rolling.

Statement by the jury
Designed with a focus on user-friendliness and reliability, the silicone layer of the Active Ball impresses regarding its functions and tactile finish.

Tratac Active Ball ist ein Vibrationsgerät, dessen hohe Intensität der Entspannung von Muskeln und Faszien dient. Mit seiner kompakten Größe leicht zu tragen, bietet es drei Vibrationsstufen an, die sich durch Druck auf den Einschaltknopf ändern lassen. In der Form einer Erdnuss hat der Active Ball die optimale Gestalt, um an schwierig zu erreichende, stabilisierende Muskeln an Wirbeln und Wirbelsäule zu gelangen. Die 4 mm dicke Silikonschicht sorgt für herausragende Elastizität, thermische Stabilität und Polsterung beim Rollen.

Begründung der Jury
Auf hohe Benutzerfreundlichkeit und Zuverlässigkeit hin konzipiert, besticht auch die Silikonschicht des Active Ball in funktionaler wie haptischer Hinsicht.

Move It
Smart Fitness Device
Smartes Fitnessgerät

Manufacturer
Eggplant Technologies, Hong Kong
In-house design
Benny Chiu
Design
Alan Tam, Hong Kong
Web
www.move-it.club
www.alantamdesign.net

Move It is a compact, smart fitness device that offers a muscle and cardio workout anywhere, and at any time. It features patent-pending intelligent handles and sensors that connect a set of various devices such as an abdominal roller, stretch bands or a skipping rope to an independent interactive workout platform. The effectiveness of the workout is enhanced by programs, developed by trainers, which give the user feedback on the exercises completed and calorie consumption via an app.

Move It ist ein kompakt gestaltetes smartes Fitnessgerät, das überall und zu jeder Zeit Muskel- und Herztrainings erlaubt. Es ist mit zum Patent angemeldeten intelligenten Griffen und Sensoren ausgestattet, die die verschiedenen Geräte wie Bauchroller, Fitnessband oder Springseil zu einer eigenständigen interaktiven Trainingsplattform verknüpfen. Die Effektivität des Trainings wird durch von echten Coaches angelegte Programme erhöht, die dem Anwender über eine App Rückmeldung über Bewegungsabläufe oder den Kalorienverbrauch geben.

Statement by the jury
Combining several elements into a fitness unit, Move It is captivating by the various effective training options available, as well as by its compact dimensions.

Begründung der Jury
Mit mehreren Elementen zu einer Fitnesseinheit zusammengefasst, überzeugt Move It durch die Vielfalt des damit möglichen, effektiven Trainings sowie durch seine kompakten Maße.

AmpliCube
Training Device
Trainingsgerät

Manufacturer
amplitrain systems GmbH,
Mannheim, Germany
In-house design
Web
www.amplitrain.de

The electric muscle activation of the AmpliCube training device relies on high technology in the form of medium frequency current, more precisely on a modulated medium frequency of 2,000 hertz. This allows a variety of training targets for the whole body. By means of a freely adjustable bioelectric impulse the device brings the body to sweat; it also offers application possibilities such as metabolic activation, relaxation and regeneration.

Statement by the jury
Tailored to individual customer requirements and training targets, the whole body can be trained with AmpliCube – using state-of-the-art technology.

Die elektrische Muskelaktivierung des Trainingsgeräts AmpliCube setzt auf Hightech in Form von mittelfrequentem Strom, genauer gesagt auf eine modulierte Mittelfrequenz von 2.000 Hertz. Damit lässt sich eine Vielzahl von Trainingszielen für den gesamten Körper erreichen. Mithilfe der frei einstellbaren bioelektrischen Impulse bringt das Gerät den Körper ins Schwitzen, bietet aber ebenso auch Anwendungsmöglichkeiten von der Stoffwechselaktivierung und Lockerung bis hin zur Förderung der Regeneration.

Begründung der Jury
Ganz auf individuelle Kundenwünsche und Trainingsziele zugeschnitten, lässt sich mit AmpliCube der gesamte Körper trainieren – und das mit Hightech nach neuestem Stand.

TOWELL+
Sports Towel
Sporthandtuch

Manufacturer
STRYVE GmbH, Hamburg, Germany
Design
THINKS Design GmbH (Florian Goecke,
Lennart Rieper), Hamburg, Germany
Web
www.stryve.de

The sports towel Towell+ makes workout more comfortable. Its sleeve keeps the towel during workout in place and prevents it from sliding off. Featuring a gym and a skin side, the towel guarantees less spreading of germs. All kinds of keys and other accessories can easily be stored in the pocket; a smartphone can be used through the touch-sensitive mesh. Thanks to its strong magnetic clip, the Towell+ can be hung virtually everywhere.

Statement by the jury
The Towell Plus sports towel concept is very well thought through, and with its various features achieves a most innovative and positive outcome.

Das Towell+ macht Workout komfortabler. So verhindert zum einen eine Art Kapuze, dass es während des Trainings wegrutscht, zum anderen sorgt die Unterscheidbarkeit von Körper- und Geräteseite für eine geringere Verbreitung von Bakterien. Spindschlüssel und andere Utensilien passen in die praktische Tasche. Befindet sich das Handy darin, bleibt es durch das touchsensible Mesh weiterhin bedienbar. Außerdem lässt sich das Towell+ durch den magnetischen Clip nahezu überall aufhängen.

Begründung der Jury
Die Idee des Sporthandtuchs Towell Plus ist sehr durchdacht und gelangt mit verschiedenen Details zu einem äußerst innovativen und formschlüssigen Ergebnis.

gripmore Golf Shoes
Golfschuh

Manufacturer
gripmore Co., Ltd., Dongguan Jianghao
Plastic Co., Ltd., Taipei, Taiwan
In-house design
James Ho, Yeitai Qin
Web
www.gripmore.net

These golf shoes, equipped with an innovative hybrid outsole, feature 21 multi-layered, flower-shaped gripmore studs, which are applied in different sizes and shapes directly onto a lightweight mesh, with hundreds of micro spikes. They distribute the bodyweight of the wearer efficiently and ensure a particularly high elasticity and stability on the golf course, as well as in the city. The upper material, of patented biomimetic snake skin, not only has a stylish look but is also protective and water repellent.

Statement by the jury
The design of the gripmore golf shoe impresses with its technically advanced outsole concept and its upper material with eye-catching snakeskin effect.

Die mit innovativer Hybridaußensohle ausgestatteten Golfschuhe weisen 21 mehrschichtige blumenförmige Gripmore-Stollen auf, die in unterschiedlicher Größe und Ausformung direkt auf ein leichtes Gewebe mit Hunderten von Mikrospikes injiziert werden. Sie verteilen das Körpergewicht des Trägers effizient und ermöglichen einen besonders hohe Elastizität und Stabilität auf dem Golfplatz wie in der Stadt. Das Obermaterial aus patentierter biomimetischer Schlangenhaut sieht schick aus, schützt und ist wasserabweisend.

Begründung der Jury
Die Gestaltung des gripmore Golfschuhs imponiert durch die ausgereift konzipierte Außensohle sowie durch das ins Auge springende schlangenhautartige Obermaterial.

Shear Reduction
Basketball Shoe
Basketballschuh

Manufacturer
Li Ning (China) Sports Goods Co., Ltd.,
Beijing, China
In-house design
Bode Oluwa, Gilbert Lam, Jiang Yuan
Web
www.li-ning.com

The Shear Reduction shoe features an outsole which reduces the shear forces within the shoe. In intense sports, sudden force movements occur in combination with many fast fine-motor movements. Therefore, the footwear must react to the movements of the athlete to avoid injuries and optimise performance. The concept of the Shear Reduction shoe entails so-called copolymers, with spiral-shaped lamellae, which can rotate up to 45 degrees as soon as the foot makes a rotary movement.

Der Shear Reduction besitzt eine Außensohle, die die Scherkräfte innerhalb des Schuhs reduziert. In intensiven Sportarten kommen plötzlich auftretende Kraftbewegungen zusammen mit vielen schnellen feinmotorischen Bewegungen vor. Daher muss das Schuhwerk auf die Bewegungen des Athleten reagieren, um Verletzungen zu vermeiden und die Leistung zu optimieren. Das Konzept des Shear Reduction sind sogenannte Copolymere mit spiralförmigen Lamellen, die sich bis zu 45 Grad mitdrehen, sobald der Fuß eine Drehbewegung macht.

Statement by the jury
With its sophisticated construction and specific material connections, the Shear Reduction shoe provides high stability and injury protection in the dynamic sport of basketball.

Begründung der Jury
Mit seiner durchdachten Konstruktion und den spezifischen Materialverbindungen bietet der Shear Reduction hohe Stabilität und Verletzungsschutz im dynamischen Basketballsport.

G Master Skyline
Running Shoes
Laufschuhe

Manufacturer
Graphene Master Holding B.V.,
Delft, Netherlands
In-house design
Shou-En Zhu, Hao-Zheng Zhu, Hol-San Tang
Design
Sketching (Koos Eissen),
The Hague, Netherlands
Web
www.agth.nl
www.gmaster.tech

The G Master Skyline running shoes were designed for runners in the city. The graphene based antistatic outsole weighs only 90 grams and has a much higher abrasion resistance than conventional EVA outsoles. The outsoles absorb the force of foot strikes, and in addition, a carbon fibre board under the foot arch stabilises the impact during running. The patterns on the outsole ensure optimal road grip in any weather. Inside the shoe, the lightweight honeycomb structured sole provides protection and efficient cooling.

Die Laufschuhe G Master Skyline wurden für Läufer in Städten konzipiert. Die graphenbasierte antistatische Außensohle wiegt nur 90 Gramm bei einer weitaus höheren Abriebfestigkeit wie bei herkömmlichen EVA-Außensohlen. Sie absorbiert die Kräfte beim Auftreten und zusätzlich stabilisiert eine Carbonfaserplatte unter dem Fußgewölbe den Aufprall beim Laufen. Die Muster auf der Außensohle bieten bestmögliche Griffigkeit bei jedem Wetter und innen sorgt die leichte wabenstrukturierte Sohle für Schutz und effiziente Kühlung.

Statement by the jury
The running shoes G Master Skyline stand out with their elaborate design which pays attention to the smallest detail, and which attaches importance to a stable, comfortable hold as well as to a good grip.

Begründung der Jury
Die Laufschuhe G Master Skyline ragen durch ihre bis ins Detail durchdachte Gestaltung heraus, die ebenso Wert auf stabilen, komfortablen Halt wie auf Griffigkeit legt.

gripmore Sock Shoe
Sock Shoes
Sockenschuhe

Manufacturer
gripmore Co., Ltd., Dongguan Jianghao
Plastic Co., Ltd., Taipei, Taiwan
In-house design
James Ho, Yeitai Qin
Web
www.gripmore.net

The gripmore sock shoes have been developed as an alternative to conventional sports shoes. They offer feet continuous support when exercising with their integral shoelace and hook and loop closure system, which are attached to the sole of the socks. The actual no-sew upper sock ensures high comfort and creates an extraordinary barefoot experience thanks to its integrated outsole. The abrasion-proof outsole, made of eco-friendly polyurethane, covers the toes and heels and protects the feet during movement.

Statement by the jury
These sock shoes are sophisticated companions for the gym; they are handy and provide the foot with secure comfort as well as maximum mobility.

Die Sockenschuhe von gripmore wurden als Alternative zu echten Sportschuhen entwickelt. Sie unterstützen die Füße mit dem an die Sohle anschließenden integralen Schnürsenkel- bzw. Klettverschlusssystem bei jeder Bewegung und Fitnessübung. Die eigentliche, nicht genähte Obersocke sorgt für hohen Komfort und vermittelt dank der integrierten Außensohle ein ungewöhnliches Barfußerlebnis. Die über Zehen und Ferse verlaufende abriebfeste Außensohle aus umweltfreundlichem Polyurethan schützt die Füße bei der Bewegung.

Begründung der Jury
Diese Sockenschuhe sind raffinierte Begleiter im Fitnessstudio: Sie sind handlich und bieten dem Fuß einen sicheren Komfort bei zugleich maximaler Beweglichkeit.

Skinners
Sock Shoes
Sockenschuhe

Manufacturer
Skinners Technologies s.r.o.,
Brno, Czech Republic
In-house design
Petr Procházka
Web
www.skinners.cc

Skinners are innovative sock shoes for travel and sport enthusiasts. They provide the maximum freedom of socks with the protective elements of shoes, offering a new joy of movement. Due to their compact dimensions, Skinners are primarily useful as handy backup footwear for outdoor activities (e.g. inline skating). The waste-free technology with a pending patent does not use adhesives or seams, guaranteeing that the abrasion-proof bottom part is neatly joined to the upper antibacterial material.

Statement by the jury
The sock shoes Skinners are characterised by being highly comfortable to wear and they are suitable for indoor as well as outdoor sports, thanks to their hard-wearing materials.

Skinners sind innovative Sockenschuhe für Reise- und Sportbegeisterte. Die Kombination der größtmöglichen Freiheit von Socken mit den Schutzkomponenten von Schuhen garantiert eine neue Bewegungsfreude. Aufgrund ihrer Kompaktheit eignen sich Skinners vor allem als handliches Ersatzschuhwerk für verschiedene Outdooraktivitäten wie etwa Inlineskating. Die zum Patent angemeldete abfallfreie Technologie gewährleistet, dass weder Klebstoff noch Nähte zum Einsatz kommen und der abriebfreie untere Teil sauber an das antibakterielle Obermaterial anschließt.

Begründung der Jury
Die Sockenschuhe Skinners zeichnen sich durch einen hohen Tragekomfort aus und eignen sich dank ihres widerstandsfähigen Materials für Indoor- wie Outdoor-Sportarten.

PUMA evoKNIT Driver Pro
Formula 1 Driver Shoe
Formel-1-Schuhe

Manufacturer
PUMA SE, Herzogenaurach, Germany
In-house design
Carl Wilkinson, Kevin Redon
Web
www.puma.com

The Puma evoKNIT Driver Pro shoe was developed especially for Formula 1 drivers. Its special feature is the fire-resistant, one-piece knitted Nomex upper material without laces, which ensures a comfortable close fit. The designers were able to produce a breathable structure with such protective properties to meet the challenging demands of Formula 1 racing. The lightweight neoprene outsole provides high grip and presents the critical interface between the driver and racing car. It facilitates lightning-quick throttle and braking reactions and gives the driver a very good feeling for the vehicle and the track.

Statement by the jury
The design of the Puma evoKNIT Driver Pro appeals both functionally and aesthetically: the fireproof knitted shoe, including a nonslip sole, adapts optimally to the driver's foot.

Der Puma evoKNIT Driver Pro wurde speziell für Formel-1-Fahrer entwickelt. Seine Besonderheit ist das feuerfeste, einteilig gestrickte Nomex-Obermaterial ohne Schnüre, das für eine bequem anliegende Passform sorgt. Den Designern gelang es, eine atmungsaktive Struktur mit schützenden Eigenschaften herzustellen, um den anspruchsvollen Anforderungen der Formel 1 gerecht zu werden. Die leichte Neopren-Außensohle bietet hohe Griffigkeit und ist die kritische Schnittstelle zwischen Fahrer und Rennwagen. Sie erleichtert blitzschnelle Drossel- und Bremsreaktionen und verschafft dem Fahrer ein sehr gutes Gefühl für Fahrzeug und Strecke.

Begründung der Jury
Die Gestaltung des Puma evoKNIT Driver Pro überzeugt funktional wie ästhetisch: Der feuerfeste Strickschuh passt sich samt griffiger Sohle dem Fuß des Fahrers optimal an.

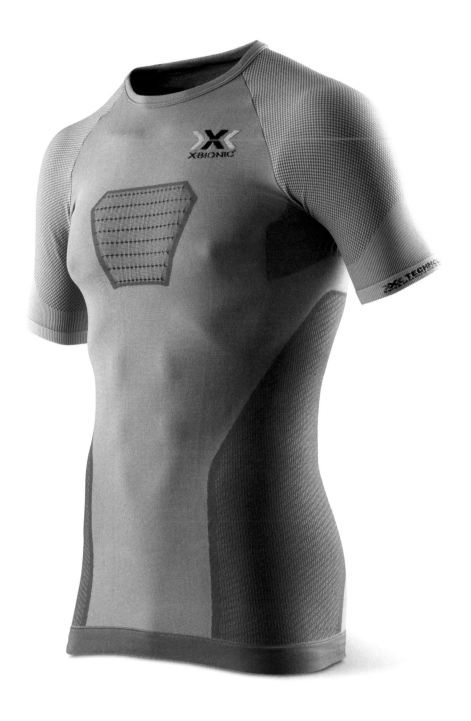

X-BIONIC® Speed EVO Shirt
Functional Sports Apparel
Sportfunktionskleidung

Manufacturer
X-BIONIC®, Asola, Italy
Design
X-Technology Swiss R&D AG,
Wollerau, Switzerland
Web
www.x-bionic.com
www.x-technology.com

The lightweight Speed Evo running shirt with integrated and patented 3D Bionic Sphere System is capable of efficiently regulating body temperature. Positioned precisely in the chest region and on the upper back, this system, which is based on scientific findings, has a profound effect on the skin. The system works by cooling wearers when they sweat and warming them when they are cold. A flexible fit ensures freedom of movement. Thanks to a newly developed yarn, the shirt weighs 33 per cent less than the already multiple awarded predecessor. In addition, the kidney and pelvis areas are protected by reinforced material.

Das sehr leichte Laufshirt Speed Evo mit integriertem und patentiertem 3D Bionic Sphere System reguliert die Körpertemperatur optimal. Genau im Brustraum und am oberen Rücken platziert, hat dieses auf wissenschaftlichen Erkenntnissen basierende System hohe Wirkung auf die Haut. Das bedeutet, es kühlt, wenn der Läufer schwitzt, und wärmt, wenn er friert. Eine flexible Passform sorgt für Bewegungsfreiheit. Dank eines neu entwickelten Garns wiegt das Shirt 33 Prozent weniger als das bereits mehrfach ausgezeichnete Vorgängermodell. Nieren und Nierenbecken sind zudem durch verstärktes Material geschützt.

Statement by the jury
The Speed Evo Shirt appeals with its intelligent use of materials, which simultaneously regulate body temperature and promote mobility and performance.

Begründung der Jury
Das Shirt Speed Evo besticht durch den intelligenten Einsatz der Materialien, die zugleich die Körpertemperatur regulieren und Beweglichkeit wie Leistung fördern.

Mugello R D-Air®
Motorcycle Racing Suit
Motorradrennanzug

Manufacturer
Dainese S.p.A., Molvena (Vicenza), Italy
In-house design
Web
www.dainese.com

The motorcycle racing suit Mugello R D-Air includes numerous technical innovations which make it a modern safety system for professional motor cycling. One of these is the patented, intelligent emergency lighting system: an LED strip that automatically activates when the driver falls thus reducing the risk of being hit by another vehicle. The remodelled architecture of the suit integrates a patented adaptive knee design, a tri-axial elastic textile and seamlessly manufactured inserts for high comfort.

Statement by the jury
The motorcycle racing suit is particularly striking with its intelligent emergency lighting system which protects the racing driver excellently in the event of a fall.

Der Motorradanzug Mugello R D-Air umfasst zahlreiche technische Innovationen, die ihn als zeitgemäßes Sicherheitssystem für professionelles Motorradfahren ausweisen. Eine davon ist das patentierte, intelligente Notlichtsystem: ein LED-Streifen, der sich beim Sturz des Fahrers automatisch aktiviert und das Risiko verringert, angefahren zu werden. Die umgestaltete Architecture des Anzugs integriert eine patentierte adaptive Kniekonstruktion, eine Dreiachselastik und nahtlos ausgefertigte Einlegestücke für hohen Komfort.

Begründung der Jury
Der Motorradanzug sticht buchstäblich durch die Besonderheit seines intelligenten Notlichtsystems ins Auge, das den Rennfahrer bei Stürzen ausgezeichnet schützt.

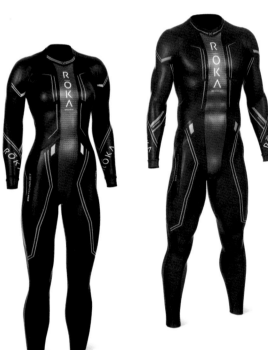

ROKA Maverick X
Wetsuit
Taucheranzug

Manufacturer
ROKA Sports, Inc., Dallas, USA
In-house design
Web
www.roka.com

Roka Maverick X redefines the performance standard of wetsuits by counteracting the number one complaint: shoulder fatigue. When wetsuits are designed with the arms hanging down, this inevitably leads to stress when the swimmer starts to crawl. In this model, the standardised paradigm was reversed by aligning the arms upwards. The result enables faster swimming, better technique and greater mobility.

Statement by the jury
This wetsuit truly embodies an innovation: with its arms pointing upwards, it is possible to simultaneously prevent shoulder pain and optimise performance.

Roka Maverick X definiert den Leistungsstandard von Taucheranzügen neu, indem er der Nummer eins der Beschwerden entgegenwirkt: Ermüdungserscheinungen in den Schultern. Wurden bisherige Taucheranzüge mit den Armen nach unten konstruiert, führt das unvermeidlich zu Anstrengung, wenn der Schwimmer zu kraulen beginnt. Bei diesem Modell wurde das standardisierte Paradigma umgekehrt, indem die Arme nach oben ausgerichtet wurden. Das Ergebnis ist, dass außerdem schnelleres Schwimmen, eine bessere Technik und mehr Mobilität möglich sind.

Begründung der Jury
Dieser Taucheranzug verkörpert in der Tat eine Innovation: Mit seinen nach oben ausgerichteten Armen lässt sich zugleich Schulterbeschwerden vorbeugen und die Leistung optimieren.

evoDISC Glove
Goalkeeper Gloves
Torwarthandschuh

Manufacturer
PUMA SE, Herzogenaurach, Germany
In-house design
James Eaton
Web
www.puma.com

The evoDISC goalkeeper gloves made of latex, polyester and neoprene are professional competition gloves. Their special feature is the new Disc closing system that allows for a custom fit around the hand and wrist. The hybrid RC/IS-Cut ensures a tight yet comfortable fit. A 4 mm thick Ultimate Grip Latex palm ensures very good grip in all weather conditions and maximum ball contact. Air Zone sections enhance breathability and the embossed Strike Zone increases protection.

Statement by the jury
The first-rate fit and selected material qualities are the outstanding features of the elaborately designed evoDISC goalkeeper gloves.

Die Torwarthandschuhe evoDISC aus Latex, Polyester und Neopren sind professionelle Wettkampfhandschuhe. Ihre Besonderheit ist das neue DISC-Verschlusssystem, das sich ausgezeichnet um Hand und Handgelenk schmiegt. Der hybride RC/IS-Cut ermöglicht dabei eine enge, dennoch komfortable Passform. Eine 4 mm dicke Ultimate-Grip-Latexschicht an der gesamten Innenfläche sorgt für sehr gute Griffigkeit bei jedem Wetter sowie für bestmöglichen Ballkontakt. Ein Air-Zone-Element erhöht die Atmungsaktivität und die geprägte Strike Zone den Schutz.

Begründung der Jury
Seine erstklassige Passform und ausgesuchte Materialqualitäten sind die hervorstechenden Merkmale des durchdacht entworfenen Torwarthandschuhs evoDISC.

Pro-Armor
Body Protector
Schutzweste

Manufacturer
Dainese S.p.A., Molvena (Vicenza), Italy
In-house design
Web
www.dainese.com

Pro-Armor is a family of body protectors that combines a special design with innovative materials. Inspired by natural fractals, such as leaves or snowflakes, the Pro-Armor pattern increases the level of protection in areas where the impact risk is high. At the same time, it provides flexibility and ventilation in other areas. This property is enhanced by the material used, a carbon-based nanometric structure, that converts impact energy into heat.

Statement by the jury
Using patterns found in nature for increased protection, and applying new materials intelligently, is evidence of an innovative design approach.

Pro-Armor ist eine Familie von Körperprotektoren, die eine besondere Formensprache mit innovativen Materialien verbindet. Von Fraktalen aus der Natur wie Blättern oder Schneeflocken inspiriert, steigert das Muster von Pro-Armor den Schutzfaktor in Bereichen, in denen das Schlagrisiko hoch ist, und bietet gleichzeitig Flexibilität und Belüftung an anderen Stellen. Diese Eigenschaft wird auch durch das verwendete Material, eine kohlenstoffbasierte nanometrische Struktur, gefördert, die die Stoßenergie in Wärme umwandelt.

Begründung der Jury
Mithilfe von Mustern aus der Natur für höheren Schutz zu sorgen und neue Materialien intelligent einzusetzen, zeugt von einem innovativen Gestaltungsansatz.

Z3 Helmet
Ski and Snowboard Helmet
Ski- und Snowboardhelm

Manufacturer
HMR Helmets®, Hammer s.r.l.,
Casazza (Bergamo), Italy
Design
Prototipi s.a.s. (Massimo Facchinetti),
Casazza (Bergamo), Italy
Web
www.hmrhelmets.it
www.prototipi.org

The Z3 ski helmet features an outer shell made of high-strength polycarbonate and an inner shell made of polystyrene foam with a ventilated structure. Two aerators in the upper area, and a vent in the rear area, ensure balanced air circulation and the removal of moist air. They comply with the class A CE standards 1077, and keep foreign particles at bay thanks to a steel net. The soft ear pads are made of thermoformed material and synthetic leather; they are protected by a net, which allows the surroundings to be easily audible.

Statement by the jury
The ski helmet Z3 appeals with a sophisticated ventilation system, which ensures that air can circulate evenly and that moisture can escape.

Der Skihelm Z3 besitzt eine Außenhülle aus hochfestem Polycarbonat und eine Innenschale aus Polystyrolschaum mit belüfteter Struktur. Eine ausgewogene Luftzirkulation und den Abtransport feuchter Luft gewährleisten zwei Belüfter im oberen und ein Entlüfter im hinteren Bereich, die den CE-Normen 1077 der Klasse A entsprechen und dank eines Stahlnetzes Fremdkörper fernhalten. Die weichen Ohrpolster sind aus thermogeformtem Material und Kunstleder gefertigt und durch ein Netz geschützt, wobei sich Außengeräusche noch gut wahrnehmen lassen.

Begründung der Jury
Der Skihelm Z3 besticht durch ein ausgeklügeltes Be- und Entlüftungssystem, das dafür sorgt, dass die Luft gleichmäßig zirkuliert und die Feuchtigkeit abfließen kann.

Pista GP-R
Motorcycle Helmet
Motorradhelm

Manufacturer
Dainese S.p.A., Molvena (Vicenza), Italy
In-house design
Web
www.dainese.com

Developed in collaboration with the MotoGP legend Valentino Rossi, Pista GP-R is characterised by a high degree of passive as well as active safety, comfort and performance. Its shell, which exceeds the safety requirements, consists of 100 % carbon and is layered with a five-density EPS structure for lightness. The 5-mm thick new Race 3 visor features a patented locking system for solid protection, as well as the Max Pinlock 120 technology for maximum vision in any weather.

Statement by the jury
In combination with its high safety standards, the quality of the materials and manufacture make the Pista GP-R the number one choice for professional helmets.

Der in Zusammenarbeit mit der MotoGP-Legende Valentino Rossi entworfene Motorradhelm Pista GP-R zeichnet sich durch ein hohes Maß an passiver wie aktiver Sicherheit, Komfort und Leistung aus. Seine Schale besteht zu 100 Prozent aus Carbon und ist mit einer 5-Dichte-EPS-Schale zu einer leichten Struktur geschichtet, die den Sicherheitsanforderungen weit übertrifft. Das 5 mm dicke New-Race-3-Visier verfügt über ein patentiertes Schließsystem für soliden Schutz sowie die Max-Pinlock-120-Technologie für maximale Sicht bei jedem Wetter.

Begründung der Jury
Die Qualität der Materialien und Verarbeitung machen den Pista GP-R zusammen mit seinen hohen Sicherheitsstandards zum Profihelm erster Wahl.

Vayu
Climbing Helmet
Kletterhelm

Manufacturer
SALEWA, Oberalp SpA, Bolzano, Italy
Design
MFOR Srl – Mind Forward, Bolzano, Italy
Web
www.salewa.com
www.mfor.eu

Vayu is a particularly lightweight, comfortable and hard-wearing climbing helmet, which is characterised by its innovative construction and the use of Carbon Nano Tech. The shock-resistant outer shell is made from high performance polymer reinforced with carbon nanotubes. It features an extremely favourable strength-to-weight ratio and therefore allows minimum wall thickness. Combined with the multi-impact shell this provides exceptional protection and in addition, the large openings ensure good ventilation.

Statement by the jury
The Vayu climbing helmet sets standards: it scores with impressive shock resistance thanks to its innovative Carbon Nano Tech and extremely low weight.

Vayu ist ein besonders leichter, bequemer und strapazierfähiger Kletterhelm, der durch seine innovative Konstruktion und den Einsatz von Carbon-Nano-Technologie gekennzeichnet ist. Die stoßfeste Außenschale aus mit Kohlenstoff-Nanoröhrchen verstärktem Hochleistungspolymer weist ein äußerst günstiges Verhältnis von Gewicht zu Festigkeit auf und erlaubt deshalb minimale Wandstärken. Kombiniert mit der Multi-Impact-Innenschale sorgt dies für eine außergewöhnliche Schutzwirkung, und die großen Öffnungen gewährleisten überdies gute Belüftung.

Begründung der Jury
Der Kletterhelm Vayu setzt Maßstäbe: Er punktet mit eindrucksvoller Stoßfestigkeit dank innovativer Carbon-Nano-Technologie und einem extrem geringen Gewicht.

N-PRO Rugby Head Guard
Medical Grade
Rugby Head Guard
Medizinischer
Rugby-Kopfschutz

Manufacturer
Contego, Galway, Ireland
In-house design
Mark Ganly
Design
Dolmen (Martin Bruggemann, Colin Conlon),
Dublin, Ireland
Thread Design & Development
(Sam Ghazaros), Cardiff, Great Britain
Web
www.n-pro.com
www.dolmen.ie
www.thread-design.co.uk

With the N-Pro Head Guard for rugby players, impact forces can be diminished considerably compared to other head protection. Classified as a non-invasive medical device, the cap consists of viscoelastic materials that reduce the G-force energy transferred to a player's head during linear and rotational impacts, major factors in sports-induced brain injury. A network of large airflow channels has been integrated into the internal surface of the head guard to improve ventilation and curtail overheating of the player.

Statement by the jury
The N-Pro Head Guard impresses with the outstanding head protection that it provides to players. A well-thought-through ventilation system regulates heat and moisture.

Mit dem N-Pro Head Guard für Rugbyspieler lassen sich Stoßkräfte im Vergleich zu anderen Kopfschutzvarianten erheblich verringern. Als nichtinvasives medizinisches Gerät eingestuft, besteht die Kappe aus viskoelastischen Materialien, die die Wirksamkeit der g-Kraft reduzieren, die bei einem linearen Aufprall oder Rotationsaufprall – Hauptursachen sportbedingter Gehirnverletzungen – auf den Kopf des Spielers übertragen wird. Ein Netzwerk großer Luftströmungskanäle wurde in die innere Oberfläche des Kopfschutzes integriert, um die Belüftung zu verbessern und die Überhitzung des Spielers zu vermindern.

Begründung der Jury
Der N-Pro Head Guard besticht durch den überragenden Kopfschutz, den er dem Spieler bietet. Ein ausgeklügeltes Belüftungssystem reguliert Wärme und Feuchtigkeit.

SHR FLEX™
Frontal Head Restraint for
Racecar Drivers
Kopf- und Nackenschutzsystem
für Rennfahrer

Manufacturer
SCHROTH Safety Products GmbH,
Arnsberg, Germany
Design
Creature LLC (Maureen Carroll),
Atlanta, USA
Web
www.schroth.com
www.creaturellc.com

When developing the SHR Flex head restraint system, the focus was on comfort, fit and agility. The result is a dynamic protection system with many technical improvements. While a low collar design works with any seating angle, the flexible shoulder system adapts to the upper body and chest area and ensures excellent stability without further padding. The patented SlipStop surface and additional "wings" for the belt guide increase comfort.

Statement by the jury
The design of the head restraint system SHR Flex has been thought through down to the detail and provides the racer with maximum protection, comfort and agility.

Bei der Entwicklung des Kopf- und Nackenschutzsystems SHR Flex standen Bequemlichkeit, Passform und Beweglichkeit im Vordergrund. Entstanden ist ein dynamisches Schutzsystem mit vielen technischen Verbesserungen. Während ein kurzer Kragen eine winkelunabhängige Sitzposition des Rennfahrers erlaubt, passen sich die biegsamen Schulterstücke seinem Oberkörper und Brustbereich an und gewährleisten ohne weitere Polsterung ausgezeichnete Stabilität. Die patentierte SlipStop-Oberfläche und zusätzliche „Flügel" für die Gurtführung erhöhen den Komfort.

Begründung der Jury
Die bis ins Detail durchdachte Konstruktion des Kopf- und Nackenschutzsystems SHR Flex bietet dem Rennfahrer größtmöglichen Schutz, Komfort und Agilität.

On Target Football
Football
Fußball

Manufacturer
On Target Football,
Maidenhead, Great Britain
In-house design
Web
www.ontargetfootball.com

The aim of the On Target Football is on the one hand to assist young players in training and improving their passing and shooting skills. On the other hand, its markings help coaches to explain and display exactly how and where players should best hit the football. Therefore, it is the ball's task to act as a guide as well as a conventional football.

Statement by the jury
The On Target football is more than a common football: thanks to its markings, it supports the training session in several respects – a real coup.

Intention des On Target Football ist es auf der einen Seite, junge Fußballer darin zu unterstützen, ihre Pass- und Schießfertigkeiten zu trainieren und zu verbessern. Auf der anderen Seite hilft er Trainern mittels der verschiedenen Markierungen dabei, den Spielern genau zu erklären und zu zeigen, wie und an welchen Stellen sie den Fußball am besten treffen sollen. So kommt diesem Ball die Aufgabe zu, als eine Art Lotse zu fungieren und zugleich als herkömmlicher Fußball zum Spielen.

Begründung der Jury
Der On Target Football ist mehr als ein üblicher Fußball: Dass er auch dank Markierungen das Training in mehrfacher Hinsicht unterstützt, ist ein wirklicher Coup.

COOLSHOT 80i VR / COOLSHOT 80 VR
Laser Rangefinders
Laser-Entfernungsmesser

Manufacturer
Nikon Vision Co., Ltd., Tokyo, Japan
In-house design
Yuki Kobayashi
Web
www.nikon.com

These laser rangefinders are equipped with Nikon's optical image stabiliser VR (vibration reduction) and provide precise distance data. Image blurring in the viewfinder due to hand movements is reduced to about one fifth or less, making accurate measurements possible more quickly. The distance to target is visually confirmed by means of the Locked On technology, even in the case of overlapping objects. The compact lightweight housing has an ergonomic design and offers convenient use with very high optical performance.

Statement by the jury
The design of these laser rangefinders blends precise measuring technology and the ergonomic usability of a handy unit into a successful device.

Die mit Nikons optischem Bildstabilisator VR (Vibration Reduction) ausgestatteten Laser-Entfernungsmesser liefern präzise Entfernungsangaben. Die durch Handbewegungen im Sucher verursachten Bildverwacklungen werden auf rund ein Fünftel oder weniger reduziert, wodurch schneller genaue Messwerte möglich werden. Mithilfe der Locked-on-Technologie wird auch bei sich überlappenden Objekten visuell die Entfernung zum Ziel bestätigt. Das kompakte und leichte Gehäuse ist ergonomisch gestaltet und bietet eine bequeme Nutzung bei sehr hoher optischer Leistung.

Begründung der Jury
In der Gestaltung dieser Laser-Entfernungsmesser verschmelzen präzise Messtechnik und ergonomische Bedienbarkeit der handlichen Geräte zu einer gelungenen Einheit.

Adidas progressor splite
Goggles
Skibrille

Manufacturer
Silhouette International, Linz, Austria
In-house design
Roland Keplinger, Kristof Retezár
Web
www.adidassporteyewear.com
www.silhouette-international.com

Weighing only 80 grams, the Adidas progressor splite goggles prove to be very lightweight and flexible. Their large field of vision, thanks to the reduced frame, creates ideal viewing conditions making them highly suitable for ski tours. The innovative Climacool ventilation system, with integrated rib structure, provides efficient air circulation inside the goggles so that fogging up is reduced to a minimum. The two-layer thermally formed face foam, with an auto-fit nose part, is breathable and ensures a good fit.

Statement by the jury
The Adidas progressor splite ski goggles appeal with their conveniently large field of vision, which are both functionally and aesthetically impressive.

Die Adidas progressor splite erweist sich mit 80 Gramm als sehr leicht und flexibel. Ihr großes Sichtfeld durch den reduziert gehaltenen Rahmen schafft ideale Sehbedingungen, sodass sie auch bestens für Skitouren geeignet ist. Das innovative Climacool-Belüftungssystem mit integrierter Rippenstruktur ermöglicht eine wirksame Luftzirkulation innerhalb des Glases, sodass die Brille nur minimal beschlägt. Der zweilagige, thermisch geformte Schaumstoff mit automatisch sich anpassender Nasenpartie ist atmungsaktiv und sorgt für einen passgenauen Sitz.

Begründung der Jury
Die Skibrille Adidas progressor splite besticht durch ihr großes praktisches Sichtfeld, das zugleich funktional wie ästhetisch beeindruck

Elan Ibex 84 Carbon xlt
Ski

Manufacturer
Elan, d.o.o., Begunje na Gorenjskem, Slovenia
Design
Gigodesign d.o.o., Ljubljana, Slovenia
Web
www.elanskis.com
www.gigodesign.com

For the Elan Ibex 84 Carbon xlt of the new Ibex ski tour series the tried and tested bridge construction has been re-engineered. The solid wood core slopes from the ski centre to the edges and is reinforced by the hollow carbon tubes of TubeLite construction, which runs along both edges and the ski centre. Under the binding the VaporTip insert, which consists of a high-tech composite compound and an aluminium insert, provides for a secure hold of the binding. This particularly lightweight ski is suitable for skiers who are not put off by long climbs.

Statement by the jury
The sophisticated construction of the Ibex 84 Carbon xlt provides skiers with exactly what they need for long tours: stable hold and low weight.

Für den Elan Ibex 84 Carbon xlt der neuen Ibex Skitourenlinie wurde die bewährte Bridge-Konstruktion überarbeitet. Der Vollholzkern fällt von der Skimitte aus zu den Kanten hin ab und wird durch die aus hohlen Carbonröhren bestehende TubeLite-Konstruktion, die entlang der beiden Kanten und der Skimitte verläuft, verstärkt. Unter der Bindung sorgt das VaporTip Insert aus einer Hightech-Kompositverbindung und einer Aluminiumeinlage für sicheren Halt der Bindung. Dieser besonders leichte Ski eignet sich für Fahrer, die lange Aufstiege nicht scheuen.

Begründung der Jury
Die ausgeklügelte Konstruktion des Ibex 84 Carbon xlt bietet dem Skifahrer genau das, was er auf langen Touren braucht: stabilen Halt und wenig Gewicht.

Walther LGU Varmint
Airgun
Luftgewehr

Manufacturer
Umarex GmbH & Co. KG, Arnsberg, Germany
In-house design
Seunghan Kang
Web
www.umarex.com

The Walther LGU Varmint is a slim, powerful spring piston air rifle whose cocking lever is mounted inconspicuously but effectively under the barrel. This technology permits to use telescopic sights of almost any length. The well-designed trigger system enables to set the first stage travel and the trigger weight. The adjustable rotary piston absorbs the torsion forces of the spring. The rifle also relies on the proven Super Silent Technology and the Vibration Reduction System. It can thus be cocked with hardly any friction and fires very smoothly. Particularly eye-catching is the robust plastic thumbhole stock, which is designed according to ergonomic principles.

Beim Walther LGU Varmint handelt es sich um ein schlankes, energiestarkes Federdruckluftgewehr, dessen Spannhebel unauffällig und effektiv parallel unter dem Lauf angebracht wurde. Diese Technik erlaubt die Montage beliebig langer Zielfernrohre. Das durchdacht gestaltete Abzugssystem ermöglicht die Einstellung des Vorzugswegs und der Abzugskraft. Der einstellbare Drehkolben schluckt die Torsionskräfte der Feder, zudem kommen die bewährte Super-Silent-Technologie und das Vibration-Reduction-System zum Einsatz. Dadurch lässt sich das Luftgewehr fast reibungslos spannen und liegt im Schuss sehr ruhig. Besonders ins Auge springt der unempfindliche, nach ergonomischen Prinzipien entworfene Kunststoff-Lochschaft.

Statement by the jury
The design of the Walther LGU Varmint impresses by a made-to-measure elegance and technical and functional details, which were given great attention.

Begründung der Jury
Die Gestaltung des Walther LGU Varmint überzeugt durch eine maßgeschneiderte Eleganz sowie technische und funktionale Details, denen höchste Aufmerksamkeit zuteilwurde.

Walther KK500 Expert-E
Small-bore Sporting Rifle
Kleinkaliber-Sportgewehr

Manufacturer
Carl Walther GmbH & Co. Produktions KG,
Ulm, Germany
In-house design
Thomas Bretschneider
Web
www.carl-walther.com

The functional and clear-cut design of the Walther KK500 Expert-E contrasts the aluminium stock with the black barrel and the ergonomically shaped grip, made of blue laminated wood. With the patented AMBI Action System, the bolt lever can be moved from left to right without using any tools. An e-trigger guarantees wear-free and exact trigger settings for several hundred thousand shots. The LED charge-level indicator and the built-in rechargeable battery ensure that the rifle is quickly charged and ready to fire.

Das klar und funktional gestaltete Walther KK500 Expert-E setzt den Aluminium-schaft in Kontrast zum schwarzen Lauf und dem ergonomisch geformten Griff aus blauem Schichtholz. Mit dem patentierten AMBI-Action-System lässt sich der Kammerstängel mit wenigen Handgriffen ohne Werkzeug von links auf rechts umstellen. Ein E-Abzug gewährleistet verschleißfreie und exakte Abzugseinstellungen für mehrere hunderttausend Schuss. Die LED-Ladestandsanzeige und der eingebaute Akku stellen die Schussbereitschaft und schnelles Aufladen sicher.

Statement by the jury
With a timeless design, the KK500 Expert-E sports rifle manages to house technology, that is both modern and extremely precise, in a compact space.

Begründung der Jury
Auf kompaktem Raum und in einer zeit-losen Gestaltung gelingt es dem Sport-gewehr KK500 Expert-E, eine hochpräzise wie moderne Technik unterzubringen.

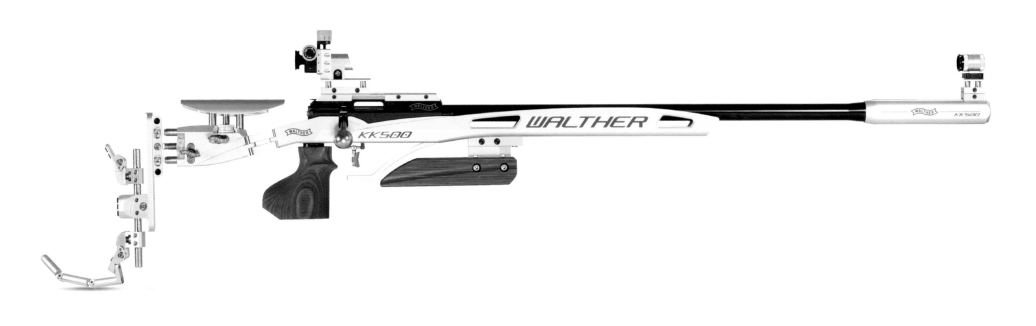

Freyr 280 titanium
Suppressor for Hunting
Schalldämpfer für Jäger

Manufacturer
Freyr Devik AS, Oslo, Norway
In-house design
Eggert Freyr Gudjonsson,
Heidi Devik Ekstrøm
Web
www.freyr-devik.no

A good suppressor not only protects the hearing of hunters and hounds but also reduces recoil and muzzle blast. This greatly improves shooting. To counteract reservations about suppressors, the design puts the focus of the Freyr 280 titanium on being user-friendly, lightweight and robust while the streamlined encapsulation fits elegantly onto the barrel of a classic hunting weapon. For its size and weight the Freyr 280 titanium offers a substantial noise reduction of up to 28 dB.

Ein guter Schalldämpfer schützt nicht nur das Gehör von Jäger und Hund, sondern reduziert auch den Rückstoß und verringert den Mündungsknall. Das verbessert das Schießen erheblich. Um Vorbehalten gegenüber Schalldämpfern entgegenzuwirken, wurde der Schwerpunkt bei der Gestaltung des Freyr 280 titanium auf Benutzerfreundlichkeit, Leichtigkeit und Robustheit gelegt. Elegant lässt sich das stromlinienförmige Gehäuse auf den Lauf einer klassischen Jagdwaffe aufsetzen. Angesichts seiner Größe und seines Gewichts beeindruckt der Freyr 280 titanium mit einer Dämpfung von bis zu 28 dB.

Statement by the jury
The design of the Freyr 280 titanium suppressor successfully reflects its highly functional quality in an aesthetic appearance.

Begründung der Jury
Bei der Gestaltung des Schalldämpfers Freyr 280 titanium ist es gelungen, seine hohe funktionale Qualität in einem ästhetischen Erscheinungsbild zu spiegeln.

ZØRE X™
Smart Lock
Intelligentes Waffenschloss

Manufacturer
ZØRE, Jerusalem, Israel
In-house design
Guni Kofman, Yalon Fishbein
Web
www.zore.life
Honourable Mention

The designers of Zøre X pursued the goal of making guns safer through a locking device that prevents unauthorised use of the firearm yet enables near-immediate usability. The lock fits inside the chamber of the gun and once unlocked, ejects immediately when charging the firearm. Its dial is designed to allow quick unlocking under any circumstances. The Zøre X can also send notifications to the holder's smartphone if someone tries tampering with the device. It is developed with great care in terms of functionality and robustness.

Zøre X wurde mit dem Ziel entworfen, Schusswaffen durch eine Sperrvorrichtung sicherer zu machen, die den unerlaubten Gebrauch der Feuerwaffe verhindert, doch deren fast unmittelbaren Einsatz zulässt. Die Sperre passt in die Kammer der Waffe und wird, sobald sie entsperrt wird, beim Laden sofort ausgeworfen. Ihr Rad ist so gestaltet, dass man die Waffe unter allen Umständen schnell entsperren kann. Sollte sich jemand an der Waffe zu schaffen machen, sendet Zøre X eine Nachricht an das Smartphone des Besitzers. Große Sorgfalt wurde bei der Entwicklung auf Funktionalität und Widerstandsfähigkeit gelegt.

Statement by the jury
The intention to make weapons safer through Zøre X deserves recognition. In its implementation, the gun lock impresses with its high functionality.

Begründung der Jury
Die Intention, Waffen mithilfe des Zøre X sicherer zu machen, verdient Anerkennung. In der Umsetzung überzeugt das Waffenschloss durch seine hohe Funktionalität.

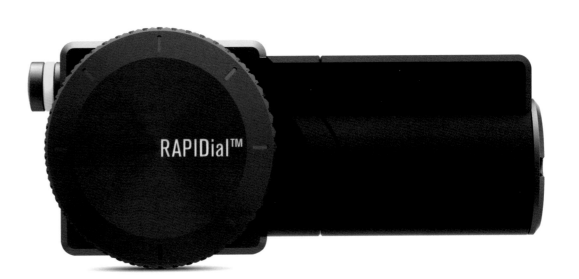

Loop 15X
Scuba regulator
Atemregler

Manufacturer
Mares S.p.A., Rapallo (Genoa), Italy
In-house design
Christof Oelrich, Gabriele Vescovi
Web
www.mares.com

The Loop 15X is all about providing a relaxed and highly comfortable way of breathing. This patented second stage is symmetrically designed with a central, vertically oriented, hose connector. The intermediate pressure hose connecting the second stage with the bottle does not run over the diver's right shoulder as customary but under the arm thus preventing the jaw muscles from getting tired. Thanks to the symmetrical structure, the Loop can be carried on the right side as well as on the left side.

Beim Loop 15X steht der entspannte hohe Atemkomfort im Vordergrund. Die patentierte zweite Stufe ist mit einem mittigen, senkrecht ausgerichteten Schlauchanschluss symmetrisch aufgebaut. Der Mitteldruckschlauch, der die zweite Stufe mit der Flasche verbindet, verläuft unter dem Arm des Tauchers und verhindert durch den sonst über die rechte Schulter geführten Schlauch, dass die Kiefermuskulatur ermüdet. Dank des symmetrischen Aufbaus kann der Loop auf der rechten wie der linken Seite getragen werden.

Statement by the jury
The design of the regulator Loop 15X impresses by the neutral positioning of the hose, which ensures natural breathing during the dive.

Begründung der Jury
Die Gestaltung des Atemreglers Loop 15X überzeugt durch die neutrale Positionierung des Schlauchs, die für natürliches Atmen während des Tauchgangs sorgt.

V-Class Vue Goggle
Unisex Swimming Goggle
Unisex-Schwimmbrille

Manufacturer
Speedo International Ltd,
Nottingham, Great Britain
In-house design
Speedo Design Team
Design
Raymont-Osman Product Design,
Leamington Spa, Great Britain
V2 Studios, London, Great Britain
Web
www.speedo.com
www.raymont-osman.com
www.v2studios.com

The V-Class Vue goggle aims to raise the bar in both styling and craftsmanship within this product category in order to make a goggle a purchase of desirability rather than just functionality. Superior anti-fog coating on the lens provides fog-free protection that is two times longer lasting than regular goggles. The IQfit technology, based on research data from global head scanning, ensures a leak-free, precise fit and helps to reduce red marks around the eyes.

Statement by the jury
The unisex swimming goggles were devised with high technical precision. They feature a coating that hardly fogs up, thus offering a very good vision in the water.

Die V-Class-Vue-Schwimmbrille zielt darauf ab, die Messlatte für Gestaltung und Verarbeitung in diesem Produktbereich höher zu legen, sodass man eine Schwimmbrille eher deshalb kauft, weil man sie einfach haben will, und nicht so sehr ihrer Funktionalität wegen. Die überragende Antibeschlagbeschichtung der Linse bietet klare Sicht, und das doppelt so lang wie normale Schwimmbrillen. Die IQfit-Technologie, der Forschungsdaten von Kopfvermessungen zugrunde liegen, sorgt für eine einlaufsichere, präzise Passform und hilft, Druckstellen um die Augen zu reduzieren.

Begründung der Jury
Die Unisex-Schwimmbrille wurde mit hoher formaler Präzision konstruiert. Sie verfügt über eine Beschichtung, die kaum beschlägt und damit sehr gute Sicht im Wasser bietet.

Tomahawk
Inflatable High Pressure Kayak
Aufblasbares Hochdruck-Kajak

Manufacturer
ORPC, Shanghai, China
Design
Pangu Design, Shanghai, China
Web
www.aquamarina.com
www.pangudesign.com

The inflatable kayak Tomahawk sets new standards in terms of rigidity, gliding properties, speed and shape. Engineered for the most challenging paddling environments in coastal regions or on big lakes, its design represents a hybrid of an inflatable kayak and classic canoe. It combines efficiency, stability, storage space and finesse. It is therefore suitable for outings with a light load, it is stable on the water and at the same time it is fast and manoeuvrable. The adjustable drop-stitch air seats, with high back support, provide hours of comfort.

Statement by the jury
The inflatable kayak Tomahawk, which manages to simultaneously fulfil high standards in terms of stability, comfort, mobility and speed, is a real innovation.

Das aufblasbare Kajak Tomahawk setzt neue Maßstäbe bezüglich Steifigkeit, Gleitfähigkeit, Geschwindigkeit und Form. Für schwierigste Paddelumgebungen in Küstennähe oder auf großen Seen konzipiert, verkörpert seine Gestaltung einen Hybrid aus aufblasbarem Kajak und klassischem Kanu. Es vereint Effizienz, Stabilität, Stauraum und Finesse: So eignet es sich für Fahrten mit leichter Last, besitzt eine gute Wasserlage, ist schnell und zugleich wendig. Die justierbaren Nadelzug-Luftsitze mit hoher Stützkraft bieten Komfort auch über Stunden.

Begründung der Jury
Das aufblasbare Kajak Tomahawk, das gleichzeitig die hohen Anforderungen an Stabilität, Komfort, Beweglichkeit und Schnelligkeit erfüllt, ist eine echte Innovation.

Mi Electric Scooter
Mi Elektroroller

Manufacturer
Xiaomi Inc., Beijing, China

In-house design
Xiaomi Inc.

Web
www.mi.com

reddot award 2017
best of the best

On the road with style

Electric scooters are popular because they are highly agile, easy to handle and environmentally friendly. Against this backdrop, the Mi Electric Scooter stands out with a remarkably self-contained look. Its purist design language with contrasting details in red lends it an overall harmonious appearance. Showcasing a clean silhouette, the batteries are placed under the deck for formal consistency. With a maximum load capacity of 150 kg, this electric scooter is also ideally suited for transporting items. It delivers a speed of 25 km/h and allows riders to easily reach a range of 30 km. Also well thought-out in terms of function, the design enhances the comfort of this easy-to-fold scooter. The folding clamp thus sits on the handlebar instead of the deck joint to reinforce security, while the bell trigger was conceived to hook the buckle on the rear mudguard when using the folding mechanism. In addition, the scooter also integrates a reliable braking system. While the front wheel is outfitted with an electronic regenerative brake, the rear wheel features strong disc braking. Both wheels have pneumatic tires so that heat produced from the braking process increases grip and safety. Projecting an attractive and highly consistent design language, this scooter truly fascinates beholders – paired with outstanding performance values, the Mi Electric Scooter has emerged as a stylistically self-reliant and highly functional means of transportation.

Mit Stil unterwegs

Elektroroller sind wegen ihrer Wendigkeit und einfachen Handhabbarkeit beliebte Fahrzeuge, die zudem sehr umweltfreundlich sind. Der Mi Elektroroller zeichnet sich vor diesem Hintergrund durch eine bemerkenswert eigenständige Gestaltung aus. Seine puristische Formensprache mit grafisch rot abgesetzten Details wirkt ausgewogen. Er zeigt eine klare Linienführung, und die Batterien wurden formal stimmig unter das Trittbrett verlegt. Er kann bis maximal 150 kg belastet werden und ist deshalb auch gut für Transportzwecke geeignet. Mit einer Geschwindigkeit von 25 km/h bietet er außerdem eine Reichweite von 30 km. Seine auch funktional sehr durchdachte Gestaltung erhöht den Komfort dieses einfach zusammenklappbaren Rollers. So sitzt der Klappmechanismus an der Lenkstange und nicht am Trittbrett, was die Sicherheit erhöht. Die Klingel wurde so gestaltet, dass beim Zusammenfalten des Rollers die Schließe am hinteren Schutzblech festgehalten wird. Das Konzept des Rollers integriert zudem ein zuverlässiges Bremssystem. Das Vorderrad ist mit einer langlebigen elektronischen Bremse ausgestattet, das Hinterrad verfügt über eine starke Scheibenbremse. Beide Räder haben Luftreifen, die beim Bremsprozess entstehende Wärme erhöht deren Griffigkeit und dadurch die Sicherheit. Mit seiner schlüssigen und attraktiven Formensprache begeistert der Mi Elektroroller den Betrachter – dies und seine Leistungswerte definieren ihn als ein stilsicheres und überaus funktionales Fortbewegungsmittel.

Statement by the jury

The Mi Electric Scooter stands out as it delivers new possibilities for using a scooter. With its high-performance characteristics and a range of up to 30 km it allows for a myriad of different usages, including that it also lends itself for transportation tasks. It features a beautiful and overall harmonious design appearance with carefully crafted details. Riding this electric scooter delivers an experience all of its own.

Begründung der Jury

Der Mi Elektroroller sticht hervor, da er neue Möglichkeiten für die Nutzung eines Rollers bietet. Er ist sehr leistungsfähig und mit einer Reichweite von 30 km kann er sehr vielseitig und auf unterschiedlichste Weise verwendet werden. Er eignet sich deshalb auch gut für den Transportbereich. Sein formschönes Design ist ausgewogen, wobei jedes Detail gut ausgeführt wurde. Das Fahren mit diesem Elektroroller ist ein besonderes Erlebnis.

Designer portrait
See page 54
Siehe Seite 54

Peugeot Micro e-Kick
Electric Hybrid Scooter
Elektrischer Hybrid-Scooter

Manufacturer
Micro Mobility Systems AG, Küsnacht, Switzerland
In-house design
Design
Peugeot Design Lab, Vélizy-Villacoublay, France
Web
www.micro.ms
www.peugeotdesignlab.com

The Peugeot Micro e-Kick is a stylish
and functional electric scooter that can
be easily folded up and stowed after
use, and it can be elegantly pulled along
thanks to its convertible handlebar
with trolley function. With 8.5 kilos it
is particularly lightweight and achieves
a range of 12 kilometres. By stepping
on the brake three times, the motor is
switched off and the Peugeot Micro
e-Kick can be ridden like a normal scooter. The vehicle is fully charged after
60 minutes.

Statement by the jury
Innovative e-mobility in urban centres –
the Peugeot Micro e-Kick makes it possible by combining mature technology
with special aesthetical and functional
details.

Der Peugeot Micro e-Kick ist ein stilvoller
und funktionaler Elektroscooter, der sich
nach seinem Einsatz problemlos zusammenklappen und verstauen oder dank der wan-
delbaren Lenkstange mit Trolleyfunktion
elegant hinterherziehen lässt. Mit 8,5 kg ist
er besonders leicht und erzielt eine Reichweite von 12 Kilometern. Bei dreimaligem
Betätigen der Bremse setzt der Motor
aus und der Peugeot Micro e-Kick kann wie
ein normaler Scooter gefahren werden.
Nach 60 Minuten ist das Fahrzeug voll
aufgeladen.

Begründung der Jury
Innovative E-Mobilität in urbanen Zentren –
das macht der Peugeot Micro e-Kick
möglich, indem er ausgereifte Technik mit
besonderen ästhetischen und funktionalen
Details verbindet.

LOU Electric Skateboard
Electric Skateboard
Elektro-Skateboard

Manufacturer
e-xperience GmbH, Flawil, Switzerland
In-house design
Web
www.e-xperience.ch

Lou looks like a normal skateboard but in fact it is a game changer. It is highly suitable for commuters as it offers a daily practical benefit as well as a pleasurable experience. The particularly lightweight, fast and easy-to-handle e-board can be driven noiselessly up to 25 km. Without effort, it accelerates up to 35 km/h. It combines state-of-the-art know-how with exceptional robustness. The Swiss crosshatch pattern on the deck ensures good grip. Except for the deck, Lou consists entirely of carbon fibres.

Statement by the jury
Highly efficient technology and a robust design for optimal functional use characterize Lou as a means of transport that is both practical and good fun.

Lou sieht aus wie ein normales Skateboard, setzt jedoch ganz neue Standards und ist sehr gut für Pendler als Kombination aus täglichem Nutzwert plus Fahrspaß geeignet. Das besonders leichte, schnelle und einfach zu handhabende E-Board lässt sich geräuschlos bis zu 25 km weit fahren und dabei ohne Anstrengung auf bis zu 35 km/h beschleunigen. Es verbindet aktuelles technisches Know-how mit außergewöhnlicher Robustheit. Das Muster mit dem Schweizerkreuz auf der Oberseite sorgt für guten Griff. Bis auf diese besteht Lou aus Carbonfasern.

Begründung der Jury
Hocheffiziente Technik und eine auf optimalen funktionalen Gebrauch setzende stabile Gestaltung kennzeichnen Lou als praktisches und viel Freude bereitendes Transportmittel.

SPECTRA
E-Mobility Tool
E-Mobilitäts-Tool

Manufacturer
Walnut Technology Limited, Hong Kong
In-house design
Yik Hang Pang
Design
Creadesign (Prof. Hannu Kähönen), Helsinki, Finland
Web
www.walnuttech.co
www.creadesign.fi

Spectra is an electric mobility tool that makes passenger transport more economical by changing the kind of locomotion. With a length of 49 cm, it is a very small and at the same time lightweight electric skateboard and is available with two direct drive motors. Spectra Pro weighs 5.5 kilos and Spectra Lite 4.5 kilos. Unlike other e-skateboards, Spectra can be controlled directly by the user's posture using an intelligent detection algorithm and pressure sensor instead of a Bluetooth remote control.

Statement by the jury
The e-skateboard Spectra is very suitable for moving around in urban areas. It is light and handy and also impresses by its control mechanism.

Spectra ist ein elektrisches Mobility Tool, das die Personenbeförderung wirtschaftlicher macht, indem es die Art unserer Fortbewegung verändert. Mit einer Länge von 49 cm ist es ein sehr kleines und dabei leichtes elektrisches Skateboard, das mit zwei Direktantriebsmotoren erhältlich ist: Spectra Pro wiegt 5,5 kg und Spectra Lite 4,5 kg. Anders als andere E-Skateboards lässt sich Spectra direkt durch die Körperhaltung des Benutzers mithilfe eines intelligenten Erkennungsalgorithmus und durch Drucksensoren statt Bluetooth-Fernbedienung steuern.

Begründung der Jury
Das E-Skateboard Spectra eignet sich sehr gut für die Fortbewegung im urbanen Raum. Es ist leicht und handlich und überzeugt zudem durch seinen Steuerungsmechanismus.

The Mellow Drive
Electric Skateboard Drive
Elektrischer Skateboardantrieb

Manufacturer
Mellow Boards GmbH, Hamburg, Germany
Design
Andi Kern, Hamburg, Germany
Christoph Philipp Schreiber, Dresden, Germany
Web
www.mellowboards.com

Only four screws are required to mount the electric Mellow Drive under any skateboard, thus presenting a compact urban e-mobility solution. The unibody magnesium frame protects the electronic system and the swappable battery pack. Two motors hide inside the wheels, which can accelerate up to 40 km/h. The user interface is just one button, surrounded by an LED ring which indicates the state of charge, an action in progress or a safety warning. The intuitive remote device with slide control accelerates when moved forward and brakes when moved backwards. It also allows to choose between four riding modes from Rookie to Pro.

Der elektrische Antrieb Mellow Drive lässt sich mit nur vier Schrauben unter jedes Skateboard montieren und stellt eine kompakte E-Mobility-Lösung für die Stadt dar. Der aus einem Stück gefertigte Magnesiumrahmen schützt die Elektronik und den auswechselbaren Batteriepack. In den Rollen verbergen sich zwei Motoren, die auf bis zu 40 km/h beschleunigen. Die Bedienoberfläche ist nur ein Knopf, umschlossen von einem LED-Ring, der den Ladezustand, einen Vorgang oder einen Sicherheitshinweis anzeigt. Die intuitive Handsteuerung mit Schieberegler gibt Gas, wenn sie nach vorn geschoben wird, und bremst beim Zurückziehen. Sie erlaubt zudem, per Knopfdruck zwischen vier Fahrmodi von Rookie bis Pro zu wählen.

Statement by the jury
As a simple and intelligent solution, the electric Mellow Drive with its remote control transforms regular skateboards into a sustainable means of transport.

Begründung der Jury
Der elektrische Mellow Drive mit seiner Handsteuerung macht als einfache und intelligente Lösung aus herkömmlichen Skateboards ein nachhaltiges Verkehrsmittel.

MODI
Modular DIY Device
Modulares Heimwerkergerät

Manufacturer
Luxrobo, Seoul, South Korea
In-house design
Jeongin Kim, Yoon Son
Web
www.luxrobo.com

The hardware platform Modi provides 13 different modules for implementable functions, which can be connected via a magnetic connector or a simple "drag and drop"-based coding tool to enable the construction of high-quality electronic devices. Everyone should be able to become an inventor when the threshold for dealing with robotics and coding is reduced. The design therefore focusses on intuitive vision and makes function and type distinguishable by colour and symbols.

Die Hardwareplattform Modi stellt 13 verschiedene Module für implementierbare Funktionen zur Verfügung, die sich über Magnetanschluss oder per einfachem „Drag and Drop"-basiertem Codierungswerkzeug anschließen lassen, um den Bau qualitativ hochwertiger elektronischer Geräte zu ermöglichen. Jeder soll zum Erfinder werden können, indem die Schwelle für die Auseinandersetzung mit Robotik und Codierung gesenkt wird. Die Gestaltung setzt daher auf intuitives Sehen und macht Funktion und Typ durch Farbe und Symbole unterscheidbar.

Statement by the jury
Modi scores as a sophisticated hardware platform that allows to connect different electronic components and to differentiate them easily by means of colours and symbols.

Begründung der Jury
Modi punktet als durchdachte Hardwareplattform, die verschiedene elektronische Komponenten verknüpfbar und mittels Farben und Symbolen leicht differenzierbar macht.

JIMMY'Z Shisha
Waterpipe
Wasserpfeife

Manufacturer
ConsumerNext GmbH, Next Generation
Stimulizer Products, Haren/Ems, Germany
In-house design
Jürgen Gerdes, Meerim Hagen
Web
www.jimmyz.store

The innovations of the water pipe Jimmy'z Shisha address its user-friendliness – the capsule is simply inserted at the bottom of the device, then the start button is pressed – and its design, which is characterised by a clear, simple form. The water pipe is also very eco-friendly because the capsules contain neither tobacco nor coal or nicotine, but instead matcha and caffeine. The empty capsules can be returned to the manufacturer, so that they can be professionally recycled.

Die Innovationen der Wasserpfeife Jimmy'z Shisha liegen in ihrer hohen Nutzerfreundlichkeit – die Kapsel wird einfach an der Unterseite des Geräts eingeführt, dann wird auf den Startbutton gedrückt – und der Gestaltung, die durch eine klare, schlichte Formgebung auffällt. Zudem ist die Umweltverträglichkeit hoch, da die Kapseln weder Tabak noch Kohle oder Nikotin, sondern stattdessen Matcha und Koffein enthalten. Die leeren Kapseln können zurückgeschickt werden, damit sie der Hersteller professionell recycelt.

Statement by the jury
The attraction of this water pipe lies in its distinct, timeless form and easy handling, which makes it a modern accessory in any environment.

Begründung der Jury
Diese Wasserpfeife besticht durch eine klare, zeitlose Gestaltung und einfache Handhabung, die sie zum zeitgemäßen Accessoire in jeder Umgebung machen.

Revstar
Electric Guitar
Elektrogitarre

Manufacturer
Yamaha Corporation,
Hamamatsu, Shizuoka, Japan

In-house design
Piotr Stolarski,
Toshihide Suzuki

Design
forpeople
(Michael Tropper, Joohee Lee,
Mark Jones, Volker Pflueger),
London, Great Britain

Web
www.yamaha.com/design
www.forpeople.co.uk

reddot award 2017
best of the best

Fascinating legend

Electric guitars have always been more than just an instrument for passionate musicians. Since its invention in the 1930s, the electric guitar has been infused with a legendary image, defined last but not least by rock stars like Jimi Hendrix and their revolutionary playing style. The Revstar electric guitar boasts an aesthetic reminiscent of the 1960s. Its design has significantly drawn inspiration from the look of London and Tokyo's vintage street-racing motorbikes of the time and merges it with a clear design language that exudes outstanding elegance enhanced by high-quality details. In line with the 50-year heritage of Yamaha guitar craftsmanship, this range of stylistically distinctive electric guitars has emerged as the result of an intricate development process. The guitars are excellently engineered to adapt to the different personalities and playing styles of musicians. Each detail has been carefully crafted and honed to lend each model a unique personality and secure its place in the range. Remarkable design aspects include the curves and contours of the ground-up body shape, individual colours and finishes, as well as a choice of custom-wound pickups to perfectly match the guitar's character. In this sense, the design of the Revstar collection skilfully embodies an extension of a musical legend – comprising instruments that are as individualistic as the guitarists who play them.

Faszination eines Mythos

Die elektrische Gitarre war für Musiker schon immer mehr als nur ein Instrument. Seit ihrer Entwicklung in den 1930er Jahren haben Stars wie etwa Jimi Hendrix mit ihrem revolutionären Gitarrenspiel einen besonderen Mythos geprägt. Mit der Elektrogitarre Revstar entstand eine Gitarre, deren Ästhetik an die 1960er Jahre erinnert. Ihre Gestaltung wurde maßgeblich inspiriert von der Anmutung der Straßenmotorräder Londons und Tokios in dieser Zeit und zeigt eine klare Formensprache, die der Gitarre durch hochwertige Details eine besondere Eleganz verleiht. Im Einklang mit der seit 50 Jahren bestehenden handwerklichen Tradition der Yamaha-Gitarren entstand nach einem aufwendigen Entwicklungsprozess eine Kollektion von stilistisch unterschiedlichen Gitarren. Sie sind technisch exzellent ausgestattet, um sich den verschiedenen Stilen und Spielweisen der Musiker anzupassen. Jedes Detail wurde sorgfältig entworfen und konstruiert, um diesen Gitarren eine individuelle Persönlichkeit zu verleihen und so ihren Platz in der Kollektion zu sichern. Prägnante Aspekte des Designs sind die Kurven und Konturen der Korpusgestaltung, unverwechselbare Farben und Oberflächen sowie die auf den jeweiligen Musiker abgestimmten Tonabnehmer, die perfekt dem Charakter der Gitarre entsprechen. In diesem Sinne knüpft die Gestaltung der Revstar-Kollektion gekonnt an einen Mythos an – mit Instrumenten, die so individuell sind wie die Gitarristen, die sie spielen.

Statement by the jury

The Revstar electric guitar merges the fascinating appearance of classic guitar models with the sophisticated use of highly advanced technology. It showcases a refined design quality with perfectly implemented details and finishes. Timeless in appearance, it delivers outstanding sound quality. Firmly embedded in the Yamaha tradition of craftsmanship, this range of electric guitars manages to project a new experience of the Yamaha brand.

Begründung der Jury

Bei der Elektrogitarre Revstar verbindet sich die Faszination klassischer Gitarrenmodelle mit dem raffinierten Einsatz hochentwickelter Technologie in ihrem Inneren. Sie zeigt eine ausgereifte gestalterische Qualität, alle Details wie auch die Oberflächen sind perfekt ausgeführt. In ihrem Design zeitlos, bietet sie Musikern einen ausgezeichneten Sound. Man kann die Marke Yamaha neu erleben, und es wird zugleich eine enge Beziehung zu deren Tradition und Gitarren-Handwerkskunst etabliert.

Designer portrait
See page 56
Siehe Seite 56

Poputar P1
Smart Guitar
Intelligente Gitarre

Manufacturer
Shenzhen Shigan Culture
Technology Co., Ltd., Shenzhen, China
In-house design
Jun-Da Ye, Qi-Ran Song, Yan Huang,
Fei-Fei Li, Yu-Jie Hao
Web
www.poputar.com

Poputar was designed for beginners with
the aim to learn playing the guitar
quickly and in an entertaining way. With
120 LEDs, integrated into the neck of
the guitar, users can immediately perceive the position of the chords visually;
they need not worry about forgetting
where to put their fingers. In addition,
Poputar P1 and a corresponding app contain a sound and rhythm game with
sound recognition in real-time. Thus, it
is possible to learn how to make music
through the eyes, and it quickly sounds
like the real version of a professional
guitarist.

Statement by the jury
The guitar Poputar P1 surprises with a
truly striking innovation: by using LEDs
on the guitar neck, playing can be
learned solely visually without any conventional methods.

Poputar P1 wurde für Anfänger gestaltet
mit dem Ziel, dass sie die Fertigkeiten des
Gitarrenspiels schnell und auf unterhalt-
same Art erlernen. Anhand von 120 LEDs,
die in den Gitarrenhals integriert wurden,
können Benutzer die Position der Akkorde
sofort visuell wahrnehmen und brauchen
keine Sorge zu haben, dass sie vergessen,
wohin sie die Finger setzen müssen. Außerdem enthalten Poputar P1 und eine dazugehörige App ein Ton- und Rhythmusspiel
mit Sounderkennung in Echtzeit, mit dem
sich Musikmachen vermittelt über die
Augen lernen lässt und es schnell wie die
echte Version eines Gitarrenprofis klingt.

Begründung der Jury
Die Gitarre Poputar P1 überrascht durch
eine wahrlich auffallende Innovation: Mithilfe von LEDs auf dem Gitarrenhals lässt
sich das Spielen ganz ohne herkömmliche
Methoden rein visuell erlernen.

YEV
Electric Violin
E-Geige

Manufacturer
Yamaha Corporation, Hamamatsu, Japan
In-house design
Keizo Tatsumi
Web
www.yamaha.com

The electric violin YEV combines excellent playability and natural sound with an extraordinary design. Its remarkably open basic body consists of maple which is reinforced with mahogany bars, combined with selected spruce. The distinctive designed frame was built from five layers of laminated walnut wood formed to a Moebius strip. With approx. 550 grams, the violin hardly weighs more than an acoustic one. A piezo pick-up is integrated into the maple bridge. It renders a warm sound pattern with an overtone spectrum and produces finest play nuances. The resin tailpieces are provided with fine tuners. If required, chin and shoulder rests can be mounted.

Statement by the jury
On the one hand, the electric violin YEV inspires with its unique design and the elaborate manufacture of selected woods, and on the other hand by a sound pattern that comes close to that of an acoustic instrument.

Die elektrische Geige YEV verbindet hervorragende Spielbarkeit und natürlichen Klang mit außergewöhnlichem Design. Ihr bemerkenswert offener Grundkörper besteht aus durch Mahagonistreben verstärktem Ahorn, kombiniert mit erlesener Fichte. Der markant gestaltete Rahmen wurde aus fünf Lagen geschichtetem Walnussholz in einer Möbiusschleife angelegt. Mit ca. 550 Gramm wiegt die Violine kaum mehr als eine akustische. In den Ahornsteg wurde ein Piezo-Tonabnehmer eingebaut, der ein warmes Klangbild mit Obertonspektrum liefert und feinste Nuancen wiedergibt. Die Kunstharz-Saitenhalter sind mit Feinstimmern versehen. Bei Bedarf lassen sich Kinn- und Schulterstütze montieren.

Begründung der Jury
Die elektrische Geige YEV begeistert zum einen durch ihre eigenständige Gestaltung und die aufwendige Verarbeitung ausgesuchter Hölzer und zum anderen durch ein Klangbild, das einem akustischen Instrument nahekommt.

Delta
Musical Instrument
Musikinstrument

Manufacturer
Salvi Harps, NSM s.p.a., Piasco (Cuneo), Italy
Design
Joris Beets Design (Keri Armendariz),
London, Great Britain
Web
www.delta-harp.com

Delta combines traditional harp craftsmanship with a solid body and cutting-
edge audio technology to a professional-
sounding instrument. The placement
of the pins and levers in controversial
straight lines leads to a significant size
reduction in the string scale length so
that an extended bass range could be accommodated in a portable instrument.
The bridge pickup system provides a clean
sound across the whole frequency spectrum. Delta is compatible with all effect
processors, recording devices and PA
systems.

Delta verbindet traditionelles Harfen-
handwerk mit einem soliden Körper und
modernster Klangtechnologie zu einem
professionell klingenden Instrument. Die
Platzierung der Stifte und Hebel in kontro-
versen Geraden führt zu einer signifikanten
Größenverringerung der Saitenmaßstabs-
länge, sodass ein erweiterter Bassbereich in
einem tragbaren Instrument untergebracht
werden konnte. Das Brücken-Pickup-System
liefert einen über das gesamte Frequenz-
spektrum verteilten sauberen Klang. Delta
ist mit allen Effektprozessoren, Aufzeich-
nungsgeräten und PA-Systemen kompatibel.

Statement by the jury
The Delta harp presents an innovative
symbiosis of classical craftsmanship and
the latest technology – the result is a
compact melodic instrument.

Begründung der Jury
Die Harfe Delta stellt eine innovative
Symbiose von klassischer Handwerkskunst
und neuester Technologie dar – mit dem
Ergebnis eines kompakten, wohlklingenden
Instruments.

Roland FP-90
Digital Piano

Manufacturer
Roland Corporation,
Hamamatsu, Shizuoka, Japan

Design
GBO Innovation Makers,
Antwerp, Belgium

Web
www.roland.com
www.gbo.eu

reddot award 2017
best of the best

Luxuriously interpreted

The fast development of touch-sensitive keyboard technology in the 1970's facilitates the creation of modern digital pianos with authentic playing touch such as Roland EP-30. The recent Roland FP-90 is a contemporary digital piano with an expressively minimalist appearance. It has been designed with the objective of lending it an easy-to-read and easy-to-use interface. The digital piano's newly designed "light-guiding" lens technology ensures that each button is highly visible, even on dark stages. Elastic coil springs used within each button mechanism mean that they feel very pleasant to the touch when pushed. Another fascinating feature is the design of the speaker system and how it was integrated to fit into the compact dimension of the housing to deliver powerful, high-quality audio. By adopting high-efficiency amplifiers and by fine-tuning the bass reflex port to suit the flat cabinet, a clear and evocative sound is achieved. Another distinctive feature is the slim profile of the keyboard's end blocks, complementing the elegance of the FP-90. They underline its expressive performance as much as the recessed design, which reveals the wooden sides of the piano keys at each end of the keyboard. The design of the Roland FP-90 digital piano thus manages to bestow sophisticated technology with a timeless, high-quality appearance – an elegant look that also projects onto the musicians on stage.

Luxuriös interpretiert

Mit der rasanten Entwicklung der berührungsempfindlichen Keyboardtechnologie in den 1970er Jahren konnten moderne digitale Pianos mit einem authentischen Spielempfinden kreiert werden, wie etwa das Roland EP-30. Das aktuelle Roland FP-90 ist ein zeitgemäßes Digital-Piano mit einer ausdrucksvollen minimalistischen Formensprache. Gestaltet wurde es vor allem mit der Zielsetzung einer übersichtlichen und einfach zu bedienenden Anwenderschnittstelle. So ermöglicht eine neu konzipierte „lichtleitende" Linsentechnologie, dass jedes Bedienelement auch auf dunklen Bühnen gut sichtbar ist. In die Tastenmechanik eingepasste elastische Schraubenfedern führen dazu, dass jede Taste auch haptisch sehr angenehm anspricht. Beeindruckend ist zudem, wie das Lautsprechersystem derart gestaltet und auf die kompakten Dimensionen des Gehäuses abgestimmt wurde, dass es eine sehr leistungsstarke und qualitativ hochwertige Klangqualität liefert. Durch den Einsatz hocheffizienter Verstärker und eine Feinanpassung der Bassreflexöffnung an das flache Gehäuse wird ein klarer und eindrucksvoller Klang erreicht. Prägend für die Anmutung des FP-90 sind außerdem die schmal geformten Profile der Endblöcke der Tastatur. Sie unterstreichen seine Ausdruckskraft ebenso wie Vertiefungen, die die Holzseiten der Klaviertasten an jedem Ende der Tastatur sichtbar werden lassen. Der Gestaltung des Digital-Pianos Roland FP-90 gelingt es damit, einer ausgereiften Technologie eine zeitlose und hochwertige Form zu verleihen – mit einer Eleganz, die sich auch auf die Bühnenpräsenz der Musiker überträgt.

Designer portrait
See page 58
Siehe Seite 58

minilogue
Polyphonic Analogue Synthesizer
Polyphoner Analog-Synthesizer

Manufacturer
KORG Inc., Tokyo, Japan
In-house design
Kyosuke Kobayashi
Web
www.korg.com

Meeting the demands of today's musicians, the minilogue presents itself as a modern, fully programmable, polyphonic analogue synthesizer. In addition to newly developed analogue circuitry that produces rich sounds, its polyphonic step and motion sequencer, tape-echo-inspired delay effect, countless sound manipulation and filter options are very inspiring. The panel-mounted OLED display can also be used as an oscilloscope to view the generated waveform.

Statement by the jury
The polyphonic synthesizer minilogue fascinates with its technical power spectrum by combining the characteristic analogue sound with the advantages of digital technology.

Den Bedürfnissen der Musiker von heute entgegenkommend, präsentiert sich der minilogue als voll programmierbarer polyphoner Analogsynthesizer. Äußerst anregend sind neben einer neu entwickelten analogen Schaltungsanordnung, die für satte Sounds sorgt, die polyphonen Step- und Motion-Sequenzer, der von einem Bandecho inspirierten Delay-Effekt sowie unzählige Klangmanipulations- und Filteroptionen. Das am Schaltpult angebrachte OLED-Display kann auch als Oszilloskop verwendet werden, um die jeweils erzeugte Wellenform zu veranschaulichen.

Begründung der Jury
Der polyphone Synthesizer minilogue begeistert durch sein technisches Leistungsspektrum, indem er den unverwechselbaren analogen Sound mit den Vorteilen der digitalen Technik verknüpft.

Intellimix Desktop Mixer

Manufacturer
Yellowtec GmbH,
Monheim am Rhein, Germany
In-house design
Hanno Mahr
Web
www.yellowtec.com

The Intellimix Desktop Mixer is characterised by a very slim high-quality aluminium case with well-arranged operational elements. Conventional mechanical faders have been advanced to G-Touch faders, which represent a groove guided, finger-friendly, friction-free level sensor. Thanks to the underlying innovative technology, the faders are not only responsive but also wear- and maintenance-free. The intuitive user interface is rounded off by familiar elements in the form of a multitouch display, push buttons and a rotary control.

Statement by the jury
The Intellimix Desktop Mixer is a sophisticated product in terms of function and design that offers an innovative operational concept and exceptional haptics.

Der Intellimix Desktop Mixer zeichnet sich durch ein sehr schlankes, hochwertiges Aluminiumgehäuse mit übersichtlich angeordneten Bedienelementen aus. Konventionelle mechanische Fader wurden zu G-Touch Fadern weiterentwickelt, die sich durch ihren Führung gebenden, fingerfreundlichen und reibungsfreien Pegelsensor auszeichnen. Dank der innovativen Technologie sind die Fader nicht nur reaktionsschnell, sondern auch verschleiß- und wartungsfrei. Die intuitive Benutzeroberfläche wird abgerundet durch vertraute Elemente wie ein Multitouch-Display, Druckknöpfe und einen Drehregler.

Begründung der Jury
Der Intellimix Desktop Mixer ist ein funktional wie gestalterisch ausgereiftes Produkt, das mit einem innovativen Bedienkonzept und außergewöhnlicher Haptik überzeugt.

The Solution
Guitar Pedalboard
Gitarrenpedalboard

Manufacturer
NEXI industries B.V.,
Alphen aan den Rijn, Netherlands
Design
6'4" design manufactory
(Franziska Faoro, Martin Hajek),
Deventer, Netherlands
Web
www.nexi.eu
www.sixfoot-four.com

The Solution is a practicable pedalboard with eight effect slots for linking up individual pedals, which do not have to be wired together. Among others, it features a built-in power supply, USB sockets for charging tablets or smartphones, an integrated tuner, A/B switch for the amplifier and a three-stage booster. The foot switches are mounted underneath the pedal slots on the edge of the board. It is splash-proof and can therefore be used in the open air when it rains.

Statement by the jury
As the name implies, The Solution solves the problem of the, often large, number of individual pedals by means of an intelligent combination. Furthermore, it is splash-proof and suitable for the stage.

The Solution ist ein praxistaugliches Pedalboard mit acht Effektslots für die Verknüpfung einzelner Bodentreter, die nicht miteinander verkabelt sein müssen. Es verfügt unter anderem über ein eingebautes Netzteil, USB-Buchsen zum Aufladen von Tablets oder Smartphones, einen integrierten Tuner, A/B-Umschalter für den Amplifier und einen dreistufigen Booster. Die Fußschalter sind unterhalb der Pedalslots am Rand des Boards angebracht. Es ist spritzwassergeschützt und kann so auch open air bei Regen genutzt werden.

Begründung der Jury
Wie der Name sagt, ersetzt The Solution die oft große Anzahl von einzelnen Effektpedalen durch eine integrale Lösung. Das Board ist zudem spritzwasserdicht und bühnentauglich.

Mustang GT40
Guitar Amplifier
Gitarrenverstärker

Manufacturer
Fender Musical Instruments Corporation,
Scottsdale, USA
In-house design
Fender Musical Instruments Design Team
Web
www.fender.com

The Mustang GT40 is a powerful, compact amplifier that features two 6.5" speakers and 40 watts of power and a full colour LCD screen. In addition to numerous effects and tone controls, it is equipped with versatile on-board presets, amplifier and loudspeaker models and includes 100 programmed presets. Wirelessly via Bluetooth or WiFi or with the built-in USB port, it connects to a laptop or a mobile device. It is also compatible with Fender Tone, an app for wireless devices.

Statement by the jury
Externally compact and lightweight, the Mustang GT40 conceals numerous state-of-the art high-tech features, which hardly limit its use.

Der Mustang GT40 ist ein leistungsstarker, kompakter Verstärker mit zwei 6,5"-Lautsprechern, 40 Watt Leistung und einem farbigen LCD-Bildschirm. Neben zahlreichen Effekten und Klangregelungen ist er mit vielseitigen On-Board-Presets, Verstärker- und Lautsprecherboxmodellen bestückt und enthält 100 programmierte Voreinstellungen. Drahtlos via Bluetooth und WiFi oder mittels eingebautem USB-Port lässt er sich mit einem Laptop oder einem anderen mobilen Gerät verbinden und ist zudem mit Fender Tone, einer App für drahtlose Geräte, kompatibel.

Begründung der Jury
Äußerlich kompakt und leicht, verbirgt der Mustang GT40 zahlreiche modernste High-tech-Features, die seinem Einsatz kaum Grenzen setzen.

MA 808
Portable PA System
Tragbares Lautsprechersystem

Manufacturer
MIPRO Electronics Co., Ltd., Chiayi, Taiwan
In-house design
Web
www.mipro.com.tw

The MA 808 portable PA system accommodates several wireless microphone receivers, a mixer unit, a two-way speaker, a CD/USB player and a Bluetooth interface for effortless music streaming. Thanks to intelligent charging technology and high-performance, long-life rechargeable batteries, the system can be operated independently of a wired power supply. Quick and easy transport is facilitated by the low weight of the system, its stand and the built-in trolley system. Two hand and pocket transmitters can be comfortably stowed away in the integrated storage compartment.

Statement by the jury
With its well-conceived functions, robust workmanship and user-friendly equipment, this portable PA system is suited for a wide range of applications.

Das mobile Lautsprechersystem MA 808 beherbergt mehrere Funkmikrofonempfänger, eine Mixereinheit, 2-Wege-Lautsprecher, CD/USB-Player und eine Bluetooth-Schnittstelle für problemloses Musik-Streaming. Dank der intelligenten Ladetechnik und der langlebigen, leistungsstarken Akkus kann das System unabhängig von einer kabelgebundenen Stromversorgung verwendet werden. Das geringe Gewicht, der Stativflansch und das eingebaute Trolley-System ermöglichen einen einfachen und schnellen Transport. Je zwei Hand- oder Taschensender können bequem im integrierten Aufbewahrungsfach verstaut werden.

Begründung der Jury
Dank der durchdachten Funktionen, der robusten Ausführung und der benutzerfreundlichen Ausstattung lässt sich das mobile Lautsprechersystem vielfältig einsetzen.

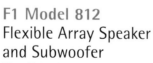

F1 Model 812
Flexible Array Speaker and Subwoofer
Flexible Array Lautsprecher mit Subwoofer

Manufacturer
Bose Design Group, Framingham, USA
In-house design
Bose Design Group
Web
www.bose.com

The portable F1 speaker system is designed for versatile use as it enables users to select four different emission angles to produce optimum sound in any spatial situation. Depending on the arrangement of the speakers, the system automatically adjusts the sound control to the existing configurations, thus ensuring optimum tonal balance for any position. The speakers are accommodated in a flexible and durable acoustic baffle with grips that facilitate convenient transport.

Statement by the jury
This speaker system shows an aesthetically appealing design and, with its sophisticated concept of adjustable emission angles, offers a high degree of flexibility.

Das tragbare F1-Lautsprechersystem lässt sich vielfältig einsetzen, denn es ermöglicht dem Anwender, vier verschiedene Abstrahlwinkel einzustellen, um den für die jeweilige Gegebenheit besten Klang zu produzieren. Je nach Anordnung der Lautsprecher passt das System automatisch die Klangregelung an die Konfiguration an und gewährleistet so die optimale Tonbalance für jede Position. Die Lautsprecher befinden sich in einer flexiblen, widerstandsfähigen Schallwand mit Griffen und können daher bequem transportiert werden.

Begründung der Jury
Das ästhetisch ansprechend gestaltete Lautsprechersystem bietet mit dem ausgeklügelten Konzept der einstellbaren Abstrahlwinkel eine hohe Flexibilität.

ST 24
Wireless Saxophone Set
Drahtloses Saxophon-Set

Manufacturer
MIPRO Electronics Co., Ltd., Chiayi, Taiwan
In-house design
Web
www.mipro.com.tw

The ST 24 saxophone set combines an instrument microphone with a wireless transmitter, allowing musicians to move around while performing, without any cables getting in the way. The soft rubber covers of the microphone clamps protect the instrument from damage and scratches, and at the same time, reduce sound distortion due to structure-borne sound. Connected to the digital sound system, the set ensures a natural and interference-free sound pick-up. The solid manufacturing of the case and high-quality rechargeable batteries provide for long-term usage.

Statement by the jury
The striking innovations of the ST 24 saxophone set are the wireless connection of the microphone with the transmitter and a design that is characterized by longevity.

Das Saxophon-Set ST 24 kombiniert ein Instrumentenmikrofon mit einem drahtlosen Sender und erlaubt es Musikern, sich bei Aufführungen ganz ohne störende Kabel zu bewegen. Die Weichgummiauflagen der Mikrofonklammer schützen vor mechanischen Beschädigungen und Kratzern am Instrument und reduzieren zugleich Klangverfälschungen durch Körperschall. An die Digitaltechnik angeschlossen, gewährleistet das Set natürliche und störungsfreie Tonabnahmen. Das Gehäuse ist solide gefertigt und hochwertige Akkus sorgen für lange Laufzeiten.

Begründung der Jury
Die hervorstechenden Innovationen des Saxophon-Sets ST 24 sind die drahtlose Verbindung des Mikrofons mit dem Sender und eine durch Langlebigkeit gekennzeichnete Gestaltung.

auna Studio-Pro
Microphone

Manufacturer
Chal-Tec GmbH, Berlin, Germany
In-house design
Web
www.chal-tec.com

The auna Studio-Pro is a large diaphragm condenser microphone designed for professional use at home or in a studio. It is suitable for recording instruments, for video blogging or for broadcast and podcast applications. Its special technical feature is a gold-coated 32 mm microphone capsule that provides a wide frequency response and a wide dynamic range. The black metal case accommodates a 3.5 mm headphone jack, as well as a matching monitor mix and volume control. Low self-noise and a high-quality AD/DA converter enable highly accurate audio signals which have captured every detail.

Statement by the jury
The condenser microphone auna Studio-Pro impresses with its versatile range of applications as well as with its high-grade recording quality.

Das auna Studio-Pro ist ein Großmembran-Kondensatormikrofon zur professionellen Nutzung im Heim- und Studiobereich, zur Abnahme von Instrumenten, für Videoblogger oder Broad- und Podcast-Anwendungen. Seine technische Besonderheit ist eine goldbedampfte 32-mm-Mikrofonkapsel, die für einen breiten Frequenzgang und hohen Dynamikumfang sorgt. Das schwarze Metallgehäuse integriert einen 3,5-mm-Klinken-Kopfhörer-Ausgang sowie einen passenden Monitor-Mix- und Lautstärkeregler. Geringes Eigenrauschen und ein qualitätvoller AD/DA-Wandler ermöglichen detailgetreue Tonsignale.

Begründung der Jury
Das Kondensatormikrofon auna Studio-Pro überzeugt durch sein vielseitiges Einsatzspektrum sowie technisch durch eine qualitativ hochwertige Aufnahmequalität.

O-WAND®
Personal Massager
Vibrator

Manufacturer
Mr & Mrs Toy Ltd, Basildon, Great Britain
In-house design
Web
www.o-wand.com

The O-Wand redefines the personal massager. Made from the highest-grade body-safe and velvet-soft silicone, the wand has full CE certification and an automatic "power off" so users never run the risk of the device overheating. Powered by a twin lithium-ion battery pack, the device has four power settings and seven pattern settings allowing the user to alter the vibrations to suit their mood. At its highest intensity, it lasts for over 40 minutes. Thanks to its waterproof, cordless design, it can be enjoyed in up to 1.2 metres of water. Four O-Wand attachments have been designed that all target different pleasure areas. Its striking manageable handle along with its black and gold design emphasises its high quality and modern stylish appearance.

Der O-Wand definiert die Intimmassage neu. Der aus erstklassigem körperfreundlichem und samtig weichem Silikon gefertigte Vibrator mit voller CE-Zertifizierung verfügt über eine Abschaltautomatik, die jede Gefahr einer Überhitzung verhindert. Er wird von einem Twin-Lithium-Ionen-Akku angetrieben, verfügt über vier Intensitätsstufen und kann auf sieben unterschiedliche Modi eingestellt werden, sodass man die Vibrationen seiner Stimmung entsprechend ändern kann. Auf höchster Stufe läuft der O-Wand mindestens 40 Minuten. Dank der wasserfesten, schnurlosen Konstruktion können die Vorteile des Vibrators auch in bis zu 1,20 Meter tiefem Wasser genossen werden. Jeder der vier Aufsätze ist für eine andere erotische Zone konzipiert. Der in Schwarz und Gold ausgeführte, beeindruckend handliche Griff unterstreicht die hohe Qualität und das zeitgemäß stilvolle Erscheinungsbild des Geräts.

Statement by the jury
The vibrator O-Wand catches the eye with its self-confident design, which combines a trend-oriented high-quality appearance with strong engine power.

Begründung der Jury
Der Vibrator O-Wand fällt durch seine selbstbewusste Gestaltung ins Auge. Sie verknüpft ein trendorientiertes hochwertiges Äußeres mit starker Motorleistung.

You can also find this product in
Dieses Produkt finden Sie auch in
Enjoying
Page 141
Seite 141

TENGA SVR
Couples' Vibrator
Partnervibrator

Manufacturer
TENGA Co., Ltd., Tokyo, Japan
In-house design
Kengo Nakamura
Web
www.tenga-global.com

Tenga SVR is a slim vibrator for partnered use, which is made of soft, dust-repellant silicone. It features a long, slim and discreet design to offer enhanced pleasure to the key points. When it was being developed, great attention was paid to the size of the ring to ensure that it does not slip or cause any discomfort to the wearer. The rechargeable, water-proof Tenga SVR is controlled by only one button; it offers five intensity levels and two pulsating options.

Statement by the jury
The Tenga SVR catches the eye with its slim shape and surprises with its dual function, which is capable of equally addressing both partners' needs.

Tenga SVR ist ein schlanker, aus weichem und staubabweisendem Silikon hergestellter Vibrator für beide Partner. Er wurde lang, schmal und dabei dezent gestaltet, um erhöhtes Vergnügen an den entscheidenden Stellen zu bieten. Während der Entwicklung wurde besonderes Augenmerk auf die Größe des Rings gelegt, um sicherzustellen, dass er nicht verrutscht und beim Träger kein Unbehagen hervorruft. Der wiederaufladbare, wasserdichte Tenga SVR lässt sich mit nur einem Knopf steuern, bietet fünf Intensitätsstufen und zwei pulsierende Varianten.

Begründung der Jury
Der Tenga SVR fällt durch seine schlanke Gestalt ins Auge und überrascht auch mit seiner Doppelfunktion, die beiden Partnern gleichermaßen gerecht wird.

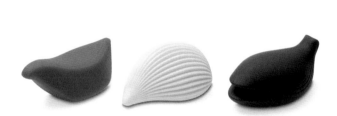

iroha+
Vibrator

Manufacturer
TENGA Co., Ltd., Tokyo, Japan
In-house design
Ayumi Mochizuki, Tomoko Nakajima
Web
www.iroha-tenga.com

The iroha+ series provides three kinds of stimulation and with three distinct shapes, a whole spectrum of sensations can be experienced. Details such as the elaborately devised tips, or a groove structure, make it easier for the users to find their preferred kind of stimulation. The device can be intuitively controlled by two buttons. The organically shaped objects, reminiscent of animals, are made of soft, dust-repellent silicone and fit comfortably in the palm of the hand.

Statement by the jury
The vibrator series iroha+ impresses with its shapely and easy to handle size, thanks to which the three units sit well in the hand. Being functionally diverse they can stimulate an array of sensations.

Die Serie iroha+ ermöglicht drei Arten der Stimulation, und mittels zusätzlicher Funktionen kann die gesamte Bandbreite der Empfindungen erlebt werden. Details wie die fein ausgearbeiteten Spitzen oder eine Rillenstruktur erleichtern es dem Nutzer, gesteuert über zwei intuitiv bedienbare Knöpfe, seine bevorzugte Art der Stimulierung zu finden. Die organisch geformten Objekte, die an Tiere erinnern, wurden aus weichem, staubabweisendem Silikon gefertigt und liegen bequem in der Hand.

Begründung der Jury
Die Vibratorserie iroha+ punktet durch die wohlgeformte handliche Größe, dank derer die drei Elemente gut in der Hand liegen. Funktional vielfältig können sie verschiedenste Empfindungen auslösen.

Animal Savior
Sex Toy

Manufacturer
Massiv Co., Taipei, Taiwan
Design
Petite Design Office (Wang Hsiao-Ching), Taipei, Taiwan
Web
www.drippp.com
www.wangching.com

The series Animal Savior was designed for modern independent women, who are tough and want more than the ordinary. In search of the perfect match, this simple, cute and ergonomically designed series offers five elements – suitable tools for individual intimate needs. Though soundless, the vibration is powerful. With only two buttons, they can be easily and intuitively controlled. The materials are FDA-approved and have a good feel.

Statement by the jury
With their intuitive control, the different versions of the compactly and exceptionally designed sex toy series are qualified to become an attractive companion of young women of today.

Die Serie Animal Savior wurde für moderne unabhängige Frauen entworfen, die tough sind und sich nicht mit Alltäglichem zufriedengeben. Auf ihrer Suche nach optimaler Übereinstimmung bietet diese schlicht, niedlich und ergonomisch gestaltete Serie mit ihren fünf Elementen passende Tools für individuelle intime Bedürfnisse. Sie sind geräuschlos bei zugleich starker Vibration und lassen sich mit nur zwei Knöpfen ohne Schwierigkeit intuitiv steuern. Die Materialien sind FDA-zugelassen und angenehm in der Haptik.

Begründung der Jury
Die verschiedenen Ausführungen der kompakt und originell gestalteten Sex-Toy-Serie eignen sich mit ihrer intuitiven Steuerung als attraktiver Begleiter junger Frauen von heute.

MysteryVibe Crescendo
Vibrator

Manufacturer
MysteryVibe, London, Great Britain
In-house design
Soumyadip Rakshit, Rob Weekly,
Stephanie Alys, Shanshan Xu
Web
www.mysteryvibe.com

MysteryVibe Crescendo is a very flexible, smart vibrator with six motors. It adapts to the body by itself, but it can also be tilted by hand to the individually most pleasant angle. Via an app, the silicone-coated and waterproof vibrator offers a variety of vibration modes for personalised pleasure. Through its targeted exploration of sensual experience, the company wants to support the medical community to address sexual problems in a positive informed way.

Statement by the jury
With its extraordinary flexibility and six motors, which allow numerous sensual experiences, the MysteryVibe Crescendo stands out in a special way.

MysteryVibe Crescendo ist ein sehr biegsamer, intelligenter Vibrator mit sechs Motoren. Er passt sich von selbst dem Körper an, lässt sich aber auch von Hand in den persönlich angenehmsten Winkel neigen. Via App bietet der silikonbeschichtete und wasserdichte Vibrator eine Vielzahl von Vibrationsarten für das jeweils individuelle Vergnügen. Mit seiner gezielten Erforschung sinnlicher Erfahrungen möchte das Unternehmen die Medizin darin unterstützen, sexuellen Problemen in einer positiv informierten Weise zu begegnen.

Begründung der Jury
Mit seiner außergewöhnlichen Biegsamkeit und sechs Motoren, die zahlreiche sinnliche Erlebnisse zulassen, ragt der MysteryVibe Crescendo besonders heraus.

Beastie CECI
Erotic Toy
Erotikspielzeug

Manufacturer
Shenzhen Divinetec Co., Ltd.,
Shenzhen, China
In-house design
Haifeng Yang, Jinkat Chen
Web
www.divinetec.cn

The characteristic features of Beastie Ceci are simplicity, elegance, functionality and longevity. It is made of one single piece of medical stainless steel and is hand polished to create a mirror effect. This makes the device pleasantly smooth and, thanks to its curved contours, it fits perfectly into a woman's hand. The seamless construction of one piece requires special manufacturing. Due to the rust-proof and antimicrobial features, Ceci is very easy to clean and can be used for many years.

Statement by the jury
Its high-quality materials and technically advanced production make Beastie Ceci an enjoyable and stylish erotic accessory.

Beastie Ceci ist durch Einfachheit, Eleganz, Funktionalität und Langlebigkeit gekennzeichnet. Er wird aus einem einzigen Stück medizinischen Edelstahls gefertigt und von Hand poliert, bis er wie ein Spiegel glänzt. Dadurch fühlt sich das Gerät angenehm glatt an und passt durch seine konturierten Rundungen genau in eine Frauenhand. Die nahtlose Konstruktion aus einem Stück erfordert spezielle Fertigungstechniken. Dank der rostbeständigen und antimikrobiellen Eigenschaften lässt sich Ceci gut sauber halten und viele Jahre lang nutzen.

Begründung der Jury
Seine hochwertigen Materialien und die technisch avancierte Herstellung machen Beastie Ceci zum angenehmen und stilvollen erotischen Accessoire.

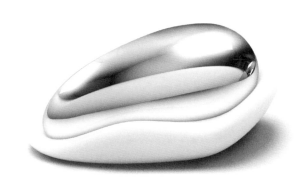

Monster Pub
Vibrator

Manufacturer
SISTALK Technology Beijing Co., Ltd.,
Beijing, China
In-house design
Bo Liu
Web
www.sistalk.cn

Embodying a further development of the traditional design of vibrators, the Monster Pub meets the needs of modern women both aesthetically and emotionally. With its curved shape, it conforms ideally to the build of female Asians. Coupled with a mobile app, it is possible to generate vibration frequencies that can be stored in the cloud and thus can be exactly repeated as well as shared anonymously.

Statement by the jury
The vibrator Monster Pub impresses with its strongly curved shape and an app that is linked to the cloud and allows the exchange of experiences among users.

Mit dem Design des Monster Pub wurde die herkömmliche Gestaltung von Vibratoren weiterentwickelt, um den Bedürfnissen moderner Frauen in ästhetischer wie emotionaler Hinsicht gerecht zu werden. Mit seiner gekrümmten Formgebung passt er sich dem Körperbau von Asiatinnen ideal an. Gekoppelt an eine mobile App, lassen sich Schwingungszahlen schaffen, die in einer Cloud aufbewahrt und dadurch immer genauso wiederholt sowie anonym geteilt werden können.

Begründung der Jury
Der Vibrator Monster Pub imponiert mit seiner stark geschwungenen Formgebung sowie einer App, die mit einer Cloud verknüpft ist und den Austausch der Nutzerinnen untereinander ermöglicht.

SenseVibe Warm
Vibrator with Heating Function
Vibrator mit Heizfunktion

Manufacturer
SenseMax Technology Ltd., Hong Kong, China
In-house design
Web
www.sensemax.net

SenseVibe Warm is a vibrator with heating function that combines a functionally and aesthetically pleasing design with innovative technology. Together with the simple and unobtrusively designed storage box, which at the same time serves as wireless charger, it has a minimalist look thus discreetly integrating into its surroundings. The equally minimalist monotone colour palette inside the box and on the device reflects the heating function. Thanks to two motors, internal and external stimulation is possible. The flexible neck part ensures that the device can be easily adapted to any body shape.

SenseVibe Warm ist ein Vibrator mit Heizfunktion, der ein funktional und ästhetisch ansprechendes Design mit innovativer Technologie vereint. Zusammen mit der schlicht und unaufdringlich gestalteten Aufbewahrungsbox, die zugleich als kabelloses Ladegerät fungiert, ist er von minimalistischer Anmutung und fügt sich so diskret in seine Umgebung ein. Die ebenso reduzierte Farbpalette spiegelt im Inneren der Box und am Gerät die spezifische Heizfunktion wider. Dank zweier Motoren sind eine innere und eine äußere Stimulation möglich und das flexible Halsstück sorgt dafür, dass sich das Gerät problemlos an jede Körperform anpassen lässt.

Statement by the jury
With SenseVibe Warm, the clear ergonomic design of the device and the elegant box is blended with a special performance spectrum and a heating function to become a strikingly distinct unit.

Begründung der Jury
Bei SenseVibe Warm verschmilzt die klare ergonomische Formgebung von Gerät und eleganter Box mit einem besonderen Leistungsspektrum samt Heizfunktion zu einer auffallend eigenständigen Einheit.

Satisfyer Pro Penguin
Pressure Wave Stimulator
Druckwellen-Vibrator

Manufacturer
EIS GmbH, Bielefeld, Germany
In-house design
Web
www.satisfyer.com

The handy design of the Satisfyer Pro Penguin wants to win over newcomers to the world of sensual games by being straightforward in its use and having an amusing shape. The curved head of the pressure wave vibrator creates special climaxes with eleven different programmes. By means of rechargeable batteries, it is quickly ready for use. Its silicone covered surface provides a soft grip and convenient handling. It is waterproof and easy to clean making the device a reliable companion.

Statement by the jury
The Satisfyer Pro Penguin not only impresses with its compact size and bright pink colour, but also with a special technology with pressure waves.

Die handliche Gestaltung des Satisfyer Pro Penguin möchte mit ihrer drolligen Form und dem unkomplizierten Gebrauch Neueinsteiger für das sinnliche Spiel gewinnen. Der gekrümmte Kopf des Druckwellen-Vibrators erzeugt besondere Höhepunkte mithilfe von elf verschiedenen Programmen. Wiederaufladbare Batterien machen ihn rasch einsatzbereit, und seine Oberfläche aus Silikon sorgt für einen weichen Griff sowie einfache Bedienbarkeit. Wasserfest und leicht zu reinigen, erweist er sich so als verlässlicher Gefährte.

Begründung der Jury
Der Satisfyer Pro Penguin imponiert nicht nur durch seine kompakte Größe und das knallige Pink, sondern auch durch die spezielle Druckwellentechnik.

Satisfyer 1
Pressure Wave Stimulator
Druckwellen-Vibrator

Manufacturer
EIS GmbH, Bielefeld, Germany
In-house design
Web
www.satisfyer.com

The original Satisfyer 1 was created for globetrotters. Its slim, round shape makes the pressure wave vibrator a sophisticated companion for the road. Using an innovative technology, with eleven powerful levels from tender to intense, it stimulates the clitoris without touch. It massages in a particularly pleasant way by means of low pressure paired with exciting pulsations. At the push of a button, the battery operation allows touch-free pleasure at any time.

Statement by the jury
The fetching design makes the slim Satisfyer 1 an eye-catcher. It is also technically interesting since it works with pressure waves.

Der originelle Satisfyer 1 wurde für Weltenbummler konzipiert. Seine schlanke, runde Form macht den Druckwellen-Vibrator zum raffinierten Begleiter für unterwegs. Durch eine innovative Technik in elf kraftvollen Stufen von zärtlich bis intensiv stimuliert er die Klitoris ohne Berührung. Durch einen Unterdruck gepaart mit spannungsvollen Pulsationen wird sie auf besonders angenehme Weise massiert. Der Batteriebetrieb ermöglicht jederzeit berührungsloses Vergnügen auf Knopfdruck.

Begründung der Jury
Durch seine einprägsame Formgebung wird der schlanke Satisfyer 1 zum Blickfang. Dass er via Druckwellen funktioniert, macht ihn auch technisch bemerkenswert.

partner
Couples' Vibrator
Partnervibrator

Manufacturer
EIS GmbH, Bielefeld, Germany
In-house design
Web
www.satisfyer.com

The partner vibrator allows both partners to simultaneously have intensive stimulation whilst making love. Its ergonomic design in the shape of a U comfortably adapts to the woman's body. There is a choice of three vibration intensities and seven vibration rhythms at the push of a button. The device is made of waterproof skin-friendly silicone, which is easy to clean and has a very pleasant feel. It is charged by means of an integrated battery and the supplied USB charging cable.

Statement by the jury
This vibrator captivates with simultaneous sensual pleasure for both partners. Thanks to its silicone surface, it is also very comfortable to handle.

Der Partnervibrator ermöglicht beiden Partnern zugleich eine intensive Stimulation beim Liebesspiel. Seine ergonomische Gestaltung in der Form eines U passt sich dem Körper der Frau komfortabel an. Per Knopfdruck kann man aus drei Vibrationsintensitäten und sieben Vibrationsrhythmen wählen. Das Gerät wurde aus wasserdichtem, hautfreundlichem Silikon gefertigt, das leicht zu pflegen und haptisch sehr angenehm ist, und wird mittels integriertem Akku und dem mitgelieferten USB-Ladekabel aufgeladen.

Begründung der Jury
Dieser Vibrator besticht dadurch, dass er beiden Partnern gleichzeitig sinnliches Vergnügen bereitet. Dank seiner Silikonoberfläche ist er zudem angenehm zu handhaben.

partner plus
Couples' Vibrator
Partnervibrator

Manufacturer
EIS GmbH, Bielefeld, Germany
In-house design
Web
www.satisfyer.com

The couples' vibrator, partner plus, has quite a few extras to offer. With its two very powerful motors, it lends itself as an exciting toy for sensual experiences of varying intensity. Its ergonomic design is precisely adapted to the anatomy of the woman and is capable of stimulating both internally and externally at the same time. The soft, body-friendly silicone surface of the partner plus is easy to clean and waterproof, so that it can be used in the tub and shower.

Statement by the jury
The outstanding characteristics of the partner plus couples' vibrator are the two powerful motors and its design which precisely adapts to the woman's body.

Der Partnervibrator partner plus zeigt so manches Extra. Mit seinen zwei sehr starken Motoren bietet er sich als spannendes Toy für verschieden intensive sinnliche Erfahrungen an. Seine ergonomische Gestaltung ist genau auf die Anatomie der Frau abgestimmt und vermag sie gleichzeitig außen wie innen zu stimulieren. Die weiche, aus körperfreundlichem Silikon hergestellte Oberfläche des partner plus ist leicht zu reinigen und wasserdicht, sodass er auch in Wanne und Dusche verwendet werden kann.

Begründung der Jury
Die herausragenden Kennzeichen des Partnervibrators partner plus sind die zwei starken Motoren und eine Formgebung, die sich dem Körper der Frau exakt anpasst.

Foldable Leaf Waterer
Portable Pet Water Dispenser
Tragbare Tiertränke

Manufacturer
Super Design Manufacture Co., Ltd.,
Zhongshan, China
In-house design
Tianle Yang, Sandy Zeng
Web
www.superdesign.cc

The Foldable Leaf Waterer is a portable drinking vessel for animals during walks or travels. The design was inspired by nature and past times, when people used leaves as vessels. Combined with a hand-crafted look, the special shape of a leaf as a vital natural element is an expression of the good relationship between man, animal and nature. The water is first poured into the leaf where it collects and from which the dog can comfortably drink. The bottle, which can easily be hung and transported in a belt loop, also serves as water reservoir.

Der Foldable Leaf Waterer ist ein tragbares Trinkgefäß für Tiere auf Spaziergängen oder auf Reisen. Die Inspiration zu seiner Gestaltung entstammt der Natur und vergangenen Zeiten, als Menschen Blätter als Gefäße nutzten. Die besondere Form des Blattes als vitales Naturelement, kombiniert mit kunsthandwerklicher Anmutung, drückt zudem die gute Beziehung zwischen Mensch, Tier und Natur aus. Das Wasser wird zunächst in das Blatt gekippt, wo es sich sammelt und woraus der Hund bequem trinken kann. Die Flasche, die sich ganz einfach in eine Gürtelschlaufe hängen und transportieren lässt, dient dabei zugleich als Wasserreservoir.

Statement by the jury
The foldable pet water dispenser does justice to the fact that pets like dogs do not always come across water: This ergonomic bottle with a nicely shaped leaf as receptacle offers an effective solution.

Begründung der Jury
Die faltbare Tiertränke wird dem Umstand gerecht, dass Haustiere wie Hunde unterwegs nicht immer Wasser vorfinden: Dafür gibt es diese ergonomische Flasche mit formschönem Blatt als Behältnis.

Reversible Silicone Travel Feeder
Portable Pet Bowl
Tragbarer Futternapf

Manufacturer
Super Design Manufacture Co., Ltd.,
Zhongshan, China
In-house design
Tianle Yang, Sandy Zeng
Web
www.superdesign.cc

The Reversible Silicone Travel Feeder is a portable pet bowl for on the way. It does justice to the fact that it is often difficult to have pet food ready to hand. At the closure of the bottle-like vessel, it features a flap in the form of a leaf that can be unfolded. With the bottle turned upside down, the food is simply poured into it. The animal can thus feed as usual from a dish. The idea for the leaf is inspired by nature and underscores the relationship that human beings have with their pets.

Der Reversible Silicone Travel Feeder ist eine tragbare Futterschale für unterwegs. Er kommt dem Umstand entgegen, dass es dabei oft schwierig ist, die Tiernahrung griffbereit und praktisch zur Hand zu haben, und besitzt am Verschluss des flaschenartigen Gefäßes eine Lasche in der Form eines Blatts, die ausgeklappt werden kann. Das Futter schüttet man bei umgedrehter Flasche einfach hinein und lässt das Tier wie gewohnt aus einer Schale fressen. Die Idee zu dem Blatt ist von der Natur inspiriert und unterstreicht die Beziehung des Menschen zu seinem Tier.

Statement by the jury
It is easy to feed one's pet on trips with this bowl whose form of a leaf emphasises the natural handling.

Begründung der Jury
Sein Haustier auf Reisen unkompliziert zu füttern, fällt mit diesem Futternapf ausgesprochen leicht. Die Schale in Form eines Blatts betont die natürliche Handhabung.

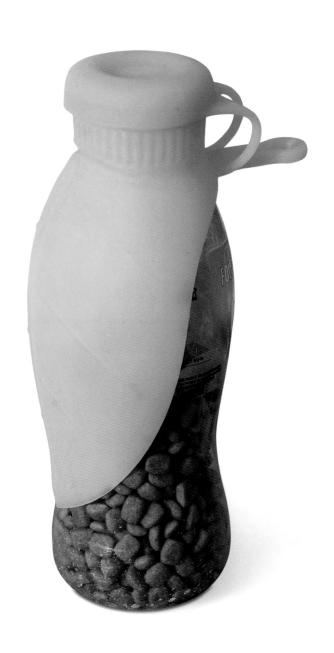

EVERSWEET Travel
Travel Bottle for Dogs
Reiseflasche für Hunde

Manufacturer
PETKIT Network Technology (Shanghai) Co.,
Ltd., Shanghai, China
In-house design
JC Zhang, Yiwei Zhang, Xiaoqing Ma
Web
www.petkit.com

With this water bottle for pets, only one hand is required to give the dog water on the way. By simply pressing the middle button with one hand, the water flow can be controlled and the amount of water measured out. Turning the button closes the bottle and safely prevents leakage. The built-in carbon filter is extracted from coconut shells; the water container is made of Tritan, and the antibacterial mouthpiece is BPA-free.

Statement by the jury
Eversweet Travel combines an ergonomic design with functional use making it easy to dispense water and close the bottle safely.

Die Wasserflasche für Haustiere sorgt dafür, dass nicht beide, sondern nur eine Hand erforderlich ist, um dem Hund unterwegs Wasser zu geben. Durch einfaches Drücken der mittleren Taste mit einer Hand lässt sich der Wasserfluss kontrollieren und die -menge dosieren. Dreht man die Taste, schließt die Flasche und verhindert Auslaufen auf sichere Weise. Der eingebaute Kohlefilter wurde aus Kokosnussschale gewonnen, der Wasserbehälter aus Tritan und das antibakterielle Mundstück sind BPA-frei.

Begründung der Jury
Eversweet Travel verbindet eine ergonomische Gestaltung mit einer funktionalen Handhabung, sodass die Wassergabe und das sichere Verschließen leicht von der Hand gehen.

EVERSWEET
Smart Drinking Fountain
Intelligenter Trinkbrunnen

Manufacturer
PETKIT Network Technology (Shanghai) Co.,
Ltd., Shanghai, China
In-house design
JC Zhang, Yiwei Zhang, Xiaoqing Ma
Web
www.petkit.com

This fountain features a triple filter system. In addition to the screen cover at the top, it has an activated carbon layer for reducing chlorine and an ion exchange resin for filtering heavy metals in the water. This ensures the provision of tasty water. The water bubbles dynamically upwards, which increases the oxygen content and stimulates the pet to drink more water. A low safety voltage and various alarm messages facilitate the handling of the fountain.

Statement by the jury
The feature of the fountain to provide filtered and oxygen-enriched water is truly aimed at the health of the animal.

Dieser Brunnen wurde mit einem Dreifach-Filtersystem ausgestattet, das neben der Siebabdeckung ganz oben eine Aktivkohleschicht zur Reduktion von Chlor sowie ein Ionenaustauscherharz zur Ausfilterung von Schwermetallen im Wasser umfasst. Auf diese Weise wird die Bereitstellung wohlschmeckenden Wassers gewährleistet. Durch das dynamische Sprudeln des Wassers nach oben wird sein Sauerstoffgehalt erhöht und das Haustier angeregt, mehr Wasser zu trinken. Eine niedrige Sicherheitsspannung und verschiedene Alarmmeldungen erleichtern den Umgang mit dem Brunnen.

Begründung der Jury
Die Qualität des Trinkbrunnens, gefiltertes und mit Sauerstoff angereichertes Wasser bereitzustellen, zielt ganz auf die Gesundheit des Tieres ab.

Pinnn Litter Box
Katzentoilette

Manufacturer
Petion Technology Company Limited,
Hong Kong
In-house design
Hao Yang, Shih-Hong Chiang, Siyan Yuan
Web
www.petion.pet

The Pinnn Litter Box features a three-tray sifting system and ergonomic handles, which makes cleaning cat litter scoopless without cumbersome shovelling. After lifting the upper container, the waste can be separated from the clean litter by means of sifting. The tray is then turned by 90 degrees, and the two other tablets are slipped on top. The hydrophobic surface is nano-coated so that waste is easy to remove. The bottom bolts fit exactly into the screen holes so that clogging in the holes will be pressed out when the trays are restacked.

Statement by the jury
The design of the cat litter box impresses with an ingenious construction and the used material which makes the usual shovelling unnecessary.

Die Streubox Pinnn ist durch ein Siebsystem aus drei Tabletts mit ergonomischen Griffen gekennzeichnet, mit dem sich Katzenstreu ohne lästiges Schaufeln säubern lässt. Nach Abheben des oberen Behälters lässt sich der Abfall durch Sieben vom sauberen Streu trennen. Anschließend dreht man das Tablett um 90 Grad und steckt die beiden anderen Tabletts wieder auf. Die hydrophobe Oberfläche wurde nanobeschichtet, sodass Abfälle leicht entfernt werden können. Die Bodenpinne passt genau in die Siebbohrungen, was bewirkt, dass Verstopfungen in den Löchern beim erneuten Stapeln der Tabletts herausgedrückt werden.

Begründung der Jury
Die Gestaltung dieser Katzentoilette überzeugt durch eine ausgeklügelte Konstruktion samt Materialeinsatz, dank derer das übliche Schaufeln unnötig ist.

GO
Smart Pet Leash
Intelligente Haustierleine

Manufacturer
PETKIT Network Technology (Shanghai) Co.,
Ltd., Shanghai, China
In-house design
JC Zhang, Yiwei Zhang, Xiaoqing Ma
Web
www.petkit.com

The smart leash features a shock-absorbing, fluorescent handle fulfilling the demands of animal owners on different functions and situations. Connected via Bluetooth, it can be synchronised with an app, which can be used to set the destinations of one's daily walks. That way, detailed roadmaps are generated and the walking routes are clearly displayed. The handle vibrates in case of incoming calls and messages. In addition, it offers an excellent feel.

Statement by the jury
The pet leash Go appeals by its interchangeable, highly functional ropes and the numerous options offered by its digital extras.

Mit stoßdämpfendem und fluoreszierendem Handgriff erfüllt die intelligente Leine die Anforderungen der Tierhalter an verschiedene Funktionen und Situationen. Sie ist über Bluetooth mit einer App synchronisierbar, mit der die Ziele der täglichen Spaziergänge eingestellt werden können. So werden detaillierte Umgebungskarten erzeugt und die Routen der Spaziergänge klar dargestellt. Bei eingehenden Anrufen oder Benachrichtigungen vibriert der Griff. Zudem bietet dieser eine herausragende Haptik.

Begründung der Jury
Die Haustierleine Go besticht durch die austauschbaren, äußerst zweckmäßigen Seile und die zahlreichen Möglichkeiten, die ihre digitalen Extras bieten.

Joey
Pet Sofa for Dogs
Hundesofa

Manufacturer
9House Pet, Kaohsiung, Taiwan
In-house design
Yingying Lee, Yulin Chen
Web
www.9housepet.com

The dog sofa Joey was developed to accommodate the natural needs of dogs. Suitable for two types of a canvas cover that is both scratch-resistant and washable, the closable cover provides security and enables an alternative seat height. The sofa also provides improved aeration and a wide field of view when the cover is open. Both versions allow for a comfortable place like a kind of hammock that can be quickly removed from the beech wood frame.

Statement by the jury
In line with the different needs of dogs for retreat or curiosity, Joey offers suitable versions of a comfortable dog sofa.

Das Hundesofa Joey wurde gestaltet, um den natürlichen Bedürfnissen von Hunden Rechnung zu tragen. Geeignet für zwei Arten eines jeweils kratzfesten und waschbaren Segeltuchbezugs, gibt die schließbare Abdeckung Sicherheit und ermöglicht eine alternative Sitzhöhe. Zugleich bietet das Sofa bei geöffneter Abdeckung bessere Luftzufuhr und ein größeres Sichtfeld für das Tier. Beide Varianten ermöglichen einen bequemen Platz in der Art einer Hängematte, die sich schnell von dem Holzrahmen aus Buche lösen lässt.

Begründung der Jury
An den unterschiedlichen Bedürfnissen von Hunden wie Rückzug oder Neugierde orientiert, bietet Joey passende Varianten eines komfortablen Hundesofas.

Babies and children
Baby und Kind

MIOS
Stroller
Kinderwagen

Manufacturer
CYBEX GmbH,
Bayreuth, Germany

In-house design
Petra Napier, Ralf Holleis

Web
www.cybex-online.com

reddot **award** 2017
best of the best

Solid lightness
Strollers face many kinds of strain in everyday use and have to stand up to many challenges on a daily basis. Paying homage to the innovative spirit of designers Ray and Charles Eames, the MIOS stroller aims at demonstrating that design can not only function but should also provide enjoyment in use. Its design is based on an X-bracing construction, which is widely used in architecture and interior design. This approach led to a perfect combination of high stability coupled with low weight through a reduced use of materials. MIOS features a static chromed aluminium frame that makes it look as if it is almost floating. This visual appearance of lightness is further enhanced by retro-modern design elements that underline the stroller's clear elegance. A breathable mesh material helps to regulate the body temperature of the child. The self-explanatory functionality of this ergonomically highly advanced stroller offers a myriad of customisation options that allow it to be easily adapted to different needs and demands: with the matching carry cot featuring a soft memory foam mattress, it delivers a high degree of comfort and safety, while an infant car seat turns it into a complete travel system. The MIOS stroller is thus perfectly prepared for all eventualities. It fascinates with high agility, uncomplicated ease of use and high stability.

Solide Leichtigkeit
Ein Kinderwagen wird im Alltag viel beansprucht und muss sich täglich aufs Neue bewähren. Als Hommage an die Innovationskraft der Designer Ray und Charles Eames will der Kinderwagen MIOS zeigen, dass Design nicht nur funktionieren, sondern auch Spaß machen kann. Seine Gestaltung basiert auf der in Architektur und Interior Design häufig eingesetzten Konstruktion der Kreuzverstrebung. Dieser Ansatz führte zu einer perfekten Kombination von hoher Stabilität und geringem Gewicht bei einem gleichzeitig reduzierten Materialeinsatz. MIOS hat ein statisches Gestell aus verchromtem Aluminium, das ihn nahezu schwebend erscheinen lässt. Diese optische Leichtigkeit wird gestalterisch unterstützt durch Retro-Elemente, die seine klare Eleganz unterstreichen. Atmungsaktives Mesh-Material verbessert zudem die Klimaregulierung für das Kind. Die selbsterklärende Funktionalität des auch ergonomisch hochentwickelten Kinderwagens erlaubt zahlreiche Individualisierungsmöglichkeiten, wodurch er gut unterschiedlichen Anforderungen angepasst werden kann: Mit Kinderwagenaufsatz und weicher Memory-schaum-Matratze bietet er ein hohes Maß an Bequemlichkeit und Schutz, mit einer passenden Babyschale wird er zum Reisesystem. Der Kinderwagen MIOS ist damit für alle Eventualitäten gerüstet. Durch seine Agilität begeistert er ebenso wie durch seine unkomplizierte Handhabung und Solidität.

Statement by the jury
The MIOS stroller convinces with a sophisticated design. Ideally tailored towards living with children, it is reliable, comfortable and very light. It can be folded up in seconds to a compact format and fascinates with an extraordinarily stable construction as well as a highly detailed functionality that offers a multitude of customisation options. This distinctive stroller merges practicability with a stylish elegance.

Begründung der Jury
Der Kinderwagen MIOS überzeugt durch eine ausgereifte Designqualität. Ausgezeichnet dem Leben mit Kindern angepasst, ist er zuverlässig, bequem und sehr leicht. In Sekundenschnelle lässt er sich auf ein kompaktes Format zusammenfalten und verblüfft durch seine außerordentlich stabile Konstruktion sowie eine bis ins Detail durchdachte Funktionalität, die zahlreiche Möglichkeiten der Individualisierung bietet. Dieser prägnante Kinderwagen vereint Praktikabilität mit stylischer Eleganz.

Designer portrait
See page 60
Siehe Seite 60

Evalite™ Duo
Tandem Duo Pushchair
Geschwisterwagen

Manufacturer
Joie Children's Products Co., Limited, United Kingdom
In-house design
Web
www.joiebaby.com

The special feature of the Evalite Duo
tandem two-child pushchair is its low
weight of only 11 kg. Furthermore, it can
be compactly folded up with one simple
hand movement, so that it takes up
no more space than a normal stroller.
Evalite Duo offers two fully-fledged
seat units with several relaxing positions.
For transporting younger children, the
rear seat can be adjusted stagelessly to a
fully reclining position. By means of an
innovative spring lock, a baby shell seat
can also be attached to the rear seat.

Statement by the jury
Compact folded dimensions, light weight
and many functional details make the
Evalite Duo a practical, everyday
companion.

Das Besondere an dem Geschwisterwagen
Evalite Duo ist sein mit nur etwa 11 kg sehr
geringes Gewicht. Zudem lässt er sich mit
einem einfachen Handgriff so kompakt zusammenfalten, dass er nicht mehr Platz
benötigt als ein normaler Buggy. Evalite Duo
bietet zwei vollwertige Sitzeinheiten mit
mehreren Ruhepositionen. Für den Transport
von jüngeren Kindern kann der hintere Sitz
stufenlos bis hin zur flachen Liegeposition
verstellt werden, mittels eines innovativen
Schnappverschlusses lässt sich am Rücksitz
auch eine Babyschale befestigen.

Begründung der Jury
Kompakte Faltmaße, ein geringes Gewicht
sowie viele funktionale Detaillösungen
machen den Evalite Duo zu einem praktischen Begleiter im Alltag.

Mytrax™
Pushchair
Kinderwagen

Manufacturer
Joie Children's Products Co.,
Limited, United Kingdom
In-house design
Web
www.joiebaby.com

The Mytrax pushchair is a 3-in-1 system which can quickly be converted from a stroller to a pram, thanks to its easily removed seat unit and canopy and adapters for the attachment of a baby seat or carrycot. A one-hand folding mechanism in the middle of the seat makes it easy to fold up the pushchair quickly; an automatic fold lock assures that the compact package can stand freely. Pneumatic rear wheels, swivel and lockable front wheels, and a one-touch brake assure a pleasant pushing experience for the parents and the child.

Der Kinderwagen Mytrax ist ein 3-in-1-System, das sich dank leicht abnehmbarer Sitzeinheit und Verdeck sowie Adaptern, mit denen sich Babyschale oder -wanne befestigen lassen, schnell vom Sport- zum Kinderwagen umbauen lässt. Ein Ein-Hand-Faltmechanismus in der Sitzmitte ermöglicht ein schnelles Zusammenfalten des Wagens, eine automatische Faltverriegelung sorgt dafür, dass das kompakte Paket auch frei steht. Luftgefüllte Hinterräder und schwenk- und feststellbare Vorderräder sowie eine One-Touch-Bremse erlauben ein für Eltern wie Kind angenehmes Schieben.

Statement by the jury
Mytrax combines great flexibility and easy operation with skilled workmanship and elegant, high-quality aesthetics.

Begründung der Jury
Mytrax verbindet hohe Flexibilität und eine einfache Bedienung mit einer sorgfältigen Verarbeitung und einer eleganten und hochwertigen Ästhetik.

iCoo Acrobat XL Plus Trio Set
Stroller Set
Kinderwagenset

Manufacturer
hauck GmbH & Co. KG, Sonnefeld, Germany
In-house design
Design
Richard Mitzman architects llp
(Richard Mitzman), London, Great Britain
Web
www.icoo.de
www.richardmitzman.com

The special feature of the Acrobat XL Plus Trio Set is its innovative one-handed folding mechanism, by means of which the stroller, including the seat unit, can be very compactly folded so that it fits into every car boot. The stroller set has three attachments which can be mounted directly onto the aluminium chassis: a carrycot, a car seat with side impact protection, and a reversible seat unit with leg cover and reclining function. Thus, the set can be used for a child from birth up to the age of about two and a half years.

Statement by the jury
The individual elements of this compact stroller set are well conceived to the finest detail and perfectly coordinated to one another.

Das Besondere an dem Acrobat XL Plus Trio Set ist sein innovativer Einhand-Faltmechanismus, durch den sich der Kinderwagen inklusive Sportsitz sehr kompakt zusammenlegen lässt und in jeden Kofferraum passt. Das Kinderwagenset hat drei Aufsätze, die sich direkt auf dem Aluminiumfahrgestell montieren lassen: eine Babywanne, einen Autositz mit Seitenaufprallschutz und einen umsetzbaren Sportwagensitz mit Beindecke und Liegefunktion. Damit kann das Set von Geburt des Kindes an und bis zu einem Alter von etwa zweieinhalb Jahren genutzt werden.

Begründung der Jury
Die einzelnen Elemente dieses kompakten Kinderwagensets sind bis ins Detail durchdacht und funktional wie ästhetisch perfekt aufeinander abgestimmt.

NOVA
Stroller
Kinderwagen

Manufacturer
Maxi-Cosi, Dorel Juvenile Europe,
Cholet, France
Design
eliumstudio, Paris, France
Web
www.maxi-cosi.com
www.eliumstudio.com

The special feature of the Nova stroller is its sophisticated folding mechanism which makes it possible to fold the stroller without using the hands. For this, it is only necessary to step on the corresponding pedal at the back of the stroller, and the pushchair folds up automatically. The stroller becomes even more compact by pressing the additional folding button. With a width of only 52 cm, it can then fit into the boot of a small car.

Statement by the jury
The Nova stroller delights with a comfortable and well-conceived folding mechanism which makes handling particularly easy.

Das Besondere an dem Kinderwagen Nova ist sein ausgefeilter Faltmechanismus. Dieser ermöglicht es, den Kinderwagen zusammenzufalten, ohne die Hände zu benutzen. Dafür wird einfach das entsprechende Pedal an der Rückseite des Wagens heruntergetreten, und der Kinderwagen klappt sich automatisch zusammen. Noch kompakter wird der Kinderwagen, wenn der zusätzliche Faltknopf gedrückt wird, sodass er mit einer Breite von nur 52 cm auch in den Kofferraum von Kleinwagen passt.

Begründung der Jury
Der Kinderwagen Nova begeistert mit einem komfortablen und durchdachten Faltmechanismus, der die Handhabung besonders einfach macht.

Albert
Infant Car Seat
Babyschale

Manufacturer
Suzhou Swandoo Children's Articles Co., Ltd.,
Suzhou, China
In-house design
Nicolas Gonzalez Garrido
Web
www.swandoo.com

The infant seat Albert is characterised by its innovative plastic shell construction which offers not only a great deal of safety and comfort but also defines the modern appearance of the seat with its harmonious proportions. An integrated sun canopy protects the baby from UV rays; the headrest can be adjusted to the size of the infant, and the handle can be set to four different positions. Details such as a seatbelt which glows in the dark contribute to a high degree of user-friendliness.

Der Babysitz Albert ist gekennzeichnet durch seine innovative Schalenkonstruktion aus Kunststoff, die nicht nur besonders viel Sicherheit und Komfort bietet, sondern auch das moderne Erscheinungsbild des Sitzes mit seinen harmonischen Proportionen prägt. Ein integriertes Sonnensegel schützt das Baby zudem vor UV-Strahlen, die Kopfstütze lässt sich auf die Größe des Kindes anpassen und der Griff in vier verschiedenen Positionen fixieren. Details wie ein im Dunkeln leuchtender Gurtverschluss tragen zur hohen Bedienfreundlichkeit bei.

Statement by the jury
This infant seat makes a strong and protective impression at first glance, and this impression is also confirmed in its functional aspect.

Begründung der Jury
Diese Babyschale vermittelt bereits auf den ersten Blick einen soliden und schützenden Eindruck und wird dem auch in funktionaler Hinsicht gerecht.

Thule Yepp Nexxt Maxi
Child Bike Seat
Fahrrad-Kindersitz

Manufacturer
Thule Group, Malmö, Sweden

Design
Vanderveer Designers,
Geldermalsen, Netherlands

Web
www.thule.com
www.vanderveerdesigners.nl

reddot award 2017
best of the best

Cosy and safe

Infant seats play a significant role in mobility with children. Bringing kids to kindergarten by bicycle or enjoying bike riding together is an easy and environmentally friendly alternative to going by car. The design of the Thule Yepp Nexxt Maxi incorporates an impressive reinterpretation of a child bike seat that combines many advantages. It showcases a contemporary use of forms paired with many well-thought-out details. At first glance its clear lines look unusual and strike the eye with a novel appeal. This design is inspired by modern bike helmets, resulting in a highly sporty appearance that matches well with almost all bicycle types and models. The seat features sophisticated ergonomics and offers comfortable seating for children at all times thanks to an innovative design with padded and shock absorbing materials. Available in five colours, the Thule Yepp Nexxt Maxi bike seat is solid yet lightweight. It is rear-mountable and provides a stable and secure ride for both babies and toddlers. The innovative five-point safety harness ensures additional safety. A smart magnetic safety buckle makes the harness snap firmly and stably into place by itself and keeps it secure while riding – parents and children can thus enjoy every single ride in relaxation and safety.

Sicher und geborgen

Für die heutige Mobilität spielt der Kindersitz eine wichtige Rolle. Kinder mit dem Fahrrad in den Kindergarten zu bringen oder auf einen Ausflug mitzunehmen, ist eine einfache und umweltfreundliche Alternative zum Auto. Die Gestaltung des Thule Yepp Nexxt Maxi stellt eine beeindruckende Neuinterpretation des Fahrrad-Kindersitzes dar, die viele Vorteile in sich vereint. Dieser Kindersitz zeigt eine zeitgemäße Formensprache und zahlreiche gut durchdachte Details. Auf den ersten Blick fällt seine ungewöhnliche und in ihrer Anmutung neue Linienführung auf. Die Formgebung erinnert an moderne Fahrradhelme, weshalb der Kindersitz eine sehr sportliche Anmutung hat, die sich gut allen Fahrradmodellen anpasst. Er weist eine hochentwickelte Ergonomie auf und dank seiner innovativen Gestaltung mit stoßabsorbierenden und gepolsterten Materialien sitzt das Kind zu jeder Zeit bequem. Die Sitzschale des in fünf Farben erhältlichen Thule Yepp Nexxt Maxi ist solide und leicht. Rückwärtig montiert, bietet sie einen stabilen und sicheren Halt für Babys und Kleinkinder. Der innovative 5-Punkt-Sicherheitsgurt erhöht die Sicherheit zusätzlich. Eine intelligente Magnet-Sicherheitsschnalle ermöglicht es, dass sich der Gurt von alleine fest und stabil verschließt und auch verschlossen bleibt – Eltern und Kind können so jede einzelne Fahrt sorgenfrei und entspannt genießen.

Statement by the jury

Following an innovative design approach has made the Thule Yepp Nexxt Maxi emerge as a child bike seat with outstanding characteristics. Based on a successful interplay of all elements it is comfortable and robust, fulfilling the highest demands on safety. It incorporates an overall convincing solution. With its fresh appeal and sophisticated functionality, it sets new standards in the field of child bike seats.

Begründung der Jury

Beim Thule Yepp Nexxt Maxi führt ein innovativer Gestaltungsansatz zu einem Kindersitz mit beeindruckenden Eigenschaften. Auf der Basis eines gelungenen Zusammenspiels aller Elemente ist er komfortabel und stabil, wobei höchster Wert auf die Sicherheit gelegt wurde. Insgesamt stellt er eine rundum gelungene Lösung dar. Mit seiner frischen Anmutung und durchdachten Funktionalität beschreitet er neue Wege im Bereich der Fahrrad-Kindersitze.

Designer portrait
See page 62
Siehe Seite 62

Spin 360™
Child Car Seat
Kinderautositz

Manufacturer
Joie Children's Products Co., Limited, United Kingdom
In-house design
Web
www.joiebaby.com

The Spin 360 is a very light and compact child car seat. Thanks to a specially developed seat shape with protection against rebound on impact, no extra rebound bar is needed, and the seat takes up less space. The Spin 360 adjusts flexibly to the size of the child and can be revolved 360 degrees on its base to allow easy entry and exit as well as change of driving direction. In the seat, children from newborn up to a weight of 18 kg can be transported seated backwards, from 9 kg also forwards, in each case in five different reclining and sitting positions.

Der Spin 360 ist ein sehr leichter und kompakter Kinderautositz. Dank einer speziell entwickelten Sitzschale mit Rückprallschutz bedarf es keines zusätzlichen Rückprallbügels, sodass der Sitz weniger Platz einnimmt. Der Spin 360 lässt sich flexibel auf die Körpergröße des Kindes anpassen und auf seiner Basis um 360 Grad drehen, um Ein- und Ausstieg sowie den Wechsel der Fahrtrichtung zu erleichtern. In dem Sitz können Kinder von Geburt an bis zu einem Gewicht von 18 kg rückwärts, ab 9 kg auch vorwärts in jeweils fünf verschiedenen Liege- und Sitzpositionen befördert werden.

Statement by the jury
This child car seat combines a sophisticated safety concept with many clever functions which make the use of the seat for parents and child convenient.

Begründung der Jury
Dieser Kinderautositz verbindet ein ausgereiftes Sicherheitskonzept mit vielen cleveren Funktionen, die die Nutzung des Sitzes für Eltern und Kind komfortabel machen.

Nuna RAVA™
Child Car Seat
Kinderautositz

Manufacturer
Nuna International BV, Erp, Netherlands
In-house design
Web
www.nuna.eu

This convertible child car seat, in which children up to 22 kg can be transported in a rearward as well as forward position, is easy to install and, thanks to a clear visual guide, can be intuitively operated. The RAVA design is intentionally minimalist, having details constructed in a manner so that extras such as bubble level guides are not needed as all is engineered into the seat. The individually adaptable system grows with the child from the birth up to 29 kg. It offers plenty of legroom and, thanks to advanced side impact protection with SIP housing and energy absorbing materials, it is very safe.

Dieser flexible Kindersitz, in dem Kinder bis 22 kg sowohl rückwärts als auch vorwärts befördert werden können, lässt sich unkompliziert installieren und dank klarer visueller Hinweise intuitiv bedienen. RAVA ist bewusst minimalistisch und mit vielen durchdachten Details gestaltet, sodass auf Extras wie die Integration einer Wasserwaage verzichtet werden konnte, weil alles bereits in den Sitz eingebaut ist. Das individuell anpassbare System wächst von der Geburt bis 29 kg mit, bietet viel Beinfreiheit und ist dank fortschrittlichen Seitenaufprallschutzes mit SIP-Gehäuse und energieabsorbierenden Materialien sehr sicher.

Statement by the jury
The RAVA child car seat impresses by its simple handling and offers many options for individual adaption, so that it grows extensively with the child.

Begründung der Jury
Der Kindersitz RAVA beeindruckt durch eine einfache Handhabung und bietet viele Möglichkeiten der individuellen Anpassung, sodass er lange mitwächst.

Vaya i-Size
Child Car Seat
Kinderautositz

Manufacturer
gb GmbH, Bayreuth, Germany
Design
Koncern Design Studio s.r.o.,
Prague, Czech Republic
Web
www.cybex-online.com

The new Vaya i-Size child seat of the
"gb Platinum" collection is compatible
with present safety standards and
offers simple-to-use technology. For instance, the Vaya i-Size, thanks to its
360-degrees rotation function, makes it
easy to change between rear-facing
and forward-facing positions – without
removal of the seat. Thus, it makes getting in and out of the child seat comfortable, promotes the child's self-confidence
and allows convenient fastening, tighten-
ing and release of the five-point seatbelt
system.

Statement by the jury
Vaya i-Size is designed ergonomically,
crafted in high quality and makes a luxurious impression. At the same time, it
complies with high demands of comfort
and safety.

Der neue Kindersitz Vaya i-Size aus der
„gb Platinum"-Kollektion wird aktuellen
Sicherheitsstandards gerecht und bietet
einfach zu bedienende Technologien. So
ermöglicht der Vaya i-Size dank seiner
360-Grad-Rotationsfunktion einen einfachen Wechsel zwischen rückwärts und
vorwärts gerichteter Position ohne Ausbau
des Sitzes. Er erleichtert so das Ein- und
Aussteigen aus dem Kindersitz, fördert die
Selbstständigkeit des Kindes und sorgt
für ein komfortables Anlegen, Straffen und
Lösen des 5-Punkt-Gurtsystems.

Begründung der Jury
Vaya i-Size ist ergonomisch gestaltet,
hochwertig verarbeitet und hat eine luxuriöse Anmutung. Gleichzeitig erfüllt er
hohe Ansprüche an Komfort und Sicherheit.

Studio ID Baby Seat
Photographer Baby Seat
Babysitz für Fotografen

Manufacturer
Générale de téléphone, La Plaine Saint-Denis, France
Design
Pars Pro Toto, Ghent, Belgium
Web
www.generaledetelephone.com
www.parsprototo.be

This baby seat was developed to make high-quality passport photos of babies and toddlers in the shortest possible time. The Studio ID Baby Seat is stable and consists of three-dimensionally moulded foam and felt. A soft surface coating provides further comfort. The special feature of the seat is a headrest with a recess which allows the baby's head to stay directed towards the camera. The height-adjustable and magnetically attached headrest also serves as a grey photographic background.

Statement by the jury
The Studio ID Baby Seat convinces by its sophisticated functionality and is designed to provide babies with the highest degree of comfort when being photographed.

Dieser Babysitz wurde entwickelt, um in möglichst kurzer Zeit qualitativ hochwertige Passbilder von Babys und Kleinkindern machen zu können. Der Studio ID Baby Seat ist stabil und besteht aus dreidimensional geformtem Schaumstoff und Filz. Eine weiche Oberflächenbeschichtung bietet zusätzlichen Komfort. Die Besonderheit des Sitzes ist ein Kopfteil mit Vertiefung, durch die der Babykopf zur Kamera hin ausgerichtet bleibt. Gleichzeitig dient das mit Magneten befestigte und höhenverstellbare Kopfteil als grauer Fotohintergrund.

Begründung der Jury
Der Studio ID Baby Seat überzeugt durch eine ausgereifte Funktionalität und ist gleichzeitig so gestaltet, dass er Babys bei Fotoaufnahmen größtmöglichen Komfort bietet.

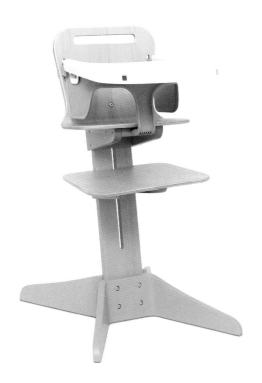

sagepole
High Chair
Hochstuhl

Manufacturer
Petit Elin, Seoul, South Korea
In-house design
Jihye Han
Web
www.petitelinstore.com

The sagepole high chair is continuously adjustable in height so that it can be optimally adapted to the environment. Its reduced and modern design is based on the form of a tree: the seat is enthroned on one single "tree trunk", a solid wooden element, and four horizontally protruding feet resting on the floor provide stability. The sitting height is set along the central column via a screw fixture, without the need for additional tools; at any time a securing lock assures that the seat cannot accidently slip down.

Statement by the jury
sagepole is a high chair with a simple as well as well-conceived design. It grows with the child and is characterised by a high level of user-friendliness.

Der sagepole-Hochstuhl ist stufenlos höhenverstellbar, sodass er optimal an die Umgebung angepasst werden kann. Sein reduziertes und zeitgemäßes Design ist an die Form eines Baumes angelehnt: Auf einem einzelnen „Stamm", einem massiven Holzelement, thront der Sitz, und zum Boden hin sorgen vier ausladende Füße für Stabilität. Die Sitzhöhe wird entlang der Mittelschiene ohne zusätzliches Werkzeug mittels eines Schraubgriffs fixiert; eine Sicherung sorgt dafür, dass der Sitz zu keinem Zeitpunkt versehentlich herunterrutschen kann.

Begründung der Jury
sagepole ist ein ebenso schlicht wie durchdacht gestalteter Hochstuhl. Er wächst mit und zeichnet sich durch eine hohe Benutzerfreundlichkeit aus.

Frrrniture
Children's Furniture
Kindermöbel

Manufacturer
Mizarstvo Florjančič, Novo Mesto, Slovenia
Design
Studijo Andaluzia d.o.o. (Lucija Vodopivc), Ljubljana, Slovenia
Web
www.florjancic.eu
www.frrrniture.com

This children's furniture collection consists of six chairs and a table. Whereas the table is a simple design, the chairs represent various characters. They are individually formed and colourfully designed. By this means, they attract the children's attention, are integrated into games and promote children's imagination. The wooden surfaces are coated with a semi-transparent, water-based and environmentally friendly finish which emphasises the structure of the wood.

Statement by the jury
Frrrniture gains merit with a loving, child-friendly and simultaneously environmentally friendly design as well as skilful workmanship, which contributes to the long life of the furniture.

Diese Kindermöbel-Kollektion setzt sich aus sechs Stühlen und einem Tisch zusammen. Während der Tisch schlicht gehalten ist, stellen die Stühle verschiedene Charaktere dar und sind alle unterschiedlich geformt und farbenfroh gestaltet. Auf diese Weise ziehen sie die Aufmerksamkeit der Kinder auf sich, werden in Spiele mit eingebunden und fördern die kindliche Phantasie. Die Holzoberflächen sind mit einer halbtransparenten, wasserbasierten und umweltfreundlichen Schicht versehen, die die Struktur des Holzes betont.

Begründung der Jury
Frrrniture punktet mit einer liebevollen, kindgerechten und zugleich umweltfreundlichen Gestaltung sowie einer sorgfältigen Verarbeitung, die zur Langlebigkeit der Möbel beiträgt.

Tinkle-Pop
Children's Furniture
Kindermöbel

Manufacturer
iloom furniture company, Seoul, South Korea
In-house design
Jungsoo Huh, Inhwan Woo
Web
www.iloom.com

Tinkle-Pop is a series of children's furniture which attracts attention due to its coherent colour concept and gently curved lines. The system is very variable; for instance, the table legs can be pulled out to three lengths according to the size of the child, while the beds can be set up either as bunk beds or individually. All furniture is so conceived that children have all important items at eye level and can reach them easily, thus promoting independence.

Tinkle-Pop ist eine Kindermöbelserie, die mit einem stimmigen Farbkonzept und einer sanft geschwungenen Linienführung auf sich aufmerksam macht. Das System ist sehr variabel; so lassen sich die Beine des Tischs je nach Größe des Kindes in drei verschiedenen Längen ausziehen, während die Betten als Etagenbett oder einzeln aufgestellt werden können. Sämtliche Möbel sind so konzipiert, dass Kinder alles Wichtige auf Augenhöhe haben und es gut erreichen können, um ihre Selbstständigkeit zu fördern.

Statement by the jury
Wonderful colours and coherent proportions characterise the impression of this lovingly crafted and yet sturdy children's furniture series.

Begründung der Jury
Wunderschöne Farben und stimmige Proportionen prägen die Anmutung dieser liebevoll gestalteten und zugleich robusten Kindermöbelserie.

FLEXA Popsicle
Children's Bed
Kinderbett

Manufacturer
Flexa4Dreams, Hornsyld, Denmark
In-house design
Kristine Schmidt
Design
Herman Studio (Helle Herman Mortensen,
Jonas Herman Pedersen), Aarhus, Denmark
Web
www.flexaworld.com
www.hermanstudio.dk

The design of the children's bed of the Flexa Popsicle collection is inspired by an ice lolly as the epitome of a happy childhood. This is shown in various details, for instance, the rounded bedposts which remind of lolly sticks, overall soft lines, and the combination of wood and sorbet colours. The bed is constructed of solid oak, robust and safe. It is available in three colours: kiwi green, cherry pink and blueberry blue.

Das Design des Kinderbetts der Flexa Popsicle-Kollektion ist von einem Eis am Stiel als dem Inbegriff einer glücklichen Kindheit inspiriert. Das zeigt sich in verschiedenen Details wie beispielsweise den abgerundeten Bettpfosten, die an Holzstiele erinnern, einer insgesamt weichen Linienführung oder auch in der Kombination von Holz und Sorbetfarben. Das Bett ist aus massivem Eichenholz gefertigt, robust und sicher. Es ist in den drei Farbtönen Kiwi-Grün, Cherry-Rosa und Blueberry-Blau erhältlich.

Statement by the jury
The Popsicle children's bed is based on an enchanting design idea which is implemented very coherently in its lines, colours and choice of materials.

Begründung der Jury
Dem Popsicle-Kinderbett liegt eine bezaubernde Gestaltungsidee zugrunde, die in Linienführung, Farb- und Materialwahl sehr stimmig umgesetzt wurde.

Ggumbi Legend Bumper Bed – New Moon
Play Mat and Bed
Spielmatte und Bett

Manufacturer
Ggumbi, Daejeon, South Korea
In-house design
Zinhi Choi
Web
www.ggumbi.com

The Legend Bumper Bed – New Moon consists of two mats, each divided into five parts. Because of this, it can be folded in various ways, no matter how much or little room is available. The bed can be arranged in twelve different forms, for example, it can be folded into a baby bed with a surrounding edge 44 cm high, a play mat or a playing house, each held in place by a Velcro fastener. The mats are 4 cm thick and made of a material with impact absorbing properties so that children will not be injured even when romping wildly on the mat.

Das Legend Bumper Bed – New Moon besteht aus zwei fünffach unterteilten Matratzen. Dadurch lässt es sich, in Abhängigkeit vom zur Verfügung stehenden Platz, auf verschiedene Weise falten. Das Bett kann zwölf verschiedene Formen annehmen, unter anderem kann es zu einem Babybett mit 44 cm hoher Umrandung, einer Spielmatte oder einem Spielhaus gefaltet und jeweils mit Klettverschluss fixiert werden. Die Matratzen sind 4 cm dick und aus einem Material, das stoßabsorbierend wirkt, sodass Kinder sich auch bei wildem Toben auf der Matte nicht verletzen.

Statement by the jury
This bed delights with its versatility which is based on an idea that is as simple as it is convincing. The discreet colouring and the image of the rising moon promote tranquillity.

Begründung der Jury
Dieses Bett begeistert mit seiner Vielseitigkeit, die auf einer ebenso einfachen wie überzeugenden Idee beruht. Die dezente Farbgebung und das Bild des aufgehenden Mondes vermitteln Ruhe.

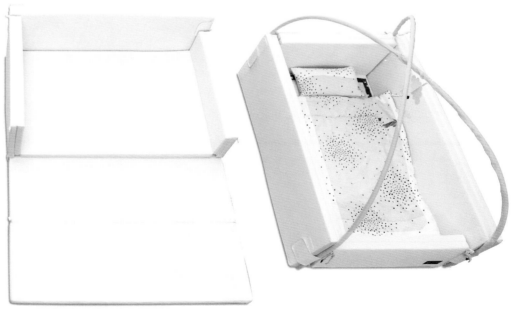

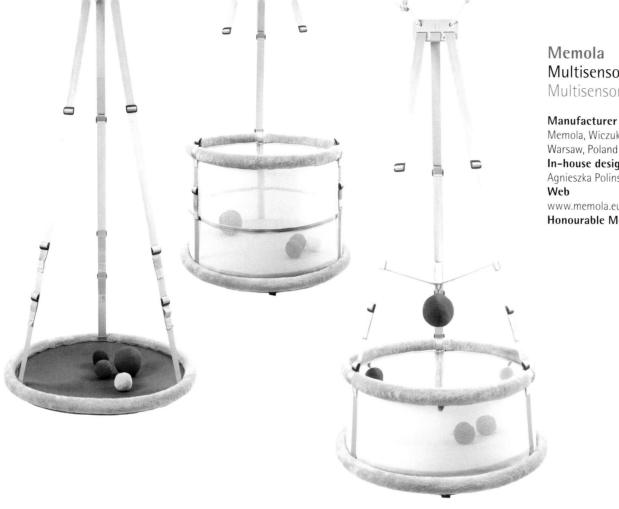

Memola
Multisensory Cradle
Multisensorische Wiege

Manufacturer
Memola, Wiczuk-Polinski Sp. z o.o.,
Warsaw, Poland
In-house design
Agnieszka Polinski
Web
www.memola.eu
Honourable Mention

Memola is a multisensory cradle which promotes several aspects of children's development. Transparent side panels allow the baby to lie on the tummy, to swing and to notice the surroundings. It is thereby encouraged to lift its head alone and to interact with its environment, thus strengthening the neck muscles and balance skill and promoting the motoric system. The cradle can be adapted easily to a basket and later to a swing so that it can be used a long time by the child.

Statement by the jury
The Memola cradle convinces from functional aspects since with its special design it purposefully promotes the child's development.

Memola ist eine multisensorische Wiege, die mehrere Aspekte der Kindesentwicklung fördert. Durchsichtige Seitenwände ermöglichen es dem Baby, gleichzeitig in Bauchlage zu liegen, zu schaukeln und die Umgebung wahrzunehmen. So wird es dazu angeregt, selbstständig den Kopf zu heben und mit seiner Umwelt zu interagieren, was die Nackenmuskulatur und die Balancefähigkeit stärkt und die Motorik fördert. Die Wiege lässt sich einfach zum Korb und später zur Schaukel umbauen, sodass sie das Kind lange begleitet.

Begründung der Jury
Die Wiege Memola überzeugt unter funktionalen Gesichtspunkten, denn mit ihrer besonderen Gestaltung fördert sie gezielt die kindliche Entwicklung.

Done by Deer
Little interiors
Children's Furniture
Kindermöbelserie

Manufacturer
Done by Deer, Silkeborg, Denmark
In-house design
Helene Hjorth, Line Kastberg
Web
www.donebydeer.com

Designed and produced in Denmark, the child furniture series "Little interiors" combines the workmanship quality of the 1950s and 1960s with a modern Scandinavian furnishing style. The series consists of furniture pieces for sleeping, nappy changing and storing, all designed with great attention to details. The baby cot converts to accommodate the child's needs and development from birth up through the toddler years. The storage rack offers plenty of space and easy access and by adding the top changer it serves as a cosy and practical changing station.

Statement by the jury
"Little interiors" has been designed with a lot of love towards detail. Its flexible functionality is combined with a timeless-classical appearance.

Die in Dänemark entworfene und produzierte Kindermöbelserie „Little interiors" kombiniert die Verarbeitungsqualität der 1950er und 1960er Jahre mit einem modernen skandinavischen Einrichtungsstil. Die Serie besteht aus mit viel Liebe zum Detail gestalteten Möbelstücken zum Schlafen, zur Aufbewahrung und zum Wickeln. Das Kinderbett lässt sich anpassen, sodass es von Geburt an bis ins Kleinkindalter genutzt werden kann. Das Regal dient in Kombination mit dem separaten Wickelaufsatz auch als gemütliche und praktische Wickelkommode und bietet viel Stauraum.

Begründung der Jury
Die Kindermöbelserie „Little interiors" ist mit viel Liebe zum Detail gestaltet. Ihre flexible Funktionalität verbindet sich mit einem zeitlos-klassischen Erscheinungsbild.

Link
Bassinet
Babywiege

Manufacturer
babyhome, babynow S.L.,
Sabadell (Barcelona), Spain
In-house design
Web
www.babyhome.es

Link is a versatile product designed to take on different functions. It seems to be simply a baby cradle or a travel cot, but it is much more. It can be opened to side-attach it to the parents' bed as an adjacent cot. Thanks to the handlebar, Link can also be used as a carrycot for moving or travelling. The side walls can be folded down turning the cradle into a play mat with a toy bar, where rattles or similar toys can be attached.

Link ist ein vielseitiges Produkt, das so konzipiert ist, dass es verschiedene Funktionen übernehmen kann. Auf den ersten Blick scheint es eine einfache Babywiege oder ein Reisebett zu sein, es ist aber mehr. Link kann seitlich zum elterlichen Bett hin geöffnet werden und dient dann als Beistellbettchen. Dank des Bügelgriffs lässt sich Link auch als Babytragetasche für unterwegs nutzen. Die Seitenwände lassen sich zudem herunterklappen, sodass aus der Wiege eine Spieldecke mit Spielbogen wird, an dem sich Rasseln oder ähnliches Spielzeug befestigen lassen.

Statement by the jury
This bassinet convinces with an innovative concept by which it is versatile in use. Its modern design appeals particularly to young families.

Begründung der Jury
Dieser Babykorb überzeugt mit einem innovativen Konzept, durch das er vielseitig einsetzbar ist. Mit seiner zeitgemäßen Gestaltung spricht er insbesondere junge Familien an.

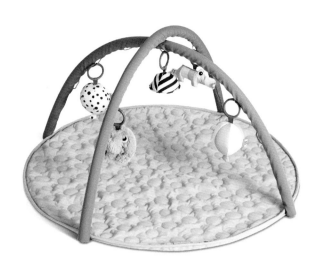

Activity Play Mat
Activity Arch
Spielbogen

Manufacturer
Done by Deer, Silkeborg, Denmark
In-house design
Helene Hjorth, Line Kastberg
Web
www.donebydeer.com

The Activity Play Mat is a subtly designed playing arch with monochrome colours which integrates harmoniously in the modern living environment. The baby's senses are stimulated by five activity toys that are easy to grasp and can be repositioned on the arches: Croco, a crackling crocodile, Elphee, a rattling elephant, a little mirror, a balloon with a chime and another one with a bell. The Velcro attachable arches can easily be removed so the soft quilted mat can be used on its own.

Statement by the jury
This activity arch with its discreet and high-quality appearance is a tasteful alternative to the classical, colourful variants.

Die Activity Play Mat ist ein subtil gestalteter Spielbogen, der sich mit seinen monochromen Farbtönen harmonisch ins moderne Wohnumfeld integriert. Die Sinne des Babys werden mithilfe von fünf herabbaumelnden, leicht zu greifenden und einfach zu verschiebenden Spielzeugen stimuliert: Croco, einem knisternden Krokodil, Elphee, einem rasselnden Elefanten, einem kleinen Spiegel, einem Ballon mit Geläut sowie einem weiteren mit Glocke. Die mit Klettverschluss angebrachten Bögen lassen sich leicht entfernen, sodass die weiche Steppdecke alleine verwendet werden kann.

Begründung der Jury
Dieser Spielbogen ist mit seinem dezenten und hochwertigen Erscheinungsbild eine geschmackvolle Alternative zu den klassischen, farbenfrohen Varianten.

My Rabbit Pet
Wooden Development Toy
Holz-Lernspielzeug

Manufacturer
Su Sang Int'l Co., Ltd., New Taipei City, Taiwan
In-house design
Duncan Hsieh
Web
www.hf-kids.com

My Rabbit Pet is a trailing toy on a lead which is in the form of a rabbit. When being pulled along, the smaller front and larger rear wheels rotate, giving the impression that the rabbit is hopping along behind the child. When standing still, it either sits upright on its back legs or stands on all four. This toy is made of wood; head, ears and stubby tail are movable.

Statement by the jury
This lovably designed and carefully made toy enchants by its hopping motion which is caused by wheels of different sizes.

My Rabbit Pet ist ein Nachziehspielzeug, das die Form eines Kaninchens hat. Wird es gezogen, rotieren das kleinere Vorder- und das größere Hinterrad so, dass der Anschein entsteht, als ob das Kaninchen dem Kind hinterherhoppeln würde. Wird es nicht bewegt, sitzt es entweder aufrecht auf den Hinterbeinen oder steht auf allen Vieren. Das Spielzeug ist aus Holz gefertigt, Kopf, Ohren und Stummelschwanz sind beweglich.

Begründung der Jury
Dieses liebevoll gestaltete und sorgfältig gefertigte Holzspielzeug bezaubert durch seine Hoppelbewegung, die durch unterschiedlich große Räder hervorgerufen wird.

Plattenbau
Learning Material and Toy
Lernmittel und Spielzeug

Manufacturer
Plattenbau, Erfurt, Germany
In-house design
Julia Heinemann
Web
www.plattenbau.design

Plattenbau is a cube assembled from 25 softly polished fine wood components. It is both a learning element and a toy at the same time. Its individual components can be assembled and combined in all different ways. Due to the haptic and intelligent construction of ever new forms, not only the perception of space qualities and the orientation in space are trained, but also the skills in abstract and strategic thinking. Plattenbau sees itself as an homage to the space concept of early Bauhaus and as a learning tool which serves the comprehension of complex relativities.

Statement by the jury
This toy and learning aid impresses with its simplified new interpretation of the well-known modular principle by means of which the spatial imagination is trained.

Plattenbau ist ein Kubus, der sich aus 25 weich polierten Edelholzteilen zusammensetzt und zugleich Lernmittel und Spielzeug ist. Seine Einzelteile lassen sich auf immer wieder neue Art und Weise zusammensetzen und kombinieren. Durch das haptische und gedankliche Konstruieren immer neuer Formen werden sowohl das Erfassen von Raumqualitäten und die Orientierung im Raum geschult als auch die Fähigkeit des abstrakten und strategischen Denkens. Plattenbau versteht sich als eine Hommage an das Raumkonzept des jungen Bauhauses und als Lernmittel, das dem Begreifen komplexer Zusammenhänge dient.

Begründung der Jury
Dieses Spiel- und Lernmittel beeindruckt mit seiner schlichten Neuinterpretation des bekannten Baukastenprinzips, durch das das räumliche Vorstellungsvermögen geschult wird.

ooh noo Toy Pram
Doll's Pram
Puppenwagen

Manufacturer
Wilsonic Design, Trzin, Slovenia
In-house design
Nina Mihovec, Peter Rojc
Web
www.wilsonicdesign.com

The ooh noo toy pram is a modern interpretation of the traditional doll's pram. It is made from natural materials such as bent birch wood and is produced entirely in Europe. The design of the pram is purist and timeless; at the same time it is extremely stable as well as sturdy and can be manoeuvred easily with its narrow rubber wheels. Due to its contemporary aesthetics, it fits harmoniously into the modern living environment.

Statement by the jury
The use of natural materials and a timeless design make the ooh noo toy pram a charming new interpretation of the doll's pram.

Der ooh noo Toy Pram ist eine moderne Interpretation des traditionellen Puppenwagens. Er ist ausschließlich aus natürlichen Werkstoffen wie gebogenem Birkenholz gefertigt und wird komplett in Europa produziert. Die Gestaltung des Puppenwagens ist puristisch und zeitlos, gleichzeitig ist er äußerst stabil und robust und lässt sich mit seinen schmalen Gummireifen leicht manövrieren. Mit seiner zeitgemäßen Ästhetik fügt er sich harmonisch ins moderne Wohnumfeld ein.

Begründung der Jury
Der Einsatz natürlicher Materialien sowie eine zeitlose Gestaltung machen den ooh noo Toy Pram zu einer charmanten Neuinterpretation des Puppenwagens.

Ramp Racer
Wooden Toy
Holzspielzeug

Manufacturer
Plan Creations Co., Ltd., Bangkok, Thailand
In-house design
Web
www.plantoys.com

This wooden car racetrack for young children convinces with its reserved design. Only the small cars in yellow, blue and red are brightly coloured, with the result that even the smallest children can follow them easily with their eyes while the cars race downwards. The track with four levels in cascade style is robust and manufactured from natural materials. It stimulates hand-eye coordination, which is an advantage when the children later start to paint, read and write, as well as gaining an initial understanding of the principle of cause and effect.

Statement by the jury
The Ramp Racer is sturdy and yet elegantly designed. The visual contrast between the wooden track and the coloured racing cars makes it easy for children to follow the speedy cars.

Diese Autorennbahn aus Holz für Kleinkinder überzeugt mit einer zurückgenommenen Gestaltung. Einzig die kleinen Autos in Gelb, Blau und Rot zeigen kraftvolle Farben, weshalb schon die Kleinsten sie auf ihrem rasanten Weg nach unten gut mit den Augen verfolgen können. Die Bahn mit vier Ebenen im Kaskadenstil ist stabil und aus natürlichen Materialen gefertigt. Sie fördert die Hand-Auge-Koordination, was den Kindern später beim Malen, Lesen und Schreiben zugutekommt, ebenso wie ein erstes Verständnis für das Prinzip von Ursache und Wirkung.

Begründung der Jury
Der Ramp Racer ist zugleich robust und anmutig gestaltet. Der visuelle Kontrast zwischen Holzbahn und farbigem Rennwagen erleichtert Kindern das Verfolgen der flinken Autos.

Zoo
Wooden Toy
Holzspielzeug

Manufacturer
SHUSHA, Moscow, Russia
In-house design
Anastasia Sherbakova, Vasily Perfilyev
Web
www.shusha-toys.ru
Honourable Mention

Zoo is a wooden construction toy with which various animals can be built. It is made from natural materials, such as solid beech. It is composed of a basic body with suggested legs and various ears, noses, beaks etc. which are held to the body by means of magnets. Children from the age of two years can let their fantasies run freely and create funny animals. While playing they also train their imagination and their motoric skills.

Statement by the jury
This attractive toy is based on an original idea and offers childish fantasy a lot of space for free development.

Zoo ist ein Konstruktionsspiel aus Holz, mit dem verschiedene Tiere gebaut werden können. Es wird komplett aus natürlichen Materialien wie Buchenholz gefertigt. Zoo setzt sich zusammen aus einem Basiskörper mit angedeuteten Beinen und verschiedenen Ohren, Schnauzen, Schnäbeln etc., die mithilfe von Magneten an der Basis halten. Kinder ab zwei Jahren können damit ihrer Phantasie freien Lauf lassen und lustige Tiere erschaffen, während sie beim Spielen ihre Vorstellungskraft und ihre motorischen Fähigkeiten trainieren.

Begründung der Jury
Dieses sympathische Holzspielzeug basiert auf einer originellen Idee und bietet der kindlichen Phantasie viel Raum zur Entfaltung.

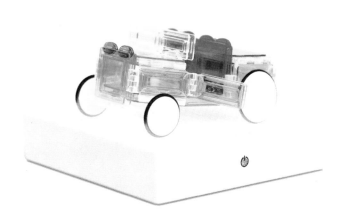

TWIPEA
Toy Blocks
Bausteine

Manufacturer
Da-Na Play, Yongin, South Korea
In-house design
Doo Hyun Hwang, Hae Young Song,
Chanu Hwang, Giuseppe Vitale
Web
www.danaplay.com
Honourable Mention

Twipea is a jointing toy which consists of a transparent receiver base (TWI stands for transparent window) and jointing blocks reminiscent of peanuts (PEA for peanut). Both together offer endless possibilities for people of all ages, alone or in company, to play, build or assemble small works of art. A particularly pleasing effect is created when the translucent constructions are stood on an illuminated box.

Statement by the jury
This jointing toy is attractive due to its translucent elements and when backlit has a special fascination.

Twipea ist ein Steckspiel, das sich aus einem transparenten Steckfeld (TWI für Transparent Window) und aus Steckbausteinen zusammensetzt, die an Erdnüsse erinnern (PEA für Peanut). Beides zusammen bietet Menschen aller Altersstufen zahllose Möglichkeiten, um damit alleine oder gemeinsam zu spielen, zu bauen oder kleine Kunstwerke zusammenzusetzen. Ein besonders schöner Effekt entsteht, wenn die transluzenten Bauwerke auf einen Leuchtkasten gestellt werden.

Begründung der Jury
Dieses Steckspiel gefällt mit seinen transluzenten Elementen und birgt hinterleuchtet eine besondere Faszination.

Robopal
Programming Blocks
Educational Toy
Lernspielzeug

Manufacturer
Suzhou Robopal Co., Ltd., Suzhou, China
Design
ECOVACS Robotics Co., Ltd., Suzhou, China
Web
www.robopal.cn
www.ecovacs.com

Robopal Programming Blocks is an innovative programming game, by which children can playfully learn to program, based on the concepts underlying the programming languages. At the same time, their analytic thinking is trained, and their comprehension of mathematics, informatics, natural sciences, and technology is taught. The programming modules can be used with various interactive programming toys which give sensor-based feedback in the form of motions, tones or light signals.

Statement by the jury
This toy familiarises children in a playful manner with the basic steps of programming and convinces from a design viewpoint with an easily understood user interface.

Robopal Programming Blocks ist ein innovatives Programmierspiel, mit dem Kinder spielerisch das Programmieren auf Basis der den Programmiersprachen zugrundeliegenden Konzepte erlernen. Gleichzeitig wird ihr analytisches Denken trainiert und ihr Verständnis für Mathematik, Informatik, Naturwissenschaften und Technik geschult. Die Programmierbausteine können mit verschiedenen interaktiven Spielzeugen genutzt werden, die sensorbasierte Feedbacks in Form von Bewegungen, Tönen oder Lichtsignalen geben.

Begründung der Jury
Dieses Spielzeug bringt Kindern auf spielerische Weise die Grundzüge des Programmierens nahe und überzeugt in gestalterischer Hinsicht mit einer leicht verständlichen Benutzeroberfläche.

Neurons
Educational Toy
Lernspielzeug

Manufacturer
Makeblock Co., Ltd., Shenzhen, China
In-house design
Yiyue Zheng, Lian Liu, Wei Xie
Design
IU+DESIGN (Jiye Shen, Shenghui Jia,
Junyao Li, Haiwei Wu, David Juan, Liang Wang,
Yajuan Huai, Zheyang Cai), Shenzhen, China
Web
www.makeblock.com
www.iuplus-design.com

Neurons is a modular system with colourful, electronic components which have been specially developed to educate children and juveniles in the STEM field. The construction kit contains 30 blocks with various functions which are all connected quite simply using magnets to create an electronic network. On the basis of data flow orientation and graphic programming, children are enabled to develop and implement their own ideas, for instance, in the field of smart homes or the Internet of Things.

Neurons ist ein modulares System mit farbigen elektronischen Bausteinen, das speziell entwickelt wurde, um Kinder und Jugendliche im MINT-Bereich zu fördern. Der Baukasten beinhaltet mehr als 30 Blöcke mit unterschiedlichen Funktionen, die ganz einfach mithilfe von Magneten miteinander verbunden werden, um ein elektronisches Netzwerk zu bilden. Auf Basis von datenflussorientierter und grafischer Programmierung werden die Kinder so in die Lage versetzt, eigene Ideen etwa im Bereich des Smart Homes oder des Internets der Dinge zu entwickeln und umzusetzen.

Statement by the jury
The design of this educational toy is so simple and intuitive that it enables children to acquire a basic knowledge of electronics independently in an experimental way.

Begründung der Jury
Dieses Lernspielzeug ist so einfach und selbsterklärend gestaltet, dass es Kinder dazu befähigt, sich eigenständig auf eine experimentelle Art Basiswissen aus der Elektronik anzueignen.

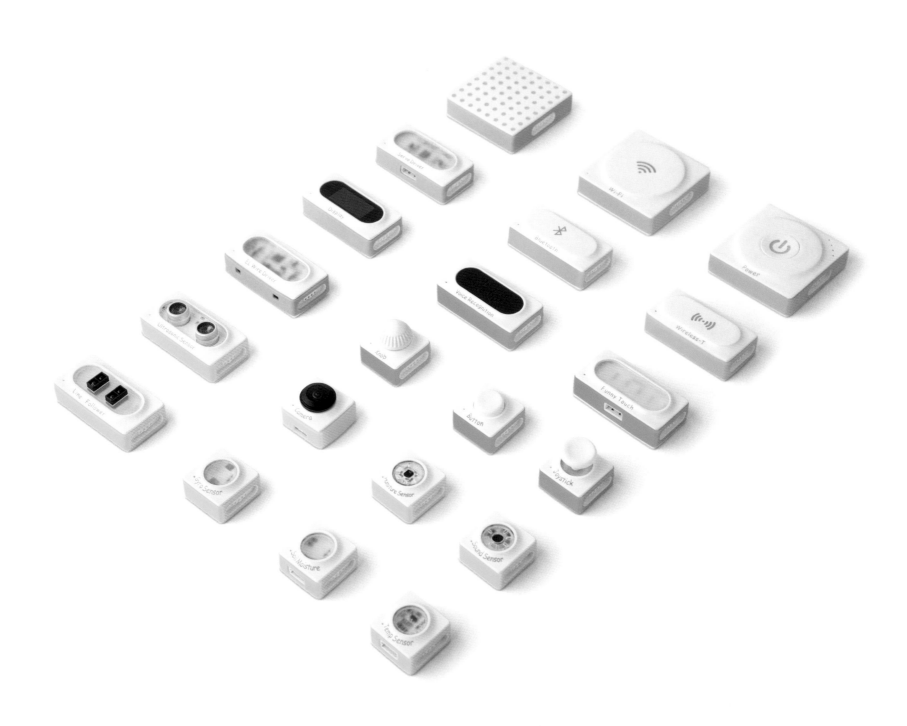

Cana
Toy Watering Can
Spielzeug-Gießkanne

Manufacturer
Quut Toys, Ghent, Belgium
Design
Pars Pro Toto, Ghent, Belgium
Web
www.quuttoys.com
www.parsprototo.be

The Cana toy is a watering can with two separate, distinctively coloured outlets. From one of them, the water is sprayed through a shower opening; on the other side, a spout allows accurate watering. In this way, children have not only twice as much fun playing with the can either in the bath or the garden but also train their motoric skills.

Statement by the jury
Cana delights with an unusual design which gives this toy watering can a high visual individuality.

Cana ist eine Spielzeug-Gießkanne, die zwei unterschiedliche, farblich markant hervorgehobene Ausgüsse hat. An der einen Seite rieselt das Wasser durch eine Brauseöffnung heraus, auf der anderen Seite ermöglicht eine Tülle ein präzises Ausgießen. Dadurch haben Kinder nicht nur doppelt so viel Spaß beim Spielen mit der Kanne in der Badewanne oder im Garten, sie trainieren gleichzeitig auch ihre Feinmotorik.

Begründung der Jury
Cana begeistert mit einer ungewöhnlichen Gestaltung, die dieser Spielzeug-Gießkanne eine hohe visuelle Eigenständigkeit verleiht.

Yummy+
Childrens Tableware
Kindergeschirr

Manufacturer
Done by Deer, Silkeborg, Denmark
In-house design
Helene Hjorth, Line Kastberg
Web
www.donebydeer.com

The Yummy+ children's tableware consists of a cup, a bowl, a plate, and a spoon and fork set, all with anti-slip and easy-grip silicone. Black polka dots and the cheerful elephant, Elphee, decorate the dinnerware and provide good fun for children. Soft tones of powder, blue or grey contribute to a balanced overall impression. The cutlery features the animal friends Elphee and Nozo or Elphee and Ozzo, and the thick handles make it easy for small children to eat on their own.

Statement by the jury
Yummy+ is optimally conceived for the needs of children and delights the eyes of adults with a tasteful design.

Das Kindergeschirr Yummy+ besteht aus einem Becher, einer Schüssel, einem Teller sowie Gabel- und Löffelset. Alle Produkte sind mit rutschfestem und angenehmem Silikon beschichtet. Ein schwarzweißes Pünktchen-Muster und Elphee, der fröhliche Elefant, zieren das Geschirr und verbreiten gute Laune. Zarte Pastellfarben wie Rosa, Blau und Grau tragen zu einem ausgewogenen Gesamteindruck bei. Das Besteckset ist mit den Markentieren Elphee und Nozo oder Elphee und Ozzo erhältlich und erleichtert kleinen Kindern durch die dicken Griffe das selbstständige Essen.

Begründung der Jury
Yummy+ ist optimal auf kindliche Bedürfnisse abgestimmt und erfreut auch die Augen der Erwachsenen mit einer geschmackvollen Gestaltung.

My Bendy Straw Cup Range
Drinking Cup
Trinkbecher

Manufacturer
Philips, Eindhoven, Netherlands
In-house design
Philips Design
Web
www.philips.com

These cups with straw for children aged from twelve months were developed specifically by a multidisciplinary team required to design a product which was both spill-proof and dentally friendly. The result is a series of colourful drinking cups with an hourglass form, optimally shaped for the hands of infants. The cap and the soft, palate-friendly drinking straw are so designed that, thanks to an innovative valve, they are absolutely leak-proof when inactive.

Statement by the jury
Thanks to their well-conceived ergonomic design, My Bendy Straw Cups are both good for the jaw and especially good to hold.

Diese Trinkbecher mit Trinkhalm für Kinder ab einem Alter von zwölf Monaten wurden eigens in einem multidisziplinären Team entwickelt, um ein Produkt zu gestalten, das zugleich auslaufsicher und zahnfreundlich ist. Das Ergebnis ist eine Serie farbenfroher Becher, die mit ihrer Sanduhrform optimal auf kleine Kinderhände zugeschnitten sind. Der Deckel und der weiche, gaumenfreundliche Trinkhalm sind so konzipiert, dass sie in inaktivem Zustand dank eines innovativen Ventils absolut dicht sind.

Begründung der Jury
Dank ihrer durchdachten ergonomischen Gestaltung sind die My Bendy Straw Cups sowohl gut für den Kiefer als auch besonders gut zu greifen.

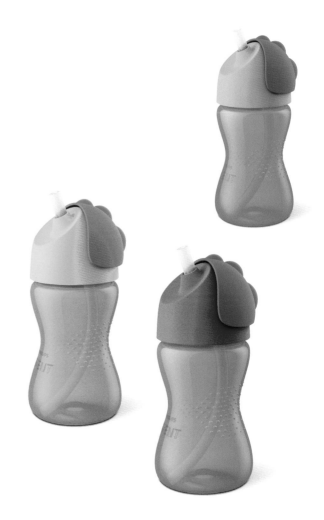

Philips Avent Essential Baby Food Maker
Baby Food Maker
Babynahrungszubereiter

Manufacturer
Philips, Eindhoven, Netherlands
In-house design
Philips Design
Web
www.philips.com

This baby food maker combines a steam cooker with a blender in one device and thus facilitates the preparation of home-made baby food. In the design, everything unnecessary has been omitted, so that only a few moves are necessary to assemble, disassemble and clean the device. A clear and understandable user interface makes operation easy and intuitive. Thanks to a special integrated technology, steam circulates from below upwards, so that the food is heated evenly and gently.

Statement by the jury
A sophisticated functional concept and a high degree of user-friendliness characterise this baby food maker which also displays a pleasantly reduced design.

Dieser Babynahrungszubereiter vereint Dampfgarer und Pürierstab in einem Gerät und erleichtert so die Zubereitung von selbstgemachter Babykost. Bei der Gestaltung wurde auf alles Überflüssige verzichtet, sodass nur wenige Handgriffe erforderlich sind, um das Gerät zusammenzusetzen, auseinanderzunehmen und zu reinigen. Eine klare und verständliche Bedienoberfläche macht die Anwendung einfach und intuitiv. Der Dampf zirkuliert dank einer besonderen integrierten Technologie von unten nach oben, sodass die Nahrung gleichmäßig und schonend erhitzt wird.

Begründung der Jury
Ein ausgereiftes Funktionskonzept und eine hohe Benutzerfreundlichkeit zeichnen diesen Babynahrungszubereiter aus, der zudem mit einer reduzierten Gestaltung gefällt.

Philips Avent Natural Electric Breast Pump Range
Breast Pump
Milchpumpe

Manufacturer
Philips, Eindhoven, Netherlands

In-house design
Philips Design

Web
www.philips.com

reddot award 2017
best of the best

Relaxation and comfort

Breast milk has been proven to be the healthiest nutrition for babies and toddlers. In order to bridge longer working periods, many mothers use milk pumps, as they allow them to remain more independent. The Philips Avent Natural Electric Breast Pump was thus developed to respond to this need and is tailor-made to exactly satisfy the demands of both mother and baby. Its design subtly interprets the natural process of breastfeeding. Working with the knowledge that relaxation enhances milk flow, the pump design explicitly focuses on comfort and absolute simplicity in use. Pleasant to the touch and quiet in use, it offers an innovative rhythmic massaging approach for effective pumping of breast milk that feels more natural. The pump features a compact form and a design idiom of feminine appeal with floral motifs that work harmoniously to deliver an effective interaction, reminiscent of a lifestyle product. It is light, made of materials that are pleasing to the touch and simple to use even when on the go. The process of expressing milk is facilitated by a clearly arranged user interface that can be customised to the specific needs of the user. The relaxing experience of comfort and ease of use make Philips Avent lend the milk pump a new image. Expressing breast milk is thus turned into a positive experience and a process that is easy to plan for active mums.

Ruhe und Komfort

Das Stillen ist für Babys und Kleinkinder die gesündeste Art der Ernährung. Um längere Zeitspannen etwa im Berufsleben zu überbrücken, nutzen viele Mütter eine Milchpumpe, da sie auf diese Weise unabhängiger sind. Die Philips Avent Natural Electric Breast Pump wurde nahe an den damit verbundenen Bedürfnissen entwickelt und ist exakt den Anforderungen von Mutter und Kind angepasst. Ihre Gestaltung interpretiert feinsinnig den natürlichen Vorgang des Stillens. Davon ausgehend, dass eine ruhige Atmosphäre automatisch den Milchfluss bei der Mutter fördert, legte sie den Schwerpunkt auf den Komfort und eine möglichst einfache Handhabung. Diese angenehme und auch leise Milchpumpe ermöglicht durch eine innovative rhythmische Massagefunktion ein zuverlässiges und natürlich wirkendes Abpumpen. Kompakt gestaltet, begeistert sie durch eine feminin anmutende Formensprache mit floralen Motiven. Diese stehen in einer harmonischen Interaktion mit der Form und verleihen ihr die Anmutung eines Lifestyleprodukts. Sie ist leicht, besteht aus haptisch angenehmen Materialien und lässt sich auch unterwegs unkompliziert benutzen. Den Vorgang des Abpumpens erleichtert ein klar aufgebautes User Interface, das sich entsprechend den jeweiligen Bedürfnissen individualisieren lässt. Durch das eindringliche Erlebnis von Komfort und Einfachheit verleiht Philips Avent der Milchpumpe ein neues Image. Das Abpumpen wird für aktive Mütter zu einem positiv besetzten und gut planbaren Vorgang.

Statement by the jury

The Philips Avent Natural Electric Breast Pump embodies an impressive innovation. It is also aesthetically pleasing and responds to the lifestyle of modern mums. The milk pump exemplifies that good design can manage to convey a new sense of lightness. Each detail of it is well conceived and perfected on a very high level. The design idiom of this milk pump appeals to the emotions and the materials are of high quality and skin-friendly.

Begründung der Jury

Die Philips Avent Natural Electric Breast Pump stellt eine beeindruckende Innovation dar. Sie ist auch ästhetisch ansprechend und entspricht dem modernen Lebensgefühl der Mütter. Beispielhaft wird aufgezeigt, dass durch gutes Design eine neue Leichtigkeit vermittelt werden kann. Jedes ihrer Details wurde durchdacht und auf einem hohen Level perfektioniert. Die Formensprache dieser Milchpumpe emotionalisiert, die Materialien sind qualitativ hochwertig und hautfreundlich.

Designer portrait
See page 64
Siehe Seite 64

Opro9 SmartDiaper
Nappy Wet Sensor
Feuchtigkeitssensor für Windeln

Manufacturer
CviLux Corporation, New Taipei City, Taiwan
In-house design
Luke Wu
Web
www.opro9.com
Honourable Mention

Opro9 SmartDiaper is a flat wetness sensor for nappies and is connected via Bluetooth 4.0 with the parents' smartphone. When the nappy is wet, the sensor sends a signal immediately. The corresponding SmartDiaper app, which can be linked to five such sensors, also indicates the degree of wetness and the temperature in the nappy and memorises how often a child wets it. Both the sensor and its soft silicone holder are easy to clean.

Opro9 SmartDiaper ist ein flacher Feuchtigkeitssensor für Windeln, der via Bluetooth 4.0 mit dem elterlichen Smartphone verbunden wird. Wird die Windel feucht, sendet der Sensor sofort eine Benachrichtigung. Die entsprechende SmartDiaper-App, die mit bis zu fünf solcher Sensoren gekoppelt werden kann, zeigt zudem Feuchtigkeitsgrad und Temperatur in der Windel an und hält die Information bereit, wie oft ein Kind einnässt. Sowohl der Sensor als auch seine weiche Silikonhülle sind leicht zu reinigen.

Statement by the jury
Behind the Opro9 SmartDiaper lies a good idea, which decidedly also has the potential for application in medical care.

Begründung der Jury
Hinter dem Opro9 SmartDiaper steckt eine gute Idee, die durchaus das Potenzial in sich birgt, auch im Bereich der medizinischen Pflege zur Anwendung zu kommen.

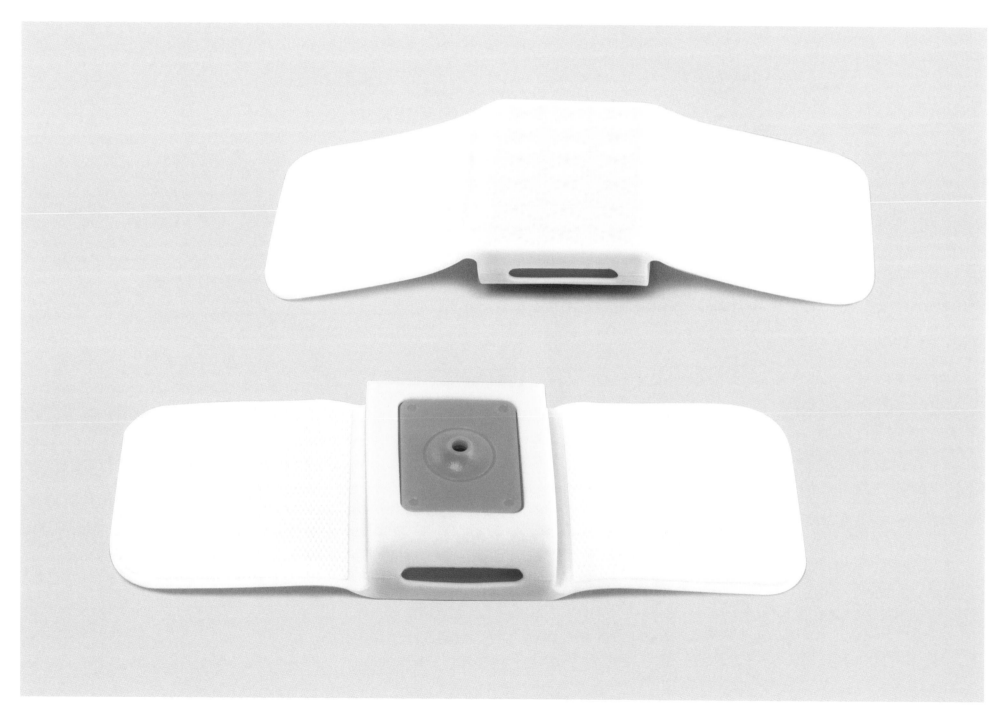

Cupcake
Baby Monitor
Babyfon

Manufacturer
Shenzhen Unixe Electronic Technology Co., Ltd.,
Shenzhen, China
Design
inDare Design Strategy Limited, Shenzhen, China
Web
www.indare.love

Cupcake is a device for supervision of babies. It conveys confidence with its soft, rounded form. The monitor includes a camera and can be networked with the smartphone so that images of the child can be streamed live and photos can be saved or shared. An integrated time function provides a report on when the baby slept or drank and when it was last changed. The device can also play lullabies, has a two-way talking function and monitors room temperature and noises.

Cupcake ist ein Gerät zur Überwachung von Babys, das mit seiner weichen, abgerundeten Formgebung vertrauenerweckend wirkt. Das Babyfon hat eine Kamera und lässt sich mit dem Smartphone vernetzen, sodass Bilder des Kindes live gestreamt und Fotos gespeichert oder geteilt werden können. Eine Zeitfunktion erlaubt es nachzuvollziehen, wann das Baby geschlafen oder getrunken hat und wann es zuletzt gewickelt wurde. Das Gerät kann zudem Schlaflieder abspielen, hat eine Gegensprechfunktion und überwacht Raumtemperatur und Geräusche.

Statement by the jury
This smart baby monitor offers many functions in one housing of minimalist design, which due to its organic form integrates harmoniously into the nursery environment.

Begründung der Jury
Dieses intelligente Babyfon bietet zahlreiche Funktionen in einem minimalistisch gestalteten Gehäuse, das sich mit seiner organischen Formensprache harmonisch in die Kinderzimmerumgebung integriert.

lovestruck
Swaddles
Pucktücher

Manufacturer
aden + anais, London, Great Britain
Design
aden + anais, New York, USA
Web
www.adenandanais.co.uk
www.adenandanais.com

lovestruck is a collection of four swaddles, each with the sizes 120x120 cm, made of 100 per cent cotton muslin. The fabric is soft and breathable and thus protects against overheating. The swaddle can be wrapped around the baby without being too restrictive; it can, however, also be used as nursing protection, bib or comforter, as sun protection or changing mat. Four different patterns in metallic, black and white, including stripes, checks and stylised skulls, characterise the contemporary design of the collection.

Statement by the jury
The soft, multifunctional swaddles of the lovestruck collection are attractive due to their graphic patterns and thus appeal to fashion-conscious young parents.

lovestruck ist eine Kollektion von vier Pucktüchern mit einer Größe von jeweils 120x120 cm, die aus hundertprozentigem Baumwollmusselin bestehen. Das Gewebe ist weich und atmungsaktiv und schützt so vor Überhitzung. Das Pucktuch kann um das Baby gewickelt werden, ohne es einzuengen, es kann aber auch als Stillschutz, Lätzchen oder Schmusetuch, als Sonnenschutz oder Unterlage verwendet werden. Vier verschiedene Muster in Schwarz-Weiß-Metallic, darunter Streifen, Karos und stilisierte Totenköpfe, prägen das zeitgemäße Design der Kollektion.

Begründung der Jury
Die weichen, multifunktionalen Pucktücher der lovestruck-Kollektion gefallen mit ihren grafischen Mustern und richten sich damit an modebewusste junge Eltern.

PLAY JELLO Picnic Bag
Toddler Rucksack
Kleinkind-Rucksack

Manufacturer
Play Jello, Seoul, South Korea
In-house design
Youngjin Seo, Ujin Kim
Web
www.play-jello.com

Picnic Bag is a rucksack for toddlers and pre-schoolers and is characterised by its simplicity. Only its bright colour and the simple lines which give it the shape of a rabbit are conspicuous. The reduction in colour and lines has been intentionally chosen since they are basic elements of visual art. The intention is to stimulate the children's fantasy and to promote their creative and emotional development. The rucksack is very light, conforms to present safety standards and, thanks to a waterproof coating, is easy to clean.

Statement by the jury
The Picnic Bag rucksack impresses by its charming shape and its overall refreshingly reduced and simultaneously child-friendly design.

Picnic Bag ist ein Rucksack für Klein- und Vorschulkinder, der durch seine Schlichtheit gekennzeichnet ist. Einzig seine leuchtende Farbe und einfache Linien, die ihm die Form eines stilisierten Kaninchens verleihen, sind auffällig. Die Reduzierung auf Farbe und Linien wurde bewusst gewählt, da sie die grundlegenden Elemente der bildenden Künste sind. Auf diese Weise soll die Phantasie der Kinder angeregt und ihre kreative sowie emotionale Entwicklung gefördert werden. Der Rucksack ist sehr leicht, entspricht aktuellen Sicherheitsstandards und ist dank einer wasserfesten Beschichtung einfach zu reinigen.

Begründung der Jury
Der Rucksack Picnic Bag besticht durch seine charmante Formgebung und seine insgesamt erfrischend reduzierte und gleichzeitig kindgerechte Gestaltung.

LÄSSIG Mini Backpack
About Friends
Children's Backpack
Kinderrucksack

Manufacturer
Lässig GmbH, Babenhausen, Germany
In-house design
Christina Driessen, Claudia Lässig
Web
www.laessig-fashion.de

The Mini Backpack About Friends is conspicuous due to its highly contrasting design. The grey blend of the material is accentuated by elements in neon colour. One-third of the material is made from Repreve, a polyester produced from recycled PET bottles. The children's backpack also carries a message: The five fantasy animals which are displayed on the outside and on the inner lining symbolise the five continents and represent friendship, open-mindedness and international cooperation.

Statement by the jury
This environmentally friendly backpack carries not only children's belongings but also the nice message that cross-border friendship is possible.

Der Mini Backpack About Friends fällt durch eine kontrastreiche Gestaltung auf. Das Grau-Melange des Stoffes wird durch Elemente in Neonfarben akzentuiert. Ein Drittel des eingesetzten Stoffes ist aus Repreve, einem aus recycelten PET-Flaschen gewonnenen Polyester, gefertigt. Der Kinderrucksack trägt zudem eine Botschaft: Die fünf Fantasietiere, die außen sowie auf dem Innenfutter zu sehen sind, symbolisieren die fünf Kontinente und stehen für Freundschaft, Weltoffenheit und internationalen Zusammenhalt.

Begründung der Jury
Dieser umweltfreundliche Rucksack transportiert nicht nur die Sachen der Kinder, sondern auch die schöne Botschaft, dass Freundschaft über Grenzen hinweg möglich ist.

LÄSSIG Saddle Bag
Spin Dye
Nappy Bag
Wickeltasche

Manufacturer
Lässig GmbH, Babenhausen, Germany
In-house design
Bettina Svojanovski, Claudia Lässig
Web
www.laessig-fashion.de

The Saddle Bag Spin Dye nappy bag is an attractive, well-conceived and long-lasting accessory for mothers. Its outer appearance is characterised by the specially developed "Spin Dye" fabric in discreet, muted colours, contrasted by powerful accents from the natural material cork. The special feature of "Spin Dye" material is that it is spun from already coloured granulate, whereby the otherwise usual dye bath is omitted, thus saving water and energy. Inside the bag, there are a generously dimensioned main compartment and many further pockets for accessories.

Statement by the jury
The use of natural and environmentally friendly produced materials characterises the appearance of this nappy bag and also adds particular sustainability.

Die Wickeltasche Saddle Bag Spin Dye ist ein schönes, durchdachtes und nachhaltiges Accessoire für Mütter. Ihr Äußeres ist geprägt durch den speziell entwickelten „Spin Dye"-Stoff in dezenten, gedeckten Farben, der durch kräftige Akzente aus dem Naturmaterial Kork kontrastiert wird. Das Besondere an dem „Spin Dye"-Stoff ist, dass er aus bereits eingefärbtem Granulat gesponnen wird, wodurch das sonst übliche Färbebad entfällt und Wasser und Energie eingespart werden. Innen hat die Tasche ein großzügiges Hauptfach und viele weitere Fächer für Zubehör.

Begründung der Jury
Die Verwendung von natur- und umweltschonend produzierten Materialien prägt das Erscheinungsbild dieser Wickeltasche und macht sie zudem besonders nachhaltig.

LÄSSIG Rosie Bag
Nappy Bag
Wickeltasche

Manufacturer
Lässig GmbH, Babenhausen, Germany
In-house design
Christina Driessen, Claudia Lässig
Web
www.laessig-fashion.de

The Rosie Bag nappy bag combines an unusual design for this type of bag with a high degree of functionality. The trapeze-shaped Rosie Bag offers clearly arranged inside compartments with many sections and accessories. It is available in the colours rose, mint, anthracite glitter and blue. Shiny rosé-gold elements contribute to the elegant appearance. An additional, length-adjustable strap offers the options of carrying it as a handbag, shoulder bag or as a rucksack.

Statement by the jury
The Rosie Bag successfully combines the functionality of a nappy bag with the look of a lifestyle accessory.

Die Wickeltasche Rosie Bag vereint ein für diese Art von Taschen außergewöhnliches Design mit hoher Funktionalität. Die trapezförmige Rosie Bag bietet eine übersichtliche Innenaufteilung mit vielen Fächern und Zubehör und ist in den Farben Rosé, Mint, Anthrazit-Glitter und Blau erhältlich. Glänzende Roségoldelemente tragen zum eleganten Erscheinungsbild bei. Ein zusätzlicher, längenverstellbarer Gurt ermöglicht es, die Tasche wahlweise als Hand- oder Umhängetasche oder als Rucksack zu tragen.

Begründung der Jury
Die Rosie Bag kombiniert auf gelungene Weise die Funktionalität einer Wickeltasche mit dem Erscheinungsbild eines Lifestyle-Accessoires.

Woom 2
Children's Bicycle
Kinderfahrrad

Manufacturer
woom GmbH, Klosterneuburg, Austria
In-house design
Web
www.woombikes.com

Woom 2 is a child's bicycle which is tailored exactly to children's anatomy and needs. 85 per cent of the bicycle's components have been manufactured specifically for this model. This learning bicycle for children aged from three to four and a half years weighs about 40 per cent less than other children's bicycles available on the market and is thus exceptionally light. This also results in easier riding so that the children learn it in a shorter time.

Woom 2 ist ein Fahrrad für Kinder, das genau auf ihre Anatomie und Bedürfnisse zugeschnitten ist. 85 Prozent der Fahrradbauteile wurden speziell für dieses Modell gefertigt. Das Lernfahrrad für Kinder im Alter von drei bis viereinhalb Jahren wiegt rund 40 Prozent weniger als andere auf dem Markt erhältliche Kinderräder und ist damit außergewöhnlich leicht. Das hat zur Folge, dass auch das Radfahren leichter wird und die Kinder es in kürzerer Zeit erlernen.

Statement by the jury
This children's bicycle for beginners convinces by its geometry which is especially well adapted to the child's body. It gains additional merit with its many well-considered details.

Begründung der Jury
Dieses Kinderfahrrad für Anfänger überzeugt mit einer Geometrie, die besonders gut an den Kinderkörper angepasst ist. Es punktet zudem mit vielen durchdachten Details.

Fashion, lifestyle and accessories
Mode, Lifestyle und Accessoires

REI – A symphony of wood and horn
Handcrafted Eyewear
Handgefertigte Brillen

Manufacturer
GABE Eyewear,
Strom Eyewear GmbH,
Linz, Austria

In-house design
Gabriel Kirschner, Ralf Kropf,
Simon Klein, Mike Milkowski

Web
www.gabe-eyewear.com

reddot award 2017
best of the best

With style and concision
What was obvious, for example, with the striking cat-eye glasses of some Hollywood stars in the 1950s, is still valid today: glasses define personal style. The design objective of REI is to underline the wearer's personal charisma. These frames are handcrafted with high precision from the natural materials wood and horn, combining unique shapes with the use of modern technologies. Since the glasses are very light, the wearer hardly feels them. The main focus of their sophisticated functionality is the innovative "Snap Joint" hinge. This screwless designed joint made of water buffalo horn also acts as a characteristic, highly recognisable feature of the entire eyewear collection. It is maintenance-free and optician-friendly, since it allows an easy upgrade with the fully adaptable temples made of horn or a combination of wood and horn. This innovative joint thus solves one of the main problems of wooden frames. Especially when working with natural materials, high-grade components are the key to durability and longevity of a product. All elements of REI are therefore carefully selected and precisely assembled by hand. Thus, each piece is also an expression of individual craftsmanship representing a particular quality that proves itself in everyday use.

Mit Stil und Prägnanz
Was beispielsweise in den 1950er Jahren mit den markanten Katzenaugen-Brillen mancher Hollywoodstars offensichtlich war, gilt auch heute noch: Die Brille prägt den eigenen Stil. Das Ziel der Gestaltung von REI ist es, die persönliche Ausstrahlung des Trägers zu unterstützen. Diese Brillengestelle werden mit hoher Präzision von Hand aus den natürlichen Materialien Holz und Horn gefertigt, wobei sich eine unverwechselbare Formgebung mit dem Einsatz moderner Technologien verbindet. Da die Brillen sehr leicht sind, spürt der Träger sie kaum. Im Mittelpunkt ihrer ausgefeilten Funktionalität steht das innovative „Snap Joint"-Scharnier. Dieses schraubenlos konzipierte Gelenk aus Wasserbüffelhorn fungiert zugleich als charakteristisches, gut wiedererkennbares Merkmal der gesamten Brillenkollektion. Es ist wartungsfrei und optikerfreundlich, da es eine einfache Nachrüstung erlaubt mit den sich nahtlos anpassenden Bügeln aus Horn oder einer Kombination von Holz und Horn. Das innovative Gelenk löst damit eines der wesentlichen Probleme bei Holzgestellen. Bei natürlichen Materialien sind besonders hochwertige Komponenten ausschlaggebend für die Haltbarkeit und Langlebigkeit eines Produkts. Alle Elemente von REI werden deshalb speziell ausgewählt und anschließend präzise von Hand verarbeitet. Jede Brille ist daher stets auch ein Ausdruck individueller Kunstfertigkeit – und repräsentiert eine besondere Qualität, die sich im Alltag bewährt.

Statement by the jury
The design of these glasses applies the natural materials of wood and horn in a markedly skilful manner. It offers wearers a maximum of ergonomics and individual expression. The extremely precise handcrafted manufacturing of REI is consistent with a sophisticated, highly developed functionality. The captivatingly innovative solution of the "Snap Joint" hinge leads to more flexibility and a more uncomplicated use.

Begründung der Jury
Die Gestaltung dieser Brille setzt die natürlichen Materialien Holz und Horn ausgesprochen gekonnt ein. Ihrem Träger bietet sie ein Höchstmaß an Ergonomie und individueller Ausdrucksmöglichkeit. Die äußerst präzise handwerkliche Ausführung von REI steht im Einklang mit einer durchdachten, hochentwickelten Funktionalität. Die bestechend innovative Lösung des „Snap Joint"-Scharniers führt dabei zu mehr Flexibilität und unkomplizierterem Gebrauch.

Designer portrait
See page 66
Siehe Seite 66

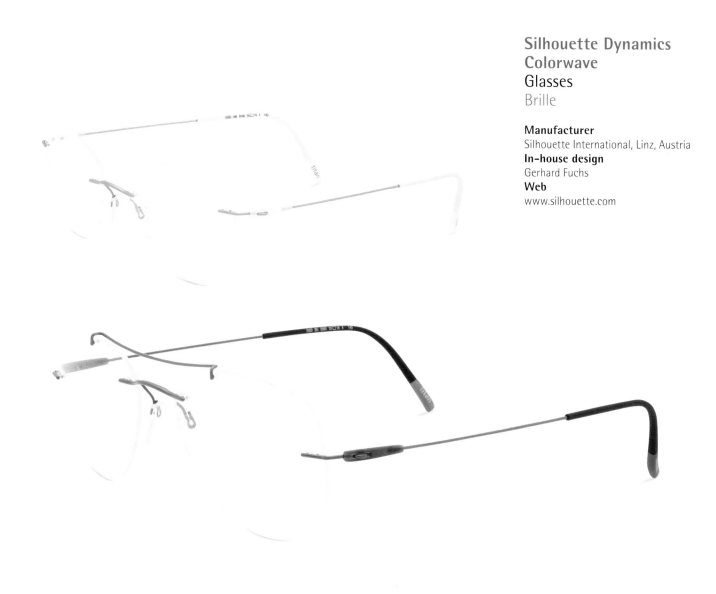

Silhouette Dynamics Colorwave
Glasses
Brille

Manufacturer
Silhouette International, Linz, Austria
In-house design
Gerhard Fuchs
Web
www.silhouette.com

Reduction, lightness and variable colour options define the concept of the Silhouette Dynamics Colorwave. The delicately built titanium frame is combined with very small SPX elements. The temple ends are manufactured in a special multi-component injection moulding process. The result is a frameless, transparent material which can be adjusted to a comfortable wearing feel. Lively colours and modern lens shapes give a young touch to the minimalist design.

Statement by the jury
Thanks to the sophisticated manufacturing process, the Silhouette Dynamics Colorwave convinces, giving a good hold without pressure.

Reduktion, Leichtigkeit und variable Farboptionen bestimmen das Konzept der Silhouette Dynamics Colorwave. Der zierliche Titaniumrahmen ist mit sehr kleinen SPX-Elementen kombiniert. Die Bügelenden sind in einem speziellen Mehrkomponenten-Spritzgussverfahren gefertigt. Dadurch entsteht ein rahmenloses, transparentes Material, das sich für einen guten Tragekomfort frei justieren lässt. Lebendige Farben und moderne Linsenformen verleihen dem minimalistischen Design einen jungen Touch.

Begründung der Jury
Dank des ausgeklügelten Herstellungsverfahrens überzeugt die Silhouette Dynamics Colorwave mit gutem Sitz ohne zu drücken.

Silhouette Atelier G700
Glasses
Brille

Manufacturer
Silhouette International, Linz, Austria
In-house design
Roland Keplinger
Web
www.silhouette.com

With the combination of titanium and real gold, these glasses impart a noble impression. Solid elements of 18-carat gold are incorporated securely in the temples by means of a special, mechanical clamping technique. The novel, matt DLC coating offers very good haptic properties and provides an elegant contrast to the polished elements made of precious metal. No screws are used in the easily adjustable frame, thus reducing the need for maintenance.

Statement by the jury
By using high-quality materials and a screw-free frame, the Silhouette Atelier G700 succeeds as a modern interpretation of sportive luxury.

Die Kombination von Titan und Echtgold verleiht dieser Brille eine edle Anmutung. Solide Elemente aus 18-karätigem Gold sind durch ein spezielles mechanisches Klemmverfahren sicher in die Bügel eingearbeitet. Die neuartige matte DLC-Oberfläche bietet eine sehr gute Haptik und verleiht einen edlen Kontrast zu den polierten Elementen aus Edelmetall. In dem gut justierbaren Rahmen werden keine Schrauben verwendet, was die Wartungsanfälligkeit der Brille reduziert.

Begründung der Jury
Durch die Verwendung hochwertiger Materialien und einen schraubenfreien Rahmen gelingt mit der Silhouette Atelier G700 die moderne Interpretation von sportivem Luxus.

Marc O'Polo 503111 60
Glasses
Brille

Manufacturer
Eschenbach Optik GmbH,
Nuremberg, Germany
In-house design
Web
www.eschenbach-optik.com

The Marc O'Polo 503111 60 glasses present the new interpretation of a classical design from the 1940s. Two incorporated rivets at the front provide the frame with an authentic vintage look which is further emphasised by the metal parts shining through the translucent material of the temples. In their clear and calm form, the glasses can be used as a unisex model. The frame colour becomes lighter towards the bottom and gives the glasses a friendly and modern look.

Statement by the jury
Colour and style of the Marc O'Polo 503111 60 provide an unpretentious glasses solution which can be combined with many styles and still appears fashionable.

Die Brille Marc O'Polo 503111 60 stellt die Neuinterpretation eines klassischen Designs aus den 1940er-Jahren vor. Zwei eben eingearbeitete Nieten an der Front verleihen dem Gestell einen authentischen Vintage-Look, der durch die aus dem transluziden Material der Brillenbügel hervorleuchtenden Metallteile noch verstärkt wird. In ihrer klaren und ruhigen Formgebung ist die Brille als Unisexmodell einsetzbar. Die nach unten hin heller verlaufende Rahmenfarbe lässt die Brille freundlich und modern erscheinen.

Begründung der Jury
Farbe und Fasson der Marc O'Polo 503111 60 ergeben eine unprätentiöse Brillenlösung, die sich zu vielen Stilen kombinieren lässt und dennoch zeitgemäß wirkt.

MONOCEROS Ara
Glasses
Brille

Manufacturer
ROLF – Roland Wolf GmbH,
Weißenbach, Austria
In-house design
Marija Iljazovic
Web
www.monoceros.cc

The unisex frame of the Monoceros Ara corresponds to a modern interpretation of the classical horn-rimmed glasses. The buffalo horn is bent by a specially developed technology. This manufacturing process using one single piece assures that the structure and colour of the horn is sustained throughout the whole frame. This clear design conveys a contemporary stylish, casual impression. The differing material thickness at the front of the frame emphasises the flowing lines and facilitates a pleasant wearing experience. The horn material also adjusts quickly to the body heat.

Statement by the jury
The Monoceros Ara implements the casually modern, new version of the horn-rimmed glasses masterfully. Moreover, the pleasant feel of the natural material is enjoyable.

Die Unisex-Fassung der Monoceros Ara entspricht einer modernen Interpretation der klassischen Hornbrille. Das Büffelhorn wird mittels einer eigens entwickelten Technologie gebogen. Diese Fertigung aus einem einzigen Stück gewährleistet, dass Struktur und Farbe des Horns über die gesamte Brille verlaufen. Diese klare Gestaltung vermittelt eine zeitgemäß stilvoll-legere Anmutung. Die unterschiedliche Materialdicke an der Fassungsfront unterstreicht die fließende Linienführung und ermöglicht ein angenehmes Tragegefühl. Zudem passt sich das Material Horn rasch der Körperwärme an.

Begründung der Jury
Mit der Monoceros Ara wurde die lässig-moderne Neuauflage der klassischen Hornbrille souverän umgesetzt. Zudem gefällt die angenehme Haptik des Naturmaterials.

MOREL
Glasses
Brille

Manufacturer
Morel, Morbier, France
In-house design
Web
www.morel-france.com

The bridge of these glasses is made of titanium and is manufactured in one piece, shaped in an arch. It has a patent, built-in hinge which needs no screws. This makes an elegant connection with the temples, so that the mechanical parts are not visible. Each temple consists of three, separately milled wooden blades. These are fastened at the ends in such a way that there is a space between them. The glasses thereby impart a particularly light impression.

Statement by the jury
The Morel glasses impress by their clever material mix of titanium and wood as well as by their functional and aesthetically well processed hinge.

Der Steg dieser Brille besteht aus Titanium und ist in einem durchgehenden Stück gefertigt, welches eine flache Kurve beschreibt. Darin eingebaut ist ein patentiertes Scharnier, bei dem keine Schrauben benötigt werden. Dies ermöglicht eine elegante Verbindung mit den Bügeln, die mechanische Teile nicht sichtbar werden lässt. Die Bügel bestehen aus jeweils drei separat gefrästen Holzstegen. Diese sind an den Enden so miteinander fixiert, dass zwischen ihnen Raum frei bleibt. Dadurch erhält die Brille eine besonders leichte Anmutung.

Begründung der Jury
Die Brille Morel besticht durch den gekonnten Materialmix von Titan und Holz sowie durch das funktionell wie ästhetisch gut ausgearbeitete Scharnier.

Glens
Backup Reading Glasses
Ersatzlesebrille

Manufacturer
Glens OÜ, Tallinn, Estonia
In-house design
Andrei Astapenko
Web
www.glens.com

Glens are prefabricated spare pair of glasses for near sight. They are manufactured from high-quality Copolyester and weigh less than one gram. Their dimensions are less than those of a credit card and therefore they can be carried in a supplied case e.g. inside the card compartment of a wallet. They lie well on the nose in almost any position, special pads protect from unpleasant pressure or slipping. Three small knobs on the bridge of the nose assure good grip and provide easy position adjustment.

Glens ist eine vorgefertigte Ersatzlesebrille für die Nahsicht. Sie ist aus hochwertigem Copolyester gefertigt und wiegt weniger als ein Gramm. Ihre Maße unterschreiten die einer Kreditkarte, daher kann sie in einem mitgelieferten Etui auch im Kartenfach etwa eines Portemonnaies untergebracht werden. Sie sitzt in fast jeder Position gut auf der Nase, spezielle Polster vermeiden unangenehmen Druck und das Verrutschen. Drei kleine Knöpfe am Nasenrücken sorgen für eine gute Haftung und ermöglichen die einfache Lageanpassung.

Statement by the jury
Glens can be carried like a credit card: with this surprisingly simple and innovative idea, a situation can hardly occur when one is on the move without reading glasses.

Begründung der Jury
Glens lässt sich wie eine Scheckkarte einstecken: Mit dieser verblüffend einfachen und innovativen Idee ist man in kaum einer Lebenslage mehr ohne Lesehilfe unterwegs.

NOOZ
Backup Reading Glasses
Ersatzlesebrille

Manufacturer
Binoptics SPRL, Brussels, Belgium
Design
Ixiade, Grenoble, France
Web
www.nooz-optics.com
www.ixiade.com

NOOZ weighs only six grams and is provided with a case which is precisely shaped, in which the backup reading glasses can be carried everywhere with you. By means of a small eyelet, the cover, which is supplied in various, fashionable colours, can be attached to the key ring or hung around the neck. The bridge is of non-slip elastomer and assures reliable, pressure-free grip on almost any nose shape. The glasses do not need a frame. The lenses are made of clear polycarbonate and are treated with scratch protection.

NOOZ wiegt nur sechs Gramm und wird in einem genau angepassten Gehäuse geliefert, in dem sich die Ersatzlesebrille überallhin einfach mitführen lässt. Mittels einer kleinen Öse kann die Umhüllung, die in verschiedenen modischen Farben angeboten wird, auch am Schlüsselbund oder an einer Halskette befestigt werden. Der Steg aus rutschfestem Elastomer sorgt für zuverlässigen, druckfreien Halt auf nahezu allen Nasenkonturen. Die Brille kommt ohne Rahmen aus. Die Linsen sind aus klarem Polykarbonat gefertigt und mit Kratzschutz versehen.

Statement by the jury
You should not have to look long for your backup reading glasses when they are needed – NOOZ presents here a clever solution, which also looks good.

Begründung der Jury
Eine Ersatzlesebrille will man im Bedarfsfall nicht lange suchen müssen – mit NOOZ ist hier eine clevere Lösung gelungen, die noch dazu gut aussieht.

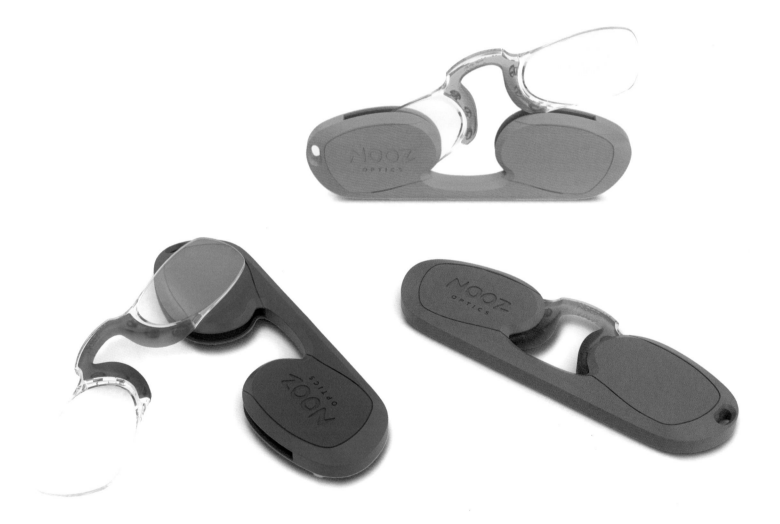

LINDBERG sirius titanium
Glasses
Brille

Manufacturer
LINDBERG, Aabyhøj, Denmark
In-house design
Web
www.lindberg.com

The rounded frame shape of these glasses is recreated from earlier models of the legendary Danish Sirius Patrol. These were needed to protect the wearer in extreme weather conditions from light reflected from the snow. In this modern variant, the lenses can be changed by means of a simple snap system. The inner lens frame can also be optionally exchanged for a form with reinforced side protection. Lenses with a single focal value or multifocal lenses as well as models without vision correction can be inserted. A hard-shell case is supplied for each frame as well as a soft pocket for a cleaning cloth and two pairs of replacement lenses.

Statement by the jury
Whether used for reading or long-distance vision while doing sports, only a single spectacle frame is needed: an impressive solution for the widespread problem of having to constantly change glasses.

Die gerundete Rahmenform dieser Brille ist den früheren Modellen der legendären dänischen Sirius-Patrouillen nachempfunden. Diese mussten ihre Träger bei extremen Wetterbedingungen vor dem reflektierenden Schneelicht schützen. Bei diesen modernen Varianten können die Linsen mit einem einfachen Schnappsystem gewechselt werden. Auch der innere Linsenrahmen kann optional gegen eine Form mit verstärktem Seitenschutz ausgetauscht werden. Als Linsen sind Einstärken- oder Gleitsichtgläser sowie Modelle ohne Korrekturfunktion einsetzbar. Zu jedem Rahmen wird ein Hartschalen-Etui geliefert sowie eine weiche Tasche für ein Reinigungstuch und zwei Paar Extralinsen.

Begründung der Jury
Ob beim Lesen oder für die Fernsicht beim Sport, hier genügt eine einzige Brillenfassung: eine eindrucksvolle Lösung für das verbreitete Problem, ständig Brillen wechseln zu müssen.

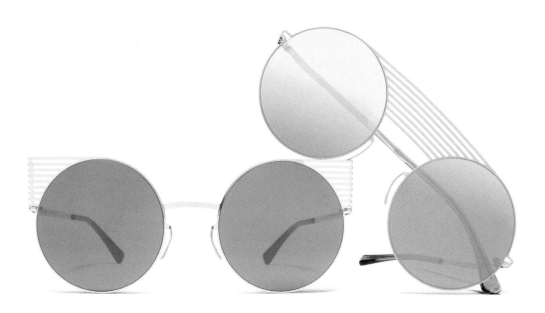

MYKITA STUDIO 1.1 & 1.2
Sunglasses
Sonnenbrillen

Manufacturer
MYKITA, Berlin, Germany
In-house design
Web
www.mykita.com

The Mykita Studio 1.1 & 1.2 sunglasses present contemporary functionality, combining with style elements of art deco. Both models display an uncompromisingly graphic design in which horizontal lines set a distinctive basic tone. Round lenses in a paper-thin frame of stainless steel underline the futuristic impression. The dark, matt outer components contrast with the metallic internal elements of the frame.

Statement by the jury
Both sunglass models Mykita Studio 1.1 & 1.2 convince due to perfectly balanced geometric aesthetics. Shape, material and expression merge into an impressing balanced composition.

Bei den Sonnenbrillen Mykita Studio 1.1 & 1.2 treffen zeitgemäße Funktionalität und Stilelemente des Art déco aufeinander. Beide Modelle folgen einer konsequent grafischen Gestaltung, in der horizontale Linien einen markanten Grundton setzen. Runde Linsen in einem papierdünnen Rahmen aus Edelstahl verstärken die futuristische Anmutung. Die dunklen, matten äußeren Komponenten kontrastieren zu den metallischen innenliegenden Elementen des Rahmens.

Begründung der Jury
Die beiden Sonnenbrillen Mykita Studio 1.1 & 1.2 überzeugen in ihrer perfekt ausbalancierten geometrischen Ästhetik. Form, Material und Ausdruck verbinden sich zu einer beeindruckenden Komposition.

Nine Golf Model 2317
Glasses
Brille

Manufacturer
nine eyewear, Aarhus, Denmark
In-house design
Jens William Sørensen
Web
www.nine-eyewear.com

These glasses were designed especially with golf in mind. The frame without lenses weighs only nine grams. The temples are just 4.5 mm wide and are cut by laser from titanium which has a thickness of only 0.7 mm. The temple ends are formed in such a way that they remain in place, even when taking a swing. Compared with usual sunglass lenses, the ProGolf glasses have no light-dimming properties. Instead, they increase the contrast by selective absorption and provide a very good vision for the golfer.

Statement by the jury
The construction of these glasses meets the special requirements on the golf course in a convincing way; also, the quality of the ProGolf special lenses impresses.

Diese Brille wurde speziell für die Verwendung beim Golfsport konzipiert. Die Fassung wiegt ohne Gläser lediglich etwa neun Gramm. Die Bügel sind nur 4,5 mm breit und werden mit einem Laser aus nur knapp 0,7 mm dickem Titan geschnitten. Die Bügelenden sind so geformt, dass die Brille auch bei ausholenden sportlichen Bewegungen gut sitzt. Im Vergleich zu herkömmlichen Sonnenschutzgläsern haben die ProGolf-Gläser keine lichtabschwächende Wirkung. Stattdessen verstärken sie den Kontrast durch selektive Absorption und bieten Golfsportlern sehr gute Sicht.

Begründung der Jury
Die Konstruktion dieser Brille kommt auf überzeugende Weise den speziellen Erfordernissen auf dem Golfplatz entgegen, auch die Qualität der ProGolf-Spezialgläser beeindruckt.

The Flamboyant
Sunglasses
Sonnenbrille

Manufacturer
Powder & Heat, Erding, Germany
In-house design
Georg Vollmer
Web
www.powder-heat.de

Since the frame is drawn strongly to the rear, these sunglasses protect the face from wind and glare particularly well. The Flamboyant is manufactured using laser sintering technology, whereby its construction is made very light and which, in addition, facilitates a precise adjustment. Thus, the distinctive, sportive T-profile at the front and the sides can still come off thin-walled. The discreet brand label on the inside of the temple underlines the high-quality overall impression.

Statement by the jury
In its distinctive and aesthetically sophisticated form, the Flamboyant protects sensitive eyes in an impressively effective way.

Durch den besonders stark nach hinten gezogenen Rahmen wird das Gesicht mit dieser Sonnenbrille besonders gut vor Wind und grellem Lichteinfall geschützt. Die Flamboyant wird mittels Lasersintertechnologie hergestellt, wodurch ihre Konstruktion besonders leicht ausfällt und zudem eine präzise Justierung ermöglicht wird. Das markante, sportive T-Profil an der Front und die Seitenwände können so dennoch dünnwandig ausfallen. Das diskrete Markenlabel an der Bügelinnenseite unterstreicht den hochwertigen Gesamteindruck.

Begründung der Jury
In ihrer markanten wie ästhetisch ausgereiften Formgebung schützt die Flamboyant empfindliche Augen auf beeindruckend wirkungsvolle Weise.

Adidas Zonyk
Sport Glasses
Sportbrille

Manufacturer
Silhouette International, Linz, Austria
In-house design
Roland Keplinger
Web
www.silhouette.com

The sweeping, continuous shape of the Adidas Zonyk sport glasses creates a very wide and uninterrupted field of vision. At the same time, this form protects athletes from sunlight, wind and impact. The light and simultaneously sturdy SPX frame with integrated Climacool ventilation system is available in two sizes. Comfortable positioning is aided by the Double-Snap Nose Bridge; temples with adjustable Flex Zones increase grip when on the move. The lenses are quickly and easily changed by means of the special Lens Lock system. Reflecting elements on the frame and sweat blocker assure safety.

Statement by the jury
The Adidas Zonyk sport glasses convince with a wide field of vision, well-considered functionality and style, no matter which callenges the athlete has to face.

Die geschwungene und durchgehende Kontur der Sportbrille Adidas Zonyk schafft ein sehr breites und irritationsfreies Sichtfeld. Zugleich schützt diese Form den Athleten vor Sonnenlicht, Wind oder Stößen. Der leichte und zugleich robuste SPX-Rahmen mit integriertem Climacool-Ventilationssystem wird in zwei Größen angeboten. Die Double-Snap Nose Bridge unterstützt einen bequemen Sitz; Bügel mit justierbaren Flex Zones verstärken den Halt in der Bewegung. Mittels speziellem Lens-Lock-System werden die Linsen einfach und schnell ausgetauscht. Für Sicherheit sorgen reflektierende Elemente auf dem Rahmen und dem Schweißblocker.

Begründung der Jury
Die Sportbrille Adidas Zonyk überzeugt mit breitem Blickfeld, durchdachter Funktionalität und Stil, egal welchen Herausforderungen der Athlet sich stellt.

Adidas Zonyk Aero
Sport Glasses
Sportbrille

Manufacturer
Silhouette International, Linz, Austria
In-house design
Roland Keplinger
Web
www.silhouette.com

The construction of the Adidas Zonyk Aero takes into account the high speeds reached in competitive cycling. The frame makes a wide field of vision possible, enabling the riders to recognise other cyclists quickly and thus contributing to safety on the track or road. The reduced design shows clear lines with an expressive silhouette and seamlessly integrated functions. Thanks to the special Vario technology, the lense has the ability to change automatically between light and dark tint within seconds.

Statement by the jury
With sophisticated functions and fast adaptability to changing weather conditions, the Adidas Zonyk Aero clearly fits into the professional segment.

Die Adidas Zonyk Aero ist in ihrer Konstruktionsweise auf hohe Geschwindigkeit beim Radsport ausgelegt. Der Rahmen ermöglicht ein sehr weites Sichtfeld, dadurch lassen sich andere Fahrer schnell erkennen und dies führt zu mehr Sicherheit auf der Strecke. Die reduzierte Gestaltung zeigt klare Linien mit einer ausdrucksstarken Silhouette und nahtlos integrierten Funktionen. Dank der speziellen Vario-Technologie wechselt das Glas automatisch zwischen einem hellen und einem dunklen Farbton innerhalb von Sekunden.

Begründung der Jury
Mit ausgefeilten Funktionen und schneller Anpassungsfähigkeit an wechselnde Wetterbedingungen platziert sich die Adidas Zonyk Aero deutlich im Profisegment.

PUMA Winterized Backpack
Backpack
Rucksack

Manufacturer
PUMA SE,
Herzogenaurach, Germany

In-house design
PUMA SE

Web
www.puma.com

reddot award 2017
best of the best

Perfectly equipped

Backpacks are a piece of gear that is popular with all age groups, having to withstand many different challenges and changing weather conditions. The PUMA Winterized Backpack is therefore equipped with fascinating features that are perfectly attuned to modern-day living. It is waterproof, keeping its contents dry at all times. Furthermore, it is lightweight, folding up easily and perfect for travelling. The sporty colouring is a striking feature that defines the backpack, bringing performance and trend together. The innovative design of the backpack additionally convinces through high functionality and sophisticated ergonomics. Thanks to a centralised pocket made of a four-way stretch fabric, the water bottle is secure and stabilising during one's run. A fully waterproof zip pocket ensures that smaller items are always at hand when on the go. Padded mesh zoning on the back provide comfort, shock protection and breathability, while lombard and sternum straps offer additional support and stability. For safety at night, the backpack is equipped with 360 reflective elements and laser-cut lash tabs for optional light fixing. A design that is prepared for all eventualities, making this a highly contemporary companion.

Perfekt gerüstet

Der in allen Altersgruppen beliebte Rucksack muss den unterschiedlichsten Herausforderungen und wechselnden Wetterbedingungen gewachsen sein. Der PUMA Winterized Backpack besitzt dafür bestechende Eigenschaften, die für das Leben in unserer Zeit perfekt durchdacht sind. Er ist wasserfest, weshalb sein Inhalt nicht nass werden kann. Er ist außerdem sehr leicht, lässt sich gut zusammenlegen und ist perfekt geeignet für Reisen. Auffällig ist die sportive Farbgebung, die ihn als praktisch und zeitgemäß definiert. Die innovative Gestaltung des Rucksacks überzeugt zudem durch eine hohe Funktionalität und ausgereifte Ergonomie. Dank einer zentralen Halterung aus einem 4-Wege-Stretchstoff beispielsweise ist die Wasserflasche auch beim Laufen sicher und stabil fixiert. Eine vollständig wasserdichte Reißverschlusstasche sorgt dafür, dass kleinere Gegenstände unterwegs immer griffbereit sind. Gepolsterte Elemente aus einem Meshgewebe auf der Rückseite geben Komfort, schützen vor Stößen und sind luftdurchlässig, Lombard- und Brustgurte bieten dem Träger zusätzlichen Halt sowie Stabilität. Für die Sicherheit bei Nacht ist der Rucksack ausgestattet mit 360 reflektierenden Elementen und lasergeschnittenen Schnurklemmen. Sein an alle Eventualitäten angepasstes Design macht ihn zu einem sehr zeitgemäßen Begleiter.

Statement by the jury

This extraordinary backpack is suited to everyday activities just as well as for spontaneous trips. It fascinates with clever and carefully realised details. The PUMA Winterized Backpack is extremely light, trendy in form and colour, and with a softness of material that wants to be touched. It is robust and waterproof. Highly functional and comfortable, it is a lot of fun to use.

Begründung der Jury

Dieser außergewöhnliche Rucksack eignet sich für den Alltag ebenso wie für die spontane Reise. Er begeistert mit cleveren und sorgfältig ausgeführten Details. Der PUMA Winterized Backpack ist extrem leicht, trendy in seiner Form- und Farbgebung und die Weichheit des Materials lädt zum Anfassen ein. Er ist wasserdicht und strapazierfähig. Sehr funktional und komfortabel bereitet er seinem Nutzer großen Spaß.

Designer portrait
See page 68
Siehe Seite 68

PUMA Ferrari
Transform Backpack
Rucksack

Manufacturer
Dongguan Jia Xin Handbag
Company Limited, Dongguan, China
Design
PUMA SE, Herzogenaurach, Germany
Web
www.puma.com

The PUMA Ferrari Transform Backpack reflects in its construction the variety of climatic conditions, under which the Formula 1 races take place – from the night race in Malaysia to the glowing heat of the midday sun in Dubai. The rucksack is treated with thermo-chromatic pigment print which reacts to heat with colour change. At temperatures above 20 degrees Celsius the rucksack shows a shining Rosso Corsa colour. A reflecting cord on the seams increases safety in the night.

Statement by the jury
A successful, innovative idea which will delight not only Ferrari fans: when under the influence of heat, the rucksack adapts an exciting Rosso Corsa colour.

Der PUMA Ferrari Transform Backpack spiegelt in seiner Konstruktion die unterschiedlichen Klimabedingungen wider, unter denen die Rennen der Formel 1 stattfinden – vom Nachtrennen in Malaysia bis hin zur gleißenden Mittagssonne in Dubai. Der Rucksack ist mit thermochromatischem Pigmentdruck behandelt, der auf die Hitze der Sonne mit Farbveränderung reagiert. Bei Temperaturen über 20 Grad Celsius zeigt der Rucksack ein strahlendes Rosso Corsa. Eine reflektierende Kordel auf den Nähten erhöht die Sicherheit bei Nacht.

Begründung der Jury
Ein gelungener innovativer Einfall, der nicht nur Ferrari-Fans begeistert: Unter Hitzeeinwirkung nimmt der Rucksack ein aufregendes Rosso Corsa an.

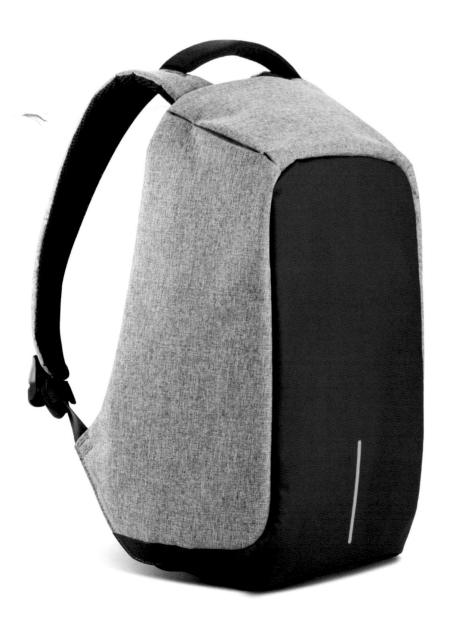

Bobby Anti-Theft Backpack
Rucksack

Manufacturer
Xindao BV, Rijswijk, Netherlands
In-house design
Thomas Droze
Web
www.xindao.com

The sturdy material protects the thief-proof, fashionably designed rucksack from cuts. Furthermore, the zip fasteners are not recognisable as such from the outside. At the sides and at the rear, pockets are located which can be accessed without having to take the rucksack off. Items which are often needed to be taken out for everyday use can be stowed in the straps. An integrated USB charger, water-repellent fabric and illuminating safety strips complete the equipment.

Statement by the jury
The Bobby Anti-Theft Backpack provides clever solutions for effective theft protection. It also satisfies the demands of fashionable, urban aesthetics.

Das robuste Material schützt den diebstahlsicheren, modisch gestalteten Rucksack vor Schnitten. Zudem sind Reißverschlüsse von außen nicht als solche erkennbar. An den Seiten und im hinteren Bereich befinden sich Taschen, auf die man unterwegs zugreifen kann, ohne den Rucksack abnehmen zu müssen. Im Riemen lassen sich Dinge verwahren, die man im Alltag immer wieder hervorholen muss. Eine integrierte USB-Ladestation, wasserabweisendes Material und leuchtende Sicherheitsstreifen runden die Ausstattung ab.

Begründung der Jury
Der Bobby Anti-Theft Backpack bietet clevere Lösungen für einen wirkungsvollen Diebstahlschutz. Zugleich wird er den Ansprüchen modisch-urbaner Ästhetik gerecht.

Intelligence Music Backpack
Musik-Rucksack

Manufacturer
Zhejiang Tao Culture Development Co., Ltd.,
Hangzhou, China
Design
Taodesign (Licheng Li), Hangzhou, China
Web
www.h3c.com.cn
www.tao-design.cn
www.toout.com

The main function of the Intelligence Music Backpack is to provide sufficient storage space for music equipment, playback options and charging functions. By means of these tools, music can be played any time and everywhere in public places. With its design as geometric, sharp-edged item, the rucksack follows a futurist keynote. Due to its sturdy construction, the components carried and integrated in it are optimally protected.

Statement by the jury
In its sharp-edged and sturdy form, the Intelligence Music Backpack emphasises the personality of the users who play music in public places.

Die Hauptfunktionen des Intelligence Music Backpack bestehen darin, adäquaten Stauraum für das Musikequipment, Abspielmöglichkeiten sowie Ladefunktionen zu bieten. Mittels dieser Tools kann Musik jederzeit und überall im öffentlichen Raum abgespielt werden. In seiner Gestaltung als geometrisch, scharfkantig geschnittenes Objekt folgt der Rucksack einem futuristischen Grundgedanken. Durch die robuste Bauart werden die mitgeführten und integrierten Bestandteile optimal geschützt.

Begründung der Jury
In seiner scharfkantigen und robusten Formgebung unterstreicht der Intelligence Music Backpack die Persönlichkeiten seiner User, die Musik im öffentlichen Raum abspielen.

Walnutt Commuter Backpack
Skateboard Backpack
Skateboard-Rucksack

Manufacturer
Walnut Technology Limited,
Hong Kong
In-house design
Yik Hang Pang
Design
Hefei XIVO Design Co., Ltd.
(Wei Gu, Jiao Ge, Chao Jing),
Hefei, China
Web
www.walnuttech.co
www.xivodesign.com

Ever more often people use the skateboard as a daily means of transport to work, to school or to university. In contrast to the usual very sporty appearance of accessories, this skateboard backpack is adapted in style to fashionable, urban demands. In addition to a simply adjusted Velcro fastener for attaching to the board, the rucksack can accommodate a laptop, tablet, books and writing materials. It can also be easily attached to a suitcase.

Statement by the jury
The Walnutt Commuter Backpack makes the skateboard as means of transport in urban environments suitable for daily use from an aesthetic as well as a formal viewpoint.

Immer häufiger benutzen Menschen das Skateboard als tägliches Transportmittel zum Arbeitsplatz, zur Schule oder Universität. Anders als das üblicherweise sehr sportive Aussehen dazu passender Accessoires ist dieser Skateboard-Rucksack in seiner Gestaltung modisch-urbanen Ansprüchen angepasst. Neben einer einfach handhabbaren Klettvorrichtung zur Anbringung des Boards können in dem Rucksack ein Laptop, Tablet, Bücher und Schreibmaterialien verstaut werden. Er lässt sich auch einfach mit einer Kofferstange verbinden.

Begründung der Jury
Der Walnutt Commuter Backpack macht das Skateboard als Transportmittel im urbanen Raum alltagstauglich, in ästhetischer wie in formaler Hinsicht.

HP Powerup Backpack
Backpack with Charging Function
Rucksack mit Ladefunktion

Manufacturer
HP Inc., Palo Alto, USA
In-house design
HP Inc. PS Industrial Design Team
Web
www.hp.com

A heavy-duty battery is integrated into
the HP Powerup Backpack, with the
capacity to charge a laptop up to 17,3",
a tablet and a smartphone. With power
priority, the order in which the devices
are charged can be controlled by the
user. Straps and eyelets ensure orderly
cable arrangement, allowing a smartphone to be used while it is being charged
and the user is underway with the
backpack. The exterior of the backpack
is made of heavy-duty canvas, while
the interior padding and durable straps
provide comfort. Temperature sensors
prevent the devices from overheating.

Statement by the jury
The HP Powerup Backpack is characterised by a sophisticated orderly structure.
It convinces with well-conceived, practical details and it also has a stylish look.

In dem HP Powerup Backpack ist eine
hochleistungsfähige Batterie integriert,
mit der ein bis zu 17,3"-Laptop, ein Tablet und ein Smartphone geladen werden
können. Der Nutzer bestimmt selbst,
welchen Geräten beim Ladevorgang Priorität eingeräumt wird. Schlaufen und Ösen
sorgen für eine ordentliche Kabelführung
und ermöglichen es auch, dass das Smartphone genutzt werden kann, während
es geladen wird und der Nutzer mit dem
Rucksack unterwegs ist. Die Außenseite
des Rucksacks ist aus robustem Segeltuch
gefertigt, Polsterungen im Inneren und
stabile Gurte sorgen für Komfort. Tempera-
tursensoren verhindern ein Überhitzen der
Geräte.

Begründung der Jury
Der HP Powerup Backpack zeichnet sich
durch eine ausgeklügelte Ordnungsstruktur
aus. Er überzeugt mit durchdachten praktischen Details und sieht außerdem flott aus.

Manfrotto Pro Light 3N1-36
Camera Backpack
Kamerarucksack

Manufacturer
Manfrotto, Cassola (Vicenza), Italy
In-house design
Web
www.manfrotto.com

The rucksack is designed for the many varied requirements of photographers, who often need a whole mix of camera and video equipment or drones during an assignment. For this purpose, provision is made in the internal compartments for various types of film material in differing sizes and numbers. The Camera Protection System in the inside can be rearranged time and again and adapted. The variable harness allows carrying on the back, as sling rucksack or crossback.

Statement by the jury
The Manfrotto Pro Light 3N1-36 can be packed in an impressive variety of ways and is very useful when out and about. In this way, it supports professional photographers and film makers convincingly.

Der Rucksack ist auf die vielseitigen Ansprüche von Fotografen ausgelegt, die in einem Arbeitseinsatz oftmals Kamera, Videoausstattung oder Drohnen benötigen. Zu diesem Zweck lassen sich in der Tasche verschiedene Typen an Filmmaterial in unterschiedlicher Größe und Anzahl unterbringen. Das Camera Protection System im Inneren kann immer wieder umgestaltet und angepasst werden. Das variable Gurtsystem ermöglicht das Tragen auf dem Rücken, als Sling-Rucksack oder Crossback.

Begründung der Jury
Der Manfrotto Pro Light 3N1-36 lässt sich beeindruckend variabel bepacken und ist unterwegs von hohem Nutzen. Damit unterstützt er Profifotografen und -filmer auf überzeugende Weise.

Manfrotto Manhattan Collection
Camera Bags
Kamerataschen

Manufacturer
Manfrotto, Cassola (Vicenza), Italy
In-house design
Web
www.manfrotto.com

The Manfrotto Manhattan Collection comprises three models of camera bags – a backpack, a 3-way shoulder bag and a messenger. For the daily commute to the office and back as well as for photo shoots in between, e.g. by foot, bike or many other means of transportation, the bags are designed to be highly functional. The innovative removable Manfrotto Insert System safeguards photography gear inside. The Flexy Camera Shell divider system combines protection with flexibility, securing most current DSLR or CSC models. Moreover, a multipurpose webbing and straps fasten a tripod, a helmet, a jacket and other bulky items. Non-slip bumpers provide extra stability in use.

Statement by the jury
The models of the Manfrotto Manhattan Collection prove to be functionally convincing tools for photographers who must protect their equipment well, but must be able to reach for it quickly.

Die Manfrotto Manhattan Collection umfasst drei Modelle von Kamerataschen – einen Rucksack, eine 3-Way Shoulder Bag und einen Bodybag. Die Gestaltung der Taschen ist auf hohe Funktionalität hin ausgelegt – für den täglichen Arbeitsweg wie auch für Fotoshootings dazwischen, ob diese nun zu Fuß, mit dem Rad oder anderen Transportmitteln erreicht werden. Das innovative herausnehmbare Manfrotto Insert System sichert die Fotoausrüstung im Inneren. Das Trennsystem Flexy Camera Shell kombiniert Schutz und Flexibilität und sichert die gängigen DSLR- oder SCS-Modelle. Ein Vielzweck-Gurtband und Schlaufen fixieren ein Stativ, einen Helm, eine Jacke und andere sperrige Gegenstände. Rutschfeste Puffer sorgen für besondere Stabilität während der Nutzung.

Begründung der Jury
Die Modelle der Manfrotto Manhattan Collection beweisen sich als funktional überzeugende Tools für Fotografen, die ihre Ausrüstung stets gut geschützt, aber auch schnell zur Hand haben müssen.

Alta Sky 51D
Camera Backpack
Kamerarucksack

Manufacturer
Vanguard World, Whitmore Lake, USA
In-house design
Bellina Israel
Web
www.vanguardworld.com

The Alta Sky 51D was designed for the transport of photographic gear and other work equipment and, thanks to ⅓-⅔ division and adjustable inner life, can be individually loaded. It is designed in such a way that it has room for one or two DSLRs with fitted lenses, three to four additional lenses, a flash unit or a drone, each with accessories, as well as a compact system camera including lens. In addition, a 15" notebook and/or a tablet can be stowed and a tripod can be attached using one of the various straps at the side.

Statement by the jury
The Alta Sky 51D convinces with a well-conceived design which is exactly tailored to the equipment it transports and keeps it safe and stable.

Der Alta Sky 51D wurde für den Transport von Fotoausrüstung oder anderen Arbeitsmitteln entworfen und kann dank ⅓-⅔-Aufteilung und anpassbarem Innenleben individuell bestückt werden. Er wurde so gestaltet, dass darin ein bis zwei DSLRs mit aufgesetztem Objektiv, drei bis vier zusätzliche Objektive, ein Blitzgerät oder eine Drohne, jeweils mit Zubehör, sowie eine kompakte Systemkamera samt Objektiv Platz finden. Außerdem lassen sich ein 15"-Laptop und/oder ein Tablet darin verstauen und ein Stativ an einem der verschiedenen seitlichen Riemen befestigen.

Begründung der Jury
Der Alta Sky 51D überzeugt mit einer durchdachten Gestaltung, die exakt auf ihr Transportgut zugeschnitten ist und dieses sicher und stabil verwahrt.

VEO Discover 46
Camera Backpack
Kamerarucksack

Manufacturer
Vanguard World, Whitmore Lake, USA
In-house design
Bellina Israel
Web
www.vanguardworld.com

The VEO Discover 46 is providing space for a camera, up to four lenses, a flashlight, a 13" notebook and a tripod. It can be quickly transformed from a normal backpack into a side-access sling rucksack without taking it off. The spacious top compartment can be used to stow away personal items or accessories, while the secure rear compartment is reserved for a laptop. A secret compartment close to the body protects a wallet and documents from unauthorised access.

Statement by the jury
The VEO Discover 46 is a nice example of well-conceived partitioning of storage space. Everything that needs to be taken along finds its optimal place.

Der VEO Discover 46 bietet Platz für eine Kamera, bis zu vier Objektive, einen Blitz, ein 13"-Notebook und ein Stativ. Er lässt sich schnell von einem normalen Rucksack in einen Sling-Rucksack mit seitlichem Zugriff verwandeln, ohne dass man ihn abnehmen muss. Im geräumigen Fach an der Oberseite werden persönliche Dinge oder Zubehör verstaut, das geschützte Fach im Rücken ist für einen Laptop reserviert, ein Geheimfach nah am Körper schützt Geldbörse und Papiere vor Zugriff.

Begründung der Jury
Der VEO Discover 46 ist ein schönes Beispiel für eine durchdachte Aufteilung von Stauraum. Alles, was man mitnimmt, findet seinen optimalen Platz.

CARGO by OWEE REFLECTIVE
Bag Collection
Taschenkollektion

Manufacturer
CARGO by OWEE, Anna Migacz-Lesińska,
Warsaw, Poland
In-house design
Web
www.cargobyowee.com
Honourable Mention

Cargo by Owee Reflective is the collection of three items – a tote bag, a hip bag and a backpack. The bags are made of the durable fabric Cordura combined with a reflective thread. That makes the products glow in the dark as the thread reflects light even from 150 metres. It means impressive visibility especially for bikers and pedestrians in the night. Every piece of the collection is comfortable and very convenient thanks to handy handles, adjustable and detachable strips as well as zipped pockets.

Cargo by Owee Reflective ist eine dreiteilige Kollektion, bestehend aus Tragetasche, Hüfttasche und Rucksack. Die Taschen sind aus langlebigem Cordura-Stoff hergestellt, der mit einem reflektierenden Garn kombiniert wurde. Auf diese Weise leuchten die Produkte im Dunkeln, da das Garn das Licht selbst aus einer Entfernung von 150 Metern reflektiert. Dadurch bleiben vor allem Radfahrer und Fußgänger bei Nacht sehr gut sichtbar. Jedes Teil der Kollektion ist bequem und sehr praktisch dank handlicher Griffe, verstellbarer und abnehmbarer Streifen sowie Reißverschlusstaschen.

Statement by the jury
The bags of the Cargo by Owee Reflective collection convince due to the well-conceived use of materials which assures safety and long durability.

Begründung der Jury
Die Taschen der Kollektion Cargo by Owee Reflective überzeugen aufgrund eines durchdachten Materialeinsatzes, der für Sicherheit und Langlebigkeit sorgt.

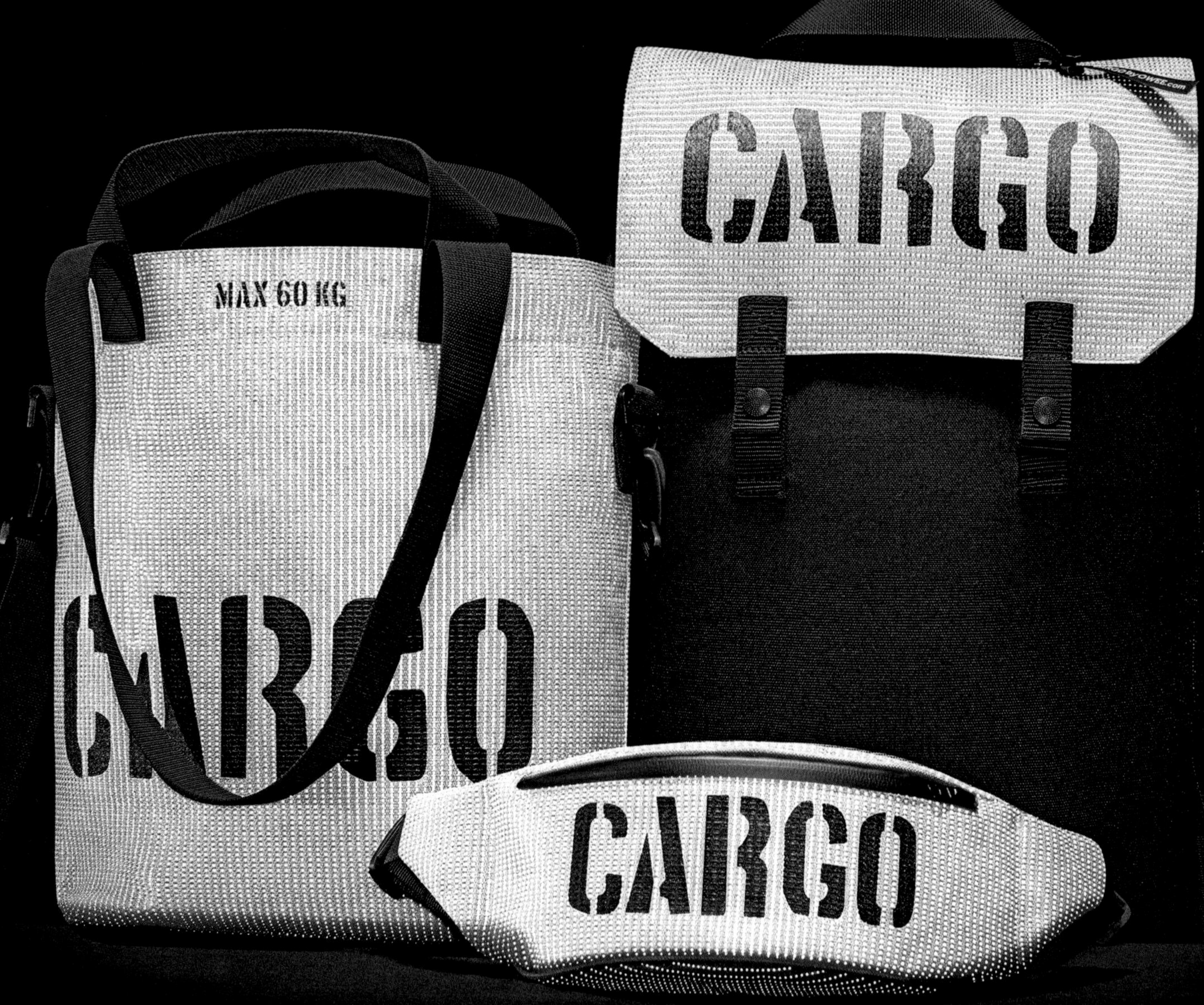
CARGO
MAX 60 KG
CARGO
CARGO

Scout Genius
Schoolbag
Schulranzen

Manufacturer
Alfred Sternjakob GmbH & Co. KG, Frankenthal, Germany
Design
Vistapark GmbH, Wuppertal, Germany
Web
www.scout-schulranzen.de
www.vistapark.de

Apart from the magnetic lock and the base trough, no plastic components of this schoolbag are visible. The lid is formed robustly, so that it closes automatically when folded down. Thanks to the water-tight, sturdy base trough with feet, the Scout Genius can be set down on wet ground without affecting the contents. The Scout carrying strap system with its wide shoulder straps shaped like an "S" and waist strap fits the back ergonomically all primary school years. The back is upholstered with breathable 3D mesh fabric.

Bei diesem Schulranzen sind außer dem Magnetschloss und der Bodenwanne keine Kunststoffteile sichtbar. Der Deckel ist stabil geformt, dadurch schließt das Magnetschloss beim Herunterklappen von selbst. Dank der wasserfesten, robusten Bodenwanne mit Füßen kann man den Scout Genius auf nassem Untergrund abstellen, ohne dass der Inhalt beeinträchtigt wird. Das mitwachsende Scout-Tragegurtsystem mit breiten Schultergurten in S-Form und Hüftgurt passt sich dem Rücken durch die gesamte Grundschulzeit hindurch ergonomisch an. Der Rücken ist mit atmungsaktivem 3D-Mesh-Gewebe gepolstert.

Statement by the jury
The Scout Genius adapts to the reality of the school day with clever details – from the automatically closing lid to the water-tight base, protecting notebooks and pens safely.

Begründung der Jury
Der Scout Genius geht mit raffinierten Details auf die Realitäten im Schulalltag ein – vom selbstschließenden Deckel bis hin zum wasserfesten Boden, der Hefte und Stifte sicher schützt.

Tokyo
Handbag
Handtasche

Manufacturer
mossy jewels, immenwerk GmbH,
Bad Schönborn, Germany
In-house design
Imme Vogel
Web
www.mossyjewels.com

The structure of this handbag was designed by experimenting with folding paper and is characterised solely by its folding radius. Since the leather is stiffened without additional, external materials, it feels soft and smooth. The lining is made of neoprene, assuring the necessary stability. A red rubber band on the inside holds cosmetics and pens in place and avoids troublesome searching. Three straps of different lengths can be easily changed as needed, using the button rivets on the sides.

In Faltexperimenten mit Papier entwickelt, existiert die Struktur dieser Handtasche nur durch den Biegeradius. Da das Leder ohne zusätzliches Fremdmaterial versteift ist, fühlt es sich weich und angenehm an. Das Innenfutter aus Neopren sorgt für die nötige Standfestigkeit. Ein rotes Gummiband im Inneren hält Kosmetika und Stifte an ihrem Platz und verhindert lästiges Suchen. Drei unterschiedlich lange Trageriemen können über die seitlichen Knopfnieten je nach Anlass leicht gewechselt werden.

Statement by the jury
The Tokyo handbag convinces due to its innovative construction in which only leather is used. That also assures a pleasant haptic.

Begründung der Jury
Die Handtasche Tokyo überzeugt durch ihre innovative Konstruktionsweise, bei der nur Leder eingesetzt wird. Das sorgt zugleich für eine angenehme Haptik.

N über C – Cork Collection
Bag Collection
Taschenkollektion

Manufacturer
frisch Beutel, Frisch & Pfaff GbR, Frankfurt/Main, Germany
Design
Peter Schmidt Group (Larissa von der Heide, Marija Zurak),
Frankfurt/Main, Germany
Web
www.frisch-shop.de
www.peter-schmidt-group.de
Honourable Mention

The bags of this collection are a limited edition of 100 pieces. They are made of cork and printed in a screen process with an abstract pattern taken from the maritime flag alphabet: hoisting „N above C" in this language is the distress at sea signal. The combination of the floating material cork and the symbolism of the flags sets a signal for refugees in distress at sea. At the same time the entire proceeds are donated to the corresponding aid organisation.

Die Taschen dieser Kollektion bestehen aus einer limitierten Auflage von 100 Stück. Sie sind aus Kork gefertigt und im Siebdruck-verfahren mit einem abstrahierten Muster aus dem Flaggenalphabet bedruckt: Mit „N über C" wird in dieser Sprache das See-notsignal gehisst. Die Verbindung aus dem schwimmfähigen Material Kork und der Flaggensymbolik setzt ein Zeichen für in Seenot geratene Flüchtlinge. Zugleich kommt der gesamte Erlös einer entsprechend tätigen Hilfsorganisation zugute.

Statement by the jury
The bag collection makes good use of its idealistic content in a playful way. The innovative material cork convinces from a functional viewpoint.

Begründung der Jury
Die Taschenkollektion weiß auf spielerische Weise mit ihrem ideellen Gehalt umzugehen. Das innovative Material Kork überzeugt auch in funktionaler Hinsicht.

senseBag Shopper

Manufacturer
Holtz Office Support, Wiesbaden, Germany
In-house design
Tobias Liliencron
Web
www.holtzofficesupport.com

The senseBag Shopper, made of cream coloured linen, has a particularly inviting design and can thus hold many items which have to be carried when out and about – from the daily shopping to a laptop. The carrying handle, made of bamboo, is comfortable to hold and the contents remain safely packed due to the stable pushbutton under it. If required, the bag can be carried on the shoulder, due to adjustable straps which are attached simply with snap hooks. Since the bag has a stiff base, it can also be set down and used as a clothes basket or wastepaper basket.

Der senseBag Shopper aus cremefarbenem Leinen ist besonders ausladend gestaltet und kann daher viele Gegenstände aufnehmen, die unterwegs mitgenommen werden müssen – von den Tageseinkäufen bis hin zu einem Laptop. Der Tragegriff aus Bambus liegt gut in der Hand, durch den darunter angebrachten stabilen Druckknopf bleibt der Inhalt sicher verwahrt. Bei Bedarf lässt sich die Tasche auch mit verstellbaren Riemen, die einfach mit Karabinerhaken montiert werden, über der Schulter tragen. Die Tasche kann wegen ihres festen Bodens auch aufgestellt und als Wäsche- oder Papierkorb genutzt werden.

Statement by the jury
The senseBag Shopper impresses with its versatility, thanks to which it is a practical everyday aid. The mix of environmentally friendly materials is a great advantage.

Begründung der Jury
Der senseBag Shopper beeindruckt mit seiner Vielseitigkeit, dank der er sich als praktische Hilfe im Alltag erweist. Auch der Mix aus umweltverträglichen Materialien nimmt für ihn ein.

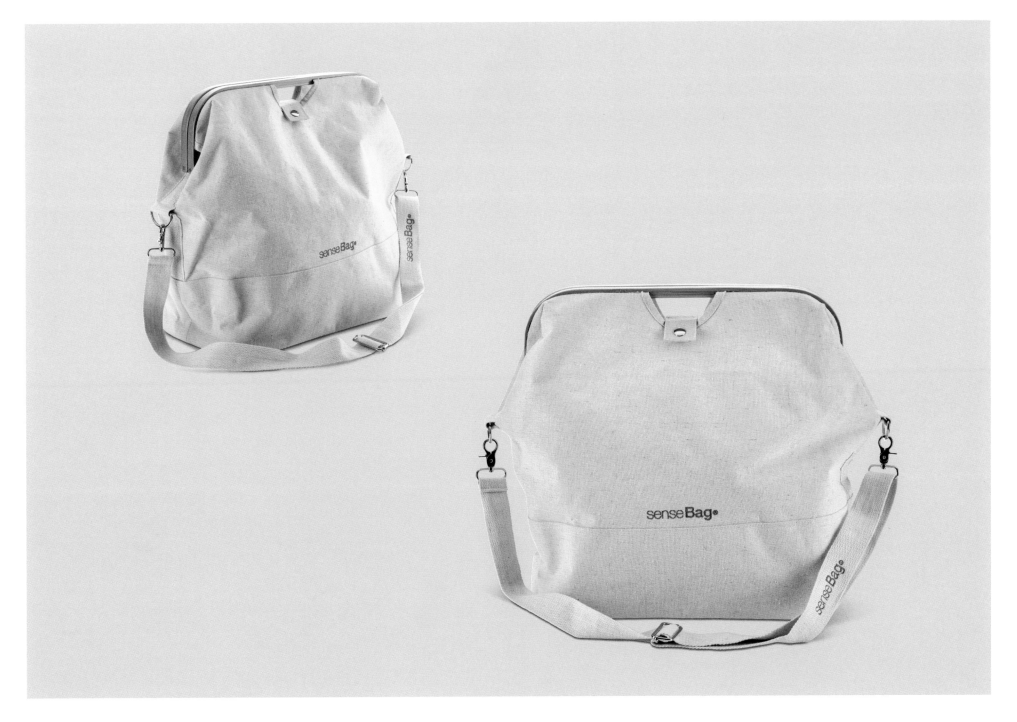

S Cart
Shopping Trolley
Einkaufstrolley

Manufacturer
Demby Development Co., Ltd.,
New Taipei City, Taiwan
In-house design
Demby Design Team (Tsung-Hsiang Wang), Taiwan
Web
www.dembygroup.com

The shopping trolley can be used as a
seat on the move when required by
pushing a large button on the side. When
it stands still, the wheels are clear of
the ground, so that it cannot run away
when used as a seat. When the S Cart
is moved over the ground, the curved
structural bars of the trolley prevent the
necessity of pulling it over the steps.
The trolley is rust-resistant and light,
yet also stable and can accept loads up
to 200 kg. Various bags for different
purposes can be carried on it as required.

Statement by the jury
The integrated seat system and the
attention to safety given to the S Cart
indicate sensitive consideration for the
requirements of elderly people.

Durch einen großen seitlichen Knopf wird
der Einkaufstrolley unterwegs bei Bedarf
zu einem Sitz. Im stehenden Zustand befinden sich die Laufräder auf Abstand zum
Boden, wodurch ein Wegrollen beim Benutzen der Sitzfläche verhindert wird. Wenn
der S Cart über Treppen bewegt wird, ver-
meidet die Bogenform, dass die Gerüst-
stangen über den Untergrund gezogen
werden müssen. Der Trolley ist rostfrei und
leicht, aber dennoch sehr stabil und kann
mit bis zu 200 kg belastet werden. Je nach
Bedarf lassen sich verschiedene Taschen
anbringen.

Begründung der Jury
Die integrierte Sitzvorrichtung und das Augenmerk auf Sicherheit beim S Cart zeugen
von der einfühlsamen Berücksichtigung der
Bedürfnisse älterer Personen.

eGeeTouch Smart Travel Padlock
Reiseschloss

Manufacturer
JSB Tech Pte Ltd, Singapore
Design
Digipas Technologies Inc., Irvine, California, USA
Web
www.egeetouch.com

This travel padlock functions without
a key. It communicates via a Bluetooth
enabled smartphone (iOS or android),
a smart watch or an NFC-enabled key
fob and thus locks and unlocks luggage.
A special proximity tracking setting
sends a notification when the case or bag
exceeds a maximum distance of nine
metres from the user. The smart padlock
is recognised and accepted by the U.S.
agency TSA, enabling the custom officer
to open and examine the luggage without damaging the lock.

Statement by the jury
Thanks to the innovative, intelligent
means of communication of the eGee-
Touch Smart Travel Padlock, fumbling
with the key and forgotten codes are a
thing of the past.

Dieses Reiseschloss funktioniert ohne
Schlüssel. Es kommuniziert mit einem
Bluetooth-fähigen Smartphone (iOS oder
Android), einer Smart Watch oder einem
NFC-fähigen Anhänger und ver- bzw. ent-
sperrt so das Gepäckstück. Eine spezielle
Proximity-Tracking-Einstellung sendet eine
Mitteilung, sobald der Koffer oder die
Tasche einen Maximalabstand von etwa
neun Metern zum Nutzer überschreitet.
Das System ist bei den US-Behörden der
TSA verzeichnet und anerkannt, Zollbeamte
können das Gepäckstück somit öffnen
und kontrollieren, ohne das Schloss dabei
zu zerstören.

Begründung der Jury
Dank der innovativen intelligenten Kom-
munikationsweise des eGeeTouch Smart
Travel Padlock gehören das Herumnesteln
mit dem Schlüssel und vergessene Codes
der Vergangenheit an.

Curio
Luggage Collection
Kofferkollektion

Manufacturer
Samsonite Asia Limited, Hong Kong
In-house design
Nobuo Maeda
Web
www.americantourister.com

The luggage collection is made of high-quality polypropylene and catches the eye due to its prominent colours. The sides and the logo are constructed of glossy material; the ribbed pattern on the front is matt. The cases can be expanded in the centre to accommodate additional luggage. A mesh dividing system inside allows easy sorting. Locks conforming to TSA are concealed elegantly in the hard shell material.

Die Kofferkollektion aus hochwertigem Polypropylen sticht durch ihre Ausführung in auffälligen Farben hervor. Die Seitenteile und das Logo sind in glänzendem Material ausgeführt, das gerippte Muster an der Vorderseite ist matt. Die Koffer können in der Mitte erweitert werden, um zusätzliches Gepäck aufzunehmen. Im Inneren ermöglicht ein Trennsystem aus Maschenstoffen einfaches Sortieren. TSA-konforme Schlösser sind elegant in das Hartschalenmaterial eingelassen.

Statement by the jury
The Curio luggage collection, with its lively design in prominent colours catches the eye immediately and makes its users convey a brilliant impression.

Begründung der Jury
Die Kofferkollektion Curio fällt mit ihrer lebhaften Gestaltung in auffälligen Farben sofort ins Auge und sichert ihren Benutzern einen glänzenden Auftritt.

7R Master
Luggage Collection
Kofferkollektion

Manufacturer
Samsonite NV, Oudenaarde, Belgium
In-house design
Erik Sijmons
Web
www.samsonite.com
www.hartmannluggage.eu

The shell form of the luggage collection 7R Master is made of high-quality aluminium and has a nostalgic appeal. The material is resilient and gives the case a classical elegance, providing a pleasant appearance and even more character over time. It is characterised by elaborate craftsmanship, with over 250 individual processes needed to create one unique product. Shock-absorbing, smoothly gliding and quiet running wheels provide easy handling.

Statement by the jury
The 7R Master models impress by their innovative idea of objectively using aluminium in the design. Every sign of wear adds to the character of the case.

Die Schalenform der Kofferkollektion 7R Master ist aus hochwertigem Aluminium gefertigt und zeigt nostalgischen Anklang. Das Material ist widerstandsfähig und verleiht dem Koffer klassische Eleganz, das gibt ihm ein ansprechendes Erscheinungsbild, dessen Charakter sich mit der Zeit noch erhöht. Er ist gekennzeichnet von aufwendiger Handarbeit, 250 einzelne Arbeitsschritte sind nötig, um ein unverwechselbares Produkt zu erzeugen. Stoßdämpfende, sanft gleitende und geräuscharme Rollen unterstützen ein einfaches Handling.

Begründung der Jury
Die Modelle des 7R Master bestechen durch die innovative Idee, Aluminium bewusst zur Gestaltung einzusetzen: Jede Gebrauchsspur verleiht dem Koffer zunehmend Charakter.

Plutus
Luggage Collection
Kofferkollektion

Manufacturer
Samsonite Asia Limited, Hong Kong
In-house design
Nobuo Maeda
Web
www.samsonite.com

With its aesthetic design and its components, the Plutus luggage collection satisfies high demands. The robust shells display an elegant prism pattern, logos and zip fasteners are finished in premium gold-metallic materials. In their interior the suitcases offer a good number of separate pockets which help to stow high-quality shoes and clothing safely and make packing in general easy. Furthermore, the collection is equipped with a TSA-conforming lock and high-quality double wheels.

Statement by the jury
With its high-quality and aesthetically balanced design as well as its functionally well-conceived stowing room, Plutus can clearly claim its place in the premium segment.

In ihrer ästhetischen Gestaltung sowie in ihren Komponenten kommt die Kofferkollektion Plutus den gehobenen Ansprüchen entgegen. Der robuste Mantel zeigt jeweils ein elegantes Prismenmuster, Logos und Zips sind mit edlen golden-metallischen Materialien versehen. Im Inneren halten die Koffer eine Fülle an getrennten Taschen bereit, die auch hochwertige Schuhe und Kleidungsstücke sicher zu verwahren helfen und das Packen allgemein erleichtern. Weiter verfügt die Kollektion über ein TSA-konformes Schloss und hochwertige Doppelräder.

Begründung der Jury
In seiner hochwertigen und ästhetisch ausgewogenen Gestaltung sowie mit einem funktional gut durchdachten Stauraum platziert sich Plutus eindeutig im Premiumsegment.

The Carry-On
Luggage
Koffer

Manufacturer
Arlo Skye, Travel Goods, New York, USA
In-house design
Mauricio Issa
Web
www.arloskye.com

This suitcase is constructed using a light aluminium-magnesium alloy. The interior is clad with an anti-bacterial fabric. Adjustable compartments and fastening straps, make packing easily versatile. Thanks to specially made wheels, the case rolls extremely quietly. A built-in lithium ion battery for two USB connections is incorporated. This system, installed seamlessly under the handle, can be removed without the need to open the case. Four wheels with 360-degree radius make transport easy.

Statement by the jury
The special feature of The Carry-On is the charger which is easily accessible – a functionally convincing tool for remaining always contactable when travelling.

Dieser Koffer ist mit einer leichten Aluminium-Magnesium-Legierung versehen. Im Inneren ist er mit antibakteriell wirksamen Stoffen ausgekleidet. Verstellbare Fächer und Schließbänder ermöglichen flexibles Packen. Dank speziell gefertigter Rollen lässt sich der Koffer besonders leise bewegen. In das Gehäuse ist ein tragbarer Lithium-Ionen-Akku für zwei USB-Anschlüsse eingearbeitet. Diese nahtlos unterhalb des Griffes eingebaute Vorrichtung kann herausgenommen werden, ohne dass der Koffer geöffnet werden muss. Vier Räder mit 360-Grad-Radius erleichtern den Transport.

Begründung der Jury
Der besondere Pluspunkt des Carry-On ist das Ladegerät, auf das einfach zugegriffen werden kann – ein funktional überzeugendes Tool, um unterwegs stets erreichbar zu bleiben.

Prodigy
Cabin Luggage
Kabinengepäck

Manufacturer
Samsonite NV, Oudenaarde, Belgium
In-house design
Adrien Lefebvre
Web
www.samsonite.com

Prodigy has been especially designed for uncomplicated handling of cabin luggage. Airport processes such as check-in and security checks are made easier due to the large-capacity, recessed pocket at the front. In this, all items, which you need to take out several times, can be stored – e.g. electronic devices or travel documents. Handle and lock are recessed in the body with rounded corners, making storage in the overhead compartment easier.

Statement by the jury
Prodigy provides a functionally well-considered solution, especially for the use of hand luggage. Convenience and aesthetics combine due to the elegant design.

Prodigy ist speziell für die unkomplizierte Verwendung als Handgepäck konstruiert. Prozesse am Flughafen wie das Einchecken und der Security Check werden durch eine geräumige, an der Front eingelassene Tasche erleichtert. Darin können alle Gegenstände, die man mehrfach herausnehmen muss, gut verstaut werden – etwa elektronische Geräte oder Reiseunterlagen. Griff und Verriegelung sind in den Körper mit abgerundeten Ecken eingelassen, was das Verstauen im Gepäckfach vereinfacht.

Begründung der Jury
Prodigy bietet eine funktional gut durchdachte Lösung speziell bei der Verwendung als Handgepäck. Komfort und Ästhetik finden durch die elegante Ausführung zusammen.

Lite-Box
Luggage Collection
Kofferkollektion

Manufacturer
Samsonite NV, Oudenaarde, Belgium
In-house design
Erik Sijmons
Web
www.samsonite.com
Honourable Mention

The shell of the Lite-Box luggage collection is made from durable Curv material. For this process, woven fibres produce a self-reinforced material which is very light and at the same time robust. The satin-finishing on the shell surface conveys a premium impression. From a design viewpoint, the voluminous, box-shaped construction with a dynamical vertical concept, as well as the reinforced shell corners are eye-catching. An additional luggage item with Smartsleeve function can be attached to the convenient, long extendable handle.

Statement by the jury
Critical travellers who desire a combination of high-quality materials and classical design will find in Lite-Box a convincing solution.

Die Schale der Kofferkollektion Lite-Box ist aus dauerhaftem Curv-Material gefertigt. Dabei ergeben gewebte Fasern ein eigenverstärktes Material, das sehr leicht und zugleich robust ist. Die satinierte Ausführung der Schalenoberfläche vermittelt eine gehobene Anmutung. Gestalterisch fallen der voluminöse kastenförmige Aufbau mit dynamischer vertikaler Ausrichtung sowie die verstärkten Kanten ins Auge. An dem komfortablen, weit ausziehbaren Griff kann ein zusätzliches Gepäckstück mit Smartsleeve-Funktion befestigt werden.

Begründung der Jury
Anspruchsvolle Reisende, die eine Kombination aus hochwertigen Materialien und klassischem Design wünschen, finden mit Lite-Box eine überzeugende Lösung.

Ultimax Collection
Luggage Collection
Kofferkollektion

Manufacturer
PROKAS Luggage by Traveler's Choice Travelware,
Los Angeles, USA
In-house design
Joseph Chen
Web
www.prokas.com
www.travelerchoice.com

The design of the Ultimax Collection takes inspiration from classic trunk suitcases. Its functional construction is oriented towards the demands of modern, everyday travel. The luggage is equipped with a comfortably gripped, patented T-Cruiser handle and patented dual Cyclone Spherical Spinner Wheel System that makes maneuvering in a 360-degree angle easy and smooth gliding. In addition to its many compartments for shoes or dirty clothing articles, a transparent bag for liquids can be removed by unzipping. All suitcases are equipped with a TSA-conforming lock.

Gestalterisch ist die Ultimax Collection inspiriert von den klassischen Schrankkoffern. Im funktionalen Aufbau orientiert sie sich an den Ansprüchen des modernen Reisealltags. Die Koffer sind mit angenehm gerippten, patentierten T-Cruiser-Griffen ausgestattet, durch das patentierte duale Cyclone-Spherical-Spinner-Wheel-System gelingt einfaches und sanft gleitendes Manövrieren im 360-Grad-Winkel. Neben zahlreichen praktischen Fächern für Schuhe oder Schmutzwäsche kann eine transparente Tasche für Flüssigkeiten mittels Zip einfach herausgenommen werden. Alle Koffer sind mit einem TSA-konformen Schloss versehen.

Statement by the jury
The Ultimax Collection convinces with its many, well-considered functions which ease not only packing but also manoeuvring and thereby facilitate everyday travel enormously.

Begründung der Jury
Die Ultimax Collection überzeugt mit vielen durchdachten Funktionen, die sowohl das Packen wie auch das Manövrieren unterstützen und dadurch den Reisealltag enorm erleichtern.

Fuze
Luggage Collection
Kofferkollektion

Manufacturer
Samsonite NV, Oudenaarde, Belgium
In-house design
Federica Mucci
Web
www.samsonite.com

The name of the luggage collection is taken from the word "fuse" and indicates the fusing of hard and soft materials used in these luggage items. The moulded hard shell brings stability and protection, whereas the soft additional outside pockets allow more flexibility. Various compartments and inside pockets enable clear and practical partition of the luggage.

Statement by the jury
Fuze makes the advantages of hard and soft luggage materials skilfully useful and proves to be a practical travel companion.

Der Name der Kofferkollektion leitet sich von dem englischen Verb „fuse" ab und verweist auf die Verbindung von hartem und weichem Material bei diesen Gepäckstücken. Die gegossenen Hartschalenteile verleihen Stabilität und Schutz, während die weichen Zusatztaschen außen erhöhte Flexibilität zulassen. Verschiedene Fächer und Innentaschen ermöglichen eine übersichtliche und praktische Aufteilung des Gepäcks.

Begründung der Jury
Fuze macht sich die Vorteile harten wie weichen Koffermaterials gekonnt zunutze und bewährt sich als praktischer Reisebegleiter.

Veron
Business Collection
Businesskollektion

Manufacturer
Samsonite Asia Limited, Hong Kong
Design
Cristian Righetti
Web
www.samsonite.com

Veron is designed especially for the demands of business travellers. All units are constructed of fine leather in combination with sturdy nylon. The collection consists of five variations, from slim briefcase for short trips via rucksack version up to the comprehensive mobile office version. All luggage components contain well-conceived functions for support in today's business working day, and with their high-quality appearance provide a professional impression.

Statement by the jury
The Veron business collection convinces by its versatility. Business travellers will always find the functionally suitable companion among the five well-conceived models.

Veron ist ganz auf die Bedürfnisse von Geschäftsreisenden ausgelegt. Alle Stücke sind in feinem gestanztem Leder in Verbindung mit robustem Nylon ausgeführt. Die Kollektion umfasst fünf Variationen, vom Slim Briefcase für Kurzreisen über eine Ausführung als Rucksack bis hin zur umfassenden Mobile-Office-Version. Alle Gepäckstücke verfügen über durchdachte Funktionen zur Unterstützung im modernen Berufsalltag und ermöglichen in ihrer hochwertigen Ausführung ein professionelles Auftreten.

Begründung der Jury
Die Businesskollektion Veron überzeugt durch ihre Vielseitigkeit. Geschäftsreisende finden unter den fünf gut durchdachten Modellen immer den funktional passenden Begleiter.

Departure HD511
Suitcase
Koffer

Manufacturer
Departure International Co., Ltd.,
Taipei, Taiwan
In-house design
Kevin Wu
Web
www.departure-travel.com

In the case of the Departure HD511 suitcase, the front attachment can be removed with a few hand motions and replaced with a different design. By this means the design can be adapted to the individual requirements of the various travellers, for instance within a family. The removable front pocket can also be used separately, as handbag or rucksack with various functions. Even when it is attached to the suitcase, various functional components can be selected for the front pocket. The well-conceived outer properties provide the suitcase with good impact resistance and make the entire construction very firm and stable.

Bei dem Koffer Departure HD511 kann der vordere Aufsatz mit wenigen Handgriffen abgenommen und durch ein anderes Design ersetzt werden. Dadurch geht die Gestaltung auf die individuellen Bedürfnisse der verschiedenen Reisenden, etwa innerhalb einer Familie, ein. Die abnehmbare Vordertasche kann auch ganz für sich alleine verwendet werden, als Handtasche oder Rucksack mit unterschiedlichen Funktionen. Auch am Koffer montiert können unterschiedliche Funktionsteile für die Vordertasche ausgewählt werden. Die durchdachte Oberflächenbeschaffenheit verleiht dem Koffer eine gute Schlagfestigkeit und macht den gesamten Aufbau sehr fest und stabil.

Statement by the jury
The Departure HD511 can be redesigned individually according to taste. Furthermore, the idea that the front component can be used individually is impressive.

Begründung der Jury
Der Departure HD511 lässt sich je nach Geschmack individuell umgestalten. Zudem beeindruckt die Idee, dass das Vorderteil auch einzeln verwendet werden kann.

WRAD Graphi-Tee
T-Shirt

Manufacturer
WRAD Srl, Monticello Conte Otto
(Vicenza), Italy

In-house design
WRAD Srl

Web
www.wradliving.com

reddot award 2017
best of the best

New cycles

Sustainability is a topic of high importance in the textile industry since worldwide it constantly produces many harmful substances. In search of an exemplary circular production process for the Graphi-Tee t-shirt, the design was inspired by a traditional technique. The idea for this textile goes back to a process, already common in ancient Roman times and from the 15th to the 19th century in southern Italy, to dye fabrics with graphite. However, the graphite powder used for the Graphi-Tee (up to ten grams per t-shirt) is a waste product from today's technology industry. It is recovered for processing, creating a closed and sustainable cycle. The special processing lends the textile expressive aesthetics and a highly pleasant feel. Since graphite is also a lubricant, the bio-cotton jersey of the Graphi-Tee is very soft and smoothly fits to the body. Consistent with the pursuit of sustainable processes in the fashion industry, the Graphi-Tees are made with a GOTS-certified (Global Organic Textile Standard) organic cotton in Italy and furthermore use a cutting technique that reduces fabric waste. The use of the non-toxic graphite powder presents a meaningful alternative to the use of harmful chemical substances in the fashion industry. With its pioneering design, the Graphi-Tee inspires people to think – and the wearer of this stylish piece of clothing becomes an ambassador for more sustainability.

Neue Kreisläufe

Das Thema der Nachhaltigkeit ist in der Textilindustrie von großer Bedeutung, da hier weltweit regelmäßig viele Schadstoffe anfallen. Auf der Suche nach einer vorbildlichen zirkulären Produktionsweise für das T-Shirt Graphi-Tee ließ man sich von einem traditionellen Verfahren inspirieren. Die Idee für diese Textilie geht zurück auf eine im südlichen Italien schon in der Antike und vom 15. bis 19. Jahrhundert übliche Praxis, Stoffe mit Graphit zu färben. Das für das Graphi-Tee genutzte Graphitpulver (bis zu zehn Gramm je T-Shirt) ist jedoch ein Abfallprodukt aus der heutigen technischen Industrie. Es wird für die Veredelung zurückgewonnen – wobei ein geschlossener, nachhaltiger Kreislauf geschaffen wird. Die besondere Veredelung verleiht dieser Textilie eine expressive Ästhetik und Haptik. Da Graphit auch ein Schmierstoff ist, ist der Biobaumwoll-Jersey des Graphi-Tee sehr weich und schmiegt sich sanft an den Körper an. Im Einklang mit dem Streben nach nachhaltigen Prozessen in der Modebranche werden die Graphi-Tees aus einer GOTS-zertifizierten (Global Organic Textile Standard) Biobaumwolle in Italien hergestellt. Bei ihrem Zuschnitt wird zudem eine Technik eingesetzt, die Stoffabfälle vermindert. Die Nutzung des ungiftigen Graphitpulvers zeigt eine sinnvolle Alternative zum Einsatz chemischer Substanzen in der Textilindustrie auf. Mit seiner wegweisenden Gestaltung regt das Graphi-Tee zum Nachdenken an – und der Träger wird mit diesem stylischen Kleidungsstück zum Botschafter für mehr Nachhaltigkeit.

Statement by the jury

With its distinctive processing, the Graphi-Tee stands as an example of a way of thinking that looks beyond the field of the textile industry, since this beautiful fashion product emphatically draws attention to the necessity of sustainable processes. The graphite material lends it its very unique character and a fascinatingly sensuous feel. This t-shirt demonstrates that design points with new ideas at ways into the future.

Begründung der Jury

Das Graphi-Tee steht durch seine auffällige Veredelung exemplarisch für ein Denken, das über den Bereich der Textilindustrie hinausweist. Denn das schöne Fashionprodukt macht eindringlich auf die Notwendigkeit nachhaltiger Prozesse aufmerksam. Das Material Graphit verleiht ihm eine ganz eigene Note sowie eine faszinierend sinnliche Haptik. Dieses T-Shirt zeigt, dass Design mit neuen Ideen Wege in die Zukunft weist.

Designer portrait
See page 70
Siehe Seite 70

Cosy Winter Tights by ITEM m6
Compression Tights
Kompressionsstrumpfhose

Manufacturer
medi GmbH & Co. KG, Bayreuth, Germany
In-house design
Dieter Friedmann, Sonja Schmidt
Web
www.medi-corporate.com
www.item-m6.com

The compression tights are manufactured in an innovative plush technique. In the manufacture, special "heat loops" are formed on the inside of the tights. These keep the legs pleasantly warm even in severe cold. Thanks to a sophisticated compression technology, silhouette and legs are impressively formed. The pressure profile is precisely defined. By this means, slipping or constriction are avoided, so that the wearer experiences a feeling of lightness and good fit.

Statement by the jury
With these compression tights, women need not do without a good fit or wearing comfort and they keep pleasantly warm at low temperatures.

Die Kompressionsstrumpfhose wird in einem innovativen Plüschverfahren gefertigt. Spezielle „Heat Loops" werden bei der Herstellung auf der Strumpfinnenseite geformt. Diese halten die Beine auch bei starker Kälte angenehm warm. Dank einer ausgefeilten Kompressionstechnologie werden Silhouette und Beine eindrucksvoll geformt. Der Druckverlauf ist exakt definiert. Dadurch wird das Rutschen oder Einengen vermieden, sodass die Trägerin ein Gefühl von Leichtigkeit und guter Passform wahrnimmt.

Begründung der Jury
Mit dieser Kompressionsstrumpfhose müssen Frauen nicht auf gute Passform oder Tragekomfort verzichten und bei kalten Temperaturen hält sie angenehm warm.

Reflective Hands
Gloves
Handschuhe

Manufacturer
Moiko, Moi & Co Oy, Helsinki, Finland
In-house design
Anu Saari, Mari Heinonmäki
Web
www.moiko.fi
Honourable Mention

In the dark time of the year, reflectors are an effective aid for pedestrians in traffic. The basic idea behind the collection of Reflective Hands was to assure this safety factor and, at the same time, to provide an innovative design for everyday use. The reflecting parts are printed on the gloves; various patterns and fabric qualities are offered. The models are comfortable to wear.

Statement by the jury
The Reflective Hands provide a comfortable feel when worn in inclement weather conditions. This is combined with a smart optical idea which also increases personal safety.

Während der dunklen Jahreszeit sind Reflektoren eine wirksame Unterstützung für Fußgänger im Verkehrsgeschehen. Grundgedanke hinter der Kollektion von Reflective Hands war, diesen Sicherheitsfaktor zu gewährleisten und gleichzeitig ein innovatives Design für den Alltag zu bieten. Die reflektierenden Teile sind im Printverfahren auf den Handschuhen angebracht, es werden verschiedene Muster und Stoffqualitäten angeboten. Die Modelle bieten ein angenehmes Tragegefühl.

Begründung der Jury
Die Reflective Hands bereiten ein komfortables Tragegefühl bei unliebsamen Wetterbedingungen. Dies ist verbunden mit einer smarten optischen Idee, die zugleich die Sicherheit erhöht.

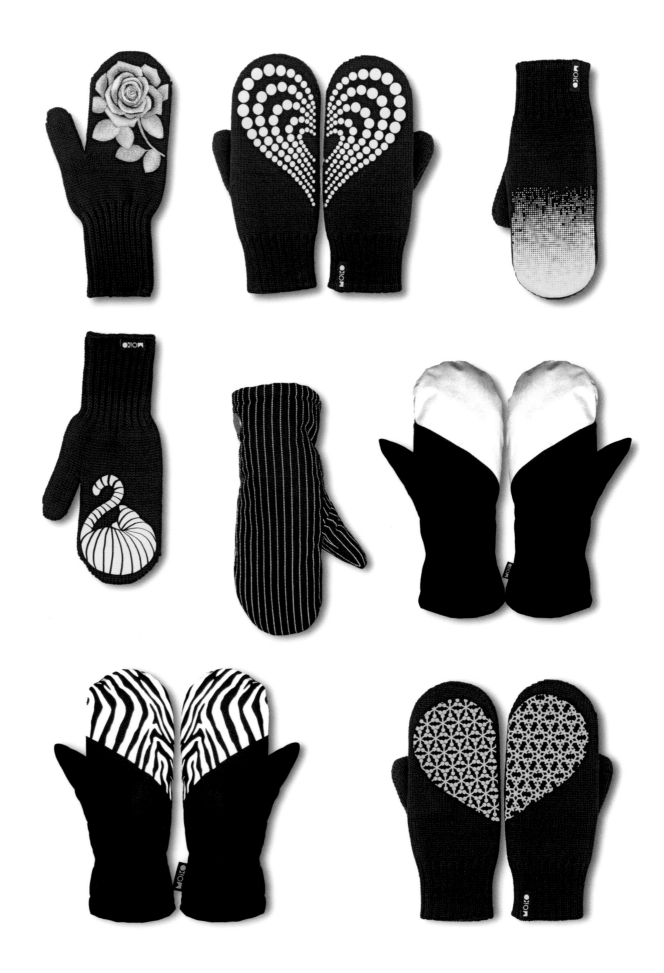

Fred and Matt Overshoes
Galoshes
Überschuhe

Manufacturer
Fred and Matt AB, Stockholm, Sweden
In-house design
Barbro Berlin
Web
www.fredandmatt.com

The galoshes surround the entire shoe and are fastened easily with a zip. The black exterior material is waterproof, stretchable and breathable, whereby the lining provides a pleasant feel when worn. If heavily dirtied, they can be washed in the washing machine. Penetration from gravel is prevented, thereby saving the shoe surface. The hand-moulded sole as well as the zip are available in three fashionable colours.

Die Überschuhe umhüllen den gesamten Straßenschuh und werden einfach mit einem Zip verschlossen. Das schwarze Außenmaterial ist wasserbeständig, dehnbar und atmungsaktiv, während das Innenfutter ein angenehmes Tragegefühl bereitet. Bei starker Verschmutzung können die Schuhe in der Waschmaschine gewaschen werden. Das Eindringen von Kies wird verhindert und dadurch die Oberfläche des Straßenschuhs geschont. Die von Hand gegossene Sohle sowie der Zip sind in drei modischen farblichen Ausführungen erhältlich.

Statement by the jury
Even in rain or slush, the galoshes allow a reputable appearance. Their comfort when worn as well as their cleaning qualities are also impressive.

Begründung der Jury
Auch bei Regen oder Schneematsch sorgen die Überschuhe für ein ansehnliches Auftreten. Beeindruckend sind zudem der Tragekomfort sowie die Pflegeeigenschaften.

PUMA Mostro
Shoes
Schuhe

Manufacturer
PUMA SE, Herzogenaurach, Germany
In-house design
Prof. Daniel Taylor
Web
www.puma.com

This version of the PUMA Mostro is a relaunch of the model first introduced in 1999. Being one of the first shoes in the sport sector it was so designed that it could be worn for everyday use. The raised sole with nub profile assures stable standing and is still very flexible in movement. An asymmetrical Velcro fastener assures quick opening and closing as well as reliable adjustment. The shoe is available in black leather as well as in many fashionable colours.

Statement by the jury
The PUMA Mostro has a design which is already defined almost as classical and it fits well; its functional qualities are convincing.

Diese Version des PUMA Mostro ist ein Relaunch des im Jahr 1999 auf den Markt gebrachten Modells. Als einer der ersten Schuhe auf dem Sportsektor war er so gestaltet, dass er auch im Alltag getragen werden konnte. Die hochgezogene Sohle mit Noppenprofil sorgt für stabilen Stand, ist in der Bewegung dennoch sehr flexibel. Ein asymmetrischer Klettverschluss ermöglicht schnelles Öffnen und Schließen sowie eine zuverlässige Justierung. Der Schuh ist in schwarzer Lederausführung und in vielen modischen Farben erhältlich.

Begründung der Jury
Der PUMA Mostro ist in seiner Gestaltung fast schon als Klassiker zu bezeichnen und auch seine Passform sowie seine funktionalen Qualitäten überzeugen.

DA.AI Eco Puncture-proof Casual Shoes
Freizeitschuhe

Manufacturer
Everbrands Co., Ltd., Guangzhou, China
Design
DA.AI Technology Co., Ltd. (Ya-Li Hsu), Taipei, Taiwan
Web
www.daait.com
Honourable Mention

The DA.AI Eco Puncture-proof Casual Shoes are part of a basic concept that converts PET bottles into daily eco-apparel and accessories. All proceeds are donated to the Buddhist Compassion Relief Tzu Chi Foundation, an international humanitarian aid charity organisation. The puncture-proof casual shoes are made with breathable and elastic recycled material. The sole has good cushioning properties. From a design viewpoint, the shoe can be worn in everyday situations.

Statement by the jury
The casual shoes prove to be an impressive contribution to waste disposal issues and to raw material recycling.

Die DA.AI Eco Puncture-proof Casual Shoes sind Teil eines Grundkonzeptes, das PET-Flaschen in Ökobekleidung für den Alltag und in Accessoires verwandelt. Sämtliche Erlöse kommen der Buddhist Compassion Relief Tzu Chi Foundation zugute, einer internationalen humanitären Hilfsorganisation. Diese durchschlagsicheren Freizeitschuhe werden mit atmungsaktivem und elastischem recycelten Material hergestellt. Die Sohle zeigt gute Dämpfungseigenschaften. In gestalterischer Hinsicht kann der Schuh in vielen Alltagssituationen getragen werden.

Begründung der Jury
Die Freizeitschuhe erweisen sich als beeindruckender Beitrag zu Entsorgungsfragen und zur Rohstoffrückgewinnung.

JS shoe
Shoes
Schuhe

Manufacturer
JS shoe, Calabasas, USA
In-house design
Design
2-LA LLC, Escondido, USA
Web
www.jsshoe.com
www.2-la.com

The JS shoe is manufactured in an innovative 3D knitting process. They are ordered online, whereby the buyer can select sizes and colours according to his individual wishes. The shoes are particularly light and, thanks to their special manufacturing process, have fewer seams. The sole does not cover the bottom completely and thus allows the foot more freedom of movement. Because of these properties, the JS shoe is particularly suitable for driving, for long sedentary work in the office and for travelling.

Statement by the jury
Use of the 3D manufacturing process for a shoe indicates a high degree of innovation for the product. The JS shoe thereby also manages with fewer seams.

Der JS shoe wird in einem innovativen 3D-Strickverfahren hergestellt. Die Bestellung erfolgt online, dabei kann der Konsument Maße und Farben nach individuellen Wünschen auswählen. Die Schuhe sind besonders leicht und weisen dank des speziellen Herstellungsverfahrens weniger Nähte auf. Die Sohle ist nicht durchgängig und lässt dem Fuß daher viel Bewegungsspielraum. Durch diese Eigenschaften eignet sich der JS shoe besonders für Autofahrten, bei längerem Sitzen im Büro oder auf Reisen.

Begründung der Jury
Das 3D-Verfahren für die Herstellung eines Schuhs anzuwenden, zeugt vom hohen Innovationsgrad des Produkts. Der JS shoe kommt dadurch zudem mit weniger Nähten aus.

HICKIES Lacing System
No-Tie Shoelaces
Schnürlose Schuhbänder

Manufacturer
HICKIES, Inc., New York, USA
In-house design
Web
www.hickies.com
Honourable Mention

When using the Hickies Lacing System, many problems experienced with conventional shoelaces can be avoided. Made from a patented thermoplastic material, the flexible laces are drawn through each pair of lace holes and fastened to each other simply by using pressure. Once installed, a shoe can be pulled on and off without tying or loosening laces each time. By use of various fastening options, the tightness can be customised to fit the foot, the shoe or the individual requirements of the user for personalised comfort. The front of the shoelaces show a distinctive and aesthetically sophisticated oval form.

Mit dem Hickies Lacing System lassen sich viele Probleme vermeiden, die bei konventionellen Schnürsenkeln auftreten können. Flexible Bänder aus patentiertem thermoplastischem Material werden durch jeweils ein Paar Schnürösen gezogen und ineinander einfach durch Druck befestigt. Einmal fixiert, kann ein Schuh an- und ausgezogen werden ohne Maschen binden bzw. lösen zu müssen. Durch unterschiedliche Verknüpfungsvarianten wird die Bindungsstärke dem Fuß, dem Schuh oder den individuellen Ansprüchen des Nutzers angepasst. Die Vorderseiten der Schuhbänder zeigen eine markante und ästhetisch ausgereifte ovale Form.

Statement by the jury
The Hickies Lacing System proves to be an innovative alternative to the conventional shoelace. Tangled knots, poor fit and tripping are reliably avoided.

Begründung der Jury
Das Hickies Lacing System beweist sich als innovative Alternative zum herkömmlichen Schnürsenkel. Unlösbare Knoten, schlechter Sitz und Stolpern werden zuverlässig vermieden.

Jimmy'z Vape
Vaporizer
E-Zigarette

Manufacturer
ConsumerNext GmbH, Next Generation
Stimulizer Products, Haren/Ems, Germany
In-house design
Meerim Hagen
Web
www.jimmyz.store

This vaporiser consists of a body of anodised aluminium and exchangeable capsules, which are available in various flavours. To change the recyclable capsules the device is taken apart by means of an easily used magnet fastener and closed again. Material and form of the outer cover provide a pleasant haptic and a modern style. The flavourings contain no nicotine but instead alternative stimulants such as matcha or caffeine.

Diese E-Zigarette besteht aus einem Körper aus eloxiertem Aluminium sowie austauschbaren Kapseln, die in verschiedenen Geschmacksrichtungen angeboten werden. Zum Wechsel der recycelbaren Kapseln wird das Gerät mittels einfach handhabbarem Magnetverschluss auseinandergenommen und wieder verschlossen. Material und Form der Ummantelung sorgen für angenehme Haptik und eine moderne Anmutung. Bei den Aromastoffen wird auf Nikotin verzichtet zugunsten alternativer Stimulanzien wie Matcha oder Koffein.

Statement by the jury
In both its aesthetics and the innovative aromas, the vaporiser conveys a modern lifestyle. The closure is impressive due to its functionality.

Begründung der Jury
Sowohl in ihrer Ästhetik als auch durch die innovativen Aromen vermittelt die E-Zigarette ein modernes Lebensgefühl. Der Verschluss beeindruckt durch seine Funktionalität.

sen7 twist
Refillable Perfume Atomiser
Wiederbefüllbarer Parfümzerstäuber

Manufacturer
Max Time GmbH, Straubenhardt, Germany
In-house design
Karl Alexander Kähler
Web
www.sen7.com

Fragrances in often fragile and unmanageable bottles can be transferred into these refillable perfume atomisers of anodised aluminium and therefore be used when you are out and about. After removing the spray head of the original container, the desired amount is pumped into the reservoir with one hand. A lockable spray head and a safety valve prevent undesired leakage of perfume into the bag. Because of the plain form, the atomiser is a unisex product.

Düfte aus oftmals zerbrechlichen und unhandlichen Flakons können in diesen wiederbefüllbaren Parfümzerstäuber aus eloxiertem Aluminium umgefüllt und damit unterwegs benutzt werden. Nach Abnehmen des Spraykopfes des Originalbehältnisses wird die gewünschte Menge mit einer Hand in das Reservoir gepumpt. Ein feststellbarer Sprühkopf und ein Sicherheitsventil verhindern unbeabsichtigtes Austreten von Parfum in der Tasche. Die klare Formgebung macht den Zerstäuber zu einem Unisex-Produkt.

Statement by the jury
Refilling perfume from bottles which are often fragile into the sen7 twist can be done with one hand and is surprisingly easy. The safety features against leakage are also convincing.

Begründung der Jury
Das Umfüllen von Parfüm aus oftmals fragilen Fläschchen in den sen7 twist gelingt mit einer Hand erstaunlich einfach. Auch die Sicherungen gegen Flüssigkeitsaustritt überzeugen.

BMW Iconic Regenschirm
Umbrella

Manufacturer
BMW Group, Munich, Germany
Design
BMW Group / doppler
Web
http://shop.bmw.com

The umbrella is part of the BMW Lifestyle Iconic Collection. The form of the handle is elegantly linear and it is partially covered in fine leather. This provides a high quality impression and assures pleasant handling. The car manufacturer's logo is incorporated in the umbrella surface by means of Jacquard technology, giving the product an additional, exclusive touch. An elegant sleeve is provided, made of the same material as the umbrella.

Statement by the jury
The high-quality as well as aesthetically elegant umbrella fits in very well with the range of products of the BMW brand.

Der Regenschirm ist Teil der Kollektion BMW Lifestyle Iconic. Der Griff zeigt eine elegante geradlinige Form und ist teilweise mit feinem Leder umwickelt. Dies erzeugt eine hochwertige Anmutung und sorgt für ein angenehmes Handling. In der Schirmfläche ist mittels Jacquardtechnik das Logo des Automobilherstellers eingearbeitet, was dem Produkt zusätzlich einen exklusiven Touch verleiht. Die elegante Hülle ist aus demselben Material wie der Schirmkörper gefertigt.

Begründung der Jury
Der hochwertige wie ästhetisch elegante Regenschirm fügt sich sehr gut in die Produktperipherie der Marke BMW ein.

The Words Of Bamboo Q1
Umbrella
Schirm

Manufacturer
Hangzhou Teak Culture Investment & Planning Co., Ltd., Hangzhou, China
Design
AOZHI Hefei Industrial Design Company (You Li, Wei Zhang), Hefei, China
Web
https://tkjjry.tmall.com

Weighing only 400 grams, The Words Of Bamboo Q1 is very light. All twelve struts are constructed from the same part of a bamboo plant, so that the tension is spread evenly over the umbrella. The umbrella is easily opened and closed gently by means of a magnetic mechanism. The transparent cover gives additional emphasis to the aesthetic lightness of the bamboo material. This effect is further underlined by the handle which remains very plain.

Statement by the jury
The Words Of Bamboo Q1 umbrella imparts cheerful aesthetics. It convinces with regard to functionality due to its stable construction of very light bamboo.

Mit nur 400 Gramm Gewicht ist The Words Of Bamboo Q1 sehr leicht. Alle zwölf Streben sind aus demselben Teil einer Bambuspflanze konstruiert, damit sich die Spannung gleichmäßig auf dem Schirmkörper verteilt. Durch einen Magnetmechanismus wird der Schirm einfach und sanft aufgespannt und wieder zugeklappt. Der transparente Stoff unterstreicht zusätzlich die ästhetische Leichtigkeit des Materials Bambus. Weiter unterstrichen wird dieser Effekt durch den sehr schlicht gehaltenen Griff.

Begründung der Jury
Der Schirm The Words Of Bamboo Q1 vermittelt eine unbeschwerte Ästhetik. In funktionaler Hinsicht überzeugt er durch den stabilen Aufbau aus sehr leichtem Bambus.

Drift Wood
Umbrella
Schirm

Manufacturer
Hangzhou Teak Culture Investment & Planning Co., Ltd.,
Hangzhou, China
Design
Zhejiang University City College (You Li, Feidi Hu,
Chong Zhan, Qiong Wu, Jing Zhang), Hangzhou, China
Web
https://tkjjry.tmall.com

Handle and shaft of the Drift Wood are made of the traditional materials wood and brass. The mechanism for opening and closing, on the other hand, is adapted to modern requirements. The handle consists of two identically incorporated notches, allowing the umbrella to be held pleasantly in the hand. Additionally, a cavity is inserted in it where small items can be stored. It serves in particular as a practical storage space for the umbrella sleeve.

Griff und Stock von Drift Wood sind aus den traditionellen Materialien Holz und Messing gefertigt. Der Mechanismus zum Aufspannen und Schließen ist hingegen modernen Anforderungen angepasst. Der Griff zeigt zwei gleichförmige eingearbeitete Einkerbungen, wodurch der Schirm gut in der Hand gehalten werden kann. Zusätzlich ist darin ein Hohlraum eingearbeitet, in dem sich kleinere Gegenstände verstauen lassen. Insbesondere dient er als praktisches Depot für den Schirmüberzug.

Statement by the jury
Drift Wood impresses with the creative and functionally impressive idea of incorporating a storage space in the handle.

Begründung der Jury
Drift Wood besticht durch die kreative und funktional eindrucksvolle Idee eines im Griff eingearbeiteten Stauraums.

RADO

SWISS MADE

Watches and jewellery
Uhren und Schmuck

Big Bang Meca-10 Magic Gold
Wristwatch
Armbanduhr

Manufacturer
Hublot SA, Nyon, Switzerland

In-house design
Hublot SA

Web
www.hublot.ch

reddot award 2017
best of the best

Magical timepiece

Wristwatches, like hardly any other piece of jewellery, are an expression of the wearer's sense of style. They are much more than a means to measure time, as an exclusive wristwatch also represents the wearer's personality. The Big Bang Meca-10 Magic Gold wristwatch showcases a highly distinctive design appearance that places the movement and the materials used centre stage. Inspired by the architecture of well-known Meccano construction kits, it fascinates with innovative mechanics. The movement for this watch was entirely overhauled to make the mechanism visible from the outside. Doing without a dial, the watch allows seeing straight into the 79-piece mechanism housed below the hands. Wearers thus can see and immediately experience the vibrant process of measuring time. Another innovation of the Big Bang Meca-10 Magic Gold is found in the unusual choice of material used. The movement rests in a housing made of "Magic Gold", an innovative fusion of 24-carat gold and ceramic. This scratch-resistant and very hard gold alloy was created by Hublot in collaboration with the École polytechnique fédérale de Lausanne (EPFL). Complemented by the spectacular movement, this patented material defines the special appeal of this wristwatch. The watch thus confirms a pioneering spirit directly reflected in the design with a choice of material that has emerged as an endless source of possibilities and the opportunity to escape watchmaking norms.

Magischer Zeitmesser

Eine Armbanduhr repräsentiert wie kaum ein anderes Schmuckstück das Stilempfinden ihres Trägers. Sie ist dabei viel mehr als nur ein Zeitmesser, eine exklusive Uhr ist für ihren Besitzer ein Ausdruck seiner Persönlichkeit. Die Big Bang Meca-10 Magic Gold stellt eine in ihrer Erscheinung überaus markante Armbanduhr dar, wobei bei ihrer Gestaltung insbesondere die Mechanik und Materialgebung im Mittelpunkt standen. Inspiriert von der Bauweise der bekannten Meccano-Metallbaukästen, fasziniert sie mit einer innovativen Konstruktion. Das Werk wurde für diese Uhr eigens neu konstruiert, um so die Mechanik von außen sichtbar zu machen. Sie hat kein Zifferblatt, sondern man blickt zwischen den Zeigern in das aus 79 Teilen bestehende Uhrwerk hinein. Auf diese Weise erlebt der Betrachter unmittelbar den lebendig anmutenden Vorgang der Zeitmessung. Eine weitere Innovation der Big Bang Meca-10 Magic Gold ist ihre ungewöhnliche Materialgebung. Die Mechanik sitzt in einem Gehäuse aus „Magic Gold", einer innovativen Verbindung von 24-karätigem Gold und Keramik. Diese kratzfeste und äußerst harte Goldlegierung wurde von Hublot in Zusammenarbeit mit der École polytechnique fédérale de Lausanne (EPFL) entwickelt. Das patentierte Material prägt ebenso wie die spektakuläre Mechanik die besondere Anmutung dieser Uhr. Seine Entwicklung steht zudem für einen Pioniergeist, den die Uhr widerspiegelt: Die Materialgebung wird zu einer Quelle unendlicher Möglichkeiten, um den gängigen Normen der Uhrengestaltung zu entfliehen.

Statement by the jury

The Big Bang Meca-10 Magic Gold demonstrates how much fun a mechanical wristwatch can be. The specially developed movement with direct view into the mechanism is as fascinating as the innovative gold alloy that safely protects the watch against scratches. Sophisticated and coherently crafted detail solutions, such as the easy-to-swap wristband, come together to define the outstanding comfort of this wristwatch. This watch embodies a convincing evolution of an archetypical product.

Begründung der Jury

Die Big Bang Meca-10 Magic Gold zeigt, wie viel Freude eine mechanische Armbanduhr bereiten kann. Das für sie eigens konstruierte Uhrwerk mit direktem Blick auf die Mechanik begeistert ebenso wie ihre innovative Goldlegierung, mit der sie sicher vor Kratzern geschützt ist. Ausgereifte und in sich schlüssige Detaillösungen, wie das sehr leicht auswechselbare Armband, definieren den besonderen Komfort dieser Uhr. Mit ihr wird ein archetypisches Produkt auf bestechende Weise weiterentwickelt.

Designer portrait
See page 72
Siehe Seite 72

Mirrored Force Resonance
Wristwatch
Armbanduhr

Manufacturer
Armin Strom AG, Biel, Switzerland
In-house design
Claude Greisler
Web
www.arminstrom.com

The watch face of the Mirrored Force
Resonance offers a view of the complex,
sophisticated mechanism of its movement. Two independent but symmetrically
arranged oscillators are linked via a resonance clutch spring and stabilise each
other. This innovative mode of operation
ensures a high precision of the watch
movement. The wristwatch has an hour
and a minute hand, a twin display for
the seconds, as well as a domed, scratchproof sapphire glass.

Statement by the jury
The design of this wristwatch manages to
convey the high art of watchmaking that
is behind the innovative construction of
the Mirrored Force Resonance.

Die Mirrored Force Resonance erlaubt auf
der Zifferblattseite einen Blick auf den
komplexen, anspruchsvollen Mechanismus
ihres Manufakturkalibers: Zwei voneinander
unabhängige, symmetrisch gespiegelte
Oszillatoren werden über eine Resonanz-
Kupplungsfeder miteinander verbunden
und stabilisieren sich gegenseitig. Diese innovative Funktionsweise sorgt für die hohe
Präzision des Uhrwerks. Die Armbanduhr
ist mit einer Stunden-, einer Minuten- und
einer Zwillingsanzeige der Sekunden
sowie mit einem gewölbten, kratzfesten
Saphirglas ausgestattet.

Begründung der Jury
Die Gestaltung dieser Armbanduhr
kommuniziert auf faszinierende Weise die
hohe Uhrmacherkunst, die sich hinter der
innovativen Bauweise der Mirrored Force
Resonance verbirgt.

Masterpiece Skeleton
Wristwatch
Armbanduhr

Manufacturer
Maurice Lacroix SA, Biel, Switzerland
In-house design
David Sanchez
Web
www.mauricelacroix.com

The design of the mechanical, open-worked Masterpiece Skeleton watch allows viewers to see the ML134 movement. No dial hides the inner workings, so the full horological mastery with its mainspring, balance, winding and numerous other microscopically small components is revealed. The positioning of the individual elements has been meticulously planned and recalls a spoke-like arrangement that can be viewed from all sides. The blue colouring of certain parts gives the watch an almost avant-garde appearance.

Statement by the jury
High horological skill comes to the fore in the design of the Masterpiece Skeleton wristwatch. In addition, its contrasting use of colour is an eye-catching feature.

Die Gestaltung der mechanischen, offen gearbeiteten Armbanduhr Masterpiece Skeleton gewährt einen Blick auf das Manufakturwerk ML134. Kein Zifferblatt verdeckt das Innenleben und so zeugen die Uhrfeder, die Unruh, die Spulen und zahlreiche weitere, teils mikroskopisch kleine Einzelteile von hoher Uhrmacherkunst. Die Anordnung der einzelnen Elemente ist sorgfältig durchdacht; sie erinnert an ein sprossenähnliches Gebilde, das von allen Seiten eingesehen werden kann. Dass einzelne Teile blau eingefärbt sind, verleiht der Uhr ein geradezu avantgardistisches Aussehen.

Begründung der Jury
Hohe Handwerkskunst spiegelt sich in der Gestaltung der Armbanduhr Masterpiece Skeleton wider. Aufmerksamkeit erregt sie zudem durch ihr kontraststarkes Farbspiel.

Masterpiece Chronograph Skeleton

Manufacturer
Maurice Lacroix SA, Biel, Switzerland
In-house design
David Sanchez
Web
www.mauricelacroix.com

The Masterpiece Chronograph Skeleton combines the technical requirements of a mechanical, open-worked movement with a beneficial complication – the chronograph. This stands out for its luxurious treatment including damascening of the bridges and the oscillating mass. The 45 mm case is available either in black PVD or in a stainless steel version. The combination of brushed satin and polished surfaces creates a contrasting look. The hour and minute hands have a luminescent coating.

Statement by the jury
The design draws attention to the technically sophisticated inner workings of the Masterpiece Chronograph Skeleton and appeals with its stylish aesthetics.

Der Masterpiece Chronograph Skeleton vereint die technischen Anforderungen eines mechanischen, offen gearbeiteten Uhrwerks mit einer nützlichen Komplikation, dem Chronographen. Letzterer zeichnet sich durch eine Hochveredelung, einschließlich Damaszierung der Brücken und der Schwungmasse, aus. Das 45 mm große Gehäuse ist in einer schwarzen PVD- oder in einer Edelstahl-Ausführung erhältlich. Die Kombination von satinierten und polierten Oberflächen erzeugt dabei eine spannungsvolle Anmutung. Die Stunden- und Minutenzeiger sind mit einer Leuchtbeschichtung versehen.

Begründung der Jury
Die Gestaltung setzt eindrucksvoll das technisch ausgereifte Innenleben des Masterpiece Chronograph Skeleton in Szene und überzeugt mit einem stilvollen Aussehen.

Autavia Calibre Heuer 02 Chronograph

Manufacturer
TAG Heuer, Branch of LVMH
Swiss Manufactures SA,
La Chaux-de-Fonds, Switzerland
In-house design
Web
www.tagheuer.com

The Autavia Calibre Heuer 02 is a modified remake of a model from the 1960s. However, in contrast to the original, the three white chronograph counters on this watch have been spaced slightly further apart which makes the opaline dial more balanced and easier to read. New features include a date window and water resistance to 100 metres. The diameter of the watch has been increased from 38 mm to 42 mm, in order to give it a more distinctive, modern appearance – an impression that is accentuated by the black aluminium bezel.

Statement by the jury
Thanks to an eye-catching redesign and the addition of useful new functions, the Autavia Calibre Heuer 02 chronograph satisfies even demanding expectations.

Die Autavia Calibre Heuer 02 ist eine modifizierte Neuauflage eines Modells aus den 1960er Jahren. Im Gegensatz zum Original wurden bei dieser Armbanduhr die drei weißen Chronographenzähler etwas voneinander abgerückt, was das opalisierende Zifferblatt optisch ausgeglichener und besser ablesbar macht. Neue Details sind ein Datumsfenster und eine Wasserdichte bis 100 Meter. Der Durchmesser der Uhr wurde von 38 mm auf 42 mm vergrößert, um ihr eine markantere und modernere Ausstrahlung zu verleihen – die Lünette aus schwarzem Aluminium unterstreicht diesen Eindruck.

Begründung der Jury
Dank einer augenfälligen Neugestaltung und der Ergänzung um nützliche Funktionen wird der Chronograph Autavia Calibre Heuer 02 auch gehobenen Ansprüchen gerecht.

Monaco Calibre 11 Chronograph

Manufacturer
TAG Heuer, Branch of LVMH
Swiss Manufactures SA,
La Chaux-de-Fonds, Switzerland
In-house design
Web
www.tagheuer.com

The waterproof Monaco Calibre 11 chronograph is a reinterpretation of the original from 1969. All the typical features, such as the crown on the left, the legendary petroleum blue dial with two white counters, or the Calibre 11 movement with chronograph function, automatic winding and date display, are still there. What is new is that the shape of the case is slightly squarer. Both the push-buttons on the sides are rectangular and the lugs are larger. The back is transparent to allow sight of the movement.

Statement by the jury
The distinctive design of the Monaco Calibre 11 chronograph skilfully combines established traditions with innovation and thus achieves a contemporary interpretation of a watch classic.

Der wasserdichte Chronograph Monaco Calibre 11 ist eine Neuinterpretation des Originals von 1969. Alle typischen Merkmale, wie etwa die Krone auf der linken Seite, das legendäre petrolblaue Zifferblatt mit den beiden weißen Zählern oder das Uhrwerk Calibre 11 mit Chronographenfunktion, automatischem Aufzug und Datum, sind vorhanden. Neu ist, dass die quadratische Form des Edelstahlgehäuses stärker betont wird. Die beiden seitlichen Drücker sind viereckig, die Gehäuseanstöße massiver. Die Rückseite ist transparent und gewährt Sicht auf das Uhrwerk.

Begründung der Jury
Die markante Gestaltung des Chronographen Monaco Calibre 11 vereint gekonnt Bewährtes mit Neuem und stellt so eine zeitgemäße Interpretation eines Uhrenklassikers dar.

Flying Regulator
Wristwatch
Armbanduhr

Manufacturer
Chronoswiss AG, Lucerne, Switzerland
In-house design
Web
www.chronoswiss.com

The Flying Regulator watch comes equipped with a 3D regulator watch face. The floating minute scale and Guilloche wicker-patterned sub dial for seconds and hours are held in the air by screw-fastened bases. The specially developed bezel as well as the domed sapphire glass make a feature of the watch's three-dimensional nature while the glass base allows for a view of the C.122 movement.

Statement by the jury
The striking design of the Flying Regulator wristwatch combines horological tradition and technical innovation on a high level.

Die Armbanduhr Flying Regulator ist mit einem 3D-Regulator-Zifferblatt ausgestattet. Über einer unteren Ebene, die in einem komplexen Korb-Guilloche-Muster gestaltet ist, werden die schwebend konstruierte Minuterie sowie das Hilfszifferblatt für Stunden und Sekunden auf verschraubten Sockeln in der Luft gehalten. Die speziell entwickelte Lünette sowie das gewölbte Saphirglas bringen die Dreidimensionalität dieser mechanischen Uhr eindrucksvoll zur Geltung. Durch den Glasboden lässt sich das Manufakturkaliber C.122 beobachten.

Begründung der Jury
Die ausdrucksstarke Gestaltung der Armbanduhr Flying Regulator vereint auf hohem Niveau horologische Tradition und technische Innovation.

Metro neomatik nachtblau
Wristwatch
Armbanduhr

Manufacturer
NOMOS Glashütte/SA, Roland Schwertner KG,
Glashütte, Germany
Design
Berlinerblau GmbH, Berlin, Germany
Studio Mark Braun (Mark Braun),
Berlin, Germany
Web
www.nomos-glashuette.com
www.markbraun.org

The slim Metro neomatik nachtblau wristwatch has very clear, distinctive minute markers and delicate hands, and, as the name indicates, the watch face is midnight-blue. In combination with subtle detailing in green and orange, the design achieves a cosmopolitan look with urban flair. The manufacturer's proprietary DUW 3001 movement, featuring automatic winding, combines high-tech production methods with meticulous craftsmanship, finishing and assembly. Precision is guaranteed by the NOMOS swing system with blue tempered balance spring.

Statement by the jury
The design of the Metro neomatik nachtblau wristwatch makes an impression with its elegant and urbane aesthetics and well-engineered construction.

Die flach gebaute Armbanduhr Metro neomatik nachtblau besitzt eine gleichermaßen klare wie auch markante Minuterie sowie schlanke Zeiger. Ihr Zifferblatt ist, wie bereits der Name andeutet, mitternachtsblau. Im Zusammenspiel mit subtilen Details in Grün und Orange erzeugt die Gestaltung einen großstädtischen, kosmopolitischen Charakter. Das herstellereigene Manufakturkaliber mit Automatikaufzug, DUW 3001, verbindet Hightech-Fertigungstechniken mit sorgfältiger Handarbeit, Veredelung und Montage. Für Präzision sorgt das NOMOS-Swing-System mit temperaturgebläuter Unruhspirale.

Begründung der Jury
Mit ihrer Eleganz und Urbanität ausstrahlenden Ästhetik und ihrer ausgereiften Bauweise überzeugt die Gestaltung der Armbanduhr Metro neomatik nachtblau.

Classic Slim Watch
Wristwatch
Armbanduhr

Manufacturer
Zeon Ltd., London, Great Britain
Design
Braun Design Team,
Kronberg im Taunus, Germany
Web
www.zeonltd.co.uk
www.braun.com

The Classic Slim Watch is a modern interpretation of the manufacturer's traditional design philosophy. It was developed to ensure comfort on the wrist. Its design is so lightweight and slim, that this wristwatch is barely noticeable to the wearer. The transition between the watchcase and the black Milanese strap is seamless. Both are made of stainless steel. The Classic Slim Watch features a matt black 38 mm clock face and the iconic yellow second hand.

Statement by the jury
The Classic Slim Watch is characterised by its high degree of wearing comfort combined with a minimalist yet striking appearance.

Die Classic Slim Watch ist eine moderne Interpretation der herstellereigenen Gestaltungsphilosophie. Die Armbanduhr wurde entwickelt, um einen guten Sitz am Handgelenk zu gewährleisten. Sie ist so flach und leicht konstruiert, dass der Träger sie kaum bemerkt. Ein fließender Übergang verbindet das Uhrengehäuse nahtlos mit dem schwarzen Milanese Armband – beide gefertigt aus Edelstahl. Die Classic Slim Watch verfügt über ein matt schwarzes 38 mm Zifferblatt und den ikonischen gelben Sekundenzeiger.

Begründung der Jury
Ein hoher Tragekomfort, gepaart mit einem gleichermaßen minimalistischen wie ausdrucksvollen Erscheinungsbild, zeichnen die Armbanduhr Classic Slim Watch aus.

Rado Ceramica
Wristwatch
Armbanduhr

Manufacturer
Rado Watch Co. Ltd., Lengnau, Switzerland
In-house design
Rado Design Team
Design
Konstantin Grcic Industrial Design
(Konstantin Grcic), Munich, Germany
Web
www.rado.com
www.konstantin-grcic.com

Due to the careful reinterpretation of this watch classic, the new Rado Ceramica includes all the characteristic features of the original: a minimalist, geometric shape as well as the use of high-quality, high-tech ceramic. At the heart of the redesign is the case which is slightly larger and harmoniously curved at the edges where it connects with the strap. The velvety matt finish, as well as the eye-catching typography on the dial, creates a contemporary appearance.

Statement by the jury
With its simple, distinctive shape, the Rado Ceramica is true both to its heritage as a wristwatch classic and to the standards of today.

Aufgrund der behutsamen Neugestaltung des Uhren-Klassikers weist auch die neue Rado Ceramica die typischen Merkmale des Originalmodells auf: eine minimalistische, geometrische Formensprache sowie der Einsatz hochwertiger Hightech-Keramik. Im Mittelpunkt des Redesigns steht das Gehäuse, das hier etwas größer gebaut ist und von den Kanten aus harmonisch geschwungen in das Armband übergeht. Das samtig matte Finish sowie die aufmerksamkeitsstarke Typografie auf dem Zifferblatt erzeugen ein zeitgemäßes Erscheinungsbild.

Begründung der Jury
Mit ihrer schlichten, ausdrucksstarken Formensprache wird die Rado Ceramica dem Erbe eines Uhren-Klassikers sowie den zeitgemäßen Ansprüchen an eine Armbanduhr gerecht.

The Innovative Anti-Seismic Mechanical Watch
Wristwatch
Armbanduhr

Manufacturer
Shenzhen Ciga Design Co., Ltd., Shenzhen, China
In-house design
Jianmin Zhang, Xin Jiang
Web
www.cigadesign.com

The design of this mechanical men's watch with skeleton structure draws attention to its innovative inner workings. The usual fixing connection between mechanical movement and case has here been replaced by a flexible connection. This acts as a buffer and increases the shock resistance qualities of the watch. A heavy-duty ceramic case, thick sapphire glass and the hard-wearing nylon strap provide added durability. The contrast between the square case and the round elements of the movement give the watch its distinctive appeal.

Gebaut als skelettiertes Modell richtet die Gestaltung den Fokus auf das innovative Innenleben dieser mechanischen Herren-Armbanduhr. Die übliche Verbindung zwischen Uhrwerk und Gehäuse wurde hier durch eine flexible Verbindung ersetzt. Diese wirkt als Puffer und erhöht so die Schockfestigkeit der Uhr. Robustheit erlangt sie zudem durch das strapazierfähige Keramikgehäuse, das dicke Saphirglas und das verschleißfeste Nylon-Armband. Der Kontrast zwischen dem quadratischen Gehäuse und den runden Teilen der Mechanik erzeugt eine unverwechselbare Anmutung.

Statement by the jury
Due to its innovative construction, this wristwatch is robust and very versatile. Furthermore, its striking appearance provides added appeal.

Begründung der Jury
Dank ihrer innovativen Bauweise ist diese Armbanduhr robust und vielseitig tragbar. Darüber hinaus überzeugt ihr prägnantes Erscheinungsbild.

Niessing Mirage
Pendant
Anhänger

Manufacturer
Niessing Manufaktur GmbH &
Co. KG, Vreden, Germany

In-house design
Nina Georgia Friesleben

Web
www.niessing.com

reddot award 2017
best of the best

Play of illusions

Natural phenomena such as Fata Morgana mirages are a type of illusion that fools the eye into perceiving a false reality. The design of the Mirage pendant skilfully plays with such optical phenomena. The design started with the question whether precious metal can be processed to acquire an iridescent transparency, creating the illusion of a mirage. Using an innovative laser method and new manufacturing techniques, this pendant has emerged as a highly expressive piece of jewellery. Taking inspiration from the natural structures of leaves, feathers and dragonfly wings, the basic circular and oval shapes of Mirage are spanned by slender strips of increasing thickness. Each individual piece of jewellery features two basic shapes that are inserted into each other using a clever technique. Their lamellar strips thus overlap and create the illusion of a transparent body with air inside that seems to shimmer and flicker. The result is an iridescent and translucent effect that lends the gold and platinum materials a highly enticing appearance. Light as a feather and vibrant with each touch, these delicate pieces of jewellery also create an unusual tactile experience: they feel surprisingly soft and smooth. The pieces of jewellery are worn on the Niessing Coil, which visually disappears in the shimmering inside the pendant. The design of the Mirage pendant thus manifests itself as a fascinating play of illusions – a shape that projects the vision of weightlessness in gold or platinum.

Spiel mit der Illusion

Bei natürlichen Erscheinungen wie der Fata Morgana wird der sinnlichen Wahrnehmung eine scheinbare Realität vorgegaukelt. Die Gestaltung des Anhängers Mirage spielt gekonnt mit solchen Phänomenen. Ausgangspunkt war die Frage, ob sich Edelmetall so verarbeiten lässt, dass es schillernd und durchscheinend wirkt und dabei die Illusion einer Luftspiegelung erzeugen kann. Mittels einer innovativen Lasertechnik sowie neuer Fertigungsverfahren entstand ein Schmuckstück von besonderer Ausdruckskraft. Inspiriert von den natürlichen Strukturen von Blättern, Federn und Libellenflügeln, bestehen die Grundformen von Mirage, Kreise und Ovale, aus feingliedrigen, in ihrer Stärke anwachsenden Lamellen. Für jedes einzelne Schmuckstück werden zwei Formen mithilfe einer geschickten Technik ineinandergesteckt. Durch Überlagerung erzeugen die Lamellen die Illusion eines Glaskörpers, die Luft im Inneren der Schmuckstücke scheint zu flirren. Dies bedingt einen schillernden und durchscheinenden Effekt, der den Materialien Gold und Platin eine besondere Wirkung verleiht. Federleicht und bei jeder Berührung schwingend, bieten die zarten Schmuckobjekte auch ein haptisches Erlebnis: Mirage fühlt sich samtweich und geschmeidig an. Getragen wird der Anhänger an der Niessing Schnur, die dabei völlig im flirrend anmutenden Inneren des Schmuckstückes verschwindet. Was sich in der Gestaltung des Anhängers Mirage manifestiert, ist ein faszinierendes Spiel mit der Illusion – eine formgewordene Vision von Schwerelosigkeit in Gold und Platin.

Statement by the jury

Wearers of this jewellery enter into a special relationship. The Mirage pendant is an expression of the Niessing company tradition of constantly translating new techniques into unusual shapes to emotionally touch the senses. This pendant exudes a fascinating vision of timelessness and can easily stand by itself. It makes wearers perceive and feel both the underlying design intention and the creative inventiveness behind it.

Begründung der Jury

Wer diesen Schmuck trägt, geht eine besondere Beziehung ein. Der Anhänger Mirage ist Ausdruck der Tradition des Unternehmens Niessing, beständig neueste Techniken in außergewöhnliche Formen zu überführen und damit die Sinne zu berühren. Dieser Anhänger ist auf bestechende Weise neu wie zeitlos, da er auch stets für sich stehen kann. Man sieht und spürt die Intention seiner Gestaltung sowie die kreative Energie, die sich dahinter verbirgt.

Designer portrait
See page 74
Siehe Seite 74

Chinese Zodiac
Brooch Series
Broschen-Serie

Manufacturer
Shanghai Dongzhi Jewelry, Shanghai,
China
In-house design
Zhiying Zheng
Web
www.dongzhi.vip

This collection of brooches represents the 12 signs of the Chinese zodiac. The innovative design of these characters that are well known in Chinese culture is inspired by modern oriental architecture. The brooches are very geometric in shape and achieve their spatial depth through a design made up of numerous individual elements. The linear structure of the 18-carat gold brooches expresses strength as well as simplicity.

Diese Broschen-Serie stellt die zwölf chinesischen Tierkreiszeichen dar. Inspirationsquelle für die innovative Gestaltung der in der chinesischen Kultur wohlbekannten Zeichen ist die moderne fernöstliche Architektur. Die Broschen weisen eine geometrische Form auf, Raumtiefe erlangen sie durch das aus zahlreichen Einzelelementen bestehende Design. Die lineare Struktur der aus 18-karätigem Gold gefertigten Broschen drückt sowohl Stärke als auch Schlichtheit aus.

Statement by the jury
The design of the Chinese Zodiac brooch collection is both vibrant and straightforward. Its high aesthetic quality is sure to attract attention.

Begründung der Jury
Kraftvoll und schnörkellos ist die Gestaltung der Broschen-Serie Chinese Zodiac. Als Hingucker setzt sie mit ihrer hohen ästhetischen Qualität markante Akzente.

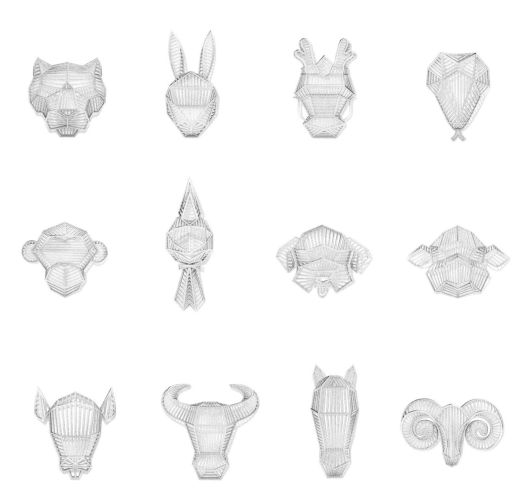

Leilana
Bangle
Armreif

Manufacturer
Bernd Wolf, Stegen, Germany
In-house design
Yvonne Wolf
Web
www.berndwolf.de
Honourable Mention

The Leilana bangle from the Flowertimes design line consists of an open-worked decoration of subtly shimmering, three-leaf blossoms. These are framed by a narrow band of sparkling, brilliant-cut zirconia. The bracelet and its flower arrangement has both a playful feminine feel, while at the same time reflecting the manufacturer's distinctive, clear-cut form. Due to its lightweight and its shape, it is very comfortable to wear. This piece of jewellery is made of sterling silver enhanced with wire-brushed high-grade 24-carat gold plating.

Der Armreif Leilana der Designlinie Flowertimes besteht aus einem durchbrochenen Ornament aus dezent schimmernden, dreiblättrigen Blüten. Diese werden von einem schmalen, glitzernden Band aus Zirkonia in Brillantschliff umrahmt. Der Armreif mit seinem Blumenarrangement ist zugleich verspielt feminin und entspricht dabei der herstellertypischen, geradlinigen Formensprache. Aufgrund seines geringen Gewichts und seiner Form bietet er einen hohen Tragekomfort. Gefertigt ist dieses Schmuckstück aus 925er Silber mit einer hochwertigen, mattschlaggebürsteten 24-Karat Goldplattierung.

Statement by the jury
The design of the Leilana bangle radiates a vibrant lightness. With its clean lines and high-quality appearance that makes for a winning combination.

Begründung der Jury
Eine beschwingte Leichtigkeit bei gleichzeitiger Geradlinigkeit versprüht die Gestaltung des Armreifs Leilana, der zudem mit einer hochwertigen Anmutung trumpft.

Extend
Ring

Manufacturer
Atelier Schiper, Rio de Janeiro, Brazil
In-house design
Alessandra Schiper
Web
www.atelierschiper.com.br

The Extend ring was inspired by the idea to create a piece of jewellery that would be as flexible as it is versatile and that would fit every finger. It was modelled on the pantograph of astronomer and inventor Christoph Scheiner. Just like the technical instrument, the ring is composed of separate elements that flexibly interlock. It is made of 18-carat white or yellow gold and ornamented with precious stones.

Statement by the jury
The Extend ring is based on an exceptional design concept. The precious stones accentuate the sophistication of this versatile, adaptable piece of jewellery.

Der Ring Extend wurde von der Idee inspiriert, ein Schmuckstück zu kreieren, das flexibel sowie vielseitig ist und sich an jeden Finger anpasst. Als Vorlage für die Umsetzung dient der Pantograph des Astronomen und Erfinders Christoph Scheiner. Wie das technische Instrument setzt sich auch der Ring aus einzelnen Elementen zusammen, die gelenkig miteinander verbunden sind. Das Schmuckstück besteht aus 18-karätigem Weiß- bzw. Gelbgold und ist mit Edelsteinen besetzt.

Begründung der Jury
Eine außergewöhnliche Gestaltungsidee liegt dem Ring Extend zugrunde. Die Edelsteine betonen dabei die Raffinesse dieses vielseitig tragbaren Schmuckstücks.

Heart Ring

Manufacturer
Six Sense Studio, Beijing, China
In-house design
Ellen Zhu

Rings are pieces of jewellery with great symbolic meaning. The ring, made of silver plated with gold, contains the Chinese character for heart, which is the focal point of this design. It can be worn on its own or be complemented by one of the other rings made of silver plated with platinum. These other rings also include characters that can be combined with the root word for heart and so create another meaning. In this way, the delicate items of jewellery are carriers of a message.

Statement by the jury
The versatile way in which these fine rings can be combined, physically, aesthetically and with regard to the symbolic character for heart, accounts for their great appeal.

Ringe sind symbolträchtige Schmuckstücke. Der aus vergoldetem Silber gefertigte Ring zeigt das chinesische Schriftzeichen für Herz, das im Mittelpunkt der Gestaltung steht. Er kann allein getragen oder mit einem der aus mit Platin überzogenem Silber gearbeiteten Ringe ergänzt werden. Letztere zeigen ebenfalls Schriftzeichen, die sich mit dem Wort Herz als Wortstamm kombinieren lassen und so zusammen eine neue Bedeutung kreieren. Auf diese Weise können die filigran anmutenden Schmuckstücke eine Botschaft vermitteln.

Begründung der Jury
Diese zart gestalteten Ringe überzeugen mit ihrer vielseitigen Kombinierbarkeit sowohl im physisch-ästhetischen Sinne als auch in Bezug auf das symbolträchtige Wort „Herz".

Niessing Solaris
Ring

Manufacturer
Niessing Manufaktur GmbH & Co. KG,
Vreden, Germany
In-house design
Nina Georgia Friesleben
Web
www.niessing.com

The Niessing Solaris gold alloy translates the blazing colours of a sunrise into precious metals. The design of the linear ring with the same name conveys energy and emotion. The colours of this piece of jewellery move smoothly from a warm red through delicate shades of peach to a vibrant yellow – these colours pervade the whole ring. The ring is made using different individual alloys which are the result of a highly sophisticated method developed specifically for this purpose by the manufacturer.

Die Goldlegierung Niessing Solaris überträgt die Farbenpracht eines Sonnenaufgangs auf Edelmetall. Die Gestaltung des gleichnamigen, geradlinigen Ringes kommuniziert Kraft und Emotionen. Das Schmuckstück zeigt einen stufenlosen Farbverlauf von einem warmen Rot über zarte Pfirsichnuancen bis hin zu strahlendem Gelb – die Farbe zieht sich durch das gesamte Material. Der Ring besteht aus verschiedenen Einzellegierungen, die in einem vom Hersteller entwickelten, aufwendigen Verfahren erzeugt werden.

Statement by the jury
Due to its emotional and exciting use of colour, the Solaris ring is bound to draw attention to itself. The clean lines of this piece of jewellery underline its expressive appearance.

Begründung der Jury
Dank seines emotionalen und aufregenden Farbspiels zieht der Ring Solaris die Blicke auf sich. Die klare Formensprache des Schmuckstücks unterstützt die expressive Anmutung.

Tsunagaru Katachi
Wedding Rings
Trauringe

Manufacturer
Mokumeganeya Co., Ltd., Tokyo, Japan
In-house design
Masaki Takahashi
Web
www.mokumeganeya.com
Honourable Mention

The Tsunagaru Katachi wedding rings –
Tsunagaru means being connected – are
made using a 400-year-old Japanese
forging technique called Mokume Gane.
The layering and then forging together
of numerous differently coloured metals
produces a pattern akin to wood grain.
This technique makes it possible to create
a unique pattern for every bride and
groom. That creates a special bond which
is strengthened when the couple itself
divides the ring to create two wedding
rings.

Statement by the jury
Sophisticated Japanese craftsmanship
comes to the fore in the design of the
Tsunagaru Katachi wedding rings whose
fine grain is unmistakable and unique.

Die Trauringe Tsunagaru Katachi – Tsunagaru
heißt Zusammensein – werden mithilfe von
Mokume Gane, einer 400 Jahre alten
japanischen Schmiedetechnik, hergestellt.
Indem zahlreiche verschiedene Farbmetalle
übereinandergeschichtet und dann zu-
sammengeschmiedet werden, entsteht ein
einer Holzmaserung ähnelndes Muster.
Diese Technik ermöglicht es, ein individu-
elles Muster für jedes Brautpaar herzustellen. Dies erzeugt eine besonders enge
Bindung, die das Paar zudem dadurch
festigt, dass es einen Ring mit den eigenen
Händen in die zwei Eheringe teilt.

Begründung der Jury
Hohe japanische Handwerkskunst spiegelt
sich in der Gestaltung der Trauringe
Tsunagaru Katachi wider, deren feine Mase-
rung unverwechselbar und individuell ist.

Alps and Cows
Ring

Manufacturer
Locherschmuck GmbH,
Ostermundigen, Switzerland
Design
Lux Goldschmiede AG (Marc Ecknauer),
St. Gallen, Switzerland
Web
www.locherschmuck.ch
www.lux-goldschmiede.ch
Honourable Mention

The Alps and Cows ring is a modern
version of the so-called "Chüeli" ring
whose origins lie in Swiss folklore. Traditionally, farmers drive their cattle up
into the mountains in spring and back
down to the valley in autumn. When they
do so, they wear particularly festive
traditional costumes which also include
a ring that represents the cattle trek.
This ring, made of carbon and 18-carat
red gold, refers to this tradition. An
optical illusion furthermore creates the
impression that the cows are ascending
and descending the mountain slopes.

Statement by the jury
The design of the Alps and Cows ring
skilfully reinterprets a folklore subject and
also displays outstanding craftsmanship.

Der Ring Alps and Cows ist eine moderne
Version eines sogenannten Chüeli-Rings.
Dessen Ursprung liegt in der Schweizer Folklore. Bauern treiben traditionell ihre Kühe
im Frühjahr in die Berge und im Herbst zurück ins Tal. Dabei tragen sie besonders
festliche Trachten, zu denen ein passender
Ring gehört, welcher den Kuh-Treck darstellt. Dieser aus Carbon und 18-karätigem
Rotgold hergestellte Ring greift das Thema
auf. Aufgrund einer optischen Täuschung
erweckt er zudem den Anschein, die Kühe
würden auf- und absteigen.

Begründung der Jury
Die Gestaltung des Rings Alps and Cows
interpretiert gekonnt ein folkloristisches
Thema neu und spiegelt zudem hohes
handwerkliches Können wider.

The jury 2017
International orientation and objectivity
Internationalität und Objektivität

The jurors of the Red Dot Award: Product Design
All members of the Red Dot Award: Product Design jury are appointed on the basis of independence and impartiality. They are independent designers, academics in design faculties, representatives of international design institutions, and design journalists.

The jury is international in its composition, which changes every year. These conditions assure a maximum of objectivity. The members of this year's jury are presented in alphabetical order on the following pages.

Die Juroren des Red Dot Award: Product Design
In die Jury des Red Dot Award: Product Design wird als Mitglied nur berufen, wer völlig unabhängig und unparteiisch ist. Dies sind selbstständig arbeitende Designer, Hochschullehrer der Designfakultäten, Repräsentanten internationaler Designinstitutionen und Designfachjournalisten.

Die Jury ist international besetzt und wechselt in jedem Jahr ihre Zusammensetzung. Unter diesen Voraussetzungen ist ein Höchstmaß an Objektivität gewährleistet. Auf den folgenden Seiten werden die Jurymitglieder des diesjährigen Wettbewerbs in alphabetischer Reihenfolge vorgestellt.

01

David Andersen
Denmark
Dänemark

David Andersen, born in 1978, graduated from Glasgow School of Art and the Fashion Design Academy in 2003. Until 2014, he developed designs for ready-to-wear clothes, shoes, perfume, underwear and home wear and emerged as a fashion designer working as chief designer at Dreams by Isabell Kristensen as well as designing couture for the royal Danish family, celebrities, artists etc. under his own name. In 2007, he debuted his collection "David Andersen". He has received many awards and grants for his designs, e.g. a grant from the National Art Foundation. David Andersen is also known for his development of sustainable clothing with his collection, Zero Waste, and has received several awards for his work on ecology and sustainable productions. Today, he works as Vice President for Design at Rosendahl Design Group, a multi-brand house with seven brands including: Rosendahl, Holmegaard, Kay Bojesen Denmark, Bjørn Wiinblad Denmark, Lyngby Porcelain, Arne Jacobsen Clocks and Juna. Furthermore, David Andersen is a guest lecturer at different schools and colleges.

David Andersen, 1978 geboren, studierte an der Glasgow School of Art und der Fashion Design Academy, wo er 2003 sein Examen machte. Bis 2014 fertigte er Designs für Konfektionsware, Schuhe, Parfüm, Unterwäsche und Homewear. Daraus entwickelte sich eine Karriere als Modedesigner und er begann, bei Dreams von Isabell Kristensen als Chefdesigner zu arbeiten sowie unter seinem eigenen Namen Couture für die dänische Königsfamilie, Prominente, Künstler etc. zu entwerfen. Im Jahr 2007 stellte er erstmals seine eigene „David Andersen"-Kollektion vor. Für seine Entwürfe hat David Andersen bereits viele Auszeichnungen und Fördergelder erhalten, darunter ein Stipendium der National Art Foundation (Nationale Kunststiftung). David Andersen hat sich auch mit „Zero Waste", einer Kollektion nachhaltiger Kleidung, einen Namen gemacht, und er hat mehrere Auszeichnungen für seine Arbeit im Bereich Umwelt und nachhaltiger Produktion erhalten. Heute arbeitet er als Vizepräsident für Design bei der Rosendahl Design Group, einem Mehrmarkenkonzern mit sieben Marken: Rosendahl, Holmegaard, Kay Bojesen Denmark, Bjørn Wiinblad Denmark, Lyngby Porzellan, Arne Jacobsen Uhren und Juna. Darüber hinaus ist David Andersen Gastdozent an verschiedenen Schulen und Hochschulen.

01 Rosendahl Penta thermos jug
With an insulating glass core and a push-button lid for easy pouring
Rosendahl Penta Thermoskanne
Mit Isolierglaskern und Druckknopfdeckel, um das Ausschenken zu erleichtern

02 Rosendahl wine ball
A multi-functional design that ingeniously combines a corkscrew, foil cutter, wine stopper and bottle opener
Rosendahl Weinkugel
Ein multifunktionales Design, das auf geniale Weise einen Korkenzieher, Folienschneider, Weinstöpsel und Flaschenöffner vereint

02

"People prefer products with an impressive history. As a designer, you need to develop products which combine design, functionality and quality."

„Menschen bevorzugen Produkte mit einer beeindruckenden Geschichte. Als Designer muss man Produkte entwickeln, die Design, Funktionalität und Qualität in Einklang bringen."

In your opinion, what makes for good design?
Good design is not only interesting because of its colour, shape or function, but because there is a story behind it. A designer must be able to take in impressions and signals from his or her daily life and then convert that into great ideas.

How has the role played by design in our everyday lives changed?
In the past, the design industry was dominated by mass production. Nowadays, we all like to show ourselves through e.g. design objects. Therefore, craftsmanship and originality have become two important factors in good design.

What attracts you to the role of Red Dot jury member?
It is very inspiring to see designs from all over the world and to follow the development. It is a pleasure to be a juror together with such competent designers.

What does winning the Red Dot say about a product?
An interesting product that has a good story and hits the zeitgeist.

Was macht Ihrer Ansicht nach gutes Design aus?
Gutes Design ist nicht nur wegen seiner Farbe, Form oder Funktion interessant, sondern weil eine Geschichte dahintersteckt. Ein Designer muss Eindrücke und Signale aus dem Alltag verwenden und in großartige Ideen verwandeln können.

Inwieweit hat sich die Rolle, die Design in unserem täglichen Leben spielt, verändert?
Früher wurde die Designbranche von Massenproduktion beherrscht. Heutzutage geben wir uns alle gerne z. B. durch Designobjekte zu erkennen. Deshalb sind Handwerkskunst und Originalität zu zwei wichtigen Faktoren für gutes Design geworden.

Was reizt Sie an der Arbeit als Red Dot-Juror?
Es ist sehr inspirierend, Entwürfe aus der ganzen Welt zu sehen und ihre Entwicklung zu verfolgen. Zudem ist es ein Vergnügen, Jurymitglied in einer Gruppe so fachkundiger Designer zu sein.

Was sagt eine Auszeichnung mit dem Red Dot über das Produkt aus?
Dass es ein interessantes Produkt ist, auf einer guten Geschichte basiert und den Zeitgeist trifft.

01

Prof. Masayo Ave
Japan/Germany

Professor Masayo Ave, an architect and designer, founded her own design studio "Ave design corporation" in 1992 and since 2001 has been a leader in advanced sensory design research. From 2004 to 2007, she had a guest professorship at the Berlin University of the Arts, where she founded the Experimental Design Institute of Haptic Interface Design. Afterwards she was professor and head of the product design department at the Estonian Academy of Arts. From 2012 to 2013, she was a guest professor at the textile and surface design department at Weißensee Academy of Art Berlin. She has also held a teaching position at the Kanazawa College of Arts in Japan, since 2009. Since 2006, her design studio "MasayoAve creation" and the Haptic Interface Design Institute have been based in Berlin. Masayo Ave is actively involved in educational design programmes for children and young people in cooperation with design institutes such as the DesignSingapore Council and the Red Dot Design Museum Essen, Germany. In October 2016, she was appointed professor and head of product design department of BAU International Berlin – University of Applied Sciences.

Professorin Masayo Ave, Architektin und Designerin, eröffnete 1992 ihr Designstudio „Ave design corporation" und nimmt seit 2001 eine Führungsposition in sensorischer Designforschung ein. Von 2004 bis 2007 hatte sie eine Gastprofessur an der Universität der Künste Berlin, wo sie das experimentelle Designinstitut „Haptic Interface Design" gründete. Anschließend war sie Professorin und Leiterin des Produktdesign-Instituts der Estonian Academy of Arts und von 2012 bis 2013 Gastprofessorin in Textildesign und Oberflächengestaltung an der Weißensee Kunsthochschule Berlin. Außerdem unterrichtet sie seit 2009 am Kanazawa College of Arts in Japan. Seit 2006 sind ihr Designstudio „MasayoAve creation" und das Haptic Interface Design Institute in Berlin ansässig. Masayo Ave beschäftigt sich mit der Designlehre von Kindern und Jugendlichen in Kooperation mit Designinstituten wie dem DesignSingapore Council und dem Red Dot Design Museum Essen. Im Oktober 2016 wurde sie zur Professorin und Leiterin der Fakultät Produktdesign an die BAU International Berlin – University of Applied Sciences berufen.

01 BLOCK
Modular sofa made from an open-cell foam based on polyester, launched in her own collection "MasayoAve creation", 1999/2000

Modulares Sofa, hergestellt aus einem offenporigen Schaum, basierend auf Polyester, erschienen in ihrer eigenen Kollektion „MasayoAve creation", 1999/2000

02 COOL
Cushions made from an open-cell foam based on polyester, launched in her own collection "MasayoAve creation", 1999/2000

Kissen, hergestellt aus einem offenporigen Schaum, basierend auf Polyester, erschienen in ihrer eigenen Kollektion „MasayoAve creation", 1999/2000

02

"Good design reduces the invisible stress of daily life."

„Gutes Design reduziert den unsichtbaren Stress des täglichen Lebens."

In your opinion, what makes for good design?
Right materials to touch, right forms to handle, the right function which follows a vision.

What attracts you to the role of Red Dot jury member?
Discovering new proposals for updating our daily life.

What does winning the Red Dot say about a product?
It allows the product to share the intercultural value of design with a wide audience across the world.

Which topics are most likely to influence design in the coming years?
Bionics, new printing and knitting technology.

Which area of design do you feel has the greatest potential for development for the future?
Sensory enhancements, such as acoustic management and haptic interfaces.

Was macht Ihrer Ansicht nach gutes Design aus?
Die richtigen Materialien zum Anfassen, die richtigen Formen für die Handhabung, die richtige Funktion, die einer Vision folgt.

Was reizt Sie an der Arbeit als Red Dot-Juror?
Neue Ideen zu entdecken, die unser tägliches Leben auf den aktuellsten Stand bringen.

Was sagt eine Auszeichnung mit dem Red Dot über das Produkt aus?
Es ermöglicht dem Produkt, den interkulturellen Wert von Design mit einem breiten Publikum in der ganzen Welt zu teilen.

Welche Themen werden das Design in den kommenden Jahren besonders beeinflussen?
Die Bionik, neue Druck- und Stricktechniken.

In welchem Designbereich sehen Sie das größte Entwicklungspotenzial für die Zukunft?
Bei Verbesserungen, die die Sinne ansprechen, wie z. B. das Akustik-Management oder haptische Schnittstellen.

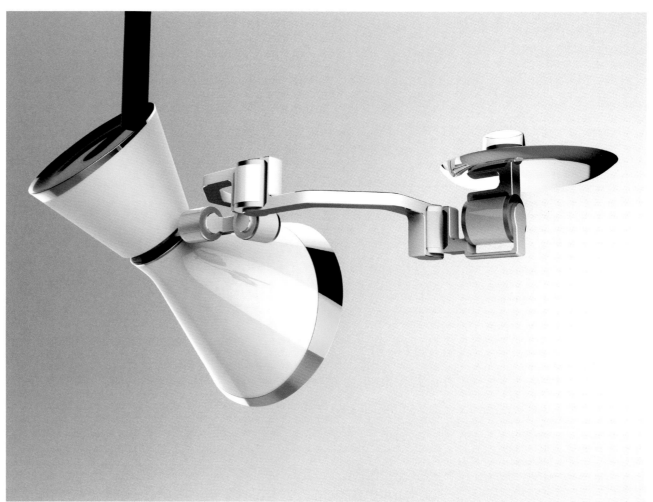

01

Chris Bangle
USA/Italy
USA/Italien

Chris Bangle studied at the University of Wisconsin, graduated from the Art Center College of Design in Pasadena, California and began his career at Opel in 1981. In 1985 he moved on to Fiat, before becoming the first American Chief of Design at BMW in 1992, where he was in charge of the designs for BMW, Mini Cooper and Rolls-Royce. In 2007 he was awarded, together with the Design Team BMW Group, the honorary title "Red Dot: Design Team of the Year" for his outstanding overall design achievements. Since leaving the automotive industry in 2009 Chris Bangle has continued his own design projects and innovations in his design studio Chris Bangle Associates s.r.l. (CBA) near Clavesana in Piemonte, Italy. As Managing Director of CBA he currently heads a team of designers and engineers, who use the studio as a design residence and creative think tank together with the staff of its clients. His 25 years of experience and competence make Chris Bangle a sought-after speaker. He frequently travels around the world to give lectures, teach design and consult clients.

Chris Bangle studierte an der University of Wisconsin, machte seinen Abschluss am Art Center College of Design in Pasadena, Kalifornien, und begann seine Karriere 1981 bei Opel. 1985 wechselte er zu Fiat, bevor er 1992 der erste „American Chief of Design" bei BMW wurde und für die Entwürfe von BMW, Mini Cooper und Rolls-Royce verantwortlich zeichnete. 2007 wurde ihm für seine herausragende gestalterische Gesamtleistung zusammen mit dem Design Team BMW Group der Ehrentitel „Red Dot: Design Team of the Year" verliehen. Seit seinem Ausstieg aus der Automobilbranche 2009 führt Chris Bangle eigene Gestaltungsvorhaben und Innovationen in seinem Studio Chris Bangle Associates s.r.l. (CBA) bei Clavesana im Piemont, Italien, fort und leitet derzeit als Managing Director von CBA ein Team von Designern und Ingenieuren, die das Studio gemeinsam mit den Mitarbeitern der Auftraggeber als Designresidenz und kreative Ideenfabrik nutzen. Seine 25-jährige Erfahrung und Kompetenz machen Chris Bangle zu einem gefragten Referenten. Er reist regelmäßig um die Welt, um Vorträge zu halten, Design zu lehren und seine Kunden zu beraten.

01 Bunny
"Bunny" is a robotic cocktail waitress in development with an Italian research centre. The project applies car design techniques and philosophy to a service robot to give it character and identity without creating a humanoid architecture and a formal solution.

„Bunny" ist eine Roboter-Cocktail-Kellnerin, die zurzeit mit einem italienischen Forschungszentrum entwickelt wird. Das Projekt basiert auf Automobildesign-Techniken und wendet die gleiche Philosophie für einen Service-Roboter an, um ihm eine Persönlichkeit und eine Identität zu geben, ohne eine menschenähnliche Architektur und eine formale Lösung zu schaffen.

02 Illusions
Collection of stones for Swarovski
Kollektion von Steinen für Swarovski

02

"I enjoy the company of these important designers in the Red Dot jury as we discuss design – it is very invigorating!"

„Mir macht die Gesellschaft dieser führenden Designer in der Red Dot-Jury große Freude. Wir unterhalten uns über Design. Das ist sehr anregend."

In your opinion, what makes for good design?
Good design is the embodiment of Truth, Beauty, and Love. By "embodiment" I mean that, when considering all the factors that went into the making of this artefact of design, it is evident that these three elements were prioritised. I am interested in the story behind the design.

How has the role played by design in our everyday lives changed?
Design has become a "thing unto itself" which of course it was never meant to be when our predecessors set out to improve their world. Through the rise of branding, the design itself has become a co-branding phenomenon and this is something we are still trying to come to grips with.

Which area of design do you feel has the greatest potential for development for the future?
I have always held that the expanded application of "car design" practices into all the other "design areas" would be a good thing for all concerned.

Was macht Ihrer Ansicht nach gutes Design aus?
Gutes Design ist die Verkörperung von Wahrheit, Schönheit und Liebe. Mit „Verkörperung" meine ich, dass diese drei Eigenschaften eindeutig bei der Gestaltung des Produkts vorrangig waren, wenn man alle Faktoren, die die Herstellung des Gegenstandes beeinflusst haben, berücksichtigt. Mich interessiert die Geschichte hinter dem Design.

Inwieweit hat sich die Rolle, die Design in unserem täglichen Leben spielt, verändert?
Design ist zu einem „Ding an sich" geworden, was natürlich niemals so beabsichtigt war, als unsere Vorgänger anfingen, ihre Welt zu verbessern. Durch zunehmendes Branding ist Design selbst zu einem Co-Branding-Phänomen geworden. Das ist etwas, was wir noch in den Griff zu bekommen versuchen.

In welchem Designbereich sehen Sie das größte Entwicklungspotenzial für die Zukunft?
Ich bin schon immer der Meinung gewesen, dass die erweiterte Anwendung von Automobildesign-Praktiken in allen anderen Designbereichen eine gute Sache für alle Beteiligten wäre.

01

Dr Luisa Bocchietto
Italy
Italien

Dr Luisa Bocchietto, architect and designer, graduated from the Milan Polytechnic. She has worked as a freelancer undertaking projects for local development, building renovations and urban planning. As a visiting professor she teaches at universities and design schools, she takes part in design conferences and international juries, publishes articles and organises exhibitions on architecture and design. Over the years, her numerous projects aimed at supporting the spread of design quality. From 2008 until 2014, she was National President of the ADI, the Italian Association for Industrial Design. Currently, she is a board member of the World Design Organization (formerly Icsid) and is President Elect for the period from 2017 to 2019.

Dr. Luisa Bocchietto, Architektin und Designerin, graduierte am Polytechnikum Mailand. Sie arbeitet freiberuflich und führt Projekte für die lokale Entwicklung, Gebäudeumbauten und Stadtplanung durch. Als Gastprofessorin lehrt sie an Universitäten und Designschulen, sie nimmt an Designkonferenzen und internationalen Jurys teil, veröffentlicht Artikel und betreut Ausstellungen über Architektur und Design. Ihre zahlreichen Projekte über die Jahre hinweg verfolgten das Ziel, die Verbreitung von Designqualität zu unterstützen. Von 2008 bis 2014 war sie Nationale Präsidentin der ADI, des italienischen Verbandes für Industriedesign. Aktuell ist sie Gremiumsmitglied der World Design Organization (ehemals Icsid) und President Elect für den Zeitraum 2017–2019.

01|02
Renovation of the Palazzo Gromo
Losa in the Piazzo historical
centre of Biella, Italy, restructur-
ing the ancient cellars into an
exhibition centre
Renovierung des Palazzo Gromo
Losa im historischen Zentrum
Piazzo in Biella, Italien, wobei die
antiken Keller in ein Ausstellungs-
zentrum umgestaltet wurden

02

"Sustainability, caring for the environment and design for all are the topics that are most likely to influence design in the coming years."

„Nachhaltigkeit, Umweltschutz und Design für alle werden die Themen sein, die das Design in den kommenden Jahren besonders beeinflussen werden."

In your opinion, what makes for good design?
Innovation, less impact on the planet, an appropriate form.

How has the role played by design in our everyday lives changed?
By contributing to the creation of a better world for everyone.

What importance does design quality have for the economic success of companies?
Great importance, because design can combine a technical and aesthetical vision and can be understood and loved by all.

Which area of design do you feel has the greatest potential for development for the future?
Service design, social design and a new form of transportation design.

Which country do you consider to be a pioneer in product design, and why?
I love Italian design, and I think that it is really always changing and redefining the goals – without limits.

Was macht Ihrer Ansicht nach gutes Design aus?
Innovation, eine geringere Auswirkung auf den Planeten, eine angemessene Form.

Inwieweit hat sich die Rolle, die Design in unserem täglichen Leben spielt, verändert?
Es trägt dazu bei, eine bessere Welt für alle zu schaffen.

Welche Bedeutung hat Designqualität für den wirtschaftlichen Erfolg von Unternehmen?
Eine große Bedeutung, denn Design kann eine technische und ästhetische Vision miteinander verbinden und von allen verstanden und geliebt werden.

In welchem Designbereich sehen Sie das größte Entwicklungspotenzial für die Zukunft?
Service-Design, Social Design und eine neue Form von Transportation Design.

Welche Nation ist für Sie Vorreiter im Produktdesign und warum?
Ich liebe italienisches Design und glaube, dass es sich kontinuierlich verändert und seine Ziele immer wieder neu definiert – ohne Grenzen.

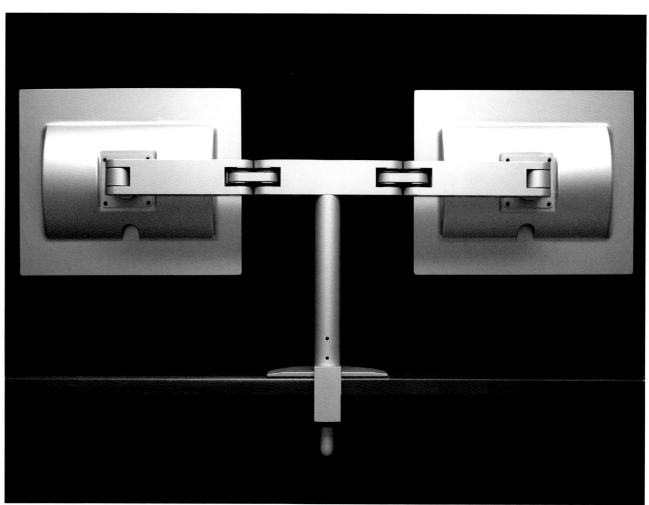

01

Gordon Bruce
USA

Gordon Bruce is the owner of Gordon Bruce Design LLC and has been a design consultant for 40 years working with many multinational corporations in Europe, Asia and the USA. He has worked on a very wide range of products, interiors and vehicles – from aeroplanes to computers to medical equipment to furniture. From 1991 to 1994, Gordon Bruce was a consulting vice president for the Art Center College of Design's Kyoto programme and, from 1995 to 1999, chairman of Product Design for the Innovative Design Lab of Samsung (IDS) in Seoul, Korea. In 2003, he played a crucial role in helping to establish Porsche Design's North American office. For many years, he served as head design consultant for Lenovo's Innovative Design Center (IDC) in Beijing. He recently worked with Bühler in Switzerland and is presently working with Huawei Technologies Co., Ltd. in China. Gordon Bruce is a visiting professor at several universities in the USA and in China and also acts as an author and design publicist. He recently received Art Center College of Design's "Lifetime Achievement Award".

Gordon Bruce ist Inhaber der Gordon Bruce Design LLC und seit mittlerweile 40 Jahren als Designberater für zahlreiche multinationale Unternehmen in Europa, Asien und den USA tätig. Er arbeitete bereits an einer Reihe von Produkten, Inneneinrichtungen und Fahrzeugen – von Flugzeugen über Computer bis hin zu medizinischem Equipment und Möbeln. Von 1991 bis 1994 war Gordon Bruce beratender Vizepräsident des Kioto-Programms am Art Center College of Design sowie von 1995 bis 1999 Vorsitzender für Produktdesign beim Innovative Design Lab of Samsung (IDS) in Seoul, Korea. Im Jahr 2003 war er wesentlich daran beteiligt, das Büro von Porsche Design in Nordamerika zu errichten. Über viele Jahre war er leitender Designberater für Lenovos Innovative Design Center (IDC) in Beijing. Bis vor Kurzem arbeitete er für Bühler, Schweiz, und ist derzeit für Huawei Technologies Co., Ltd. in China tätig. Gordon Bruce ist Gastprofessor an zahlreichen Universitäten in den USA und in China und als Buchautor sowie Publizist tätig. Kürzlich erhielt er vom Art Center College of Design den Lifetime Achievement Award.

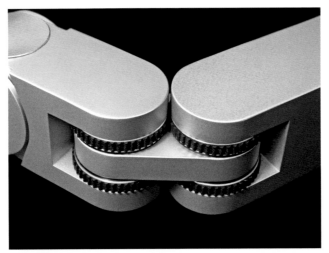

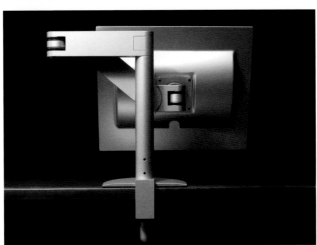

02

"Design is good when it is seamless and unintrusive in the same way that very well-designed typography becomes invisible when reading a book."

„Design ist gut, wenn es nahtlos und unaufdringlich ist, genau wie eine gut gestaltete Typografie unsichtbar wird, wenn man ein Buch liest."

In your opinion, what makes for good design?
Design is good when an idea – tangible or intangible – improves any human rituals, like reading, bicycle riding, fishing, cooking, working, education, etc., by creating a sense of fulfilment and joy while also improving the user's potential.

How has the role played by design in our everyday lives changed?
Good design continues to become more ubiquitous due to the miniaturisation and simplification of objects that embody the rapid advance of technology and the enhanced portability of power and intelligence. As such, many ideas that in the past have been separate are now coalesced.

What importance does design quality have for the economic success of companies?
Good design does many things; one of which enhances the user's experience thus creating a sense of dependability that will ultimately evolve a sense of trust. Trust is the most important quality. Trust, in turn, creates a foundation for building loyalty that enhances the economic performance of any business.

Was macht Ihrer Ansicht nach gutes Design aus?
Design ist gut, wenn eine Idee – ob konkret oder nicht – menschliche Rituale dadurch verbessert, dass ein Gefühl der Erfüllung und Freude ausgelöst und das Potenzial des Nutzers verbessert wird. Das kann Aktivitäten wie Lesen, Radfahren, Angeln, Kochen, Arbeiten, Lernen usw. einschließen.

Inwieweit hat sich die Rolle, die Design in unserem täglichen Leben spielt, verändert?
Gutes Design wird aufgrund der Miniaturisierung und Vereinfachung von Objekten, die den rasanten Fortschritt in der Technik sowie die erweiterte Mobilität von Energie und Intelligenz verkörpern, immer allgegenwärtiger. Viele Ideen, die früher unabhängig voneinander waren, sind dadurch verschmolzen.

Welche Bedeutung hat Designqualität für den wirtschaftlichen Erfolg von Unternehmen?
Gutes Design erreicht vieles. Dazu gehört ein verbessertes Nutzererlebnis, indem ein Gefühl der Zuverlässigkeit, das dann Vertrauen schafft, erweckt wird. Vertrauen ist die wichtigste Eigenschaft und bildet wiederum die Basis für die Treue, die die wirtschaftliche Leistung eines Unternehmens verbessert.

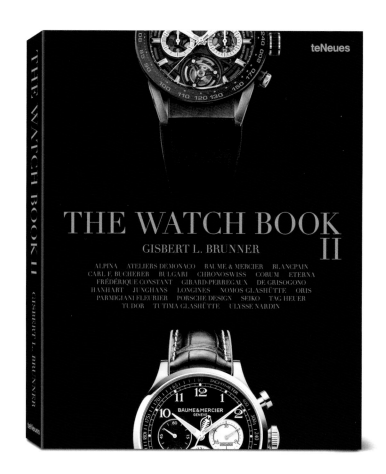

01

Gisbert L. Brunner
Germany
Deutschland

Gisbert L. Brunner, born in 1947, has been working on watches, pendulum clocks and other precision timepieces since 1964. During the quartz clock crisis of the 1970s, his love for the apparently dying-out mechanical timepieces grew. His passion as a hobby collector eventually led to the first newspaper articles in the early 1980s and later to the by now more than 20 books on the topic. Amongst others, Brunner works for magazines such as Chronos, Chronos Japan, Ganz Europa, the Handelszeitung, Prestige, Red Bulletin, Terra Mater, Uhren Juwelen Schmuck, Vectura Magazin and ZEIT Magazin. After the successful Watch Book in 2015, the teNeues publishing house published Watch Book II in 2016. In it, Gisbert L. Brunner portrays a total of 24 watch brands from Alpina to Ulysse Nardin in words and images. In June 2017, Watch Book III appeared, which was dedicated exclusively to the Rolex brand.

Gisbert L. Brunner, Jahrgang 1947, beschäftigt sich seit 1964 mit Armbanduhren, Pendeluhren und anderen Präzisionszeitmessern. Während der Quarzuhren-Krise in den 1970er Jahren wuchs seine Liebe zu den anscheinend aussterbenden mechanischen Zeitmessern. Ein leidenschaftliches Sammelhobby führte ab den frühen 1980er Jahren zu ersten Zeitschriftenartikeln und inzwischen mehr als 20 Büchern über dieses Metier. Brunner ist u. a. für Magazine wie Chronos, Chronos Japan, Ganz Europa, Handelszeitung, Prestige, Red Bulletin, Terra Mater, Uhren Juwelen Schmuck, Vectura Magazin und ZEIT Magazin tätig. Nach dem erfolgreichen Watch Book des Jahres 2015 veröffentlichte der teNeues-Verlag 2016 das Watch Book II, in dem Gisbert L. Brunner insgesamt 24 Uhrenmarken von Alpina bis Ulysse Nardin in Wort und Bild porträtiert. Im Juni 2017 erschien das ausschließlich der Marke Rolex gewidmete Watch Book III.

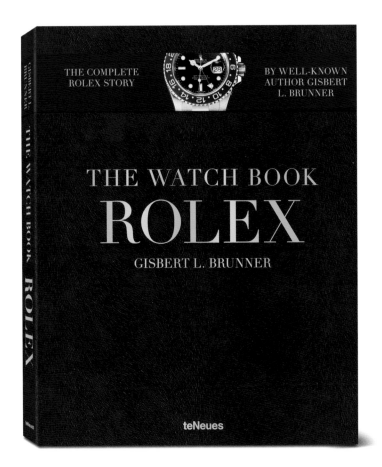

02

"Stringent corporate design and skilful product design increase brand and product awareness and that definitely leads to success."

„Stringentes Corporate Design und gekonntes Produktdesign steigern die Wahrnehmung von Marke und Produkt, was sich definitiv im Erfolg niederschlägt."

In your opinion, what makes for good design?
Good design is characterised by form following function. Good design is accompanied by a classic, but also future-oriented appearance, attracts the observer's attention and ensures intuitive handling of the product is a given.

How has the role played by design in our everyday lives changed?
Since time immemorial, every product has been inextricably linked with design, for design means nothing other than creation. Today, design has taken on a greater importance purely because many people have developed a greater awareness of what Max Bill once termed the "product form".

Which country do you consider to be a pioneer in product design, and why?
Japan has played a leading role in this area for quite a while. That's because people in the Land of the Rising Sun have traditionally focused intently on reducing function to the absolute essentials.

Was macht Ihrer Ansicht nach gutes Design aus?
Gutes Design ist dadurch gekennzeichnet, dass die Form der Funktion folgt. Gutes Design geht mit klassischem, aber auch zukunftsorientiertem Auftritt einher, weckt die Aufmerksamkeit des Betrachters und gewährleistet die intuitive Bedienung eines Produkts.

Inwieweit hat sich die Rolle, die Design in unserem täglichen Leben spielt, verändert?
Seit Menschengedenken verknüpft sich jedes Produkt mit Design, denn Design meint nichts anderes als Gestaltung. Heutzutage spielt Design jedoch allein schon deshalb eine größere Rolle, weil viele Menschen für das, was Max Bill einmal als Produktform bezeichnet hat, deutlich mehr Bewusstsein entwickelt haben.

Welche Nation ist für Sie Vorreiter im Produktdesign und warum?
Japan spielt hier schon seit Längerem eine herausragende Rolle, weil man sich im Land der aufgehenden Sonne traditionsgemäß sehr intensiv mit der Reduktion auf das für die Funktion unabdingbar Notwendige beschäftigt.

01

Rüdiger Bucher
Germany
Deutschland

Rüdiger Bucher, born in 1967, graduated in political science from Philipps-Universität Marburg and completed the postgraduate study course "Interdisciplinary studies on France" in Freiburg, Germany. Since 1995, he was in charge of "Scriptum. Die Zeitschrift für Schreibkultur" (Scriptum. The magazine for writing culture) at the publishing house Verlagsgruppe Ebner Ulm for five years where in 1999 he became editorial manager of Chronos, the leading German-language special interest magazine for wrist watches. As chief editor since 2005, Chronos has positioned itself internationally with subsidiary magazines and licensed editions in China, Korea, Japan and Poland. At the same time, Rüdiger Bucher established a successful corporate publishing department for Chronos. Since 2014, he has been editorial director and in addition to Chronos he has also been in charge of the sister magazines "Uhren-Magazin" (Watch Magazine), "Klassik Uhren" (Classic Watches) and the New York-based "WatchTime". Rüdiger Bucher lectures as an expert for mechanical wrist watches and is a sought-after interview partner for various media.

Rüdiger Bucher, geboren 1967, absolvierte ein Studium in Politikwissenschaft an der Philipps-Universität Marburg und das Aufbaustudium „Interdisziplinäre Frankreich-Studien" in Freiburg. Ab 1995 betreute er beim Ebner Verlag Ulm fünf Jahre lang „Scriptum. Die Zeitschrift für Schreibkultur", bevor er im selben Verlag 1999 Redaktionsleiter von „Chronos", dem führenden deutschsprachigen Special-Interest-Magazin für Armbanduhren, wurde. Ab 2005 Chefredakteur, hat sich Chronos seitdem mit Tochtermagazinen und Lizenzausgaben in China, Korea, Japan und Polen international aufgestellt. Gleichzeitig baute Rüdiger Bucher für Chronos einen erfolgreichen Corporate-Publishing-Bereich auf. Seit 2014 verantwortet er als Redaktionsdirektor neben Chronos auch die Schwestermagazine „Uhren-Magazin", „Klassik Uhren" sowie die in New York beheimatete „WatchTime". Als Experte für mechanische Armbanduhren hält Rüdiger Bucher Vorträge und ist ein gefragter Interviewpartner für verschiedene Medien.

02

"In a society in which many already
have everything they need, good
design creates desires among
consumers."

„In einer Gesellschaft, in der viele
schon alles haben, was sie brauchen,
weckt gutes Design zusätzliche
Begehrlichkeiten beim Konsumenten."

What importance does design quality have for the economic success of companies?
A well-designed product is regarded as more desirable by customers and at the same time strengthens the manufacturer's credibility. As a result, the manufacturer can either increase sales or justify a better price.

What attracts you to the role of Red Dot jury member?
As a journalist, I find it fascinating to be able to exchange views with so many good designers from all over the world. I learn an awful lot in the process.

What does winning the Red Dot say about a product?
Winning a Red Dot is a bit like giving a product a knighthood. The Red Dot attests that a product is good and has been designed to a high quality, that it is quite innovative and makes you feel good.

Which topics are most likely to influence design in the coming years?
In the world of watches, the link between traditional and progressive elements will become ever more prevalent.

Welche Bedeutung hat Designqualität für den wirtschaftlichen Erfolg von Unternehmen?
Ein gut gestaltetes Produkt wird vom Konsumenten stärker begehrt und stärkt zugleich die Glaubwürdigkeit des Herstellers. Dadurch kann dieser entweder mehr Produkte verkaufen oder einen höheren Preis rechtfertigen.

Was reizt Sie an der Arbeit als Red Dot-Juror?
Für mich als Journalisten ist es faszinierend, mich mit so vielen guten Designern aus aller Welt austauschen zu können. Dabei lerne ich unheimlich viel.

Was sagt eine Auszeichnung mit dem Red Dot über das Produkt aus?
Die Verleihung des Red Dot ist ein Adelsschlag für jedes Produkt und bezeugt, dass es gut und hochwertig gestaltet ist, dass es einen gewissen Innovationsgrad besitzt und positive Emotionen weckt.

Welche Themen werden das Design in den kommenden Jahren besonders beeinflussen?
Im Segment der Uhren wird man häufiger die Verbindung von traditionellen mit zukunftsgerichteten Elementen erleben.

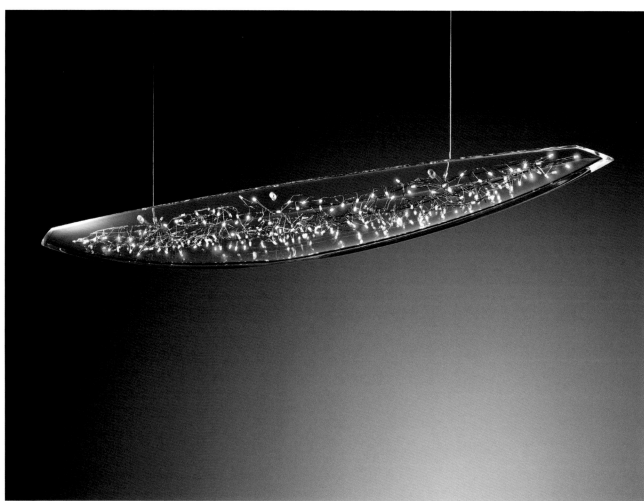

01

Prof. Jun Cai
China

Jun Cai is professor at the Academy of Arts & Design, and director of the Design Management Research Lab at Tsinghua University in Beijing. He is also external reviewer for the Aalto University and Design School of Hong Kong Polytechnic University. Professor Cai has focused on research for design strategy and design management since the 1990s. Through exploration of design-driven business innovation and user-centred design thinking by theoretical and practical research, he was a consultant for more than 60 projects for among others Motorola, Nokia, LG, Boeing, Lenovo, Coway, Fiyta and Aftershockz. Furthermore, he has published papers and publications on design research, design strategy and design management.

Jun Cai ist Professor an der Academy of Arts & Design sowie Direktor des Design Management Research Lab an der Tsinghua University in Beijing. Er ist zudem externer Referent der Aalto University und der Design-schule der Polytechnic University in Hongkong. Bereits seit den 1990er Jahren konzentriert sich Professor Cai auf die Forschung in den Bereichen Designstrategie und Designmanagement. Aufgrund seiner Erforschung von designorientierter Geschäftsinnovation und benutzerzentriertem Designdenken durch theoretische und praktische Forschung war er in mehr als 60 Pro-jekten beratend tätig, unter anderem für Motorola, Nokia, LG, Boeing, Lenovo, Coway, Fiyta und Aftershockz. Außerdem hat er bereits Abhandlungen und Veröffentlichungen über Designforschung, Designstrategie und Designmanagement verfasst.

01 Dust of Galaxy
Lighting design
Leuchtendesign

02 Journey within the air
Research and analysis framework
for a value proposition for
Chinese users on behalf of LG
Forschungs- und Analyserahmen-
konzept für das Leistungsver-
sprechen chinesischer Nutzer im
Auftrag von LG

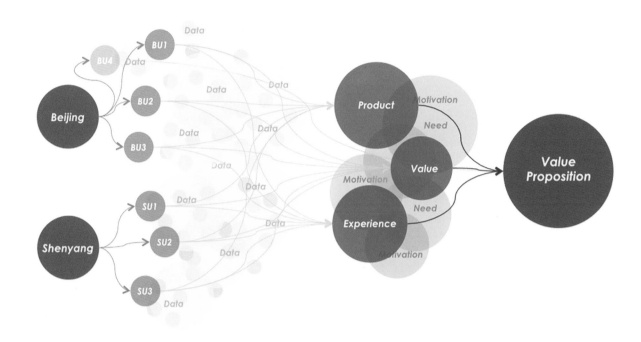

02

"Design solves problems in every
aspect of our daily life. It connects technology and aesthetics,
making everyday lives enjoyable."
„Design löst in jedem Bereich unseres
täglichen Lebens Probleme. Es
schlägt die Brücke zwischen Technik
und Ästhetik und macht unseren
Alltag angenehmer."

What importance does design quality have for the economic success of companies?
Good quality of design both in products and services can not only bring marketing success and make branding for companies reliable, but also strengthen their competitive position with regard to business development.

Which topics are most likely to influence design in the coming years?
IoT with AI technology will be a megatrend to future products from operation to interaction. Emotional feedback between human and machine will acquire more meaning and a cultural context. Lifestyle changes influenced by health, sports and sustainability will make product design more active in the future. Finally, 3D prints will offer more possibilities for product style and introduce new forms of aesthetics.

Welche Bedeutung hat Designqualität für den wirtschaftlichen Erfolg von Unternehmen?
Gute Designqualität für Produkte und Dienstleistungen kann nicht nur Erfolg im Marketing mit sich bringen und zuverlässiges Branding für ein Unternehmen schaffen, sondern auch seine Wettbewerbsposition mit Blick auf die Geschäftsentwicklung stärken.

Welche Themen werden das Design in den kommenden Jahren besonders beeinflussen?
Das Internet der Dinge mit der Technologie künstlicher Intelligenz wird sich zu einem Megatrend für die Produkte der Zukunft entwickeln, der vom Betrieb bis hin zur Interaktion alles steuert. Emotionales Feedback zwischen Mensch und Maschine wird an Bedeutung gewinnen und in einen kulturellen Kontext gesetzt werden. Lifestyle-Veränderungen aufgrund einer gesünderen, sportlicheren und nachhaltigeren Lebensweise werden dazu führen, dass das Produktdesign in Zukunft aktiver ist. Schließlich wird der 3D-Druck weitere Möglichkeiten für Stil und neue Formen der Ästhetik auftun.

01

Vivian Wai-kwan Cheng
Hong Kong
Hongkong

On leaving Hong Kong Design Institute after 19 years of educational service, Vivian Cheng founded "Vivian Design" in 2014 to provide consultancy services and promote her own art in jewellery and glass. She graduated with a BA in industrial design from the Hong Kong Polytechnic University and was awarded a special prize in the Young Designers of the Year Award hosted by the Federation of Hong Kong Industries in 1987, and the Governor's Award for Industry: Consumer Product Design in 1989, after joining Lambda Industrial Limited as the head of the Product Design team. In 1995 she finished her master's degree and joined the Vocational Training Council teaching product design, and later became responsible for, among others, establishing an international network with design-related organisations and schools. Vivian Cheng was the International Liaison Manager at the Hong Kong Design Institute (HKDI) and member of the Chartered Society of Designers Hong Kong, member of the Board of Directors of the Hong Kong Design Centre (HKDC), and is board member of the World Design Organization (formerly Icsid) from 2013 to 2017. Furthermore, she has been a panel member for the government and various NGOs.

Nach 19 Jahren im Lehrbetrieb verließ Vivian Cheng 2014 das Hong Kong Design Institute und gründete „Vivian Design", um Beratungsdienste anzubieten und ihre eigene Schmuck- und Glaskunst weiterzuentwickeln. 1987 machte sie ihren BA in Industriedesign an der Hong Kong Polytechnic University. Im selben Jahr erhielt sie einen Sonderpreis im Wettbewerb „Young Designers of the Year", veranstaltet von der Federation of Hong Kong Industries, sowie 1989 den Governor's Award for Industry: Consumer Product Design, nachdem sie bei Lambda Industrial Limited als Leiterin des Produktdesign-Teams angefangen hatte. 1995 beendete sie ihren Master-Studiengang und wechselte zum Vocational Training Council, wo sie Produktdesign unterrichtete und später u. a. für den Aufbau eines internationalen Netzwerks mit Organisationen und Schulen im Designbereich verantwortlich war. Vivian Cheng war International Liaison Manager am Hong Kong Design Institute (HKDI), Mitglied der Chartered Society of Designers Hong Kong und Vorstandsmitglied des Hong Kong Design Centre (HKDC) und ist Gremiumsmitglied der World Design Organization (ehemals Icsid) von 2013 bis 2017. Außerdem war sie Mitglied verschiedener Bewertungsgremien der Regierung und vieler Nichtregierungsorganisationen.

02

"Winning a Red Dot means the design, the making and the overall quality are of a high standard, and therefore represent top quality for consumers."

„Eine Auszeichnung mit dem Red Dot bedeutet, dass Design, Herstellung und Qualität insgesamt von einem hohen Niveau sind und daher dem Verbraucher höchste Qualität bieten."

How has the role played by design in our everyday lives changed?
Design is penetrating all dimensions of our life, and has become an important part of it. The invention of the smartphone, for example, has made entertainment accessible 24 hours a day and connects us even when we are thousands of miles away. With a smartphone, we can manage our investments, as well as our assets, use various apps to process everything from shopping to drawing, and arrange scheduling and relationships.

What attracts you to the role of Red Dot jury member?
It's always a challenge to be able to reach a good judgment at design competitions. The process is not just a competition for the entries, but also a competition for the jury members with regard to time, knowledge, and an understanding of the rapidly changing world.

Which country do you consider to be a pioneer in product design, and why?
Europe is still leading the way in the development of philosophical, technological and design practices.

Inwieweit hat sich die Rolle, die Design in unserem täglichen Leben spielt, verändert?
Design durchdringt alle Aspekte unseres Lebens und ist ein wichtiger Teil dessen geworden. Die Erfindung des Smartphones zum Beispiel macht Unterhaltung 24 Stunden am Tag zugänglich und erlaubt uns, in Verbindung zu bleiben, auch wenn wir Tausende Kilometer voneinander entfernt sind. Mit einem Smartphone können wir unsere Investitionen sowie unser Vermögen verwalten, verschiedene Apps nutzen, um vom Einkauf bis zum Zeichnen alles zu handhaben, und Terminplanung ebenso wie Beziehungen organisieren.

Was reizt Sie an der Arbeit als Red Dot-Jurorin?
Es ist immer eine Herausforderung, bei Designwettbewerben ein gutes Urteil abzugeben. Der Prozess ist für die Einsendungen, aber auch für die Juroren ein Wettbewerb in Bezug auf Zeit, Wissen und Verständnis der sich so rapide verändernden Welt.

Welche Nation ist für Sie Vorreiter im Produktdesign und warum?
Europa ist in der Entwicklung von philosophischen, technologischen und Designpraktiken immer noch führend.

01

Datuk Prof.
Jimmy Choo OBE
Malaysia/
Great Britain
Malaysia/
Großbritannien

Datuk Professor Jimmy Choo is descended from a family of Malaysian shoemakers and learned the craft from his father. He studied at Cordwainers College, which is today part of the London College of Fashion. After graduating in 1983, he founded his own couture label and opened a shoe shop in London's East End whose regular customers included the late Diana, Princess of Wales. In 1996, Choo launched his ready-to-wear line with Tom Yeardye and sold his share in the business 2001 to Equinox Luxury Holdings Ltd. He now spends his time designing shoes for private clients under his new label using his Chinese name Zhou Yang Jie. He is also passionate about promoting design education through his work as an ambassador for footwear education at the London College of Fashion. He is a spokesperson for the British Council in their promotion of British Education to foreign students and is working with the non-profit programme, Teach For Malaysia. In 2003, Jimmy Choo was honoured for his contribution to fashion by Queen Elizabeth II who appointed him "Officer of the Order of the British Empire".

Datuk Professor Jimmy Choo, der einer malaysischen Schuhmacher-Familie entstammt und das Handwerk von seinem Vater lernte, studierte am Cordwainers College, heute Teil des London College of Fashion. Nach seinem Abschluss 1983 gründete er sein eigenes Couture-Label und eröffnete ein Schuhgeschäft im Londoner East End, zu dessen Stammkundschaft auch Lady Diana, die verstorbene Prinzessin von Wales, gehörte. 1996 führte Choo gemeinsam mit Tom Yeardye seine Konfektionslinie ein und verkaufte seine Anteile an dem Unternehmen 2001 an die Equinox Luxury Holdings Ltd. Heute gestaltet er unter seinem neuen Label und seinem chinesischen Namen Zhou Yang Jie Schuhe für Privatkunden. In seiner Rolle als Botschafter für Footwear Education am London College of Fashion setzt er sich leidenschaftlich für die Förderung der Designausbildung ein. Er ist ferner Sprecher des British Council für die Förderung der Ausbildung ausländischer Studenten in Großbritannien und arbeitet darüber hinaus für das gemeinnützige Programm „Teach for Malaysia". Für seine Verdienste in der Mode verlieh ihm Königin Elisabeth II. 2003 den Titel „Officer of the Order of the British Empire".

01
Chinese flower embroidered silk sling back pump. The specific gold colour is a traditional representation of the position and wealth in Malaysia, while the Chinese flower pattern represents freedom, relaxation and flying.

Ein mit chinesischen Blumen bestickter Slingback-Pumps aus Seide. Der besondere Goldton wird in Malaysia traditionell verwendet, um Position und Reichtum darzustellen, während das chinesische Blumenmuster für Freiheit, Entspannung und Fliegen steht.

02 Maroon Kelingkan embroidered pumps
Kelingkan is a style of embroidery using gold and silver metal thread dating to the 14th century and symbolising patience, diligence, perseverance and creativity.

Mit kastanienbraunen Kelingkan bestickte Pumps
Kelingkan ist eine Stilrichtung der Stickerei, die auf das 14. Jahrhundert zurückgeht und Gold- und Silber-Metallgarn verwendet, um Geduld, Fleiß, Beharrlichkeit und Kreativität zu symbolisieren.

02

"The Red Dot Award attracts the most talented and celebrated in the world of design – both as judges and entrants."

„Der Red Dot Award zieht die Begabtesten und Prominentesten der Designwelt an – sowohl als Juroren wie auch als Bewerber."

In your opinion, what makes for good design?
To catch my eye, a product must be beautiful, useful, of the highest quality, and offer something unique in the product, design or material.

What importance does design quality have for the economic success of companies?
Great importance. If a product satisfies a need, looks beautiful, is made with high-quality materials and works perfectly, then it will be a success.

Which area of design do you feel has the greatest potential for development for the future?
In fashion, sustainable and ethical fashion is growing and can't be ignored. More brands are addressing consumers' concerns about the supply chain, the product's impact on the environment and the brand's social responsibility.

Which country do you consider to be a pioneer in product design, and why?
England, particularly London, has a rich history of producing leading design talent.

Was macht Ihrer Ansicht nach gutes Design aus?
Um meine Aufmerksamkeit zu gewinnen, muss ein Produkt schön, nützlich und von höchster Qualität sein und in Design oder Material etwas Einzigartiges bieten.

Welche Bedeutung hat Designqualität für den wirtschaftlichen Erfolg von Unternehmen?
Eine große. Wenn ein Produkt ein Bedürfnis befriedigt, schön aussieht, aus hochwertigen Materialien besteht und perfekt funktioniert, wird es ein Erfolg.

In welchem Designbereich sehen Sie das größte Entwicklungspotenzial für die Zukunft?
In der Modewelt gewinnt die nachhaltige und ethische Mode an Bedeutung und kann nicht mehr ignoriert werden. Eine wachsende Anzahl von Marken geht auf die Bedenken der Konsumenten ein, was die Lieferkette, die Auswirkungen eines Produkts auf die Umwelt und die soziale Verantwortung der Marke betrifft.

Welche Nation ist für Sie Vorreiter im Produktdesign und warum?
England, besonders London, kann auf eine lange Geschichte in der Ausbildung führender Designtalente zurückblicken.

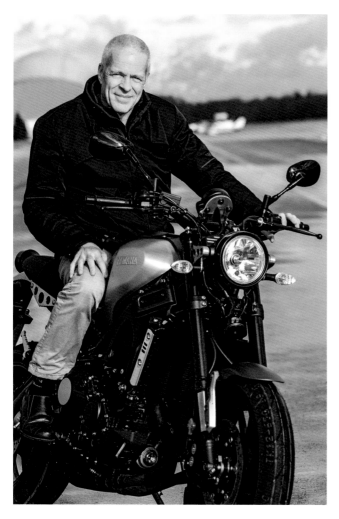

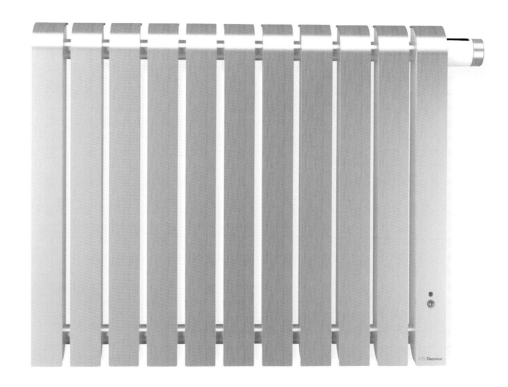

01

Vincent Créance
France
Frankreich

After graduating from the Ecole Supérieure de Design Industriel, Vincent Créance began his career in 1985 at the Plan Créatif Agency where he became design director in 1990 and developed, among other things, numerous products for high-tech and consumer markets, for France Télécom and RATP (Paris metro). In 1996, he joined Alcatel as Design Director for all phone activities on an international level. In 1999, he became Vice President Brand in charge of product design and user experience as well as all communications for the Mobile Phones BU. During the launch of the Franco-Chinese TCL and Alcatel Mobile Phones joint venture in 2004, Vincent Créance advanced to the position of Design and Corporate Communications Director. In 2006, he became President and CEO of MBD Design, one of the major design agencies in France, providing design solutions in transport design and product design. Créance is a member of the APCI (Agency for the Promotion of Industrial Creation), on the board of directors of ENSCI (National College of Industrial Creation), and a member of the Strategic Advisory Board for Strate College.

Vincent Créance begann seine Laufbahn nach seinem Abschluss an der Ecole Supérieure de Design Industriel 1985 bei Plan Créatif Agency. Hier stieg er 1990 zum Design Director auf und entwickelte u. a. zahlreiche Produkte für den Hightech- und Verbrauchermarkt, für die France Télécom oder die RATP (Pariser Metro). 1996 ging er als Design Director für sämtliche Telefonaktivitäten auf internationaler Ebene zu Alcatel und wurde 1999 Vice President Brand, zuständig für Produktdesign und User Experience sowie die gesamte Kommunikation für den Geschäftsbereich „Mobile Phones". Während des Zusammenschlusses des französisch-chinesischen TCL und Alcatel Mobile Phones 2004 avancierte Vincent Créance zum Design and Corporate Communications Director. 2006 wurde er Präsident und CEO von MBD Design, einer der wichtigsten Designagenturen in Frankreich, und entwickelte Designlösungen für Transport- und Produktdesign. Créance ist Mitglied von APCI (Agency for the Promotion of Industrial Creation), Vorstand des ENSCI (National College of Industrial Design) und Mitglied im wissenschaftlichen Beirat des Strate College.

01 Mythik
Radiator for Thermor, a company
of Groupe Atlantic
Heizkörper für Thermor, ein Unternehmen der Groupe Atlantic

02 Optifuel
Low fuel consumption trailer for
Renault Trucks
Anhänger mit geringem Kraft-
stoffverbrauch für Renault Trucks

02

"Seeing so many contemporary
objects in this fantastic exhibition
as a Red Dot juror is very refresh-
ing and has the effect of a fountain
of youth."

„Als Red Dot-Juror dieser phantastischen Ausstellung so viele zeitge-
nössische Objekte sehen zu können,
ist sehr erfrischend und hat die
Wirkung eines Jungbrunnens."

In your opinion, what makes for good design?
It's a pleasure to buy, then to use, and even causes
some sadness when you have to replace it: emotions
are always stronger than rationality when you choose
something.

**What does winning the Red Dot say about a
product?**
More than a high level of design achievement:
winning a Red Dot also gives value to design within
a company, rewards the commitment of all the con-
tributors and makes them proud of their work. Moreover, it is an efficient way to compare yourself with
competitors.

**Which topics are most likely to influence design in
the coming years?**
I think that the emerging sharing economy will
change the way in which we look at products over the
coming years. A product will no longer be designed
only for me, but also for a community. This trend will
logically reinforce sustainability expectations, and
desacralise the objects as a part of my identity.

Was macht Ihrer Ansicht nach gutes Design aus?
Es ist ein Vergnügen, es zu kaufen, dann zu benutzen,
und macht traurig, wenn es ersetzt werden muss: Emotionen sind immer stärker als die Vernunft, wenn man
etwas auswählt.

**Was sagt eine Auszeichnung mit dem Red Dot über
das Produkt aus?**
Mehr als ein hohes Maß an Designleistung: Die
Auszeichnung mit einem Red Dot verleiht dem Design-
produkt auch innerhalb des Unternehmens einen Mehrwert. Sie soll das Engagement aller Mitwirkenden
belohnen und sie stolz auf ihre Arbeit machen. Darüber
hinaus ist es eine wirksame Methode, sich mit Konkur-
renten zu messen.

**Welche Themen werden das Design in den
kommenden Jahren besonders beeinflussen?**
Ich denke, dass die aufstrebende „Sharing Economy"
unsere Perspektive auf Produkte in den kommenden
Jahren verändern wird. Ein Produkt wird nicht mehr nur
für mich, sondern auch für eine Gemeinschaft gestaltet. Dieser Trend wird Erwartungen an die Nachhaltigkeit logischerweise verstärken und den Objekten ihren
sakralen Charakter als Teil meiner Identität nehmen.

01

Martin Darbyshire
Great Britain
Großbritannien

Martin Darbyshire founded tangerine in 1989 and under his stewardship it has developed into a global strategic design consultancy that creates award-winning solutions for internationally recognised brands such as LG, Samsung, Hyundai, Toyota, Nikon, Huawei, Virgin Australia and Cepsa. Before founding tangerine, he worked for Moggridge Associates and then in San Francisco at ID TWO (now IDEO). A design leader on the international stage, Martin Darbyshire combines his work for tangerine with a worldwide programme of keynote speeches and activities promoting the importance of design. He has served as UKT&I Ambassador for the UK Creative Industries and two terms as a board member of the World Design Organization (formerly Icsid). He was also formerly a visiting professor at Central Saint Martins. Martin Darbyshire is a trustee of the UK Design Council and a juror at the Red Dot Award and China Good Design. Recently, the UK Creative Industries Council recognised his global export success awarding him the CIC International Award 2016.

Martin Darbyshire gründete tangerine 1989. Unter seiner Leitung entwickelte sich das Büro zu einem globalen strategischen Designberatungsunternehmen, das preisgekrönte Lösungen für weltweit anerkannte Marken wie LG, Samsung, Hyundai, Toyota, Nikon, Huawei, Virgin Australia und Cepsa entwickelt. Zuvor arbeitete er für Moggridge Associates und dann in San Francisco bei ID TWO (heute IDEO). Als ein weltweit führender Designer verbindet Martin Darbyshire seine Arbeit für tangerine mit einem globalen Programm von Keynote-Referaten und -Aktivitäten, um den bedeutenden Beitrag von Design hervorzuheben. Martin Darbyshire war für das Ministerium für Handel und Investition des Vereinigten Königreichs Botschafter des Bereichs Kreativindustrie und für zwei Amtszeiten Gremiumsmitglied der World Design Organization (ehemals Icsid). Er war zudem Gastdozent an der Central Saint Martins. Martin Darbyshire ist Kurator der UK Design Council sowie Juror des Red Dot Awards und China Good Design. Vor Kurzem wurde er für seinen weltweiten Exporterfolg von der UK Creative Industries Council mit dem CIC International Award 2016 ausgezeichnet.

02

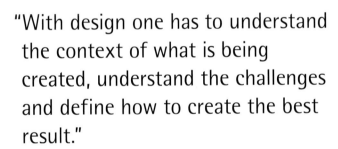

"With design one has to understand the context of what is being created, understand the challenges and define how to create the best result."

„Bei Design muss man den Kontext verstehen, in dem etwas geschaffen werden soll, und die Anforderungen bestimmen, wie man das beste Ergebnis erzielen kann."

What does winning the Red Dot say about a product?
At any stage in your career, winning a Red Dot is very special, as a designer. It is a good feeling to know that your peers have judged you worthy of an award, especially a Red Dot award which carries such prestige within the design and commercial community.

How has the role played by design in our everyday lives changed?
Looking back at the early days, the focus was on form, but now the discipline is about creating value and desirability. The discipline itself has expanded and the lead players in industrial design are talking about "experiences".

Which area of design do you feel has the greatest potential for development for the future?
Sustainability is absolutely fundamental, and an important part of design is getting rid of things that are no longer needed. Every designer has a heightened consciousness of what is going to bring a big change in the future.

Was sagt eine Auszeichnung mit dem Red Dot über das Produkt aus?
Zu jedem Zeitpunkt einer Karriere ist die Auszeichnung mit dem Red Dot für einen Designer etwas ganz Besonderes. Es gibt einem ein gutes Gefühl zu wissen, dass die Kollegen einen für eine Auszeichnung als würdig erachten, vor allem für einen Red Dot, der in der Design- und Geschäftswelt solches Prestige genießt.

Inwieweit hat sich die Rolle, die Design in unserem täglichen Leben spielt, verändert?
Schaut man auf die Anfänge zurück, war das Augenmerk eher auf die Form gerichtet. Heutzutage geht es um das Schaffen von Wert und darum, etwas begehrenswert zu machen. Die Disziplin selbst ist gewachsen und die Branchenführer im industriellen Design reden von „Erfahrungen".

In welchem Designbereich sehen Sie das größte Entwicklungspotenzial für die Zukunft?
Nachhaltigkeit ist absolut fundamental. Ein wichtiger Bestandteil von Design ist es, die Dinge loszuwerden, die nicht mehr gebraucht werden. Jeder Designer hat ein gesteigertes Bewusstsein für das, was in Zukunft große Veränderungen mit sich bringen wird.

01

Stefan Eckstein
Germany
Deutschland

Stefan Eckstein is the founder and CEO of ECKSTEIN DESIGN in Munich. The studio focuses on industrial, interaction and corporate industrial design. Stefan Eckstein studied industrial design at the Muthesius Academy of Fine Arts and Design in Kiel and ergonomics at the Anthropological Institute of the University of Kiel, Germany. Together with his design team, he has received many design awards in national and international competitions. Today, Stefan Eckstein is recognised as a renowned designer for industrial design. In line with his principle, "reduction to the essential leads to a better result", he has developed a user-driven approach to innovation, called "Agile Design Development". It combines innovative concept- and development methods in a structured thought process. Stefan Eckstein has been a member of numerous international juries, has been a member of the Association of German Industrial Designers (VDID) for 25 years and was elected president in 2012. Under his management, the VDID CODEX was developed. Today, it serves as a model for the ethical values of the profession of industrial designers.

Stefan Eckstein ist Gründer und Geschäftsführer von ECKSTEIN DESIGN, einem Studio für Industriedesign, Interaction Design und Corporate Industrial Design in München. Er studierte Industrial Design an der Muthesius-Hochschule und Ergonomie am Anthropologischen Institut der Christian-Albrechts-Universität zu Kiel. Zusammen mit seinem Designteam erhielt er zahlreiche Auszeichnungen. Heute gehört Stefan Eckstein zu den renommierten Designern im Bereich des Industrial Designs. Gemäß seiner Philosophie „Reduzierung auf das Wesentliche führt zu einem besseren Ergebnis" entwickelte er eine nutzerorientierte Innovationsmethode, die Agile Designentwicklung. In einem besonders strukturierten Denkprozess werden dabei innovative Konzept- und Entwicklungsphasen miteinander verbunden. Stefan Eckstein ist international als Juror tätig, seit über 25 Jahren Mitglied beim Verband Deutscher Industrie Designer (VDID) und seit 2012 Präsident des Verbandes. Der VDID CODEX wurde unter seiner Leitung entwickelt und steht heute als Leitbild für die ethischen Werte des Berufsstandes.

01 ECCO 75
The ECCO 75 by SmartRay is a high-definition, 3D sensor suitable for identifying smaller defects and for taking highly precise measurements
Der ECCO 75 von SmartRay ist ein hochauflösender 3D-Sensor für eine detailgetreue Inspektion und höchst genaue Messanwendungen

02|03 VDW.CONNECT Drive
A modern dental endoscopy machine for electronic depth measurement with accompanying mechanical file
Modernes Dental-Endoskopiegerät für die elektronische Tiefenmessung mit dazugehöriger mechanischer Feile

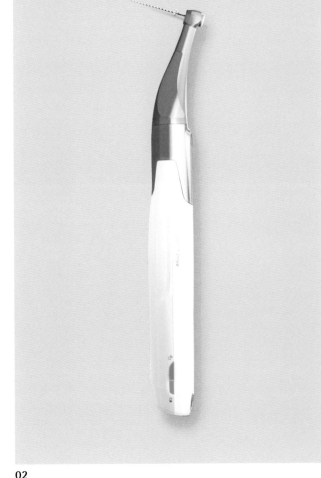

02

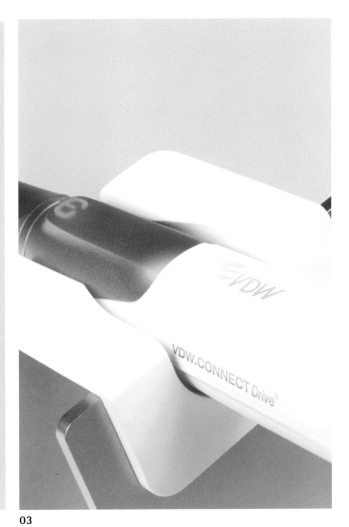

03

"In order to be able to create sophisticated design quality and functional, responsible design, we require 'new' thinking."

„Um anspruchsvolle Gestaltungsqualität und funktionales, verantwortungsvolles Design zu konzipieren, braucht es ‚neues' Denken."

In your opinion, what makes for good design?
For me, design is a means of understanding the world around us. It needs to be user-friendly, innovative, aesthetically pleasing and must appeal to the user's emotions.

How will the role played by design in our everyday lives change?
Design will play a leading role for products and (digital) systems and will take on an explanatory function in the years to come.

What importance does design quality have for the economic success of companies?
It is through design that technology becomes workable and understandable for users. Products do what they are meant to do and deliver the quality that their design promises. Therefore, design is an important economic driver.

What does winning the Red Dot say about a product?
That it successfully manages to combine ergonomics, usability, an idea, quality, function and aesthetics.

Was macht Ihrer Ansicht nach gutes Design aus?
Für mich ist Design eine Art und Weise, die Welt um uns herum zu begreifen. Es muss nutzerfreundlich, innovativ und ästhetisch sein und den Nutzer emotional ansprechen.

Inwieweit wird sich die Rolle, die Design in unserem täglichen Leben spielt, verändern?
Design wird in den nächsten Jahren eine Hauptrolle für Produkte und (digitale) Systeme übernehmen und eine erklärende Funktion haben.

Welche Bedeutung hat Designqualität für den wirtschaftlichen Erfolg von Unternehmen?
Erst durch Design wird Technologie funktional und für den Menschen verständlich. Die Produkte erfüllen ihre Aufgaben und lösen das Qualitätsversprechen ein, das ihr Design abgibt. Deshalb ist Design ein wichtiger Motor für die Wirtschaft.

Was sagt eine Auszeichnung mit dem Red Dot über das Produkt aus?
Dass es Ergonomie, Usability, Idee, Qualität, Funktion und Ästhetik gelungen miteinander verknüpft.

01

Robin Edman
Sweden
Schweden

Robin Edman has been the chief executive of SVID, the Swedish Industrial Design Foundation, since 2001. After studying industrial design at Rhode Island School of Design he joined AB Electrolux Global Design in 1981 and parallel to this started his own design consultancy. In 1989, Robin Edman joined Electrolux North America as vice president of Industrial Design for Frigidaire and in 1997, moved back to Stockholm as vice president of Electrolux Global Design. Throughout his entire career he has worked towards integrating a better understanding of users, their needs and the importance of design in society at large. His engagement in design related activities is reflected in the numerous international jury appointments, speaking engagements, advisory council and board positions he has held. Robin Edman served on the board of the World Design Organization (formerly Icsid) from 2003 to 2007, the last term as treasurer. Since June 2015, he is the president of BEDA (Bureau of European Design Associations).

Robin Edman ist seit 2001 Firmenchef der SVID, der Swedish Industrial Design Foundation. Nach seinem Industriedesign-Studium an der Rhode Island School of Design kam er 1981 zu AB Electrolux Global Design. Zeitgleich startete er seine eigene Unternehmensberatung für Design. 1989 wechselte Edman zu Electrolux North America als Vizepräsident für Industrial Design für Frigidaire und kehrte 1997 als Vizepräsident von Electrolux Global Design nach Stockholm zurück. Während seiner gesamten Karriere hat er daran gearbeitet, ein besseres Verständnis für Nutzer zu entwickeln, für deren Bedürfnisse und die Wichtigkeit von Design in der Gesellschaft insgesamt. Sein Engagement in designbezogenen Aktivitäten spiegelt sich in zahlreichen Jurierungsberufungen sowie in Rednerverpflichtungen und Positionen in Gremien sowie Beratungsausschüssen. Von 2003 bis 2007 war Robin Edman Mitglied im Vorstand der World Design Organization (ehemals Icsid), in der letzten Amtsperiode als Schatzmeister. Seit Juni 2015 ist er Präsident von BEDA (Bureau of European Design Associations).

01 EcoDesign Circle
Three-year EU project to increase
awareness of eco-design of the
Baltic Sea region's small and
medium-sized companies, designers and design organisations; in
collaboration with design organisations and universities from
Germany, Estonia, Lithuania,
Poland, Finland and Sweden,
represented by SVID collaborating
with Green Leap at KTH
Drei Jahre währendes EU-Projekt,
um Aufmerksamkeit auf das Öko-
design der kleinen und mittel-
ständischen Unternehmen, der
Designer und Designorganisationen
an der Ostsee zu lenken; in Zusammenarbeit mit Designorganisationen und Universitäten aus
Deutschland, Estland, Litauen,
Polen, Finnland und Schweden,
vertreten durch SVID in Zusammenarbeit mit Green Leap an der KTH

"Good design is seeing the
opportunities and catering to
the user needs in an intelligent
and sustainable way."

„Gutes Design ist das Erkennen von
Chancen und das Beantworten
von Verbraucherbedürfnissen in
einer intelligenten und nachhaltigen Form."

How has the role played by design in our everyday lives changed?
Design has become an absolute necessity to provide the solutions we expect and desire. The broader scope of design to embrace businesses as well as the public sector has made us request that design plays a role in the creation of products, services, strategies and processes.

What importance does design quality have for the economic success of companies?
Design efforts have a great impact on business success, profitability and repeat purchasing.

What does winning the Red Dot say about a product?
A Red Dot displays a seal of quality for the product and the efforts it takes to produce a winning design.

Which area of design do you feel has the greatest potential for development for the future?
The influence of design in the strategic development of businesses and the public sector.

Inwieweit hat sich die Rolle, die Design in unserem täglichen Leben spielt, verändert?
Design ist für die Lösungen, die wir erwarten und uns wünschen, zwingend notwendig geworden. Der breite Geltungsbereich, der sowohl die Wirtschaft als auch den öffentlichen Sektor umfasst, hat dazu geführt, dass wir verlangen, dass Design in der Herstellung von Produkten, Dienstleistungen, Strategien und Prozessen eine Rolle spielt.

Welche Bedeutung hat Designqualität für den wirtschaftlichen Erfolg von Unternehmen?
Designleistungen haben einen großen Einfluss auf den Geschäftserfolg, die Rentabilität und das markentreue Kaufverhalten.

Was sagt eine Auszeichnung mit dem Red Dot über das Produkt aus?
Der Red Dot ist ein Qualitätssiegel für das Produkt und die Arbeit, die in einem erfolgreichen Entwurf steckt.

In welchem Designbereich sehen Sie das größte Entwicklungspotenzial für die Zukunft?
Im Einfluss von Design auf die strategische Entwicklung von Unternehmen und öffentlichem Sektor.

341

01

Joachim H. Faust
Germany
Deutschland

Joachim H. Faust studied at the RWTH Aachen University as well as at the Texas A&M University in the USA with the aid of a DAAD grant. There, he obtained his diploma and masters in architecture. He has worked, among others, as design architect for Skidmore, Owings & Merrill in Houston, Texas and New York as well as for KPF Kohn, Pedersen, Fox/Eggers Group. In 1987, Joachim H. Faust took over the running of the HPP office in Frankfurt and, since 1997, has been a managing partner at the HPP Group headquarters in Düsseldorf. HPP has 400 employees and offers urban planning, architecture, interior design, general planning and project management from a total of eight offices in Germany. Internationally, HPP has independent offices in Shanghai and Istanbul. Joachim H. Faust is responsible for the company's strategic expansion in China. In 2013, he was asked to take part in the German government's reform commission for "the construction of large projects". In addition, he is an author and gives specialist lectures on architecture and interior design.

Joachim H. Faust studierte an der RWTH Aachen sowie mit einem DAAD-Stipendium an der Texas A&M University in den USA, wo er die Abschlüsse Dipl.-Ing. Architektur und Master of Architecture erlangte. Er war u. a. als Design Architect für Skidmore, Owings & Merrill in Houston, Texas, und New York tätig sowie für KPF Kohn, Pedersen, Fox/Eggers Group. 1987 übernahm Joachim H. Faust die Leitung des HPP-Büros in Frankfurt am Main, seit 1997 führt er die HPP-Gruppe am Hauptsitz Düsseldorf als geschäftsführender Gesellschafter. Mit 400 Mitarbeitern bietet HPP Stadtbereichsplanung, Architektur, Innenarchitektur, Generalplanung und Projektsteuerung in insgesamt acht Büros in Deutschland an. International ist HPP in Shanghai und Istanbul mit eigenen Gesellschaften vertreten. Joachim H. Faust begleitet die Expansion in China strategisch. 2013 wurde er in die Reformkommission „Bau von Großprojekten" der Deutschen Bundesregierung berufen. Er ist zudem als Autor tätig und hält Vorträge zu Fachthemen der Architektur und Innenarchitektur.

01 BASF Business Center D105, Ludwigshafen

The employee cafeteria in the recently completed BASF Business Center D105 offers cutting-edge island-based catering and is open to all BASF employees in the main site in Ludwigshafen, Germany.

Das Mitarbeiter-Restaurant im kürzlich fertiggestellten BASF Business Center D105 bietet modernste Inselkonzept-Gastronomie und ist offen für alle BASF-Mitarbeiter am Hauptwerk Ludwigshafen.

02 Shenzhen North Railway Station Towers

The construction of the North Railway Station Towers in the Chinese port city of Shenzhen is a multi-functional complex consisting of two towers measuring 258 and 100 metres respectively.

Der Bau der North Railway Station Towers in der chinesischen Hafenmetropole Shenzhen ist ein Multifunktionskomplex, bestehend aus zwei Türmen von 258 und 100 Metern Höhe.

02

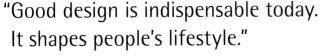

"Good design is indispensable today. It shapes people's lifestyle."

„Gutes Design ist heute unverzichtbar und prägt den Lifestyle der Menschen."

What importance does design quality have for the economic success of companies?
Good design quality is a must for economic success. Outstanding design gives people confidence in a product and leads to even greater success.

What attracts you to the role of Red Dot jury member?
The discussions with the other jury members, the breadth of their cultural, technical but also sensory experiences.

Which topics are most likely to influence design in the coming years?
In a time of limited resources and high environmental pollution, the "life cycle" or "cradle to cradle" of a product will in future become critical.

Which country do you consider to be a pioneer in product design, and why?
Italy for furniture, Japan and Germany for industrial products, and the USA and China for communication products. The reason for this is the prevalent culture of creativity and craftsmanship that, through design ideas, turns an object into a world-beater.

Welche Bedeutung hat Designqualität für den wirtschaftlichen Erfolg von Unternehmen?
Designqualität ist Pflicht für wirtschaftlichen Erfolg. Herausragendes Design schafft Produktvertrauen und damit noch größeren Erfolg.

Was reizt Sie an der Arbeit als Red Dot-Juror?
Die Diskussion mit den Jurykollegen und deren unterschiedliche kulturelle und technische, aber auch sinnliche Erfahrungshorizonte.

Welche Themen werden das Design in den kommenden Jahren besonders beeinflussen?
In Zeiten knapper Ressourcen und hoher Umweltbelastungen werden die Themen „Lebenszyklus" oder auch „Cradle to Cradle" eines Produkts in Zukunft vordringlich werden.

Welche Nation ist für Sie Vorreiter im Produktdesign und warum?
Italien bei Möbeln, Japan und Deutschland bei Industrieprodukten, USA und China bei Kommunikationsprodukten. Grund dafür ist die jeweils bestehende kreative und handwerkliche Kultur, die die Objekte durch geniale Designideen zu den weltweit besten macht.

01

Prof. Lutz Fügener
Germany
Deutschland

Professor Lutz Fügener began his studies at the Technical University Dresden, where he completed a foundation course in mechanical engineering. He then transferred to the Burg Giebichenstein University of Art and Design in Halle/Saale, Germany, where he obtained a degree in industrial design in 1995. In the same year, he became junior partner of Fisch & Vogel Design in Berlin. Since then, the firm (today called "studioFT") has increasingly specialised in transportation design. Two years after joining the firm, Lutz Fügener became senior partner and co-owner. In 2000, he was appointed as Professor of Transportation Design/3D Design by Pforzheim University and there chairs the prestigious BA degree course in transportation design. Lutz Fügener is also active as an author and journalist for a number of different daily newspapers, weekly magazines and periodicals, as well as blogs in which he writes on mobility-related design topics.

Professor Lutz Fügener absolvierte ein Grundstudium in Maschinenbau an der Technischen Universität Dresden und nahm daraufhin ein Studium für Industrial Design an der Hochschule für Kunst und Design, Burg Giebichenstein, in Halle an der Saale auf. Sein Diplom machte er im Jahr 1995. Im selben Jahr wurde er Juniorpartner des Büros Fisch & Vogel Design in Berlin. Seit dieser Zeit spezialisierte sich das Büro (heute „studioFT") mehr und mehr auf den Bereich „Transportation Design". Zwei Jahre nach seinem Einstieg wurde Lutz Fügener Seniorpartner und gleichberechtigter Mitinhaber des Büros. Im Jahr 2000 wurde er von der Hochschule Pforzheim auf eine Professur für Transportation Design/3D-Gestaltung berufen und ist Leiter des renommierten BA-Studiengangs für Fahrzeugdesign. Lutz Fügener ist als Autor und Journalist für verschiedene Tageszeitungen, Wochenmagazine, Periodika und Blogs tätig und schreibt über Themen des Designs im Zusammenhang mit Mobilität.

01|02 SpeedE project
Redesign of an experimental car
of the German Institute for
Automotive Engineering (ika) of
RWTH Aachen University in the
course of a research project
Redesign eines Experimental-
fahrzeugs des Instituts für
Kraftfahrzeuge (ika) an der
RWTH Aachen im Rahmen eines
Forschungsprojekts

02

"In my opinion, good design is
defined by a symbiotic synergy
of function and aesthetics."

„Gutes Design definiert sich aus
meiner Sicht durch ein symbio-
tisches Zusammenwirken von
Funktion und Ästhetik."

How has the role played by design in our everyday lives changed?
The superabundance in the world coexists with regions, processes and areas of work that are developing at an incredible rate. Contemporary product design must take into consideration the wide-ranging consequences of this situation.

What importance does design quality have for the economic success of companies?
Companies that are aware of the possibilities offered by design can make products that are not only aesthetically appealing, but also intuitively understandable and thereby gain a competitive advantage in the eyes of customers.

Which country do you consider to be a pioneer in product design, and why?
German designers create Asian cars just as Asian designers quite naturally work here alongside their colleagues from western countries and the Middle East.

Inwieweit hat sich die Rolle, die Design in unserem täglichen Leben spielt, verändert?
Eine Welt des Überflusses steht sich rasant in verschiedene Richtungen entwickelnden Regionen, Prozessen und Arbeitsgebieten gegenüber. Zeitgemäße Produktgestaltung muss die weitreichenden Konsequenzen dieser Situation berücksichtigen.

Welche Bedeutung hat Designqualität für den wirtschaftlichen Erfolg von Unternehmen?
Mit den Möglichkeiten des Designs vertraute Unternehmen können Produkte über einen ästhetischen Anspruch hinaus intuitiv wahrnehmbar machen und so im Wettbewerb um die Gunst des Kunden punkten.

Welche Nation ist für Sie Vorreiter im Produktdesign und warum?
Deutsche Designer gestalten asiatische Automobile ebenso wie Designer aus Asien hier selbstverständlich mit ihren Kollegen aus westlichen Ländern oder dem Nahen Osten arbeiten.

01

Hideshi Hamaguchi
USA/Japan

Hideshi Hamaguchi graduated with a Bachelor of Science in chemical engineering from Kyoto University. Starting his career with Panasonic in Japan, Hamaguchi later became director of the New Business Planning Group at Panasonic Electric Works, Ltd. and then executive vice president of Panasonic Electric Works Laboratory of America, Inc. In 1993, he developed Japan's first corporate Intranet and also led the concept development for the first USB flash drive. Hideshi Hamaguchi has over 15 years of experience in defining strategies and decision-making, as well as in concept development for various industries and businesses. As Executive Fellow at Ziba Design and CEO at monogoto, he is today considered a leading mind in creative concept and strategy development on both sides of the Pacific and is involved in almost every project this renowned business consultancy takes on. For clients such as FedEx, Polycom and M-System he has led the development of several award-winning products.

Hideshi Hamaguchi graduierte als Bachelor of Science in Chemical Engineering an der Kyoto University. Seine Karriere begann er bei Panasonic in Japan, wo er später zum Direktor der New Business Planning Group von Panasonic Electric Works, Ltd. und zum Executive Vice President von Panasonic Electric Works Laboratory of America, Inc. aufstieg. 1993 entwickelte er Japans erstes Firmen-Intranet und übernahm zudem die Leitung der Konzeptentwicklung des ersten USB-Laufwerks. Hideshi Hamaguchi verfügt über mehr als 15 Jahre Erfahrung in der Konzeptentwicklung sowie Strategie- und Entscheidungsfindung in unterschiedlichen Industrien und Unternehmen. Als Executive Fellow bei Ziba Design und CEO bei monogoto wird er heute als führender Kopf in der kreativen Konzept- und Strategieentwicklung auf beiden Seiten des Pazifiks angesehen und ist in nahezu jedes Projekt der renommierten Unternehmensberatung involviert. Für Kunden wie FedEx, Polycom und M-System leitete er etliche ausgezeichnete Projekte.

01 Cintiq 24HD
for Wacom, 2012
für Wacom, 2012

02 Toy blocks for everyone
A collection of 202 building
blocks crafted from beechwood,
available in beautifully arranged
units. Infused with the stories
of twelve elements, each unique
piece embodies a small fragment
of nature. For Felissimo, Japan,
in collaboration with Marie Uno.
Bauklötze für alle
Eine Kollektion von 202 Bauklötzen,
die aus Buchenholz gefertigt und
in attraktiv arrangierten Sets erhältlich sind. Durchtränkt mit den
Geschichten von zwölf Elementen,
verkörpert jedes einzigartige Stück
ein kleines Fragment der Natur.
Für Felissimo, Japan, in Zusammenarbeit mit Marie Uno.

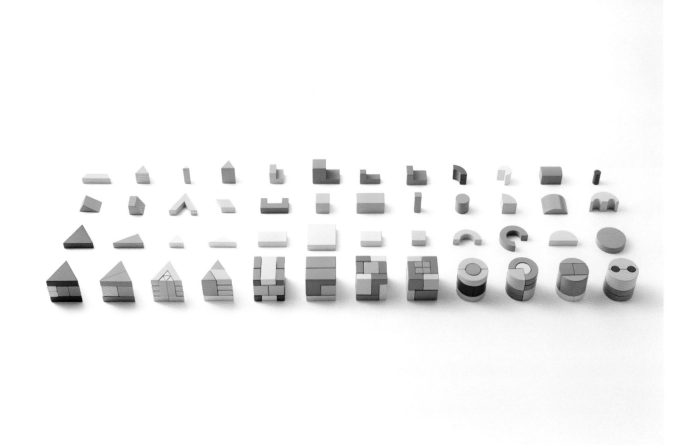

02

"Good design should be simple,
attractive and meaningful, but,
above all, it should have a beautiful
purpose."
„Gutes Design sollte schlicht, ansprechend und sinnvoll sein, aber vor
allem einen schönen Zweck haben."

How has the role played by design in our everyday lives changed?
No design, no life. Design brings stimulation to our daily life and mind.

What does winning the Red Dot say about a product?
Winning the Red Dot says the product is at its pinnacle. People can regard it as the top of a mountain and the designer can also feel as if he were at the summit.

Which area of design do you feel has the greatest potential for development for the future?
Every area has a huge potential for design development. Design development will never stop as long as humans interact with something.

Which country do you consider to be a pioneer in product design, and why?
China. Designers in China have been in a fast-learning and experimental mode for years, and this will give us a greater opportunity to develop new product design languages.

Inwieweit hat sich die Rolle, die Design in unserem täglichen Leben spielt, verändert?
Kein Design, kein Leben. Design bringt Stimulation in unser tägliches Leben und unseren Geist.

Was sagt eine Auszeichnung mit dem Red Dot über das Produkt aus?
Die Auszeichnung mit dem Red Dot bedeutet, dass ein Produkt seinen Höhepunkt erreicht hat. So können Menschen erkennen, dass es an der Spitze angekommen ist, und auch der Designer fühlt sich, als ob er den Gipfel erklommen hätte.

In welchem Designbereich sehen Sie das größte Entwicklungspotenzial für die Zukunft?
Jeder Bereich hat ein enormes Potenzial für Design-entwicklung. Die Entwicklung von Design wird nicht stillstehen, solange Menschen mit etwas interagieren.

Welche Nation ist für Sie Vorreiter im Produktdesign und warum?
China. Designer in China sind seit Jahren lern- und experimentierfreudig. So haben wir eine bessere Chance, neue Produktdesignsprachen zu entwickeln.

01

Prof. Renke He
China

Professor Renke He, born in 1958, studied civil engineering and architecture at Hunan University in China. From 1987 to 1988, he was a visiting scholar at the Industrial Design Department of the Royal Danish Academy of Fine Arts in Copenhagen and, from 1998 to 1999, at North Carolina State University's School of Design. Renke He is dean and professor of the School of Design at Hunan University and is also director of the Chinese Industrial Design Education Committee. Currently, he holds the position of vice chair of the China Industrial Design Association.

Professor Renke He wurde 1958 geboren und studierte an der Hunan University in China Bauingenieurwesen und Architektur. Von 1987 bis 1988 war er als Gastprofessor für Industrial Design an der Royal Danish Academy of Fine Arts in Kopenhagen tätig, und von 1998 bis 1999 hatte er eine Gastprofessur an der School of Design der North Carolina State University inne. Renke He ist Dekan und Professor an der Hunan University, School of Design, sowie Direktor des Chinese Industrial Design Education Committee. Er ist derzeit zudem stellvertretender Vorsitzender der China Industrial Design Association.

01 Black sand tea set
Design for the New Channel
Social Innovation Design project
by Cao Yuan
Design für das „New Channel
Social Innovation Design"-Projekt
von Cao Yuan

02 Black sand tableware
Design for the New Channel
Social Innovation Design project
by Yue Zou
Design für das „New Channel
Social Innovation Design"-Projekt
von Yue Zou

02

"Winning a Red Dot is the highest form of approval for world class design."

„Die Auszeichnung mit einem Red Dot ist die höchste Form der Anerkennung für Design von Weltklasse."

In your opinion, what makes for good design?
A user experience that surpasses the expectation of consumers.

How has the role played by design in our everyday lives changed?
The development of mobile Internet design has penetrated all aspects of our daily lives. One app design can be used all over the world simultaneously; no single physical product design was able to do that before.

What importance does design quality have for the economic success of companies?
Good design is good business; this is still a golden rule today. Design quality decides the quality of the user experiences for the products and services of any company; it is the key issue for companies' economic success.

What attracts you to the role of Red Dot jury member?
To be the first to know the best designs in the world.

Was macht Ihrer Ansicht nach gutes Design aus?
Ein Nutzererlebnis, das die Erwartungen der Verbraucher übertrifft.

Inwieweit hat sich die Rolle, die Design in unserem täglichen Leben spielt, verändert?
Die Entwicklung der Gestaltung des mobilen Internets hat alle Aspekte unseres täglichen Lebens durchdrungen. Ein App-Design kann auf der ganzen Welt gleichzeitig genutzt werden. Kein einziges physisches Produktdesign konnte das bislang schaffen.

Welche Bedeutung hat Designqualität für den wirtschaftlichen Erfolg von Unternehmen?
Gutes Design bringt wirtschaftlichen Erfolg. Das ist auch heute noch eine goldene Regel. Designqualität ist ausschlaggebend für die Art und Weise, in der der Benutzer die Produkte und Dienstleistungen eines Unternehmens qualitativ erlebt. Es ist das zentrale Thema für den wirtschaftlichen Erfolg von Unternehmen.

Was reizt Sie an der Arbeit als Red Dot-Juror?
Der Erste in der Welt zu sein, der die besten Entwürfe der Welt zu sehen bekommt.

ESCUELA DE INGENIERÍA
FACULTAD DE INGENIERÍA

01

Prof.
Carlos Hinrichsen
Chile

Professor Carlos Hinrichsen graduated as an industrial designer in Chile in 1982 and earned his master's degree in engineering in Japan in 1991. Currently, he is the Senior Managing Coordinator of Engineering Design in the School of Engineering in the P. Universidad Católica de Chile. Chile is in transition from an efficiency-based towards an innovation-based economy where the School of Engineering contributes with actions and initiatives to achieve this important aim for the country, mixing research, innovation, business, design and engineering spheres. From 2007 to 2009, Carlos Hinrichsen was president of the World Design Organization (formerly Icsid) and currently serves as senator within the organisation. In 2010, he was honoured with the distinction "Commander of the Order of the Lion of Finland". From 2014 to 2016, he was dean of the Faculty of Business, Engineering and Digital Arts at the Gabriela Mistral University in Santiago. For more than three decades he has led interdisciplinary teams to enable corporations, educational and other institutions to gain leadership and competitive positioning.

Professor Carlos Hinrichsen machte 1982 seinen Abschluss in Industriedesign in Chile und erhielt 1991 seinen Master der Ingenieurwissenschaft in Japan. Aktuell ist er leitender geschäftsführender Koordinator für Engineering Design an der P. Universidad Católica de Chile. Chile ist im Übergang von einer effizienzbasierten zu einer innovationsbasierten Wirtschaft, in der die Ingenieurschule mit Maßnahmen und Initiativen dazu beiträgt, dieses wichtige Landesziel durch eine Mischung aus Forschung, Innovation, Handel, Design und Ingenieurwesen zu erreichen. Von 2007 bis 2009 war Carlos Hinrichsen Präsident der World Design Organization (ehemals Icsid) und dient heute als Senator innerhalb der Organisation. 2010 wurde er mit der Auszeichnung „Commander of the Order of the Lion of Finland" geehrt. Von 2014 bis 2016 war er Dekan der Fakultät für Handel, Ingenieurwesen und Digitale Künste an der Gabriela-Mistral-Universität in Santiago. Seit mehr als drei Jahrzehnten leitet er interdisziplinäre Teams, um Unternehmen, Bildungsinstituten und anderen Organisationen zu helfen, eine marktführende und starke Wettbewerbsposition zu erlangen.

The School of Engineering UC with
its Faculty of Engineering of the
Pontificia Universidad Católica de
Chile where Hinrichsen acts as
Senior Managing Coordinator of
Engineering Design is committed
to interdisciplinary education as
a key area of growth and development. The future interdisciplinary
building is an evidence of this
goal.

Die Ingenieurschule UC mit der
Fakultät für Ingenieurwissenschaf-
ten der Pontificia Universidad
Católica de Chile, wo Hinrichsen als
Senior Managing Coordinator of
Engineering Design tätig ist, enga-
giert sich für eine fachübergrei-
fende Ausbildung, da sie diese als
den wichtigsten Wachstums- und
Entwicklungsbereich betrachtet.
Das künftige interdisziplinäre Ge-
bäude ist Zeugnis dieser Zielsetzung.

"The Red Dot Award is an important platform for obtaining global exposure and visibility, and is a win-win opportunity for companies and designers."

„Der Red Dot Award ist eine wichtige Plattform, um international bekannt und bemerkt zu werden. Unternehmen und Designern bietet er eine Win-win-Chance."

In your opinion, what makes for good design?
When I was child, I realised that it contributes to people's happiness, and over the years I confirmed that impression.

What importance does design quality have for the economic success of companies?
Design and innovation quality is a key factor in the fight against the general prevailing commoditisation of many product and/or service types. In this regard, those products that deserve recognition can be regarded as good evidence of a relationship between quality and a potentially successful market response.

Which area of design do you feel has the greatest potential for development for the future?
Mostly the "interdisciplinary areas" where we are able to find innovation led by design, or design led by innovation coming from the R&D sphere, and innovations associated with social and market changes, whose purpose it is to successfully respond to people's new needs and requirements.

Was macht Ihrer Ansicht nach gutes Design aus?
Schon als Kind wurde mir bewusst, dass es dazu beiträgt, Menschen glücklich zu machen. Im Laufe der Jahre hat sich dieser Eindruck bestätigt.

Welche Bedeutung hat Designqualität für den wirtschaftlichen Erfolg von Unternehmen?
Design- und Innovationsqualität ist ein zentraler Faktor für den Widerstand gegen die allgemein zunehmende Kommerzialisierung vieler Produkt- und/oder Servicetypen. In dieser Hinsicht sind die Produkte, die Anerkennung verdienen, diejenigen, die gute Beweise für einen Zusammenhang zwischen Qualität und einer potenziell erfolgreichen Marktreaktion liefern.

In welchem Designbereich sehen Sie das größte Entwicklungspotenzial für die Zukunft?
Hauptsächlich in den „interdisziplinären Bereichen", in denen wir von Design inspirierte Innovation oder von Innovation inspiriertes Design im F&E-Bereich sehen. Hinzu kommen Innovationen, die verbunden sind mit sozialen und Marktveränderungen, deren Ziel es ist, erfolgreich auf die Bedürfnisse und Anforderungen von Menschen einzugehen.

01

Simon Husslein
Germany/Switzerland
Deutschland/Schweiz

Simon Husslein was born in Werneck, Germany in 1976 and studied industrial design from 1995 to 2000 at Darmstadt University of Applied Sciences. From 2000 to 2005, he worked closely with his mentor and friend Hannes Wettstein at Wettstein's studio in Zurich. From 2005 to 2007, he completed a master's degree in Design Products at the London Royal College of Art. Subsequently, he led a number of projects in London and Shanghai and lectured at Shanghai's Tongji University. Between 2008 and 2014, he put his mark on a large number of projects at the Studio Hannes Wettstein in Zurich where he was creative director and member of the executive committee. In 2015, he founded the Atelier Simon Husslein. Simon Husslein develops products, furniture, installations and spatial design. He teaches and undertakes brand consultancy.

Simon Husslein, geboren 1976 in Werneck, studierte von 1995 bis 2000 Industrial Design an der Fachhochschule Darmstadt. Von 2000 bis 2005 arbeitete er eng mit seinem Mentor und Freund Hannes Wettstein in dessen Zürcher Studio zusammen. Von 2005 bis 2007 absolvierte er ein Masterstudium in Design Products am Royal College of Art in London. Danach betreute er eigene Projekte in London und Shanghai und unterrichtete an der Tongji-Universität in Shanghai. Zwischen 2008 und 2014 prägte er als Creative Director und Mitglied der Geschäftsleitung eine Vielzahl der Projekte des Studios Hannes Wettstein in Zürich. 2015 gründete er das Atelier Simon Husslein. Simon Husslein entwickelt Produkte, Möbel, Installationen und Raumgestaltungen. Er berät Marken und unterrichtet.

02

"No sophisticated brand can, in the long term, afford to ignore design quality."

„Keine anspruchsvolle Marke kann es sich langfristig leisten, Designqualität zu ignorieren."

How has the role played by design in our everyday lives changed?
The concentration and networking of things haven't always made everyday life easier. Design has the responsibility to provide some orientation and to create interfaces that are people-friendly.

What importance does design quality have for the economic success of companies?
Good design increases the probability that a product will be able to sustain its market position for an above-average length of time.

What attracts you to the role of Red Dot jury member?
Over the years, I have personally benefited from the attention that design prizes bring. By being a jury member and being able to contribute to the quality of the Red Dot, I am able to give something back.

Which country do you consider to be a pioneer in product design, and why?
The clarity of a classification by nation is becoming increasingly blurred.

Inwieweit hat sich die Rolle, die Design in unserem täglichen Leben spielt, verändert?
Verdichtung und Vernetzung von Dingen haben unseren Alltag nicht nur erleichtert. Design kommt die Verantwortung zu, Orientierung zu geben und Schnittstellen menschlich zu gestalten.

Welche Bedeutung hat Designqualität für den wirtschaftlichen Erfolg von Unternehmen?
Gutes Design erhöht die Chance signifikant, dass sich ein Produkt überdurchschnittlich lange in seinem Marktumfeld behaupten kann.

Was reizt Sie an der Arbeit als Red Dot-Juror?
Ich konnte in der Vergangenheit selbst wiederholt von der Aufmerksamkeit, die Designpreise auslösen, profitieren. Sich als Teil der Jury für die Qualität des Red Dot zu engagieren, gibt mir die Möglichkeit, etwas zurückzugeben.

Welche Nation ist für Sie Vorreiter im Produktdesign und warum?
Heutzutage verwischt die Klarheit einer nationalen Zuordnung.

01

Tapani Hyvönen
Finland
Finnland

Tapani Hyvönen graduated as an industrial designer from the present Aalto University School of Arts, Design and Architecture. In 1976, he founded the design agency "Destem Ltd." and was co-founder of ED-Design Ltd. in 1990. He has served as CEO and president of both agencies until 2013. He has been a visiting professor at Guangdong University of Technology in Guangzhou and Donghua University in Shanghai, China. His many award-winning designs, for which e.g. he was honoured with the Industrial Designer of the Year Award of the Finnish Association of Industrial Designers TKO in 1991 or the Pro Finnish Design Award by the Design Forum Finland, are part of the collections of the Design Museum Helsinki and the Cooper-Hewitt Museum, New York. Tapani Hyvönen was an advisory board member of the Design Leadership Programme at the University of Art and Design Helsinki 1989–2000, and a board member of the World Design Organization (formerly Icsid) 1999–2003 and 2009–2013. He was president of the Finnish Association of Designers Ornamo 2009–2012 and has been a board member of the Finnish Design Museum since 2011.

Tapani Hyvönen graduierte an der heutigen Aalto University School of Arts, Design and Architecture zum Industriedesigner. 1976 gründete er die Designagentur „Destem Ltd." und war 1990 Mitbegründer der ED-Design Ltd., die er beide bis 2013 als CEO und Präsident leitete. Er lehrt als Gastprofessor u. a. an der Guangdong University of Technology in Guangzhou und der Donghua University in Shanghai, China. Seine vielfach ausgezeichneten Arbeiten, für die er u. a. mit der Auszeichnung zum Industriedesigner des Jahres der Finnish Association of Industrial Designers TKO 1991 oder dem Pro Finnish Design Award des Design Forum Finland geehrt wurde, sind in den Sammlungen des Design Museum Helsinki und des Cooper-Hewitt Museum, New York, vertreten. Tapani Hyvönen war 1989–2000 in der Beratungskommission des Design Leadership Programme der University of Art and Design Helsinki und 1999–2003 sowie 2009–2013 Vorstandsmitglied der World Design Organization (ehemals Icsid). Er war Präsident der Finnish Association of Designers Ornamo 2009–2012 und ist seit 2011 Vorstandsmitglied des Finnish Design Museum.

02 DOSIME
A hybrid smart home and wearable device that detects and
measures ionising radiation exposure, tracks cumulative exposure
and reports in real-time. For
Mirion Technologies, 2016.
Ein hybrides tragbares Gerät für die
intelligente Haustechnik. Es erkennt
und misst die ionisierende Strahlen-
einwirkung, zeichnet die kumulative
Belastung auf und gibt dazu in
Echtzeit Bescheid. Für Mirion
Technologies, 2016.

02

"As the purpose of design is to make things understandable and easy to use, information ergonomics will have an important role to play in future design."
„Da der Sinn von Design ist, Dinge verständlich und benutzerfreundlich zu machen, wird Informationsergonomie im Design der Zukunft eine wichtige Rolle spielen."

In your opinion, what makes for good design?
The most common criteria for good design are aesthetics, user friendliness, usability, sustainability, ergonomics, general efficiency etc. In good design, all aspects are in equilibrium, but a failure of one criteria can ruin the whole design.

What importance does design quality have for the economic success of companies?
An investment in design pays back more than many other investments. When company management complains about the price of the design, I usually say: good design never costs too much, but bad design can cost everything.

Which topics are most likely to influence design in the coming years?
Service will continue to be an important part of product design. Digitalisation and the Internet of Everything will be connected to most of the products.

Was macht Ihrer Ansicht nach gutes Design aus?
Die gebräuchlichsten Kriterien für gutes Design sind Ästhetik, Nutzerfreundlichkeit, Brauchbarkeit, Nachhaltigkeit, Ergonomie, die Leistung insgesamt usw. Bei gutem Design sind alle diese Kriterien im Einklang. Wenn aber eines versagt, zerstört es das ganze Design.

Welche Bedeutung hat Designqualität für den wirtschaftlichen Erfolg von Unternehmen?
Eine Investition in Design zahlt sich mehr aus als jegliche andere Investition. Wenn die Unternehmensleitung über die Designkosten klagt, sage ich meist: Gutes Design kostet nie zu viel, doch schlechtes Design kann alles kosten.

Welche Themen werden das Design in den kommenden Jahren besonders beeinflussen?
Service wird weiterhin ein wichtiger Bestandteil von Produktdesign sein. Die Digitalisierung und das „Internet of Everything" werden mit den meisten Produkten verbunden sein.

01

Guto Indio da Costa
Brazil
Brasilien

Guto Indio da Costa, born in 1969 in Rio de Janeiro, studied product design and graduated from the Art Center College of Design in Switzerland in 1993.
He is design director of Indio da Costa A.U.D.T, a consultancy based in Rio de Janeiro, which develops architectural, urban planning, design and transportation projects. It works with a multidisciplinary strategic-creative group of designers, architects and urban planners, supported by a variety of other specialists. Guto Indio da Costa is a member of the Design Council of the State of Rio de Janeiro, former Vice President of the Brazilian Design Association (Abedesign) and founder of CBDI (Brazilian Industrial Design Council). He has been active as a lecturer and contributing writer to different design magazines and has been a jury member of many design competitions in Brazil and abroad.

Guto Indio da Costa, geboren 1969 in Rio de Janeiro, studierte Produktdesign und machte 1993 seinen Abschluss am Art Center College of Design in der Schweiz. Er ist Gestaltungsdirektor von Indio da Costa A.U.D.T, einem in Rio de Janeiro ansässigen Beratungsunternehmen, das Projekte in Architektur, Stadtplanung, Design- und Transportwesen entwickelt und mit einem multidisziplinären, strategisch-kreativen Team aus Designern, Architekten und Stadtplanern sowie mit der Unterstützung weiterer Spezialisten operiert. Guto Indio da Costa ist Mitglied des Design Councils des Bundesstaates Rio de Janeiro, ehemaliger Vizepräsident der brasilianischen Designvereinigung (Abedesign) und Gründer des CBDI (Industrial Design Council Brasiliens). Er ist als Lehrbeauftragter aktiv, schreibt für verschiedene Designmagazine und ist als Jurymitglied zahlreicher Designwettbewerbe in und außerhalb Brasiliens tätig.

02

"Good design must bring some kind of innovation that has the potential to enhance peoples' lives and thus to improve our society."

„Gutes Design muss eine Innovation mit sich bringen, die das Potenzial hat, das Leben von Menschen und die Gesellschaft an sich zu verbessern."

How has the role played by design in our everyday lives changed?
It has deeply changed. Products have become far more complex, and usability has become a major issue.

What importance does design quality have for the economic success of companies?
Design quality has become absolutely necessary and an important requirement. Therefore, the challenge of enhancing design quality has become one of the most important factors for the economic success of companies.

What attracts you to the role of Red Dot jury member?
Firstly, it is a great experience to see the worldwide vanguard of product design every year. This is an incredible picture of the worldwide outlook on design. Secondly, the interaction with the very international jury, the exchange of points of views and the qualified discussions are extremely interesting and usually lead to new understanding and new perceptions in such a fast changing world.

Inwieweit hat sich die Rolle, die Design in unserem täglichen Leben spielt, verändert?
Sie hat sich grundlegend geändert. Produkte sind viel komplexer und Nutzerfreundlichkeit ist zu einem wichtigen Thema geworden.

Welche Bedeutung hat Designqualität für den wirtschaftlichen Erfolg von Unternehmen?
Designqualität ist absolut notwendig und zu einer wichtigen Voraussetzung geworden. Daher ist die Aufgabe, die Designqualität zu verbessern, zu einem der wichtigsten Faktoren für den wirtschaftlichen Erfolg von Unternehmen geworden.

Was reizt Sie an der Arbeit als Red Dot-Juror?
Erstens ist es ein tolles Erlebnis, jedes Jahr die weltweite Avantgarde des Produktdesigns zu sehen. Dies gibt uns einen unglaublichen Einblick in die Auffassung von Design in aller Welt. Zweitens sind die Interaktion mit der sehr internationalen Jury, der Austausch von Standpunkten und die qualifizierten Diskussionen äußerst interessant und führen üblicherweise zu einem neuen Verständnis und neuen Wahrnehmungen in dieser sich rasch verändernden Welt.

01

Prof.
Cheng-Neng Kuan
Taiwan

In 1980, Professor Cheng-Neng Kuan earned a master's degree in Industrial Design (MID) from the Pratt Institute in New York. He is currently a full professor and the vice president of Shih-Chien University, Taipei, Taiwan. With the aim of developing a more advanced design curriculum in Taiwan, he founded the Department of Industrial Design, in 1992. He served as department chair until 1999. Moreover, Professor Kuan founded the School of Design in 1997 and had served as the dean from 1997 to 2004 and as the founding director of the Graduate Institute of Industrial Design from 1998 to 2007. Professor Kuan had also held the position of the 16th chairman of the board of China Industrial Designers Association (CIDA), Taiwan. His fields of expertise include design strategy and management as well as design theory and creation. Having published various books on design and over 180 research papers and articles, he is an active member of design juries in his home country and internationally. He is a consultant to major enterprises on product development and design strategy.

1980 erwarb Professor Cheng-Neng Kuan einen Master-Abschluss in Industriedesign (MID) am Pratt Institute in New York. Derzeit ist er ordentlicher Professor und Vizepräsident der Shih-Chien University in Taipeh, Taiwan. 1992 gründete er mit dem Ziel, einen erweiterten Designlehrplan zu entwickeln, das Department of Industrial Design in Taiwan. Bis 1999 war Professor Kuan Vorsitzender des Instituts. Darüber hinaus gründete er 1997 die School of Design, deren Dekan er von 1997 bis 2004 war. Von 1998 bis 2007 war er Gründungsdirektor des Graduate Institute of Industrial Design. Zudem war er der 16. Vorstandsvorsitzende der China Industrial Designers Association (CIDA) in Taiwan. Seine Fachgebiete umfassen Designstrategie, -management, -theorie und -kreation. Neben der Veröffentlichung verschiedener Bücher über Design und von mehr als 180 Forschungsarbeiten und Artikeln ist er aktives Mitglied von Designjurys in seiner Heimat sowie auf internationaler Ebene. Zudem ist er als Berater für Großunternehmen im Bereich Produktentwicklung und Designstrategie tätig.

01 KNEESUP
A knee rehabilitation system integrating smart wearable devices and a mobile application – an example of a project that was selected as the winner of Taiwan's Young Pin Design Award 2016 for being the best of the year
Knie-Rehabilitationssystem, das tragbare intelligente Geräte und eine mobile App integriert – Beispiel eines Projekts, das als Jahresbestleistung zum Gewinner des Young Pin Design Award 2016 in Taiwan gekürt wurde

02 WisFit
A piece of intelligent magnetic fitness equipment including a commercial service system and an example of a project that was selected as a winner of Taiwan's Young Pin Design Award 2016
Intelligentes magnetisches Fitnessgerät mit einem Handels-Service-System und Beispiel für ein Gewinner-Projekt des Young Pin Design Award 2016 in Taiwan

02

"The greatest potential for development for the future lies in the experience that entertains or in the entertainment design."
„Das größte Entwicklungspotenzial für die Zukunft liegt in Erfahrungen, die unterhalten, oder im Unterhaltungsdesign."

How has the role played by design in our everyday lives changed?
Instead of attracting attention, design is becoming a detector of cultural meanings.

What importance does design quality have for the economic success of companies?
Only through good design can a company succeed in being outstanding, as well as popularly accepted by the target market.

What does winning the Red Dot say about a product?
Authority. It makes one believe that quality design is truly good.

Which country do you consider to be a pioneer in product design, and why?
The United States, because they have three critical resources that hardly any other country can uphold simultaneously: a deeply embedded entrepreneurship, a dense multi-ethnic culture, and a big vibrant market.

Inwieweit hat sich die Rolle, die Design in unserem täglichen Leben spielt, verändert?
Anstatt Aufmerksamkeit zu erregen, wird Design zu einem Indikator für kulturelle Bedeutungen.

Welche Bedeutung hat Designqualität für den wirtschaftlichen Erfolg von Unternehmen?
Nur durch gutes Design kann es einem Unternehmen gelingen, herausragend zu sein und gleichzeitig in seinem Absatzmarkt auf allgemeine Akzeptanz zu stoßen.

Was sagt eine Auszeichnung mit dem Red Dot über das Produkt aus?
Autorität. Sie überzeugt einen davon, dass qualitativ hochwertiges Design wirklich gut ist.

Welche Nation ist für Sie Vorreiter im Produktdesign und warum?
Die Vereinigten Staaten, weil sie drei entscheidende Ressourcen haben, die kaum ein anderes Land gleichzeitig aufrechterhalten kann: einen tief verankerten Unternehmergeist, eine starke multiethnische Kultur und einen großen, dynamischen Markt.

01

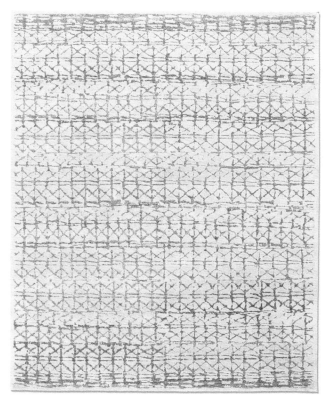

02

Kristiina Lassus
Finland/Italy
Finnland/Italien

Kristiina Lassus, born in Helsinki in 1966, graduated from the University of Industrial Arts of Helsinki with a Master of Arts in Design Leadership in 1992. This was followed by postgraduate studies in product development at the Helsinki Polytechnic in 1993, and her second MA in Interior Architecture and Furniture Design from the University of Industrial Arts in Helsinki in 1995. After working in renowned architectural practices in Finland and Australia, she developed her first products for Alessi, Poltronova and Zanotta. Her specialisation in design management and product development led to managerial positions in international design companies. She worked as Design Coordinator for Artek Oy Ab in Finland from 1994 to 1997 and as Design Manager for Alessi SpA in Italy from 1998 to 2004. In 2003, she founded Kristiina Lassus Studio which provides consultancy services in creative direction, project management, product design, brand development and design promotion. In 2007, she registered her own trademark, "Kristiina Lassus", as a symbol of independent and personal production.

Kristiina Lassus, 1966 in Helsinki geboren, graduierte 1992 an der University of Industrial Arts in Helsinki mit einem Master of Arts in Design Leadership. Ab 1993 studierte sie Product Development an der Helsinki Polytechnic und legte 1995 ihren zweiten Master of Arts in Interior Architecture und Furniture Design an der University of Industrial Arts in Helsinki ab. Sie arbeitete in renommierten Architekturbüros in Finnland und Australien, bevor sie ihre ersten Produkte für Alessi, Poltronova und Zanotta entwarf. Dank ihrer Spezialisierung auf Design Management und Product Development hatte sie geschäftsführende Positionen in internationalen Designfirmen inne. Von 1994 bis 1997 arbeitete sie als Design Coordinator für Artek Oy Ab in Finnland und von 1998 bis 2004 als Design Manager für Alessi SpA in Italien. 2003 gründete sie das Kristiina Lassus Studio, dessen Beratungstätigkeit die Bereiche Creative Direction, Projektmanagement, Produktdesign, Markenentwicklung und Designförderung umfasst. 2007 ließ sie ihre eigene Schutzmarke „Kristiina Lassus" eintragen, als Symbol einer unabhängigen und persönlichen Produktion.

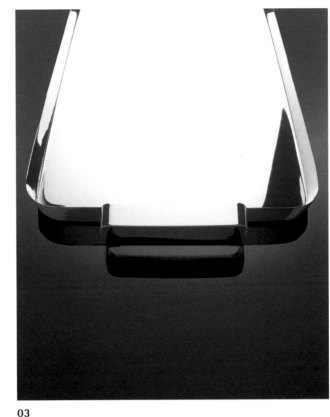

03

04

"Red Dot is a forum that helps exemplary products to stand out. It is a pleasure to be part of this jury and to give these products their well-deserved recognition."

„Red Dot ist ein Forum, das vorbildhaften Produkten hilft hervorzustechen. Es ist eine große Freude, Teil dieser Jury zu sein und diesen Produkten ihre wohlverdiente Anerkennung zu geben."

How has the role played by design in our everyday lives changed?
From concrete product design, the role of design is now moving towards abstract, intelligent and immaterial dimensions e.g. related to energy, climate, mood and atmosphere or services.

What importance does design quality have for the economic success of companies?
A fundamental importance. Design focuses on building on company strengths and opportunities and on eliminating weaknesses. It improves the overall product performance, production efficiency and the product life cycle. Research and development of new technical solutions push companies to evolve. Market leaders are innovators that have a clear mission and vision. Design quality gives companies a clear competitive advantage.

Inwieweit hat sich die Rolle, die Design in unserem täglichen Leben spielt, verändert?
Die Rolle von Design entwickelt sich vom konkreten Produktdesign weg hin zu mehr abstrakten, intelligenten und ungegenständlichen Dimensionen z. B. in Bezug auf Energie, Klima, Stimmung und Ambiente oder Dienstleistungen.

Welche Bedeutung hat Designqualität für den wirtschaftlichen Erfolg von Unternehmen?
Eine grundlegende Bedeutung. Design zielt darauf ab, auf den Stärken und Chancen eines Unternehmens aufzubauen und seine Schwächen zu beseitigen. Es verbessert die allgemeine Leistung, die Wirksamkeit und den Lebenszyklus eines Produkts. Forschung und Entwicklung neuer technologischer Lösungen treiben Unternehmen dazu an, sich weiterzuentwickeln. Marktführend sind die Unternehmen, die Wegbereiter sind und eine klare Mission und Vision haben. Designqualität gibt Unternehmen einen deutlichen Wettbewerbsvorteil.

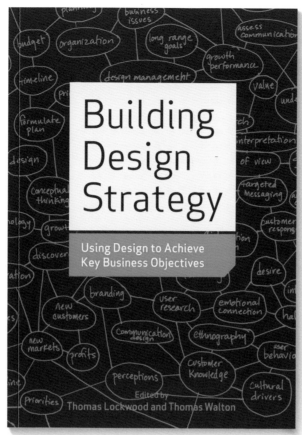

01

02

Dr Thomas Lockwood
USA

Dr Thomas Lockwood is the author of several books on design management, design strategy and design thinking. He has a PhD in design management and is recognised as a thought leader at integrating design and innovation practice into business, and building great design and UX organisations. He produced 22 conferences about design leadership, lectured and led workshops in over 20 countries, and is a design adviser to countries and companies. His design accomplishments range from creating high-tech skiwear for the US Olympic Nordic Ski Team, to corporate design programmes for Fortune 500 organisations. He is the founding partner of Lockwood Resource, an international consulting and recruiting firm specialising in design leadership. Previously he has been the president of DMI, the Design Management Institute, a corporate design director, and a partner and creative director at several design firms.

Dr. Thomas Lockwood ist der Autor mehrerer Bücher zu den Themen Designmanagement, Designstrategie und Designdenken. Er ist promovierter Designmanager und wird allgemein als Vordenker im Bereich der Integration von Design und Innovation in die Wirtschaft anerkannt. Er machte sich auch mit dem Bau von großen Design- und UX-Organisationen einen Namen. Außerdem organisierte er insgesamt 22 Konferenzen über Führung im Design, hielt in mehr als 20 Ländern Vorträge und leitete Workshops und ist als Designberater für Länder und Unternehmen aktiv. Seine Designerfolge reichen von der Gestaltung der Hightech-Skibekleidung für die olympische Nordic-Ski-Mannschaft der USA bis hin zu Corporate-Design-Programmen für Unternehmen, die zu den Fortune 500 gehören. Er ist der Gründungspartner von Lockwood Resource, einer internationalen Beratungs- und Personalbeschaffungsfirma, die sich auf Designmanagement spezialisiert hat. Davor war er Präsident des DMI (Design Management Institute), als Corporate Design Director tätig und als Partner und Creative Director bei verschiedenen Designfirmen angestellt.

01 Building Design Strategy
The book explains how to build and develop great design organisations, and synchronise design and business strategy.
Das Buch erklärt, wie große Designorganisationen auf- und ausgebaut und wie Design und Unternehmensstrategie aufeinander abgestimmt werden.

02 Innovators
The book demonstrates how the best design leaders increase the influence of design, and actually help develop corporate cultures of innovation.
Das Buch beweist, dass die führenden Köpfe im Design den Einfluss des Designs verstärken und tatsächlich dazu beitragen, Unternehmenskulturen zu entwickeln, die auf Innovation ausgerichtet sind.

"The rapidly growing international parity of design will influence the field of product design in the coming years."
„Die rasant zunehmende internationale Gleichwertigkeit von Design wird den Produktdesignbereich in den kommenden Jahren beeinflussen."

In your opinion, what makes for good design?
Good design is that which solves the right problems, with people and planet in mind.

How has the role played by design in our everyday lives changed?
Design is at the foundation of everything, and now more than ever people want to be surrounded by good design. Good design makes for good experiences; it can make us happy.

What importance does design quality have for the economic success of companies?
Design quality is fundamental to good business. Quality can be evaluated, and therefore improved, and so can design.

What attracts you to the role of Red Dot jury member?
The entire ecology – the products, process and people. Being a Red Dot judge informs my perspective of the best of global design, and stimulates my passion for design. I love the examination, the debate, the diversity of opinions, and the challenge of the entire evaluation process.

Was macht Ihrer Ansicht nach gutes Design aus?
Gutes Design löst die richtigen Probleme und verliert die Menschen und unseren Planeten nicht aus dem Blick.

Inwieweit hat sich die Rolle, die Design in unserem täglichen Leben spielt, verändert?
Design ist die Basis, auf der alles aufbaut. Mehr denn je wollen Menschen sich mit gutem Design umgeben. Gutes Design führt zu guten Erfahrungen. Es kann uns glücklich machen.

Welche Bedeutung hat Designqualität für den wirtschaftlichen Erfolg von Unternehmen?
Designqualität ist für wirtschaftlichen Erfolg von grundlegender Bedeutung. Qualität kann bewertet und daher verbessert werden. Das Gleiche gilt für Design.

Was reizt Sie an der Arbeit als Red Dot-Juror?
Die gesamte Ökologie – die Produkte, die Prozesse und die Menschen. Red Dot-Juror zu sein, beeinflusst meinen Standpunkt in Bezug auf das Beste, was globales Design zu bieten hat, und schürt meine Leidenschaft für Design. Ich liebe die Untersuchung, den Austausch, die Vielfalt der Meinungen und die Herausforderung des gesamten Bewertungsprozesses.

01

Lam Leslie Lu
Hong Kong
Hongkong

Lam Leslie Lu received a Master of Architecture from Yale University in Connecticut, USA in 1977, and was the recipient of the Monbusho Scholarship of the Japanese Ministry of Culture in 1983, where he conducted research in design and urban theory in Tokyo. He is currently the principal of the Hong Kong Design Institute and academic director of the Hong Kong Institute of Vocational Education. Prior to this, he was head of the Department of Architecture at the University of Hong Kong. Lam Leslie Lu has worked with, among others, Cesar Pelli and Associates, Hardy Holzman Pfeiffer Associates, Kohn Pedersen Fox Associates and Shinohara Kazuo on the design of the Centennial Hall of the Tokyo Institute of Technology. Moreover, he was visiting professor at Yale University and the Delft University of Technology as well as assistant lecturer for the Eero Saarinen Chair at Yale University. He also lectured and served as design critic at major international universities such as Columbia, Cambridge, Delft, Princeton, Yale, Shenzhen, Tongji, Tsinghua and the Chinese University Hong Kong.

Lam Leslie Lu erwarb 1977 einen Master of Architecture an der Yale University in Connecticut, USA, und war 1983 Monbusho-Stipendiat des japanischen Kulturministeriums, an dem er die Forschung in Design und Stadttheorie in Tokio leitete. Derzeit ist er Direktor des Hong Kong Design Institute und akademischer Direktor des Hong Kong Institute of Vocational Education. Zuvor war er Leiter des Architektur-Instituts an der Universität Hongkong. Lam Leslie Lu hat u. a. mit Cesar Pelli and Associates, Hardy Holzman Pfeiffer Associates, Kohn Pedersen Fox Associates und Shinohara Kazuo am Design der Centennial Hall des Tokyo Institute of Technology zusammengearbeitet, war Gastprofessor an der Yale University und der Technischen Universität Delft sowie Assistenz-Dozent für den Eero-Saarinen-Lehrstuhl in Yale. Er hielt zudem Vorträge und war Designkritiker an großen internationalen Universitäten wie Columbia, Cambridge, Delft, Princeton, Yale, Shenzhen, Tongji, Tsinghua und der chinesischen Universität Hongkong.

"Designs can make or break a business. User experience and functionality are keys today."

„Design ist entscheidend für Erfolg oder Misserfolg eines Unternehmens. Die Benutzererfahrung und Funktionalität sind heutzutage ausschlaggebend."

In your opinion, what makes for good design?
Form and function is still where it all starts. There is also a need for clarity – in reason, purpose, form, intuitive aspects and for me in a certain cleverness.

How has the role played by design in our everyday lives changed?
We are spoiled by mobile devices and all those apps! We now expect designs to be multi-functional and multi-use. Formal beauty is not a priority in this cycle of design evolution and less important than convenience.

What attracts you to the role of Red Dot jury member?
The humbling experience and sensory assaults when confronted with so many ideas. The experience makes you work hard to improve – it is therapy and a critique of oneself.

Was macht Ihrer Ansicht nach gutes Design aus?
Form und Funktion ist immer noch, womit alles beginnt. Es gibt auch einen Bedarf an Klarheit – bezüglich des Anlasses, des Zwecks, der Form, der intuitiven Aspekte und für mich auch einer gewissen Intelligenz.

Inwieweit hat sich die Rolle, die Design in unserem täglichen Leben spielt, verändert?
Wir werden von mobilen Endgeräten und all diesen Apps verwöhnt! Und erwarten jetzt, dass Gestaltungen multifunktional und vielseitig einsetzbar sind. Formale Schönheit hat in dieser Phase der Designentwicklung keine Priorität mehr und ist weitaus weniger wichtig als Komfort.

Was reizt Sie an der Arbeit als Red Dot-Juror?
Es ist eine Erfahrung, die einen Bescheidenheit lehrt. Man wird außerdem mit so vielen Ideen konfrontiert, dass einen die vielen sinnlichen Eindrücke überfluten. Diese Erfahrung führt dazu, dass man hart daran arbeitet, sich zu verbessern. Die Arbeit als Red Dot-Juror ist zugleich Therapie und Selbstkritik.

01

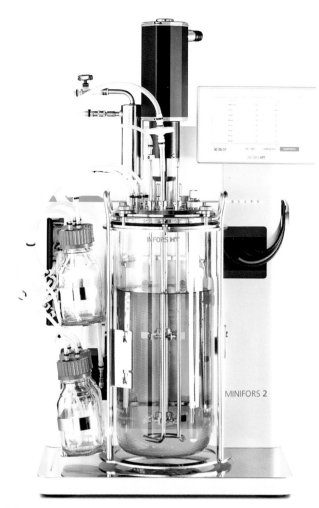

02

Wolfgang K. Meyer-Hayoz
Switzerland
Schweiz

Wolfgang K. Meyer-Hayoz studied mechanical engineering, visual communication and industrial design and graduated from the Stuttgart State Academy of Art and Design. The professors Klaus Lehmann, Kurt Weidemann and Max Bense had a formative influence on his design philosophy. In 1985, he founded the Meyer-Hayoz Design Engineering Group with offices in Winterthur, Switzerland and Constance, Germany. The design studio offers consultancy services for national as well as international companies in five areas of design competence: design strategy, industrial design, user-interface design, temporary architecture and communication design, and has received numerous international awards. From 1987 to 1993, Wolfgang K. Meyer-Hayoz was president of the Swiss Design Association (SDA). He is a member of the Association of German Industrial Designers (VDID), Swiss Marketing and the Swiss Management Society (SMG). Wolfgang K. Meyer-Hayoz also serves as juror on international design panels and supervises change management and turnaround projects in the field of design strategy.

Wolfgang K. Meyer-Hayoz absolvierte Studien in Maschinenbau, Visueller Kommunikation sowie Industrial Design mit Abschluss an der Staatlichen Akademie der Bildenden Künste in Stuttgart. Seine Gestaltungsphilosophie prägten die Professoren Klaus Lehmann, Kurt Weidemann und Max Bense. 1985 gründete er die Meyer-Hayoz Design Engineering Group mit Büros in Winterthur/Schweiz und Konstanz/Deutschland. Das Designstudio bietet Beratungsdienste für nationale wie internationale Unternehmen in den fünf Designkompetenzen Designstrategie, Industrial Design, User Interface Design, Temporäre Architektur und Kommunikationsdesign und wurde bereits vielfach ausgezeichnet. Von 1987 bis 1993 war Wolfgang K. Meyer-Hayoz Präsident der Swiss Design Association (SDA); er ist Mitglied im Verband Deutscher Industrie Designer (VDID), von Swiss Marketing und der Schweizerischen Management Gesellschaft (SMG). Wolfgang K. Meyer-Hayoz engagiert sich auch als Juror internationaler Designgremien und moderiert Change-Management- und Turnaround-Projekte im designstrategischen Bereich.

01–03 Minifors 2
Compact and easy-to-use biore-
actor for Infors AG, Switzerland –
the unique product design and
the layout of the device are optimally conceived for laboratory
work processes
Kompakter und einfach zu bedie-
nender Bioreaktor für Infors AG,
Schweiz – das einzigartige Produktdesign und das Gerätelayout
sind für die Arbeitsprozesse in
Laboratorien optimal ausgelegt

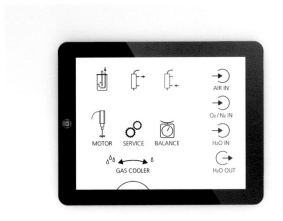

03

"Winning a Red Dot means: design quality of the highest order."

„Eine Auszeichnung mit dem
Red Dot bedeutet: Designqualität
auf höchstem Level."

How has the role played by design in our everyday lives changed?
Today, the desire for good design affects almost every aspect of life. What is different to the past is how design quality is defined by the DNA and positioning of a company.

What importance does design quality have for the economic success of companies?
My many years of experience in industry and in work-ing with small, mid-sized and large companies allow me to say that there is a proven link between pro-fessional design work and the resulting success of a company.

Which area of design do you feel has the greatest potential for development for the future?
The integration of design in companies (consulting), biotechnology and the upstream and downstream processes involved, as well as the demographic chal-lenges of the aging population in our part of the world.

Inwieweit hat sich die Rolle, die Design in unserem täglichen Leben spielt, verändert?
Der Wunsch nach guter Gestaltung hat heute praktisch alle Lebensbereiche erfasst. Was sich gegenüber früher jedoch manifestiert, ist die Definition der Designqualität über die DNA und Positionierung des Unternehmens.

Welche Bedeutung hat Designqualität für den wirtschaftlichen Erfolg von Unternehmen?
Aufgrund meiner langjährigen Erfahrung in der Indus-trie und der Zusammenarbeit mit kleinen, mittleren und großen Unternehmen kann ich sagen, dass die Kausa-lität von professioneller Designarbeit und hieraus resul-tierendem Unternehmenserfolg nachweisbar besteht.

In welchem Designbereich sehen Sie das größte Entwicklungspotenzial für die Zukunft?
In der Integration von Design in Unternehmen (Consulting), in der Biotechnologie und den hier vor- und nachgelagerten Prozessen sowie in den demografischen Herausforderungen der alternden Gesellschaft in unseren Breitengraden.

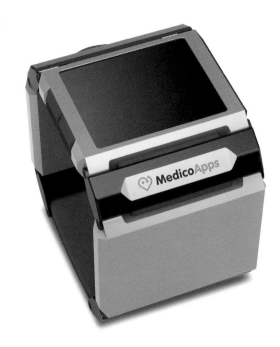

01

Prof. Jure Miklavc
Slovenia
Slowenien

Professor Jure Miklavc graduated in industrial design from the Academy of Fine Arts in Ljubljana, Slovenia and has nearly 20 years of experience in the field of design. Miklavc started his career working as a freelance designer, before founding his own design consultancy, Studio Miklavc. Studio Miklavc works in the fields of product design, visual communications and brand development and is a consultancy for a variety of clients from the industries of light design, electronic goods, user interfaces, transport design and medical equipment. Sports equipment designed by the studio has gained worldwide recognition. From 2013 onwards, the team has been working for the prestigious Italian motorbike manufacturer Bimota. Designs by Studio Miklavc have received many international awards and have been displayed in numerous exhibitions. Jure Miklavc has been involved in design education since 2005 and is currently a lecturer and head of industrial design at the Academy of Fine Arts and Design in Ljubljana.

Professor Jure Miklavc machte seinen Abschluss in Industrial Design an der Academy of Fine Arts and Design in Ljubljana, Slowenien, und verfügt über nahezu 20 Jahre Erfahrung im Designbereich. Er arbeitete zunächst als freiberuflicher Designer, bevor er sein eigenes Design-Beratungsunternehmen „Studio Miklavc" gründete. Studio Miklavc ist in den Bereichen Produktdesign, Visuelle Kommunikation und Markenentwicklung sowie in der Beratung zahlreicher Kunden der Branchen Lichtdesign, Elektronische Güter, Benutzeroberflächen, Transport-Design und Medizinisches Equipment tätig. Die von dem Studio gestalteten Sportausrüstungen erfahren weltweit Anerkennung. Seit 2013 arbeitet das Team für den angesehenen italienischen Motorradhersteller Bimota. Studio Miklavc erhielt bereits zahlreiche Auszeichnungen sowie Präsentationen in Ausstellungen. Seit 2005 ist Jure Miklavc in der Designlehre tätig und aktuell Dozent und Head of Industrial Design an der Academy of Fine Arts and Design in Ljubljana.

02

"Winning a Red Dot is primarily confirmation of an excellent quality from invaluable impartial evaluators."

„Die Auszeichnung mit dem Red Dot ist primär eine Bestätigung hochwertiger Qualität durch unbezahlbare objektive Gutachter."

In your opinion, what makes for good design?
Sometimes, the best design is of the kind that we don't even notice. It's quietly and perfectly doing its job in anonymity like a well-mannered butler. Good design also doesn't burden people and the environment.

How has the role played by design in our everyday lives changed?
I think we live in a more artificial environment than ever before in the history of humankind. Everything around us in the urban environments is designed. That is why the importance of good-quality design is even more relevant.

Which topics are most likely to influence design in the coming years?
The development of artificial intelligence, the Internet of Things and general automation will change the way we live in the future. But the most powerful change could be that design will be bolder in taking the initiative to be the crucial social and technological innovator in the society of the future.

Was macht Ihrer Ansicht nach gutes Design aus?
Manchmal ist das beste Design das, das wir nicht einmal bemerken. Es erfüllt seine Aufgabe tadellos und in stiller Anonymität, ganz wie ein wohlgesitteter Butler. Gutes Design belastet auch Mensch und Umwelt nicht.

Inwieweit hat sich die Rolle, die Design in unserem täglichen Leben spielt, verändert?
Meiner Meinung nach leben wir in einer künstlicheren Umgebung als je zuvor in der Geschichte der Menschheit. Alles, was uns in einem städtischen Umfeld umgibt, ist von Designern gestaltet. Deshalb ist qualitativ hochwertiges Design immer wichtiger.

Welche Themen werden das Design in den kommenden Jahren besonders beeinflussen?
Die Entwicklung von künstlicher Intelligenz, das Internet der Dinge und die allgemeine Automatisierung werden unsere Lebensweise in der Zukunft verändern. Aber die größte Veränderung mag dadurch verursacht werden, dass Design in Zukunft stärker die Initiative ergreift, zum entscheidenden sozialen und technologischen Innovator der künftigen Gesellschaft zu werden.

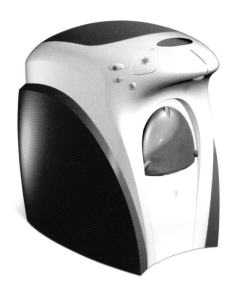

01

Prof. Ron A. Nabarro
Israel

Professor Ron A. Nabarro is an industrial designer, strategist, entrepreneur, researcher and educator. He has been a professional designer since 1970 and has designed more than 750 products to date in a wide range of industries. He has played a leading role in the emergence of age-friendly design and age-friendly design education. From 1992 to 2009, he was a professor of industrial design at the Technion Israel Institute of Technology, where he founded and was the head of the graduate programme in advanced design studies and design management. Currently, Nabarro teaches design management and design thinking at DeTao Masters Academy in Shanghai, China. From 1999 to 2003, he was an executive board member of the World Design Organization (formerly Icsid) and now acts as a regional advisor. He is a frequent keynote speaker at conferences, has presented TEDx events, has lectured and led design workshops in over 20 countries and consulted to a wide variety of organisations. Furthermore, he is co-founder and CEO of Senior-touch Ltd. and design4all. The principle areas of his research and interest are design thinking, age-friendly design and design management.

Professor Ron A. Nabarro ist Industriedesigner, Stratege, Unternehmer, Forscher und Lehrender. Seit 1970 ist er praktizierender Designer, gestaltete bisher mehr als 750 Produkte für ein breites Branchenspektrum und spielt eine führende Rolle im Bereich des altersfreundlichen Designs und dessen Lehre. Von 1992 bis 2009 war er Professor für Industriedesign am Technologie-Institut Technion Israel, an dem er das Graduiertenprogramm für fortgeschrittene Designstudien und Designmanagement einführte und leitete. Aktuell unterrichtet Nabarro Designmanagement und Design Thinking an der DeTao Masters Academy in Shanghai, China. Von 1999 bis 2003 war er Vorstandsmitglied der World Design Organization (ehemals Icsid), für die er aktuell als regionaler Berater tätig ist. Er ist ein gefragter Redner auf Konferenzen, hat bei TEDx-Veranstaltungen präsentiert, hielt Vorträge und Workshops in mehr als 20 Ländern und beriet eine Vielzahl von Organisationen. Zudem ist er Mitbegründer und Geschäftsführer von Senior-touch Ltd. und design4all. Die Hauptbereiche seiner Forschung und seines Interesses sind Design Thinking, altersfreundliches Design und Designmanagement.

02

"Design has become one of the
most important and crucial aspects
of commercial success."

„Design ist zu einem der wichtigsten
und wesentlichsten Aspekte des
wirtschaftlichen Erfolgs geworden."

In your opinion, what makes for good design?
Good design is a design that brings something important and valuable to our world. It's not just what looks good but what performs, converts, surprises, and is ethically and environmentally responsible. But first and foremost it must comply with a real need.

What attracts you to the role of Red Dot jury member?
As the winning products at the Red Dot Award set an example to the design world, the most exciting part of being a Red Dot juror is the fact that, as a juror, you can bring your values, your ethics, your experience and your knowledge to the adjudication process and, in doing so, influence the future of design.

Which country do you consider to be a pioneer in product design, and why?
As most of the production of consumer products has shifted to China, I believe that the natural next step would be for Chinese designers to be the pioneers and innovators of product design in the future.

Was macht Ihrer Ansicht nach gutes Design aus?
Gutes Design ist Design, das etwas Wichtiges und Wertvolles zu unserer Welt beiträgt. Es geht nicht nur darum, dass etwas gut aussieht, sondern dass es etwas leistet, verwandelt, dass es überrascht und ethisch und ökologisch verantwortungsvoll ist. In erster Linie muss es aber ein wirkliches Bedürfnis erfüllen.

Was reizt Sie an der Arbeit als Red Dot-Juror?
Da die Produkte, die im Red Dot Award ausgezeichnet werden, in der Designwelt eine Vorbildfunktion haben, ist der aufregendste Part der Jurorenarbeit die Tatsache, dass man als Juror seine eigenen Werte, seinen Ethos, seine Erfahrungen und sein Wissen in den Beurteilungsprozess einbringen und so die Zukunft von Design beeinflussen kann.

Welche Nation ist für Sie Vorreiter im Produktdesign und warum?
Da sich die Produktion der meisten Konsumgüter nach China verlagert hat, bin ich der Meinung, dass chinesische Designer als natürlicher nächster Schritt die Pioniere und Wegbereiter für das Produktdesign der Zukunft sein werden.

01

Prof. Dr. Ken Nah
Korea

Professor Dr Ken Nah graduated with a Bachelor of Science in industrial engineering from Hanyang University, South Korea, in 1983. He deepened his interest in human factors/ergonomics by earning a master's degree from Korea Advanced Institute for Science and Technology (KAIST) in 1985 and he gained a PhD from Tufts University in 1996. In addition, Ken Nah is also a USA Certified Professional Ergonomist (CPE). He is currently the dean of the International Design School for Advanced Studies (IDAS) and a professor of design management as well as director of the Human Experience and Emotion Research (HE.ER) Lab at IDAS, Hongik University, Seoul. Since 2002 he has been the director of the International Design Trend Center (IDTC). Ken Nah was the director general of "World Design Capital Seoul 2010". Alongside his work as a professor, he is also the president of the Korea Institute of Design Management (KIDM), vice president of the Korea Association of Industrial Designers (KAID) as well as the chairman of the Design and Brand Committee of the Korea Consulting Association (KCA).

Professor Dr. Ken Nah graduierte 1983 an der Hanyang University in Südkorea als Bachelor of Science in Industrial Engineering. Sein Interesse an Human Factors/Ergonomie vertiefte er 1985 mit einem Master-Abschluss am Korea Advanced Institute for Science and Technology (KAIST) und promovierte 1996 an der Tufts University. Darüber hinaus ist Ken Nah ein in den USA zertifizierter Ergonom (CPE). Derzeit ist er Dekan der International Design School for Advanced Studies (IDAS) und Professor für Design Management sowie Direktor des „Human Experience and Emotion Research (HE.ER)"-Labors an der IDAS, Hongik University, Seoul. Seit 2002 ist er zudem Leiter des International Design Trend Center (IDTC). Ken Nah war Generaldirektor der „World Design Capital Seoul 2010". Neben seiner Lehrtätigkeit ist er Präsident des Korea Institute of Design Management (KIDM), Vizepräsident der Korea Association of Industrial Designers (KAID) sowie Vorsitzender des „Design and Brand"-Komitees der Korea Consulting Association (KCA).

01 Design Ergonomics
Co-authored with
Prof. Dr Sungjoo Cho, 2017,
Culture Code
Verfasst zusammen mit
Prof. Dr. Sungjoo Cho, 2017,
Culture Code

02 Design Innovation Note
Co-authored with
Prof. Dr Hyunsun Kim and
Hyojin Kim, 2017, Culture Code
Verfasst zusammen mit
Prof. Dr. Hyunsun Kim und
Hyojin Kim, 2017, Culture Code

02

"Design is the most effective tool for innovation. Therefore, maintaining good design quality is a must for the economic success of a company."

„Design ist das effektivste Mittel für Innovation. Deshalb muss ein Unternehmen gute Designqualität gewährleisten können, um wirtschaftlichen Erfolg zu haben."

In your opinion, what makes for good design?
To me, good design is always the optimal balance between "it looks good" and "it works well."

What does winning the Red Dot say about a product?
It is a hallmark of good design given by international design experts. It is like an internationally recognised passport for the world of design excellence.

Which topics are most likely to influence design in the coming years?
Definitely drones and robots. In the forthcoming era of Industry 4.0, these areas will explode much faster than expected.

Which country do you consider to be a pioneer in product design, and why?
For me, the Scandinavian countries are pioneers in product design, since their living standard and the awareness of design quality that ordinary people have is the highest in the world.

Was macht Ihrer Ansicht nach gutes Design aus?
Für mich ist gutes Design immer das optimale Gleichgewicht zwischen „Es sieht gut aus" und „Es funktioniert gut".

Was sagt eine Auszeichnung mit dem Red Dot über das Produkt aus?
Es ist ein Gütezeichen für gutes Design, das von internationalen Designexperten verliehen wird. Der Red Dot ist wie ein international anerkannter Pass in der Welt des Qualitätsdesigns.

Welche Themen werden das Design in den kommenden Jahren besonders beeinflussen?
Auf jeden Fall Drohnen und Roboter. In der bevorstehenden Ära der Industrie 4.0 werden diese Bereiche viel schneller wachsen als erwartet.

Welche Nation ist für Sie Vorreiter im Produktdesign und warum?
Für mich sind die skandinavischen Länder Pioniere in der Produktgestaltung, da ihr Lebensstandard und Bewusstsein für Designqualität bei der allgemeinen Bevölkerung die höchsten weltweit sind.

01

Alexander Neumeister
Germany/Brazil
Deutschland/Brasilien

Alexander Neumeister is a high-tech industrial designer, who lives both in Germany and Brazil. A graduate of the Ulm School of Design and a one-year scholarship student at the Tokyo University of Arts, he specialised in the fields of medicine, professional electronics and transportation. Among some of his best-known works are the "Transrapid" maglev trains, the German ICE trains, the Japanese Shinkansen "Nozomi 500", as well as numerous regional trains and subways for Japan, China and Brazil, and the C1 and C2 trains for the Munich underground. Aside from working on projects for large German companies, he was design consultant for Hitachi/Japan for 21 years. From 1983 to 1987 he was board member and later vice-president of the World Design Organization (formerly Icsid). In 1992, Alexander Neumeister and his team received the honorary title "Red Dot: Design Team of the Year". In November 2011, he was awarded the design prize of the city of Munich and in January 2015, he won the EU's "European Railway Award" in recognition of his contribution to railway design.

Alexander Neumeister arbeitet als Hightech-Indus-triedesigner und ist in Deutschland wie in Brasilien zu Hause. Als Absolvent der Hochschule für Gestaltung in Ulm und Stipendiat der Tokyo University of Arts für ein Jahr spezialisierte er sich auf die Bereiche Medi-zin, Professionelle Elektronik und Verkehr. Die Magnet-schwebebahn „Transrapid", die deutschen ICE-Züge, der japanische Shinkansen „Nozomi 500", aber auch zahlreiche Regionalzüge und U-Bahnen in Japan, China und Brasilien sowie die U-Bahnen C1 und C2 für München zählen zu seinen bekanntesten Entwürfen. Neben Projekten für deutsche Großunternehmen war er 21 Jahre lang Designberater für Hitachi/Japan. Von 1983 bis 1987 war er Vorstandsmitglied und später Vizepräsident der World Design Organization (ehemals Icsid). 1992 wurden er und sein Team mit dem Ehren-titel „Red Dot: Design Team of the Year" ausgezeichnet. Im November 2011 erhielt er den Designpreis der Landeshauptstadt München und im Januar 2015 den „European Railway Award" der EU für seine Leistungen auf dem Gebiet des Railway-Designs.

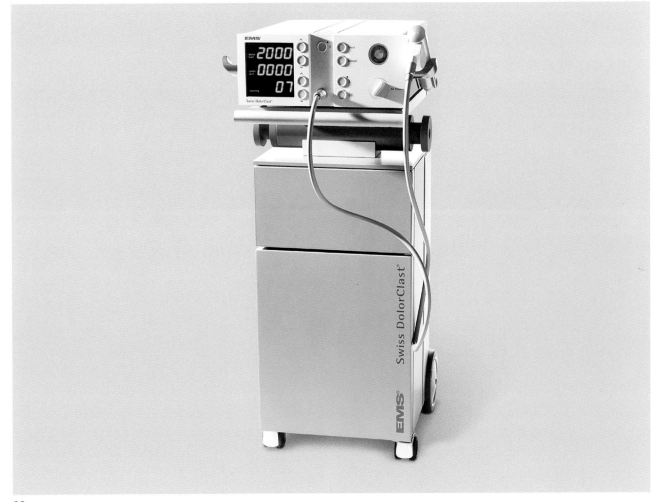

02

"In our affluent society, you will find countless alternatives for every product. Design awards help consumers to decide."

„In unserer Überflussgesellschaft gibt es für jedes Produkt unzählige Varianten. Hier helfen Designpreise dem Käufer bei der Entscheidung."

In your opinion, what makes for good design?
The successful combination of material and function. But also the avoidance of unnecessary decoration and the ability for a product to fit into different environments.

What attracts you to the role of Red Dot jury member?
The teamwork and the opportunity for exchange with the other jury members from all corners of the world.

What does winning the Red Dot say about a product?
The international composition of the jury shows that the award not only addresses regional preferences, but satisfies international standards as well.

Which area of design do you feel has the greatest potential for development for the future?
New technologies have always been my first choice as the basis for new products. This is why, in my opinion, the combination of 3D printing technologies with new energy-storage systems, linked to highly complex software has the greatest development potential.

Was macht Ihrer Ansicht nach gutes Design aus?
Die gelungene Kombination von Materialaufwand und Funktion. Aber auch der Verzicht auf unnötige Dekoration und die Fähigkeit, sich in Umgebungen einzuordnen.

Was reizt Sie an der Arbeit als Red Dot-Juror?
Die Arbeit im Team und die Möglichkeit, sich mit anderen Juroren aus unterschiedlichsten Ländern auszutauschen.

Was sagt eine Auszeichnung mit dem Red Dot über das Produkt aus?
Die international zusammengesetzte Jury belegt, dass die Auszeichnung nicht nur regionalen Präferenzen genügt, sondern internationales Niveau erfüllt.

In welchem Designbereich sehen Sie das größte Entwicklungspotenzial für die Zukunft?
Für mich standen immer neue Technologien als Basis für neue Produkte im Vordergrund. Daher hat die Kombination von 3D-Drucker-Technologien mit neuen Energiespeichern und deren Verknüpfungen durch hochkomplexe Software das optimale Entwicklungspotenzial für mich.

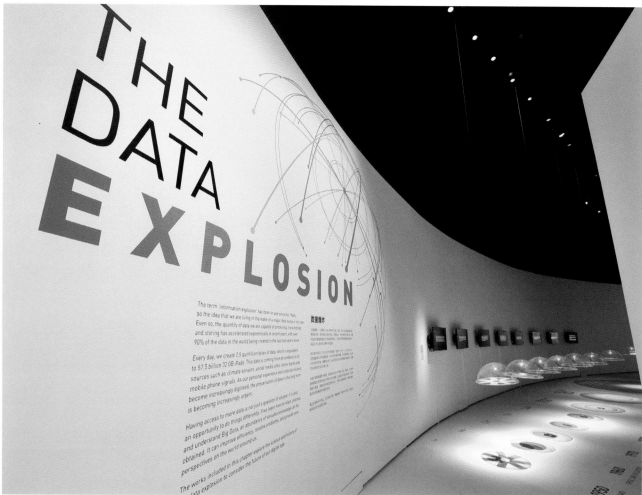

01

Simon Ong
Singapore
Singapur

Simon Ong, born in Singapore in 1953, graduated with a master's degree in design from the University of New South Wales and an MBA from the University of South Australia. He is the deputy chairman and co-founder of Kingsmen Creatives Ltd., a leading communication design and production group with 19 offices across the Asia-Pacific region and the Middle East. Kingsmen has won several awards, such as the President's Design Award, Singapore Good Design Mark, SRA Best Retail Concept Award, SFIA Hall of Fame, Promising Brand Award, A.R.E. Retail Design Award and RDI International Store Design Award USA. Simon Ong is actively involved in the creative industry as chairman of the design group of Manpower, the Skills & Training Council of Singapore Workforce Development Agency. Moreover, he is a member of the advisory board of the Singapore Furniture Industries Council, Design Business Chamber Singapore and Interior Design Confederation of Singapore. An ardent advocate of education, Simon Ong currently serves as a board director of Nanyang Academy of Fine Arts and a member of the advisory board to the School of Design & Environment at the National University of Singapore.

Simon Ong, geboren 1953 in Singapur, erhielt einen Master in Design der University of New South Wales und einen Master of Business Administration der University of South Australia. Er ist stellvertretender Vorsitzender und Mitbegründer von Kingsmen Creatives Ltd., eines führenden Unternehmens für Kommunikationsdesign und Produktion mit 19 Geschäftsstellen im asiatisch-pazifischen Raum sowie im Mittleren Osten. Kingsmen wurde vielfach ausgezeichnet, u. a. mit dem President's Design Award, Singapore Good Design Mark, SRA Best Retail Concept Award, SFIA Hall of Fame, Promising Brand Award, A.R.E. Retail Design Award und RDI International Store Design Award USA. Simon Ong ist als Vorsitzender der Designgruppe von Manpower, der „Skills & Training Council of Singapore Workforce Development Agency", aktiv in die Kreativindustrie involviert, ist unter anderem Mitglied des Beirats des Singapore Furniture Industries Council, der Design Business Chamber Singapore und der Interior Design Confederation of Singapore. Als leidenschaftlicher Befürworter von Bildung ist Simon Ong zurzeit als Vorstandsvorsitzender der Nanyang Academy of Fine Arts und als Mitglied des Beirats der School of Design & Environment an der National University of Singapore tätig.

02

"Sustainability is the key to designing for the future – especially in the areas of urban design and product design."

„Nachhaltigkeit ist der Schlüssel zur Gestaltung der Zukunft, insbesondere in den Bereichen Urban Design und Produktdesign."

In your opinion, what makes for good design?
Less is more and good design must have a purpose beyond its aesthetic value. Good design should enrich the everyday lives of end users.

How has the role played by design in our everyday lives changed?
Design permeates every aspect of our everyday lives, from urban design to product design for example. Design's role hasn't changed, but its prominence has.

Which topics are most likely to influence design in the coming years?
As the average human lifespan increases, product design will be geared towards developing solutions for aging populations. Artificial intelligence will also continue to gain momentum because the study of human behaviour is central to product design. Last but not least, sustainability will remain a priority.

Was macht Ihrer Ansicht nach gutes Design aus?
Weniger ist mehr. Gutes Design muss außerdem einen Zweck jenseits seines ästhetischen Werts erfüllen. Gutes Design sollte den Alltag des Nutzers bereichern.

Inwieweit hat sich die Rolle, die Design in unserem täglichen Leben spielt, verändert?
Design durchdringt jeden Aspekt unseres täglichen Lebens, z. B. von der Städteplanung bis zum Produktdesign. Die Rolle von Design hat sich nicht verändert, nur seine Bedeutung.

Welche Themen werden das Design in den kommenden Jahren besonders beeinflussen?
Mit dem Anstieg der durchschnittlichen menschlichen Lebensdauer wird das Produktdesign zunehmend auf die Entwicklung von Lösungen für eine alternde Bevölkerung ausgerichtet werden. Die Künstliche Intelligenz wird sich weiterhin verbreiten, weil die Untersuchung des menschlichen Verhaltens für die Produktgestaltung von zentraler Bedeutung ist. Nicht zuletzt bleibt auch die Nachhaltigkeit eine Priorität.

01

Prof. Martin Pärn
Estonia
Estland

Professor Martin Pärn, born in Tallinn in 1971, studied industrial design at the University of Industrial Arts Helsinki (UIAH). After working in the Finnish furniture industry he moved back to Estonia and undertook the role of the ambassadorial leader of design promotion and development in his native country. He was actively involved in the establishment of the Estonian Design Centre that he directed as chair of the board. Martin Pärn founded the multidisciplinary design office "iseasi", which creates designs ranging from office furniture to larger instruments and from interior designs for the public sector to design services. Having received many awards, Pärn began in 1995 with the development of design training in Estonia and is currently head of the Design and Engineering's master's programme, he established in 2010. The joint initiative of the Tallinn University of Technology and the Estonian Academy of Arts aims, among other things, to create synergies between engineers and designers.

Professor Martin Pärn, geboren 1971 in Tallinn, studierte Industriedesign an der University of Industrial Arts Helsinki (UIAH). Nachdem er in der finnischen Möbelindustrie gearbeitet hatte, ging er zurück nach Estland und übernahm die Funktion des leitenden Botschafters für die Designförderung und -entwicklung seiner Heimat. Er war aktiv am Aufbau des Estonian Design Centres beteiligt, das er als Vorstandsvorsitzender leitete. Martin Pärn gründete das multidisziplinäre Designbüro „iseasi", das Büromöbel, größere Instrumente oder Interior Designs für den öffentlichen Sektor gestaltet und Designservices anbietet. Vielfach ausgezeichnet, startete Pärn 1995 mit der Entwicklung der Designlehre in Estland und ist heute Leiter des Masterprogramms „Design und Engineering", das er 2010 aufgebaut hat. Es ist eine gemeinsame Initiative der Tallinn University of Technology und der Estonian Academy of Arts und verfolgt u. a. das Ziel, durch den Zusammenschluss Synergien von Ingenieuren und Designern zu erreichen.

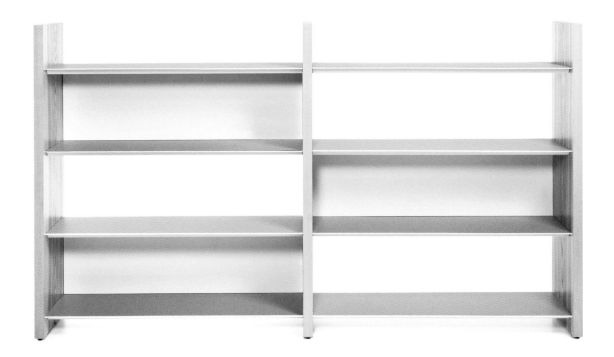

02

"I believe design at its best produces new meanings and creates promising situations that turn possible futures into pleasant everyday reality."

„Design kann im besten Falle neue Bedeutungen und verheißungsvolle Situationen schaffen, die mögliche Zukunftsszenarien zur angenehmen Realität werden lassen."

What importance does design quality have for the economic success of companies?
Design bundles the output and activities of companies together, makes these systems understandable as a whole, as well as usable and lovable. This love translates into economic success.

What attracts you to the role of Red Dot jury member?
Having been a member of the Red Dot jury for a few years in a row, gives me a fantastic archaeological overview of the changes in our everyday life. There are areas where new technologies are emerging, like robots and drones, or others where old technology is being replaced, like lighting. And, of course, sharing the judging work and experience with other judges is also a great part of being a Red Dot jury member.

Which topics are most likely to influence design in the coming years?
I believe the key role of design has always been to humanise technology. With the move towards artificial intelligence and the Internet of Things, the importance of good design will just grow.

Welche Bedeutung hat Designqualität für den wirtschaftlichen Erfolg von Unternehmen?
Design bündelt die Produktion und die Aktivitäten von Unternehmen, macht diese Systeme in ihrer Gesamtheit verständlich, verwendbar und liebenswert. Diese Liebe verwandelt sich in wirtschaftlichen Erfolg.

Was reizt Sie an der Arbeit als Red Dot-Juror?
Da ich seit einigen Jahren in Folge Mitglied der Red Dot-Jury bin, habe ich so einen phantastischen, archäologischen Überblick über die Veränderungen in unserem Alltag bekommen. Es gibt Bereiche, in denen neue Technologien entstehen, z. B. Roboter und Drohnen, oder in denen alte Technologie ersetzt wird, etwa bei der Beleuchtung. Doch auch das gemeinsame Beurteilen von Projekten und die Erfahrung mit anderen Juroren machen einen großen Teil des Reizes aus.

Welche Themen werden das Design in den kommenden Jahren besonders beeinflussen?
Ich glaube, die Schlüsselrolle des Designs war schon immer die Vermenschlichung der Technologie. Und mit dem Übergang zur künstlichen Intelligenz und dem Internet der Dinge wird gutes Design nur an Bedeutung gewinnen.

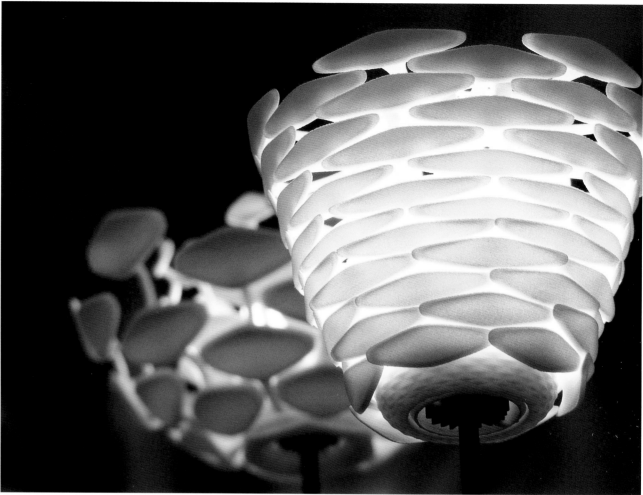

01

Dr Sascha Peters
Germany
Deutschland

Dr Sascha Peters is founder and owner of the agency for material and technology HAUTE INNOVATION in Berlin. He studied mechanical engineering at the RWTH Aachen University, Germany, and product design at the ABK Maastricht, Netherlands. He wrote his doctoral thesis at the University of Duisburg-Essen, Germany, on the complex of problems in communication between engineering and design. From 1997 to 2003, he led research projects and product developments at the Fraunhofer Institute for Production Technology IPT in Aachen and subsequently became deputy head of the Design Zentrum Bremen until 2008. Sascha Peters is author of various specialist books on sustainable raw materials, smart materials, innovative production techniques and energetic technologies. He is a leading material expert and trend scout for new technologies. Since 2014, he has been an advisory board member of the funding initiative "Zwanzig20 – Partnerschaft für Innovation" (2020 – Partnership for innovation) commissioned by the German Federal Ministry of Education and Research.

Dr. Sascha Peters ist Gründer und Inhaber der Material- und Technologieagentur HAUTE INNOVATION in Berlin. Er studierte Maschinenbau an der RWTH Aachen und Produktdesign an der ABK Maastricht. Seine Doktorarbeit schrieb er an der Universität Duisburg-Essen über die Kommunikationsproblematik zwischen Engineering und Design. Von 1997 bis 2003 leitete er Forschungsprojekte und Produktentwicklungen am Fraunhofer-Institut für Produktionstechnologie IPT in Aachen und war anschließend bis 2008 stellvertretender Leiter des Design Zentrums Bremen. Sascha Peters ist Autor zahlreicher Fachbücher zu nachhaltigen Werkstoffen, smarten Materialien, innovativen Fertigungsverfahren und energetischen Technologien und zählt zu den führenden Materialexperten und Trendscouts für neue Technologien. Seit 2014 ist er Mitglied im Beirat der Förderinitiative „Zwanzig20 – Partnerschaft für Innovation" im Auftrag des Bundesministeriums für Bildung und Forschung.

02

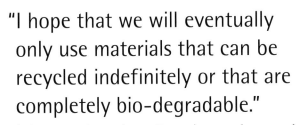

"I hope that we will eventually
only use materials that can be
recycled indefinitely or that are
completely bio-degradable."

„Ich würde mir wünschen, dass wir
nur noch Materialien verwenden,
die unendlich oft recycelt werden
können oder sich in der Natur
vollständig biologisch abbauen."

What developments do you regard as particularly positive in the area of materials?
Those material developments that attempt to imitate or copy organic and natural processes. That can only be to our benefit.

What factors should designers and manufacturers consider when selecting materials?
Aside from sustainability, it would be wonderful if we could manage to make materials work in a completely closed system, thereby avoiding the creation of waste products.

What developments do you hope for in the future of materials?
The ability to integrate functions in materials by selecting the right raw materials and combining them cleverly. The use of "smart materials" would allow us to minimise the effort needed to create certain functions. Imagine if a material could take over the role of an electric motor and produce simple movements in a product.

Welche Entwicklungen im Bereich der Materialien nehmen Sie als besonders positiv wahr?
Solche Materialentwicklungen, mit denen versucht wird, organische Vorgänge und Prozesse aus der Natur nachzuahmen bzw. zu kopieren. Davon können wir nur profitieren.

Welche Faktoren sollten Designer und Hersteller bei der Wahl ihrer Materialien beachten?
Neben der Nachhaltigkeit wäre es ganz wunderbar, wenn wir es schaffen würden, Materialien vollständig in geschlossenen Kreisläufen zirkulieren zu lassen, sodass Abfälle gar nicht erst entstehen können.

Welche Entwicklungen in der Material-Branche würden Sie sich für die Zukunft wünschen?
Dass wir es durch die verwendeten Werkstoffe und deren Kombination schaffen, Funktionen in Material zu integrieren. Denn bei der Verwendung von Smart Materials würde sich der Aufwand zur Funktionsrealisierung auf ein Minimum reduzieren. Man stelle sich nur vor, ein Material könnte die Aufgabe eines Elektromotors übernehmen und leichte Bewegungsverläufe in einem Produkt realisieren.

01

Dirk Schumann
Germany
Deutschland

Dirk Schumann, born in 1960 in Soest, studied product design at Münster University of Applied Sciences. After graduating in 1987, he joined oco-design as an industrial designer, moved to siegerdesign in 1989, and was a lecturer in product design at Münster University of Applied Sciences until 1991. In 1992, he founded his own design studio Schumanndesign in Münster, developing design concepts for companies in Germany, Italy, India, Thailand and China. For several years now, he has focused on conceptual architecture, created visionary living spaces and held lectures at international conferences. Dirk Schumann has taken part in exhibitions both in Germany and abroad with works that have garnered several awards, including the Gold Prize (Minister of Economy, Trade and Industry Prize) in the International Design Competition, Osaka; the Comfort & Design Award, Milan; the iF product design award, Hanover; the Red Dot Design Award, Essen; the Focus in Gold, Stuttgart; as well as the Good Design Award, Chicago and Tokyo. In 2015 he founded Schumann&Wang in Xiamen City, the Chinese subsidiary of Schumanndesign.

Dirk Schumann, 1960 in Soest geboren, studierte Produktdesign an der Fachhochschule Münster. Nach seinem Abschluss 1987 arbeitete er als Industriedesigner für oco-design, wechselte 1989 zu siegerdesign und war bis 1991 an der Fachhochschule Münster als Lehrbeauftragter für Produktdesign tätig. 1992 eröffnete er in Münster sein eigenes Designstudio Schumanndesign, das Designkonzepte für Unternehmen in Deutschland, Italien, Indien, Thailand und China entwickelt. Seit einigen Jahren beschäftigt er sich mit konzeptioneller Architektur, entwirft visionäre Lebensräume und hält Vorträge auf internationalen Kongressen. Dirk Schumann nimmt an Ausstellungen im In- und Ausland teil und wurde für seine Arbeiten mehrfach ausgezeichnet, u. a. mit dem Gold Prize (Minister of Economy, Trade and Industry Prize) des International Design Competition, Osaka, dem Comfort & Design Award, Mailand, dem iF product design award, Hannover, dem Red Dot Design Award, Essen, dem Focus in Gold, Stuttgart, sowie dem Good Design Award, Chicago und Tokio. 2015 gründete er mit Schumann&Wang in Xiamen City die chinesische Dependance von Schumanndesign.

01 DHE-4
Instantaneous water heater for
STIEBEL ELTRON, Germany
Durchlauferhitzer für STIEBEL
ELTRON, Deutschland

02 Victrix TT
Gas-fired boiler for
IMMERGAS, Italy
Gaswärmeerzeuger für
IMMERGAS, Italien

02

"The Red Dot conveys that a product demonstrates outstanding quality of form and function, as well as a sensible use of resources."

„Der Red Dot sagt über ein Produkt aus, dass es eine exzellente Qualität in Form und Funktion sowie einen überlegten sinnvollen Umgang mit Ressourcen aufweist."

In your opinion, what makes for good design?
Spontaneous belief in a product. An aura of quality and substance. The desire to spend time on the product.

What importance does design quality have for the economic success of companies?
Design quality is a cultural statement about the responsibility companies have – towards the users of their products. Those who assume this responsibility will be successful.

Which area of design do you feel has the greatest potential for development for the future?
Communication and networking, as these areas connect people of all age groups, cultural and social background. We therefore need to find a way of making products understandable.

Which country to you consider to be a pioneer in product design, and why?
The Asia-Pacific region, because of its openness to new concepts, ideas and because of the courage companies have to implement them in a systematic way.

Was macht Ihrer Ansicht nach gutes Design aus?
Spontanes Vertrauen in das Produkt. Ausstrahlung von Qualität und Tiefgründigkeit. Der Wunsch, sich mit dem Produkt zu befassen.

Welche Bedeutung hat Designqualität für den wirtschaftlichen Erfolg von Unternehmen?
Designqualität ist ein kulturelles Statement der Verantwortlichkeit von Unternehmen – gegenüber den Nutzern ihrer Produkte. Unternehmen, die diese Verantwortung tragen, werden damit erfolgreich sein.

In welchem Designbereich sehen Sie das größte Entwicklungspotenzial für die Zukunft?
Kommunikation und Vernetzung, da in diesen Bereichen Menschen aller Altersstufen, kultureller und sozialer Herkunft verbunden sind und hier eine übergreifende Plattform der Verständlichkeit der Produkte gefunden werden muss.

Welche Nation ist für Sie Vorreiter im Produktdesign und warum?
Der Großraum Asien, durch die offene Haltung gegenüber neuen Konzepten, Ideen und dem Mut der Unternehmen, diese gezielt umzusetzen.

01

Prof. Song Kee Hong
Singapore
Singapur

Professor Song Kee Hong is a deputy head at the Industrial Design Division, National University of Singapore. He is also the design director at cross-disciplinary consultancy Design Exchange and has more than two decades of design experience, including work at global innovation consultancy Ziba in the US and at HP. He has worked with notable brands across diverse industries including Apple, Dell, Epson, HP, Intel, Lenovo, P&G, Philips, Sanyo, Sennheiser, and WelchAllyn. His portfolio lists over twenty international design awards. Until recent Song Kee Hong was executive committee member of the Design Business Chamber Singapore and served on the advisory committees of the National University of Singapore's School of Design and Environment, and of the Singapore government's Ministry of Education's Design and Technology programme. He was furthermore a member of the advisory board for Singapore Polytechnic's School of Mechanical and Manufacturing Engineering and the Singapore Design Council.

Professor Song Kee Hong ist ein stellvertretender Leiter der Industrial Design Division an der National University of Singapore. Er ist ebenfalls Designdirektor der inter-disziplinären Unternehmensberatung Design Exchange und verfügt über mehr als zwei Jahrzehnte Design-erfahrung, u. a. durch Tätigkeiten bei der globalen Inno-vations-Unternehmensberatung Ziba in den USA und bei HP. Er arbeitete bereits mit namhaften Marken unter-schiedlicher Branchen zusammen, u. a. Apple, Dell, Epson, HP, Intel, Lenovo, P&G, Philips, Sanyo, Sennheiser und WelchAllyn. Sein Portfolio verzeichnet mehr als 20 internationale Designauszeichnungen. Bis vor Kurzem war Song Kee Hong Vorstandsmitglied der Design Busi-ness Chamber Singapore und in den Fachbeiräten der Fakultät „Design und Umwelt" an der Nationaluniversität Singapur sowie des Design- und Technologieprogramms des Bildungsministeriums aktiv. Zudem saß er im Beirat der Fachhochschule für Maschinenbau und Fertigungs-technik in Singapur sowie des landeseigenen Singapore Design Councils.

01 MX W1
Wireless earphone for Sennheiser
Drahtloser Kopfhörer für Sennheiser

02 ConnectedHealth remote
Health monitoring app
App zur Fernüberwachung
des Gesundheitszustands

02

"The role of design in our everyday lives has changed insofar as it is increasingly growing beyond aesthetics and styling."

„Die Rolle von Design hat sich insofern verändert, als es zunehmend über Ästhetik und Styling hinauswächst."

How has the role played by design in our everyday lives changed?
Design is increasingly growing beyond aesthetics and styling. I think the increasing frequency of market disruptions has created more opportunities for the design industry. These days, many designers are working on ways to improve user experience and simplify the interface between people and technology, businesses and even government policies.

What importance does design quality have for the economic success of companies?
Today, almost any company can have access to the same technology and manufacturing capability. This has lowered entry barriers and saturated markets with commodity products; thus making design quality a critical differentiator against the competition.

What attracts you to the role of Red Dot jury member?
I get to see the latest and the best products from around the world and have the rare opportunity to discuss issues on the design industry with some of the world's best design talents.

Inwieweit hat sich die Rolle, die Design in unserem täglichen Leben spielt, verändert?
Design wächst zunehmend über Ästhetik und Styling hinaus. Die immer häufigeren Marktstörungen haben zu mehr Chancen für die Designbranche geführt. Heutzutage arbeiten viele Designer daran, Nutzererfahrungen zu verbessern und die Schnittstellen zwischen Mensch und Technik, Unternehmen und sogar der Regierungspolitik einfacher zu gestalten.

Welche Bedeutung hat Designqualität für den wirtschaftlichen Erfolg von Unternehmen?
Heute kann fast jedes Unternehmen Zugang zu den gleichen Technologien und Fertigungskapazitäten haben. Das hat zu niedrigeren Eintrittsbarrieren und der Überflutung von Märkten mit Rohstoffprodukten geführt. Die Designqualität ist daher zu einem wesentlichen Unterscheidungsmerkmal gegenüber der Konkurrenz geworden.

Was reizt Sie an der Arbeit als Red Dot-Juror?
Ich habe die Chance, die neuesten und besten Produkte aus aller Welt zu sehen, und die äußerst seltene Gelegenheit, mit den weltbesten Designtalenten Themen der Designbranche zu besprechen.

01

Aleks Tatic
Germany/Italy
Deutschland/Italien

Aleks Tatic, born 1969 in Cologne, Germany, is product designer and founder of Tatic Designstudio in Milan, Italy. After his studies at the Art Center College of Design in the USA and Switzerland, he specialised in the areas of sports and lifestyle products in various international agencies in London and Milan. Afterwards, he guided the multiple award-winning Italian design studio Attivo Creative Resource to international success, leading the agency for 12 years. Together with his multicultural team of designers and product specialists, he today designs and develops – amongst others – sailing yachts, sporting goods, power tools, FMCGs and consumer electronics for European and Asian premium brands. Aleks Tatic lectures on practice-oriented industrial design and innovation management at various European universities and seminars.

Aleks Tatic, geboren 1969 in Köln, ist Produktdesigner und Gründer der Agentur Tatic Designstudio in Mailand. Nach seinem Studium am Art Center College of Design in den USA und der Schweiz hat er sich zunächst in verschiedenen internationalen Büros in London und Mailand auf das Gebiet der Sport- und Lifestyleprodukte spezialisiert. Danach führte er zwölf Jahre lang das mehrfach ausgezeichnete italienische Designbüro Attivo Creative Resource zu internationalem Erfolg. Heute gestaltet und entwickelt er mit seinem multikulturellen Team von Designern und Produktspezialisten u. a. Segeljachten, Sportgeräte, Elektrowerkzeuge, FMCGs und Unterhaltungselektronik für europäische und asiatische Premiummarken. Aleks Tatic unterrichtet an verschiedenen europäischen Hochschulen und Seminaren praxisorientiertes Industriedesign und Innovationsmanagement.

01 Bosch AQT33-11
High Pressure Washer, 2015
Hochdruckreiniger, 2015

02 Gardena
Nozzle and Sprayer Range, 2002
Spritzen- und Brausensortiment, 2002

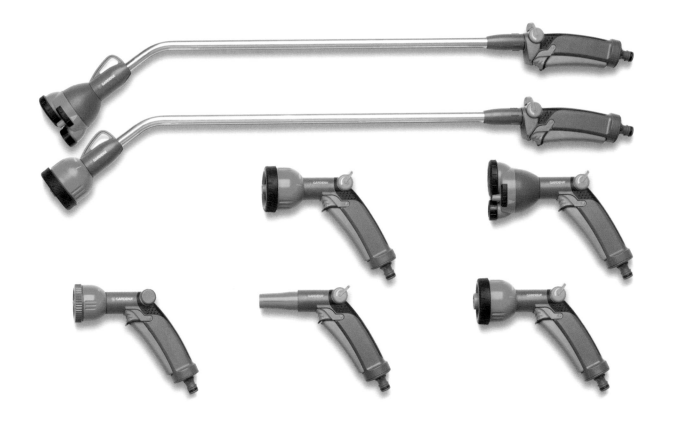

02

"Despite all the design trends, the 'Ten Principles for Good Design' by Dieter Rams have not aged at all in the last forty years."

„Trotz aller Designtrends sind die ‚Zehn Thesen für gutes Design' von Dieter Rams in den letzten vierzig Jahren kein bisschen gealtert."

How has the role played by design in our everyday lives changed?

At university, we were taught that product design would have the task to improve people's lives and work. The economic success of a company would emerge as a by-product. In the meantime, a role reversal has taken place: today, designers primarily design for the economic success of products and companies. And sometimes, a product comes out that, on the side, also improves our lives. I do not view this negatively: as companies have recognised the competitive element of design, more of design is being produced, and on all levels. Today, we are surrounded by more design, thus better products than in the past.

What does winning the Red Dot say about a product?

That the companies and the designers involved have focused on the use, handling and aesthetics of a product in an outstanding way.

Inwieweit hat sich die Rolle, die Design in unserem täglichen Leben spielt, verändert?

Im Studium wurde uns beigebracht, dass Produktdesign die Aufgabe hätte, das Leben und Arbeiten der Menschen zu verbessern, und quasi als Nebenprodukt würde der wirtschaftliche Erfolg eines Unternehmens entstehen. Inzwischen hat ein Rollentausch stattgefunden: Designer gestalten heute in erster Linie für den wirtschaftlichen Erfolg von Produkten und Unternehmen. Und manchmal kommt dabei, nebenher, ein Produkt heraus, das unser Leben verbessert. Ich sehe das nicht negativ: Dadurch, dass Unternehmen den Wettbewerbsfaktor Design erkannt haben, wird viel mehr und überall Design betrieben. Wir werden heute von mehr Design, also von besseren Produkten umgeben als früher.

Was sagt eine Auszeichnung mit dem Red Dot über das Produkt aus?

Dass sich Unternehmen und Designer ausgezeichnet mit dem Nutzen, der Handhabung und der Ästhetik eines Produktes beschäftigt haben.

01

02

Nils Toft
Denmark
Dänemark

Nils Toft, born in Copenhagen in 1957, graduated as an architect and designer from the Royal Danish Academy of Fine Arts in Copenhagen in 1986. He also holds a master's degree in Industrial Design and Business Development. Starting his career as an industrial designer, Nils Toft joined the former Christian Bjørn Design in 1987, an internationally active design studio in Copenhagen with branches in Beijing and Ho Chi Minh City. Within a few years, he became a partner of CBD and, as managing director, ran the business. Today, Nils Toft is the founder and managing director of Designidea. With offices in Copenhagen and Beijing, Designidea works in the following key fields: communication, consumer electronics, medicine, and graphic arts, as well as projects in business development, design strategy, graphic and exhibition design.

Nils Toft, 1957 in Kopenhagen geboren, machte seinen Abschluss als Architekt und Designer 1986 an der Royal Danish Academy of Fine Arts in Kopenhagen. Er verfügt zudem über einen Master im Bereich Industrial Design und Business Development. Zu Beginn seiner Karriere als Industriedesigner trat Nils Toft 1987 bei dem damaligen Christian Bjørn Design ein, einem international operierenden Designstudio in Kopenhagen, das mit Niederlassungen in Beijing und Ho-Chi-Minh-Stadt vertreten ist. Innerhalb weniger Jahre wurde er Partner bei CBD und leitete das Unternehmen als Managing Director. Heute ist Nils Toft Gründer und Managing Director von Designidea. Mit Büros in Kopenhagen und Beijing operiert Designidea in verschiedenen Hauptbereichen: Kommunikation, Unterhaltungselektronik, Medizin und Grafikdesign sowie Projekte in den Bereichen Geschäftsentwicklung, Designstrategie, Grafik und Ausstellungsdesign.

01–04
Four generations of
Wittenborg coffee machines
Vier Generationen der
Wittenborg Kaffeemaschinen

03

04

"As a designer, I love design.
Working as a Red Dot juror means
being in design heaven."

„Als Designer liebe ich Design.
Deshalb befinde ich mich durch die
Arbeit als Red Dot-Juror im siebten
Designhimmel."

In your opinion, what makes for good design?
Design is good when it tells a story that speaks to our
emotions and opens our eyes to new possibilities and
experiences.

**How has the role played by design in our everyday
lives changed?**
Today, design is no longer an exclusive experience, but
it affects all aspects of our lives. Design today can
be a personal statement, a new experience, and it may
define how you want to live your life.

**Which topics are most likely to influence design in
the coming years?**
A 360 degree range of influential topics would include
authenticity, transparency, artificial intelligence,
industry 4.0, environment and diversity.

**Which area of design do you feel has the greatest
potential for development for the future?**
In the near future, more and more products will be
autonomous and will work with artificial intelligence.
We will live alongside them and how we design them
can make a big difference.

Was macht Ihrer Ansicht nach gutes Design aus?
Design ist gut, wenn es eine Geschichte erzählt, die
uns emotional anspricht und unsere Augen für neue
Möglichkeiten und Erfahrungen öffnet.

**Inwieweit hat sich die Rolle, die Design in unserem
täglichen Leben spielt, verändert?**
Heute ist Design nicht mehr ein exklusives Erlebnis,
sondern wirkt sich auf alle Aspekte unseres Lebens aus.
Design kann heute ein persönliches Statement, eine
neue Erfahrung sein und es kann bestimmen, wie man
sein Leben leben will.

**Welche Themen werden das Design in den
kommenden Jahren besonders beeinflussen?**
Ein 360-Grad-Überblick über einflussreiche Themen
würde Authentizität, Transparenz, künstliche Intelligenz, Industrie 4.0, Umwelt und Vielfalt einschließen.

**In welchem Designbereich sehen Sie das größte
Entwicklungspotenzial für die Zukunft?**
In nächster Zukunft werden immer mehr Produkte au-
tonom und mit künstlicher Intelligenz ausgestattet sein.
Wir werden direkt neben ihnen leben und es wird einen
großen Unterschied machen, wie wir sie gestalten.

01

Cheng Chung Yao
Taiwan

Cheng Chung Yao studied at the Pratt Institute New York and graduated with a master's degree in architecture. In 1991, he founded the Department of Interior Space Design at Shih Chien University and has worked as a lecturer at the Graduate School of Architecture at Tam Kang University as well as at the Graduate School of Architecture at Chiao Tung University. In 1999, he founded "t1 design" where he heads a team of architects and interior designers as well as exhibition and graphic designers. The company's best-known products include the City Plaza of Taiwan Pavilion of the 2010 Shanghai Expo, the Taiwan Design Museum and the Taiwan Design Center. Furthermore, Cheng Chung Yao curated and designed the International Interior Design Exhibition for the Expo, was president of the Chinese Society of Interior Designers, chief executive of the Asia Pacific Space Designers Association, board member of the International Federation of Interior Architects / Designers and founder of the Taiwan Interior Design Award.

Cheng Chung Yao studierte Architektur am Pratt Institute New York und schloss sein Studium mit dem Master ab. 1991 gründete er die Fakultät für Interior Space Design an der Shih Chien University und war als Dozent an der Graduate School of Architecture der Tam Kang University sowie an der Graduate School of Architecture der Chiao Tung University tätig. 1999 gründete er „t1 design" und leitet dort ein Team aus Architekten, Innenarchitekten sowie Ausstellungs- und Grafikdesignern. Zu den bekanntesten Projekten des Büros zählen der City Plaza of Taiwan Pavilion der Expo 2010 in Shanghai, das Taiwan Design Museum und das Taiwan Design Center. Zudem kuratierte und gestaltete Cheng Chung Yao die International Interior Design Exhibition für die Expo, war u. a. Präsident der Chinese Society of Interior Designers, Hauptgeschäfts- führer der Asia Pacific Space Designers Association und Vorstandsmitglied der International Federation of Interior Architects / Designers und gründete den Taiwan Interior Design Award.

01|02 ArtBox museum
01|02 ArtBox museum
The ArtBox museum in Taipei is a building for art exhibitions and the collection of a private foundation. It is located on the banks of the Tamsui river, between two high-rise apartment buildings. It has a steel structure with a full, matt glass facade and is illuminated at night time.

Das Museum ArtBox in Taipeh ist ein Gebäude für Kunstausstellungen und für die Sammlung einer privaten Stiftung. Es liegt am Ufer des Flusses Tamsui, zwischen zwei Hochhäusern. Es hat eine Stahlstruktur mit einer vollen, mattierten Glasfassade und wird nachts beleuchtet.

02

"The different disciplines of product design are converging and will, in future, cross traditional professional boundaries."

„Die verschiedenen Disziplinen des Produktdesigns verschmelzen miteinander und werden in Zukunft traditionelle berufliche Grenzen überschreiten."

In your opinion, what makes for good design?
Good design is not just a good answer to meeting certain needs of our times; good design is also an expression of the vision of creating a better way to live our lives.

What importance does design quality have for the economic success of companies?
The design quality of a product leads to business success and improves the image of companies. With their successful products, they become icons of their industry.

What attracts you to the role of Red Dot jury member?
The Red Dot selection process presents a comprehensive expression of the global review of the design industry's creativity. It documents contemporary design history, aesthetics and philosophy in a great way.

What does winning the Red Dot say about a product?
The Red Dot award signals advanced design quality. It gives a product a worldwide image of distinction.

Was macht Ihrer Ansicht nach gutes Design aus?
Gutes Design ist nicht nur eine gute Antwort auf bestimmte Bedürfnisse unserer Zeit. Gutes Design ist auch ein Ausdruck der Vision, einen besseren Weg zu finden, unser Leben zu leben.

Welche Bedeutung hat Designqualität für den wirtschaftlichen Erfolg von Unternehmen?
Die Designqualität eines Produkts führt zu geschäftlichem Erfolg und verbessert das Image eines Unternehmens. Mit seinen erfolgreichen Produkten wird es dadurch zu einem Kultobjekt in seiner Branche.

Was reizt Sie an der Arbeit als Red Dot-Juror?
Der Red Dot-Auswahlprozess ist der allgemeine Ausdruck des globalen Urteils über die Kreativität der Designbranche. Es ist ein großartiges Dokument der zeitgenössischen Designgeschichte, Ästhetik und Philosophie.

Was sagt eine Auszeichnung mit dem Red Dot über das Produkt aus?
Der Red Dot signalisiert fortschrittliche Designqualität. Er verleiht einem Produkt weltweit ein erstklassiges Image.

Alphabetical index manufacturers and distributors
Alphabetisches Hersteller- und Vertriebs-Register

Alphabetical index designers
Alphabetisches Designer-Register

Alphabetical index designers
Alphabetisches Designer-Register

reddot edition

Editor | Herausgeber
Peter Zec

Project management | Projektleitung
Sophie Angerer

Project assistance | Projektassistenz
Maren Boots
Marie Eigner
Theresa Falkenberg
Judith Lindner
Samuel Madilonga
Vivien Mroß
Louisa Mücher
Jonas Römmer
Julia Sagner

Editorial work | Redaktion
Bettina Derksen, Simmern, Germany
Eva Hembach, Vienna, Austria
Burkhard Jacob, Essen, Germany
Karin Kirch, Essen, Germany
Karoline Laarmann, Dortmund, Germany
Bettina Laustroer, Wuppertal, Germany
Kirsten Müller, Mülheim an der Ruhr, Germany
Astrid Ruta, Essen, Germany
Martina Stein, Otterberg, Germany
Corinna Ten-Cate, Wetter, Germany

Proofreading | Lektorat
Klaus Dimmler (supervision), Essen, Germany
Mareike Ahlborn, Essen, Germany
Jörg Arnke, Essen, Germany
Wolfgang Astelbauer, Vienna, Austria
Sabine Beeres, Leverkusen, Germany
Dawn Michelle d'Atri, Kirchhundem, Germany
Annette Gillich-Beltz, Essen, Germany
Eva Hembach, Vienna, Austria
Karin Kirch, Essen, Germany
Norbert Knyhala, Castrop-Rauxel, Germany
Laura Lothian, Vienna, Austria
Regina Schier, Essen, Germany
Anja Schrade, Stuttgart, Germany

Translation | Übersetzung
Heike Bors-Eberlein, Viersen, Germany
Patrick Conroy, Lanarca, Cyprus
Stanislaw Eberlein, Viersen, Germany
William Kings, Wuppertal, Germany
Tara Russell, Dublin, Ireland
Jan Stachel-Williamson, Christchurch, New Zealand
Philippa Watts, Exeter, Great Britain
Andreas Zantop, Berlin, Germany
Christiane Zschunke, Frankfurt am Main, Germany

Layout | Gestaltung
Lockstoff Design GmbH, Grevenbroich, Germany
Judith Baumann
Susanne Coenen
Katja Kleefeld
Stephanie Marniok
Iris Mecklenburg
Lena Overkamp
Saskia Rühmkorf
Nicole Slink

Photographs | Fotos
Stefano Campo Antico (BLOCK, juror Masayo Ave)
Dragan Arrigler (Relaxroll, juror Jure Miklavc)
EcoDesign Circle (EcoDesign Circle, juror Robin Edman)
Eyelike.org – Pieter Bas Doornebal
(product photo SoilCares, Netherlands; Book Working)
Kaido Haagen (Nove / Kord, juror Martin Pärn)
Alex Muchnik (portrait juror Sascha Peters)
Chih Jung Tsai (ArtBox museum, juror Cheng Chung Yao)
Wagner Ziegelmeyer (Serelepe chair, juror Indio da Costa)
Thomas Zipf (product photo biobrush GmbH, Germany;
Book Enjoying)

Page | Seite
440 Enjoying
364 Doing
442 Working
530 Living

Name
Tokyo_Institute_of_Technology_Centennial_Hall_2009
Copyright | Urheber
Wiiii
Source | Quelle
http://commons.wikimedia.org/wiki/File:Tokyo_Institute_
of_Technology_Centennial_Hall_2009.jpg

Jury photographs | Jurorenfotos
Simon Bierwald, Dortmund, Germany
Alex Muchnik, Essen, Germany

In-company photos | Werkfotos der Firmen

Production | Produktion
gelb+, Düsseldorf, Germany
Bernd Reinkens

Lithography | Lithografie
tarcom GmbH, Gelsenkirchen, Germany
Gregor Baals
Jonas Mühlenweg
Bernd Reinkens (supervision)
Gundula Seraphin

Printing | Druck
Dr. Cantz'sche Druckerei Medien GmbH,
Ostfildern, Germany

Bookbindery | Buchbinderei
CPI Moravia Books s.r.o., Pohořelice, Czechia

Red Dot Design Yearbook 2017/2018
Living: 978-3-89939-194-7
Doing: 978-3-89939-195-4
Working: 978-3-89939-196-1
Enjoying: 978-3-89939-197-8
Set (Living, Doing, Working & Enjoying): 978-3-89939-193-0

Publisher + worldwide distribution |
Verlag + Vertrieb weltweit
Red Dot Edition
Design Publisher | Fachverlag für Design
Contact | Kontakt
Sabine Wöll
Gelsenkirchener Str. 181
45309 Essen, Germany
Phone +49 201 81418 22
Fax +49 201 81418 10
E-mail edition@red-dot.de
www.red-dot-edition.com
www.red-dot-shop.com
Book publisher ID no. | Verkehrsnummer
13674 (Börsenverein Frankfurt)

Bibliographic information published
by the Deutsche Nationalbibliothek
The Deutsche Nationalbibliothek
lists this publication in the Deutsche
Nationalbibliografie; detailed bibliographic
data are available on the Internet at
http://dnb.ddb.de
Bibliografische Information
der Deutschen Nationalbibliothek
Die Deutsche Nationalbibliothek verzeichnet
diese Publikation in der Deutschen
Nationalbibliografie; detaillierte
bibliografische Daten sind im Internet über
http://dnb.ddb.de abrufbar